WHEN
CRACK
WAS
KING

WHEN CRACK WAS KING

—

A PEOPLE'S HISTORY
OF A MISUNDERSTOOD ERA

DONOVAN X. RAMSEY

ONE WORLD

NEW YORK

Copyright © 2023 by Donovan X. Ramsey

Published in the United States by One World,
an imprint of Random House, a division of
Penguin Random House LLC, New York.

ONE WORLD and colophon are registered trademarks of
Penguin Random House LLC.

Library of Congress Cataloging-in-Publication Data

Names: Ramsey, Donovan X., author.
Title: When crack was king: a people's history of a misunderstood era /
by Donovan X. Ramsey.
Description: First edition. | New York: One World, [2023] | Includes index.
Identifiers: LCCN 2022043879 (print) | LCCN 2022043880 (ebook) |
ISBN 9780525511809 (hardcover) | ISBN 9780525511823 (ebook)
Subjects: LCSH: Crack (Drug)—United States—History—20th century. |
Cocaine—United States—History—20th century. | Drug control—United States—
History—20th century.
Classification: LCC HV5810 .R36 2023 (print) | LCC HV5810 (ebook) |
DDC 362.29/80973—dc23/eng/20230505
LC record available at lccn.loc.gov/2022043879
LC ebook record available at lccn.loc.gov/2022043880

Printed in the United States of America on acid-free paper

oneworldlit.com

2 4 6 8 9 7 5 3

First Edition

Book design by Edwin A. Vazquez

For the misunderstood,
the marginalized, and the maligned

Passion is never enough; neither is skill. But try. For our sake and yours, forget your name in the street; tell us what the world has been to you in the dark places and in the light. Don't tell us what to believe, what to fear. Show us belief's wide skirt and the stitch that unravels fear's caul.

—Toni Morrison,
Nobel Lecture (1993)

Beneath the Veil lay right and wrong, vengeance and love, and sometimes throwing aside the veil, a soul of sweet Beauty and Truth stood revealed.

—W.E.B. Du Bois,
Black Reconstruction in America (1935)

CONTENTS

WHEN
CRACK
WAS
KING

—

INTRODUCTION

I HARDLY EVER SAW MICHELLE, despite the fact that she lived just a few doors down the block from my family. I don't remember meeting her. But I learned to be afraid of her. My mom, a cautious woman who otherwise avoided gossip, would drag our house phone from room to room by its long white cord and talk at length with her friends about Michelle From Down the Street.

Michelle had too many "strange" people going in and out of her house. The neighborhood could hear her parties at all hours of the night, my mom complained. She looked "a mess." It was all just *so* sad, my mom would say with a slow shake of her head. The phone conversations would drift to other topics, but I stayed fixed on Michelle and tried to imagine what might be going on just a few feet away.

One Sunday afternoon, I was sitting on our front porch with my older sister when a van pulled up and parked in front of Michelle's place. Out of it came an older woman and a young girl, each resembling our infamous neighbor in her own way.

Because my sister knew everything, I asked her who the strangers were. "Duh! That's Michelle's family," she said. The small girl was Michelle's daughter.

"Why don't she live with her mom?" I asked.

My sister shrugged her shoulders, dismissive, then answered, "I don't know. Probably because Michelle is a crackhead."

It was 1993 or 1994, in Columbus, Ohio. I was just five or six years old but had heard the word "crackhead" countless times, usually from other kids. "Crackhead" was a go-to insult—so-and-so was "acting like a crackhead," "yo mama" was a "crackhead."

The word was popular, I assume, because it belonged to the grown-up world and using it made us feel grown. I suppose we made it a slur because we feared what it represented, a rock bottom to which any of us could sink. That's what children do when they're in search of power over things that frighten us. We reduce them to words, bite-size things that can be spat out at a moment's notice.

Still, I couldn't make sense of the fact that Michelle was a crackhead. She lived just down the street, after all, and she had a family. Crackheads were supposed to be foreigners from some netherworld, whose main activity was begging for money and otherwise disrupting community life. Then they were supposed to return to wherever they came from—alleyways, sewers, wherever the trash went after we threw it out.

I remember Michelle disappearing from the neighborhood sometime soon after that visit from her family. She was replaced in my awareness by other people who lived on the margins of our poor Black community. There was the thin light-skinned woman I'd see sometimes around the convenience store at the end of our street. Al, the older man who owned and operated the store, called her "Miss Prissy," after the skinny, frenetic chicken from the Foghorn Leghorn cartoons.

There was a man whose name I never knew who walked up and down the streets, always in a hurry and always selling something— bags of loose fireworks in the summer, brand-new down coats in the winter. As with Michelle, the adults I knew acknowledged him and

Prissy only in passing. I did the math and concluded they were also crackheads.

That type of calculus, I imagine, was common for lots of kids who grew up like me—poor and Black in the midst of the crack epidemic of the 1980s and '90s. There were things happening all around us that we knew better than to ask about, things we had to figure out for ourselves. My mother had a policy: Mind your business. That's exactly what she'd say when she'd catch me stealing glances at the older boys on the corner: "Mind your business." It was like growing up in a steel town where nobody talked about steel.

Conversations about crack became more mainstream in years to come. Our national dialogue reached its peak for me in the form of Whitney Houston sitting down for a prime-time interview to address rumors of drug use. It's a scene seared into my memory—a raspy-voiced and gaunt Houston sitting opposite Diane Sawyer. The singer is dressed entirely in white and holding a picture of herself that she's been handed by the interviewer.

"That's not just thin," Sawyer insists with a squint. "Anorexia? Bulimia?" Houston, incredulous, shakes her head. "No way." Then Sawyer gets to the reason she's really there, why we're all watching. She reads from what we're made to believe is a headline copied to the sheet of paper in her hand. "Whitney Dying, Crack Rehab Fails."

Houston leans in and uses a hand to punctuate the point. "First of all, let's get one thing straight. Crack is cheap. I make too much money to ever smoke crack. Let's get that straight. Okay? We don't do crack. We don't do that. Crack is wack."

Sawyer continued to ask if Houston indulged in alcohol, marijuana, cocaine, or pills, and Houston admitted she'd done all "at times." Crack, though? Any question of the pop superstar using that substance was settled by the simple logic that Houston was too wealthy to enjoy something so low-class.

The singer would divulge years later in an interview with Oprah Winfrey that her drug of choice had been marijuana laced with "base," short for "freebase." Neither she nor Oprah seemed aware that "freebase" and "crack" are different names for the exact same substance: smokable cocaine.

I understand now why Houston denied it. Crack left a residue on everything it touched. Anything could be done to a person associated with the evil substance. I surveyed my community and saw its effects in the way my neighborhood was policed. It was as though the police weren't satisfied until everyone I knew had been stopped, questioned, searched, detained, fined, arrested, jailed, inconvenienced, awakened in the middle of the night, humiliated. Some would end up beaten, shot, or killed. All of us would be touched.

School felt like an extension of the streets. There, it was teachers, mostly white, who did the profiling. They labeled my classmates "emotionally disturbed" or "hyperactive," diagnosed them with learning disabilities, and dismissed them accordingly. For us, Black boys mostly, it was a gradual process that sped up as we got bigger and more spirited. We didn't realize we were inside the belly of a beast that ate insubordinate Black boys whole, one that labeled us so it could consume us and that used our reaction to justify itself to itself.

My peers and I couldn't name it, but we recognized the disdain of teachers and educators and bristled at it. We avoided the police who profiled us as drug dealers and gangbangers—as "superpredators." We resisted the low expectations of teachers who regarded us as possible crack babies incapable of learning. Despite our ignorance of the greater forces, we did our best to outrun crack and its accompanying threats.

With the help of music and movies, I eventually deciphered what the grown-ups wouldn't explain. I deduced that my community was in the middle of an invisible war. When people disappeared from the neighborhood, I learned, it was because they'd been killed or locked up. Or worse, they were "on that shit," meaning they'd become addicted to crack and condemned to a life of wandering the streets like the living dead.

That was the message I got when I watched an ashy-mouthed

Chris Rock as Pookie in *New Jack City* for the first time. In the movie, Pookie finally gets clean but, in an agonizing scene, eventually relapses. "I tried to kick," he explains, "but that shit just be callin' me, man, it be callin' me, man . . . I just got to go to it!"

If that depiction didn't forever scare me off crack, there was the scene in *Jungle Fever* in which Samuel L. Jackson's Gator terrorizes his own elderly mother, played with tenderness by Ruby Dee, for money to get high. The scene ends when his father, played by Ossie Davis, happens upon the scene and shoots Gator dead after declaring his son is better off that way.

The popular music of my childhood added layers to what I saw in movies. Ice Cube asked in "A Bird in the Hand," "Do I have to sell me a whole lot of crack / for decent shelter and clothes on my back?" Tupac rhymed on "Keep Ya Head Up," "And in the end, it seems I'm headin' for the pen. / I try and find my friends, but they're blowin' in the wind." Other songs, including "Everyday Struggle" by Biggie or "Life's a Bitch" by Nas, made me certain that I not only didn't want to do drugs; I didn't want to sell them either.

As we got further away from the crack era, the panic over crack was replaced with panic over terrorism and other twenty-first-century American crises. For me, however, the questions around crack—how it disrupted whole communities and how it became a punchline—only burned stronger.

The crack epidemic ended, and I survived its fallout by some combination of striving, my mother's mothering, and God's grace. I came out relatively unscathed but not untouched, and carried the memories with me in everything I did, including my career as a journalist.

I went on to write about Black communities out of my deep respect and adoration for the beleaguered and misunderstood community that raised me. Inevitably, my work included stories about the criminal legal system. With each, I'd dig deeper and deeper—past specific situations and sources to the greater issues running through the stories. It wouldn't take much digging before I hit some crack-era law, practice, or idea.

Then, as if a spell had been broken, the nation's approach to the crack epidemic and crack-era ideas started to shift. In 2009, *The New York Times* published an article about so-called crack babies titled "The Epidemic That Wasn't." "Cocaine is undoubtedly bad for the fetus," the article stated. "But experts say its effects are less severe than those of alcohol and are comparable to those of tobacco, two legal substances that are used much more often by pregnant women, despite health warnings." In 2013, the paper followed up with another report debunking the crack baby myth. Other outlets followed suit, and slowly the process by which the crack baby had crawled into collective consciousness was revealed.

"Crack baby" had entered the lexicon alongside "crackhead." In 1985, a young neonatologist named Ira Chasnoff had published one of the earliest articles on the effects of cocaine use in pregnancy in *The New England Journal of Medicine.* Based on preliminary results from a study of just twenty-three women, he concluded that infants exposed to cocaine had "significant depression of interactive behavior and a poor organizational response to environmental stimuli." He wrote, "These preliminary observations suggest that cocaine influences the outcome of pregnancy as well as the neurologic behavior of the newborn."

Chasnoff's research, however limited, immediately found its way into the national dialogue around crack in the late 1980s. Already, a few years into the crack epidemic, conservative politicians and pundits were eager for ammunition in their war on drugs, Democrat-controlled big cities, and the poor people of color who called them home. From Chasnoff's study and some others, they conjured the "crack baby."

Crack babies were, the stories went, infants born afflicted due to their exposure to cocaine in the womb. They were the "tiniest victims" of the crack epidemic—deformed, intellectually disabled, and expected to overwhelm taxpayer-funded public services. Exactly how many crack babies were born was, it seems, secondary to the horror and resentment they could evoke.

Within a few short years, the national media was in a full-blown panic over crack babies. Some of the stories seem to have been written to evoke pity ("Crack Comes to the Nursery"), while others suggested blame and burden: "For Pregnant Addict, Crack Comes First." The stories—run by reputable outlets including *Time, The New York Times, Newsweek, The Washington Post, Rolling Stone,* and countless television programs—almost all began the same, describing scenes of underdeveloped infants struggling for life in incubators.

"Crack Kids," a 1991 article in *Time,* begins, "At a hospital in Boston lies a baby girl who was born before her time—three months early, weighing less than 3 lbs." It goes on to describe the baby as "entangled in a maze of wires and tubes that monitor her vital signs and bring her food and medicine."

Coryl Jones, a research psychologist at the National Institute of Drug Abuse in Bethesda, Maryland, was quoted in a 1989 *New York Times* article as saying crack was "interfering with the central core of what it is to be human" in exposed infants. In a 1988 interview with NBC News, George Miller, a Democratic congressman representing California's seventh district, concluded, "These children, who are the most expensive babies ever born in America, are going to overwhelm every social service delivery system that they come in contact with throughout the rest of their lives."

Washington Post columnist Charles Krauthammer wrote in a 1989 column, "The inner-city crack epidemic is now giving birth to the newest horror: a bio-underclass, a generation of physically damaged cocaine babies whose biological inferiority is stamped at birth." Later in the column, Krauthammer quoted family policy expert Douglas Besharov as saying, "This is not stuff that Head Start can fix. This is permanent brain damage. Whether it is 5 percent or 15 percent of the Black community, it is there."

Of crack babies, Krauthammer decided, "Theirs will be a life of certain suffering, of probable deviance, of permanent inferiority. At best, a menial life of severe deprivation . . . The dead babies may be the lucky ones."

Thirty years after Ira Chasnoff published his landmark study on the effects of cocaine use in pregnancy, the crack baby myth finally exploded. Hallam Hurt, a neurologist, then chair of neonatology at Philadelphia's Albert Einstein Medical Center, began researching the effects of prenatal cocaine exposure on developmental outcomes in 1988. When she finally concluded her research in 2015, the results were astounding: there were no significant differences in the development between children exposed to cocaine in utero and those who were not.

Of course, Hurt and other physicians make it a point to caution against cocaine use during pregnancy. Its effects are similar to those of tobacco. It can raise the blood pressure of expectant mothers to dangerous levels and even cause a pregnant woman's placenta to tear away from her uterine wall. For those reasons, it's associated with premature birth. (It was likely premature babies—their small size, shallow breathing, lack of interaction, and tremors—that inspired Chasnoff's conclusions.)

The *New York Times* editorial board has since officially acknowledged the paper's role in "slandering the unborn." It wrote, "News organizations shoulder much of the blame for the moral panic that cast mothers with crack addictions as irretrievably depraved and the worst enemies of their children. *The New York Times, The Washington Post, Time, Newsweek* and others further demonized Black women 'addicts' by wrongly reporting that they were giving birth to a generation of neurologically damaged children who were less than fully human and who would bankrupt the schools and social service agencies once they came of age."

Crackhead, crack baby, superpredator: these terms came to dominate the American imagination in the 1980s and 1990s. And because so much news coverage of the crack epidemic, and the debate around it, was racialized, these characters came to personify the nation's urban centers and, ultimately, Black America. Crack cast a shadow over the entire community—especially its young people.

The revelations regarding the crack baby myth were hard to accept, even for me. Despite my experience making media, and knowing how misinformation can snowball, I still could not comprehend how so many people got something so important so wrong and for so long. It was as though journalists, policymakers, and scientists didn't care enough to investigate the supposed phenomenon—or worse, that they had some vested interest in advancing the myth.

The myth of the crack baby was widely accepted as gospel, it seems, because it mapped so well onto existing ideas of Black biological inferiority and cultural pathology, and it stoked anxieties regarding violent crime and the cost of America's social safety net. Indeed, in the form of the crack baby, America was delivered a perfect symbol for its animosity toward Black America—a ticking time bomb of violence and expense created because Black mothers cared too little about themselves and their offspring.

The crack baby myth stuck, along with other myths of the crack era. That they persist and continue to distort the image of Black communities is an insult on top of the actual injury of the epidemic—trauma that has largely gone unacknowledged and is being passed down through generations. This is crack's residue.

I have come to understand the persistence of the residue as a by-product of what theorists call "transgenerational trauma" and "postmemory." "Transgenerational trauma," or "intergenerational trauma," is a psychological term for trauma that is transferred between generations. After a first generation of survivors experiences trauma, they are able to transfer their trauma to their children and further generations of offspring via complex mechanisms.

In her 2012 book *The Generation of Memory*, scholar Marianne Hirsch advances the concept of transgenerational trauma with her theory of "postmemory," which describes the relationship that the "generation after" has to the personal, collective, and cultural trauma of those who came before. "These experiences were transmitted to them so effectively and affectively as to seem to constitute memories in their own right."

However, on their own path toward healing, second-generation survivors of trauma encounter unique challenges. On the bridge between memory and history, they grapple with the chasm that exists between memories of traumas as they've been transmitted versus the way they're remembered in the larger society. It's all made more complicated by misinformation, propaganda, misremembering, and ongoing efforts to bury the past by both survivors of trauma and its perpetrators.

I still can't hear Patti LaBelle sing without thinking of Michelle. She'd blast LaBelle's "If Only You Knew" so loud each night that the muffled sound of the singer's voice would come through my bedroom windows. "'Cause you don't even suspect, could probably care less, about the changes I've been going through," Patti sings with a tear in her voice. "If only you knew." It's heartbreaking for reasons I could never explain.

Those who survived the crack epidemic, Black and brown people in particular, hardly ever talk about it. If we do, it's discussed wearily, like a trauma long accepted, in hushed voices and with thousand-yard stares. But we, survivors and second-generation survivors, want answers. We need to reconcile our memory and postmemory with all we'd learned about the crack era in popular culture. We are piecing together fragments toward a real history.

As a nation, the United States appears to be turning a corner in its war on drugs, as criticisms of marijuana prohibition are merging with criticisms from Black communities of crack-era laws and law enforcement. Indeed, works like *The Condemnation of Blackness* by Khalil Gibran Muhammad, *Stamped from the Beginning* by Ibram X. Kendi, and *The New Jim Crow* by Michelle Alexander have refined in recent years an argument I'd heard my entire life, that the U.S. criminal legal system functions as a means of social control by targeting Black communities through the war on drugs.

Tupac said as much on 1998's "Changes": "And still I see no changes, can't a brother get a little peace? / It's war on the streets and the war in the Middle East / Instead of war on poverty / They got a war on drugs so the police can bother me." About the experience of so-called superpredators, he explained on 1991's "Trapped," "How can I feel guilty after all the things they did to me? / Sweated me, hunted me, trapped in my own community / One day I'm gonna bust, blow up on this society / Why did you lie to me? I couldn't find a trace of equality."

Around 2015, I decided to dig into the crack epidemic for myself. I'd had enough speculation and innuendo. I wanted to know the facts of crack—what it was, where it came from, and how it spread. I wanted to know why my community seemed so affected by it and not others. Who were we before crack? My hope wasn't to write a book, at least not at first. Rather, I wanted to unlock some understanding that might help me better navigate a world that often made no sense.

ACT

I

–

THE ORIGINS

1

—

ELGIN

ELGIN SWIFT IS ONE FACE of the American Dream. The forty-five-year-old car salesman earns a six-figure salary and manages a staff of twenty. Just as important: Elgin is self-made, having been promoted from sales representative more than fifteen years ago. Before that, he worked his way up from busboy to manager at a small Italian restaurant.

He also has a number of successful business ventures. Elgin owns rental properties, publishes a popular podcast, and has significant investments in cryptocurrency. His success in business has provided him with all the creature comforts one could want: a luxury condo, designer clothes, and a lifestyle that includes plenty of travel, fine dining, and leisure activities.

Elgin is practically indistinguishable from the other middle-aged white men commuting into New York City every day from New Jersey. He's of average height and weight. He keeps the hair on his head and his beard closely cropped. His prominent nose and large dark eyes render him ethnically ambiguous. But upon close inspection, there are some things that set him apart. His narrow face is always framed by a neat line-up that fades to skin above the ears. He loves the boom bap of eighties hip hop, graffiti, and classic sneakers. He's also obsessed with making money, the art of the hustle.

His style and interests were formed during his childhood in crack-era Yonkers, New York. He's now years and miles away from that reality, but Elgin's past continues to color his life as much as his New York accent colors his speech.

I met Elgin Swift in my search to find people whose relatives struggled with crack addiction. I encountered hundreds after putting out an open call via social media platforms, and people shared with me things they'd never told anyone about loved ones and relationships lost to crack.

I interviewed Swift after one of his friends insisted we connect. To be honest, I was reluctant at first to include him—a white man—in a book on how the Black community survived the crack era, but I became convinced the more we talked that his story might illustrate crack's almost gravitational pull, the way it touched anyone and everyone close to poor Black and Latino people in the nation's urban centers.

Swift described the unique racial mix but broad poverty of Yonkers in the seventies and eighties. He detailed his childhood in the streets, the way he was neglected by his addict father but adopted by the Black and Latino people around him. I knew I had to write about him, however, after he shared his recurring nightmares with me, terrifying visions that illustrate the traumatic impact of the crack era. Their details vary. Sometimes they start in the apartment or in the shelter. They all end up the same. He dreamed recently that he was on vacation in Mexico walking past a tree when, suddenly, a zebra fell out of it. The zebra's legs were broken, and it was shaking uncontrollably. All Elgin could do was pet the animal in an attempt to comfort it. But eventually the police came, and they assumed that he'd broken the zebra's legs. As in all his nightmares, Elgin wound up in a prison cell. In the nightmare, his cell was a three-by-three room not even big enough to spread his arms in. He remembers thinking that he couldn't live like that, that his only option was to kill himself.

Everything comes rushing to the surface after Elgin has those nightmares. He starts to worry that maybe he spoiled his daughter, Asia, that he did her a disservice by giving her things instead of his undivided attention and time.

Then he starts thinking about his father, Stephen, and wondering whether it's worth it to give things one last try. The last he heard, the old man had been diagnosed with dementia and moved into a care center in the Bronx. Is there enough of Stephen's mind left to apologize and mean it? Would reaching out be worth the pain of seeing him like that? Will Elgin regret it forever if Stephen died and he missed his opportunity?

He could add that to his regret over how things ended with Artiesha, whom he left to chase his own happiness. A part of him wonders if karma or some higher power will allow him to be fully happy, or content at least, considering how he hurt her.

Elgin's nightmares also bring to the surface his deepest anxiety: the fear that he'll end up where he started—back in Yonkers, poor and desperate with no way out. It's in the moments after he wakes that he realizes how present that fear is in his everyday life. The nightmares call that fear forward like a word that has been on the tip of his tongue. He's waiting, he realizes, for the other shoe to drop, for the life that he's built to suddenly evaporate.

The successful salesman is in therapy now. During his first session, Elgin shared his nightmares and the details of his upbringing. The therapist offered something he hadn't given much thought to. "You have classic PTSD," she said. Elgin laughed to himself when she said it. The diagnosis was obvious, unexpected, and strangely comforting.

2

—

LENNIE

SHE'S GONE BY MANY NAMES—Lennie, Linda, Black. Today, most people call her Miss Woodley. It's a simple thing, being addressed that way. Most women merely age into "Miss." It's the step after "young lady" and right before "ma'am." Miss Woodley, on the other hand, had to earn it.

You wouldn't know it just by looking at her—she looks not unlike many other middle-aged Black women—but Miss Woodley was addicted to crack for nearly thirty years. The drug, which she started using as a teenager, almost robbed her of her very humanity. The world saw her as a crackhead, a "hooker," just about everything except "Miss."

She succumbed to addiction for decades but managed to hold on to some sense of herself—who she was before crack and who she wanted to be. So, when the smoke finally cleared, she was still standing—not diminished but fortified, strengthened in the places where she had been bruised and broken: Miss Woodley.

Miss Woodley is Los Angeles through and through. She refers to the area in South Central where she grew up as "the Hood." She calls her friends "the homies." She has the Black Angeleno accent, too, a unique blend of linguistic influences that transforms words like "party" into "poor-dy," and "folk" into "foke."

Like many Black women, she looks younger than her fifty-eight years. She's dark-skinned with a round face and big smile, not tall but not short, and loves to "dress." That means more than just putting on clothes. Miss Woodley carefully puts together her looks, favoring bold prints, cutouts, heels, and other details that make her stand out. Her hair is important, too. She changes it just about every week, and it's always neatly coiffed.

People gravitate to Miss Woodley for her flair—the way she can forge connections with strangers over the smallest things, her sense of humor, and the ease with which she talks about who and where she's been. On more than one occasion, she has found herself meeting someone, learning their darkest secrets during that meeting, then crying with them. She's like a cool auntie—stylish, self-possessed, knowing but not judgmental.

Miss Woodley regarded me cautiously when we first met. She wasn't standoffish. In fact, she was warm and open. But she also had no problem making her boundaries known and her concerns clear. She wanted to know who I was, who sent me, and what I wanted with her.

I was led to her by a series of sources, people who were in recovery. They each introduced me to others until I was presented with a profile for Miss Woodley, an L.A.-based substance abuse counselor. There were glimmers of a story in her eyes, I told her.

Her clients run the gamut. Crack fizzled out but there are a few smokers still holding on. She sees a whole lot of meth addicts. It's the new hot drug in L.A., maybe more popular than opioids, which have taken much of middle America by storm. Each client is unique. Their needs are all different. All seem to love Miss Woodley.

She can't help but laugh a little when she thinks about the buffet of services available to them, the change in attitudes regarding addiction. Miss Woodley's clients have access to several treatment options. There's an outpouring of support from the public and elected officials, including funding for programs. "It wasn't like that back in the day," she says. They also have the benefit of Miss Woodley, someone who survived the crack years and has just about seen it all.

"I'm not supposed to talk about my life, but how can I not talk about it? I been where they are," she says. "I let my clients know that was then, this is now, and there's no shame in none of that. I'm able to relate on so many levels."

3

—

KURT

THE CITIES MOST IMPACTED by crack cocaine were sites of unrest and white flight in the 1960s. The population shift in the 1970s and 1980s produced Black leadership and many elected Black mayors. Such was the case with David Dinkins in New York, Sharpe James in Newark, Tom Bradley in Los Angeles, Lionel Wilson in Oakland, Wilson Goode in Philadelphia, Marion Barry in Washington, D.C., Ernest Morial in New Orleans, Andrew Young in Atlanta, and Kurt Schmoke in Baltimore. Schmoke is not as well-known as his Black mayor peers, but his contribution to the era and the history of Baltimore are important.

Schmoke had a remarkable rise, from high school quarterback to mayor of his hometown. At a very young age, he was identified as someone with great promise. And even as he was conceiving a future for himself, there were powerful forces across Baltimore pushing him into leadership. Schmoke's intelligence was also evident. It shone through in stories about him in *The Baltimore Sun,* going as far back as his high school days.

I do not like many politicians, but I immediately connected to

Schmoke's story. He reminded me of the bookish guys I studied alongside at Morehouse whose greatest ambitions were to learn everything so they could go back home and save their communities. They—we—were community projects, full of investment from our families and friends and teachers and churches. This investment fueled us, but it could also weigh us down at times.

I'd seen guys like Schmoke soar, but I'd also seen them crash and burn. What would it mean to soar as the first Black man elected mayor of a big city, one as beleaguered as Baltimore during the crack era? What weight did Schmoke carry, I wondered, and how did he survive it?

Another thing about Schmoke intrigued me—his unusual position on drugs. Contrary to popular opinion and against the advice of many, he advocated for drug decriminalization as early as 1988. It was Schmoke's belief then that Baltimore, a city with a world-renowned medical and public-health resource in Johns Hopkins University, could serve as a model for treating addiction as a public-health issue instead of a criminal one. Schmoke's position was so well known within Baltimore that it was incorporated into a storyline on the hit HBO crime drama *The Wire* decades later. In the series, his proposal to decriminalize drugs came to life as Hamsterdam, a neighborhood created by police major Howard "Bunny" Colvin to study the potential positive effects of de facto legalization of the drug trade. The real-life Schmoke even appeared in two episodes from the third season, in a bit part as the Baltimore health commissioner.

When we eventually met in the summer of 2018 it was at the University of Baltimore, where the former mayor had been president for four years. He was remarkably clean-cut. At that point we'd gone back and forth over email, our correspondence set up and carefully moderated by his assistant at the University of Baltimore. He was formal in email and formal during our few brief phone conversations, but still, I wasn't prepared for how neat, tidy, and upright he'd be in person.

I arrived early to the Academic Center, which housed the president's office. The building looked dated but well-kept and had the smell of old books and oil soap. I was escorted to a conference room by one of Schmoke's aides. The overhead lights were off inside the room, but the midafternoon sun came in through the tall windows, casting a blue haze. It was like an old library, cool and hazy inside from a mix of daylight and dust.

I expected Schmoke to charge into the room, the way politicians tend to. Instead, he sauntered in as quiet and deliberate as a librarian, shook my hand, and sat down. Despite most students being away for the summer and the campus mostly empty, Schmoke was dressed in a stiff dress shirt and tie, pleated pants, and oxfords. What hair he had left was gray and closely cropped. He had small, alert eyes that would have disappeared if not for the thin rectangular frames that anchored them. He was clean-shaven, with big, bright teeth. He didn't attempt to make a joke or offer a practiced smile. Schmoke showed up and got to business. His unornamented presence did not inspire, but it was surprisingly grounding.

"I don't remember all of the details," he warned. "But I can give you, through memory's haze, my perspective."

From there, Schmoke rolled out in incredible detail how he'd experienced the crack years as mayor of Baltimore and just how hard it was to fight the epidemic as a Black mayor of a major city.

4

—

SHAWN

ACROSS NEWARK, PEOPLE CALL Shawn McCray "O.G." or "Coach." McCray earned the latter title as head coach of boys' basketball at Central High School, his alma mater. Over the past twenty-seven years, he's mentored countless youngsters in that role and taught them the fundamentals of a game he loves. He's bonded with them and their families, and they show McCray love as he moves through the city, stopping him on the street or yelling, "Hey, Coach," in passing. The former title, O.G., he earned by surviving the streets of Newark, first as a boy in one of the city's most infamous projects and later as a member of the Zoo Crew, Newark's most legendary ring of drug traffickers.

The still-strapping fifty-six-year-old dresses mostly in T-shirts and athletic wear and he walks like a ballplayer, taking long strides with slight dips in each step. Even when there isn't a Spalding under his arm, it looks like there should be. He has long locs and a gray beard, but a boyishness shines through from under it all. To look at him, you see the O.G., one of the few who survived the crack era in Newark. You also see the young man, the boy from the Bricks with one foot on the court and the other on the block. It's this quality that allows McCray to connect with young men. They see themselves in him and vice versa.

I met McCray after a long search for someone whose life illuminated the desires of young men who sold drugs during the crack era. I thought I'd eventually track down someone like D.C.'s Rayful Edmond, L.A.'s "Freeway" Rick Ross, or Alberto "Alpo" Martinez out of NYC—legendary men with stories that made their way into popular culture. Ricky Ross was the inspiration for the Miami rapper Rick Ross's name. Alpo was immortalized in the character of Rico in the 2002 film *Paid in Full*. And Jay-Z references Edmond on 1996's "Can I Live," rhyming, "No more Big Willie, my game has grown, prefer you call me William. / Illin' for revenues / Rayful Edmond like Channel 7 News."

However, while researching crack kingpins and reading their stories as told by *Don Diva* magazine and authors like Seth Ferranti, I came across the story of Shawn McCray, a Newark dealer who turned his life around and became a leader in his community.

"Sometimes, in the toughest of places against the longest of odds, a guy gets a break, makes a vow and keeps it. The vow takes hold and grows stronger, and everyone is better for it," read a story in *The Star-Ledger*.

I made some calls to sources around Newark and found out McCray was the real deal, not just a savvy marketer who'd honed a great personal narrative but a concerned citizen and a son of Newark who ran for city council in 2014, 2018, and 2022, self-publishing an autobiography along the way. He'd been an outspoken community leader even during the years he was selling drugs, protesting police abuse over the years and starting the Zoo Crew Summer Basketball League in 1998.

I didn't know what to expect when I finally got McCray on the phone—I wondered if he'd have a hard, intimidating quality like many of the dealers I'd read about. Instead, he had a low voice that barely modulated. It was the voice of someone who didn't get excited about much. Even the most harrowing stories from Newark during the crack era rolled off his tongue matter-of-factly, like he was reporting the weather.

He only raised his voice above a murmur when he talked about basketball or the public housing project community where he grew up. His first arrest? That was a matter-of-fact series of events. But McCray talked about his best games and Hayes Homes with a warmth and verve that most people reserve for old friends and dearly departed loved ones.

The last of the ten towers that comprised William P. Hayes Homes was demolished in 2000. Those buildings and others were the bricks that made Newark Brick City. Now they're gone from the skyline, scattering the 1,100 or so families that made up the vertical community.

"The community came together. Even though we were living in housing," he told me on our first call. "I think housing humbles people. Nowadays, especially with social media, you can run around and pretend that you're something that you're not. When we grew up in the projects, we knew everybody's parents was most likely on welfare. Everyone was receiving government assistance. So it wasn't like you can say you're doing better than me, because we're actually living in the same neighborhood under the same conditions. I remember my mother telling me she was going to a rent party. I was like, 'What's a rent party?' She was like, 'Well, somebody is short on their rent, so we're going to have a party and charge a couple dollars to get in and we're going to help them pay their rent.'" McCray chuckled. "But the mindset was different before all this."

By "this," McCray meant the crack era. It was the turning point at which he saw his community fall apart, a moment when he and his friends made some good choices but plenty of bad ones, dangerous choices that risked their lives and freedom and endangered their communities.

As someone identified as "gifted" in elementary school and who could also hoop, McCray had more options than others. His gifts opened doors for him, to private school and eventually to college, but nobody knew what to do with the gifted athlete who still had to return to the projects each night, Shawn included.

Today, McCray is unrelenting in his support for kids who remind him of himself growing up. That's where Coach and O.G. collide. He's already been where many young men in Newark are. He survived it and emerged from the wreckage of the crack era intact with something to give back. McCray is a working man.

Having spent his drug money, he doesn't have much to give, but he has basketball—its discipline and camaraderie, the way it helps players get in their bodies and out of their heads, the outlet it offers for anger and frustration, and the promise it holds for more life.

ACT

II

—

INCUBATION

5

—

DREAMS AND NIGHTMARES

ALL EVENTS ARE THE RESULT of countless others, big and small, coming together at a particular moment. They pile up like logs on a pyre. Then there's some kindling, a spark fed by the atmosphere, and, suddenly, a fire. That's how it was with what became known as the crack epidemic: one thing led to the next, and so many things happened at once that it's impossible to name just a single cause or responsible party. But as it is with fire, there were knowable elements—the substance itself, poverty, violence, grief.

Perhaps the most salient element was grief, a deep despair that drenched Black America toward the end of the twentieth century. Was it an old grief, nurtured and passed down like an heirloom? Or was it fresh, assigned by the stars to the generation that felt it? Both? Whichever, it was revealed to be vast, deep, and undeniable in the decades leading into the crack epidemic.

During those years, America was a troubled nation but one that still seemed to believe it could be a "Great Society." "You could strike sparks anywhere," journalist Hunter S. Thompson wrote of the period. "There was a fantastic universal sense that whatever we were doing was right, that we were winning . . . We had all the momentum; we were riding the crest of a high and beautiful wave."

Black America's momentum was embodied by the Civil Rights Movement. The protests, boycotts, marches have been rendered conventional by time, retelling, and repetition, but the movement was once fresh and new. Black people across the country were upsetting the country's racial hierarchy, and the country itself. For the first time since Reconstruction, there was reason for Black Americans to be hopeful. Hopeful not because the moral arc of the universe was bending toward justice but because Black Americans were actively bending it.

Imagine the restlessness of these people who, for generations, had languished in the American South just a few small steps from bondage. They'd been terrorized by America, their dreams repressed but never quite extinguished.

All they found in Los Angeles, Baltimore, and Newark was a lighter shade of Texas, South Carolina, and Georgia, as they were barred from unions, banned from neighborhoods, policed like an invading horde. Indeed, those who left the South saw the cities to which they escaped transform into facsimiles of those they had escaped from almost as fast as they arrived.

How encouraged they must have been, then, as *Brown v. Board* in 1954 dovetailed into the Montgomery bus boycott in 1955 and 1956, the desegregation of Little Rock Central High School in 1957, and the sit-ins and Freedom Rides between 1958 and 1961. That whirlwind of activity forced even the president of the United States, John F. Kennedy, to address the "rising tide of discontent" in America and declare his commitment to civil rights legislation.

"One hundred years of delay have passed since President Lincoln freed the slaves, yet their heirs, their grandsons, are not fully free," Kennedy said during a televised address on June 11, 1963. "They are not yet freed from the bonds of injustice. They are not yet freed from social and economic oppression. And this nation, for all its hopes and all its boasts, will not be fully free until all its citizens are free."

And how buoyant Black Americans must have felt when just a few months later, with the whole world watching, a personification of Black virtue stood before the nation and demanded their birthright. His address, the articulation of a Black American Dream, was so profoundly eloquent that it rose from a speech to a sermon. How could America not get religion hearing him intone of every valley exalted, every mountain made low, the rough places made plain, and the crooked places made straight? Almost exactly a year later, Congress passed the Civil Rights Act, and later the Voting Rights Act.

Still, even during these shining moments, Black folk were catching hell. From New York to Watts, they were not only suffering under the weight of white supremacy but being snuffed out by it.

Especially in northern cities, Blacks were redlined into areas of concentrated poverty and further isolated when the federal government built highways that separated them from their white neighbors. Their neighborhoods were patrolled by police departments that moved like occupying forces, with extreme prejudice and impunity. Police brutality was a regular occurrence in these places.

As early as 1963, individual run-ins with police were erupting into larger conflicts in cities across America, and the summer of 1964 saw seven riots—in Rochester, New York City, Philadelphia, Jersey City, Paterson, Elizabeth, and Chicago—events all initiated by incidents of police brutality against Blacks. The summer after Malcolm was assassinated, a massive riot erupted in Los Angeles, a city in which he'd organized against police brutality years before.

Watts, a predominantly Black section of L.A., went up in flames when residents took to the streets in response to reports that a twenty-one-year-old resident had been pulled over, beaten, and arrested by members of the California Highway Patrol. The following year, 1966, riots broke out in Cleveland, Chicago, and San Francisco.

By this point, it was clear that King's dream and the hope it represented were beginning to fade from the American consciousness. In fact, in 1966—just three years after his "I Have a Dream" speech—King himself expressed his disillusionment in an interview with CBS's

Mike Wallace. It was in this interview that he called riots "the language of the unheard." "And what is it that America has failed to hear?" he added. "It has failed to hear that the economic plight of the Negro poor has worsened over the last few years."

—

THE LONG, HOT SUMMER

THE FEDERAL GOVERNMENT RECORDED 164 "civil disorders" across thirty-four states in the first nine months of 1967, with violent protests erupting in 128 cities during the summer months. All told, at least eighty-three people were killed during that summer's riots, and thousands were injured. Property damage was estimated in the tens of millions, and in some cities, entire neighborhoods were burned to the ground.

Detroit's Twelfth Street Riot was arguably the bloodiest. It occurred after police raided an unlicensed bar at 9125 Twelfth Street on the city's Near West Side. Officers attempted to arrest everyone present, eighty-two people in total, who were at the bar to celebrate the return of two local GIs from the Vietnam War. The incident escalated into riots that lasted five days. The Long, Hot Summer, as it became known, also saw riots in Newark. Residents there clashed with authorities over the course of four days after an incident in which police officers beat and arrested a Black taxi driver.

The law-enforcement response to the events in both Detroit and Newark was staggering. In Newark, 7,917 members of the police and National Guard were deployed, leading to 1,465 arrests and twenty-six deaths. The National Guard was also deployed in Detroit in addition to local police and the United States Army's 82nd and 101st Airborne Divisions. The result was 43 dead, 1,189 injured, and more than 7,200 arrests.

On July 28, 1967, with rioting still underway in Detroit, President

Lyndon Johnson announced that he was assembling an eleven-person commission to investigate the cause of the riots and provide recommendations to prevent future unrest. The group—dubbed the Kerner Commission after Otto Kerner, Jr., then governor of Illinois and the commission chair—was charged by Johnson with answering three basic questions: What happened? Why did it happen? What can be done to prevent it from happening again and again?

The commission released its report seven months later, on February 29, 1968. The 426-page document reasoned that the riots of 1967 resulted from Black frustration with a lack of economic opportunity and access to the mainstream of American life. It called out both state and federal governments for failures in housing, education, and social services. "Our nation is moving toward two societies, one Black, one white—separate and unequal," it famously concluded.

The report's recommendations included a federal jobs program aimed at increasing Black employment, the diversification of police forces across the country, and perhaps most notably, an investment in housing programs to the tune of billions of dollars, with the goal of breaking up residential segregation in the North and South.

Interest in the Kerner Report was so high that it was published as a paperback and sold almost one million copies in the first two weeks of its release. But despite having created the commission and given it its mission, President Johnson was deeply unhappy with its work. Johnson, after all, had signed the Civil Rights Act and the Voting Rights Act into law, and the report pointed to the failures of that legislation. Simultaneously, it called out the whole of white America for its complicity in the country's system of oppression.

"What white Americans have never fully understood—but what the Negro can never forget—is that white society is deeply implicated in the ghetto," the report read. "White institutions created it, white institutions maintain it, and white society condones it."

Martin Luther King, Jr., called the report a "physician's warning of approaching death, with a prescription for life."

—

THE NIGHTMARE (1968-74)

ON APRIL 4, 1968, less than a month after the Kerner Commission report and only five years after his transcendent "I Have a Dream" speech, King was assassinated. He was shot in broad daylight on the balcony of the Lorraine Motel in Memphis. A sniper's bullet entered the thirty-nine-year-old's right cheek, breaking his jaw and several vertebrae as it traveled down his spinal cord, severing his jugular vein and major arteries before lodging in his shoulder. He was killed almost instantly.

There may be no better symbol for America's relationship to its Black citizens than King, the most widely respected member of the race, sprawled on a motel balcony in a pool of his own blood. He died a senseless and sudden death, one devoid of dignity—a Black death.

Between the evening of April 4, the day King was assassinated, and Easter Sunday, April 14, 1968, more than one hundred cities across thirty-six states and the District of Columbia rioted. Combined, 43 men and women were killed, approximately 3,500 were injured, and 27,000 were arrested. Fifty-four cities suffered at least $100,000 in property damage, with D.C. and Baltimore topping the list at approximately $15 million and $12 million in damage, respectively.

Experts called it the greatest wave of social unrest since the Civil War. "Not until over 58,000 National Guardsmen and army troops joined local state and police forces did the uprisings cease," wrote historian Peter B. Levy in his 2018 book *The Great Uprising: Race Riots in Urban America During the 1960s.*

The event is not well remembered in the American consciousness. It does not fit easily into the narrative of a triumphant Civil Rights Movement that erased the country's racism. In fact, it points to the contrary. The Holy Week Uprising, as it's called, suggests that Black Americans were so incensed by King's assassination, by what it represented, that news of it spurred a violent insurrection.

And it was in this fateful moment that the wave of hope finally broke for Black America. It rolled back to reveal deep vulnerabilities in the nation's social and moral compacts. Black America would respond to the devastation of King's death and the period of rioting with even greater militancy in the movement for Black liberation. White America would respond with increased hostility toward Black Americans, and everything associated with them: social support services, civil rights, protest, crime—what would become known as "inner-city" issues.

One measure of the shift in Black consciousness was the change exhibited by activist Stokely Carmichael. He had been an organizer in the Student Nonviolent Coordinating Committee (SNCC), which was essential to many of the major moments of the Civil Rights Movement—the sit-ins, Freedom Rides, the March on Washington, the Mississippi Freedom Summer and Selma campaigns. Founded by Ella Baker, SNCC had been led by Marion Barry, Charles F. McDew, and John Lewis before Carmichael assumed leadership in 1966 and moved the group to the left.

Soon after he was named chairman of SNCC, Carmichael began to question publicly the wisdom of nonviolent protest, and in a 1966 speech in Greenwood, Mississippi, he began using "Black Power" as a slogan. "This is the twenty-seventh time I have been arrested and I ain't going to jail no more!" he told the crowd. "The only way we gonna stop them white men from whuppin' us is to take over. What we gonna start sayin' now is Black Power!"

In 1967, while still chairman of SNCC, he joined the Black Panther Party, which was growing in Oakland and L.A. The group believed, as Carmichael did, in armed resistance to state violence and in Black independence. Later that year, he stepped down from his post with SNCC to be more active with the Panthers.

Carmichael was in D.C. when he received news of King's assassination. The next day, at a press conference held at the New School for Afro-American Thought, he voiced the anger of so many Black Americans. "When white America killed Dr. King last night, she declared war on us," Carmichael told reporters.

That declaration of war just so happened to come in an election year, further injecting the riots and civil rights issues into the national debate. On the Democratic side, the conversation was over how to best advance the Johnson administration's civil rights work and end the war in Vietnam, which the United States had been lumbering through since 1955. On the Republican side, the conversation focused on how to best deal with the antiwar left and the nation's Black population.

The Democrats were a party divided and in disarray. Johnson, facing challenges from Robert Kennedy and Wisconsin Senator Eugene McCarthy, announced just days before King's assassination that he wouldn't run for reelection. Vice President Hubert Humphrey ran instead. He and Kennedy traded primary wins over the next few months until, after winning the California primary on June 4, Kennedy was assassinated during a victory party at the Ambassador Hotel in Los Angeles.

Kennedy had a mixed record on civil rights. As attorney general, he'd both authorized the FBI surveillance of Martin Luther King, Jr., and provided protection for activists during some of the tensest moments of the movement. Nevertheless, in the wake of King's assassination, he'd become something of a last hope for Black Americans still clinging to King's memory and the promise of the Civil Rights Movement.

A poll in May 1968 showed that only 40 percent of overall respondents believed Kennedy embodied "many of the same outstanding qualities" as his late brother. Ninety-four percent of Black respondents, however, agreed with the comparison. Another poll identified Kennedy as the most likely of all the 1968 candidates to "speed up" racial progress.

At the time of his death, Kennedy was in second place behind Humphrey for the Democratic Party nomination and gaining on the vice president. He'd secured 393 delegates compared to Humphrey's 561 and McCarthy's 258. Humphrey went on to receive the party's nomination at the now-infamous Democratic National Convention in Chicago, where an estimated 10,000 protesters—antiwar activists, Black Panthers, students, and concerned citizens—clashed with 12,000 police officers, 5,000 National Guardsmen, and nearly 7,000 federal troops. The result was a deeply fractured Democratic Party organized behind Humphrey, a candidate nobody really wanted, and the protests were held up as an example to America of the violent threat presented by progressive politics.

Humphrey entered the general election and into a fight with opponents who appealed to the fears, resentments, and outright hostilities of white Americans regarding the events of 1968. He was up against Richard Nixon on the Republican ticket, and running as the American Independent Party candidate was George Wallace, the segregationist governor of Alabama.

On Election Day, Wallace carried five Southern states, winning almost 10 million popular votes and 46 electoral votes—the greatest showing of any third-party candidate in American history. Wallace remains the last non-Democratic, non-Republican candidate to win any pledged electoral votes. Still, he lost to Nixon, who received 301 electoral votes and 43.4 percent of the popular vote, just barely edging out Humphrey's 42.7 percent.

Nixon is perhaps best remembered for his corruption and the Watergate scandal, but his brand as a politician was a fierce conservatism steeped in the politics of white resentment. But unlike Wallace, who advertised his white supremacist ideologies, Nixon's approach was more insidious.

The best example is his choice of Spiro Agnew, the governor of Maryland, to be his running mate in 1968. Agnew owed his national profile to the stir he caused when he publicly dismissed the findings of the Kerner Commission report. "Why don't impoverished white Americans riot? Could it be that they know they will not meet with sympathy, that collective white lawlessness will not be tolerated?" Agnew asked in a July 1968 speech to the National Governors' Conference. "It is not the centuries of racism and deprivation that have built to an explosive crescendo but the fact that lawbreaking has become a socially acceptable and occasionally stylish form of dissent."

In the wake of the riots that leveled Baltimore after King's assassination, Agnew brought more than one hundred local Black leaders to the state capitol. Instead of engaging them in a dialogue about the riots and a path forward, as had been promised, he scolded them for failing to prevent Baltimore's Black community from rioting.

"Now, parts of many of our cities lie in ruins. You need not leave these City limits to verify the destruction and the resulting hardship to our citizens. And you know whom the fires burned out just as you know who lit the fires," he told the group, which included civil and religious leaders. "They were not lit in honor of your great fallen leader. Nor were they lit from an overwhelming sense of frustration and despair. Those fires were kindled at the suggestion and with the instruction of the advocates of violence."

Slowly, an anti-protest, anti-Black approach to policy took shape in the Nixon White House, with Agnew as its public face. The basic premise of the approach was that America had been for far too long pulled to the left by a too-vocal minority of Americans—Blacks, Latinos, women, students, pacifists, the media, and out-of-touch intellectuals. The Democratic Party's catering to these groups had resulted in little more than lawlessness, epitomized by the riots. The only way forward for America, the Nixon campaign posited, was leadership that reflected the values of the "silent majority" and a return to "law and order."

This philosophy helped Nixon win the presidential election of 1968, and in the decades to come, it would pervade American politics and animate policy. Politically, it became the foundation of the "Southern strategy," a Republican Party scheme to lock in the support of white voters in the South and other parts of America by appealing to their faith in white supremacy and anti-Blackness.

Republican strategist Lee Atwater would later summarize the Southern strategy in an interview with Alexander Lamis, a political scientist at Case Western Reserve University. "By 1968 you can't say 'nigger'—that hurts you. Backfires," Atwater said. "So you say stuff like forced busing, states' rights, and all that stuff, and you're getting so abstract. Now you're talking about cutting taxes, and all these things you're talking about are totally economic things, and a byproduct of them is, Blacks get hurt worse than whites. And subconsciously maybe that is part of it. I'm not saying that. But I'm saying that if it is getting that abstract and that coded, that we are doing away with the racial problem one way or the other."

In terms of policy, the Nixon administration's "law and order" message swept the country. Americans demanded a criminal justice system that was tough on crime. Voters rewarded politicians who promised this with electoral victories.

But it's clear from Nixon's jumbled remarks on crime at the 1968 Republican National Convention that his administration needed one issue that would organize his calls for law and order and galvanize his base.

"I pledge to you that our new attorney general will be directed by the president of the United States to launch a war against organized crime in this country," Nixon promised in the speech. "I pledge to you that the new attorney general of the United States will be an active belligerent against the loan sharks and the numbers racketeers that rob the urban poor in our cities. I pledge to you that the new attorney general will open a new front against the filth peddlers and the narcotics peddlers who are corrupting the lives of the children of this country."

In a diary entry from 1969, White House chief of staff H. R. Haldeman paraphrased Nixon's private thoughts. Referring to the president as "P," Haldeman wrote, "P emphasized that you have to face the fact that the whole problem is really the blacks. The key is to devise a system that recognizes this while not appearing to."

A 1994 interview with John Ehrlichman, counsel and assistant to the president for domestic affairs under Nixon, revealed how the administration finally arrived at drugs as a target.

"The Nixon campaign in 1968, and the Nixon White House after that, had two enemies: the antiwar left and Black people," Ehrlichman told *Harper's* writer Dan Baum. "We knew we couldn't make it illegal to be either against the war or blacks, but by getting the public to associate the hippies with marijuana and blacks with heroin, and then criminalizing both heavily, we could disrupt those communities. We could arrest their leaders, raid their homes, break up their meetings, and vilify them night after night on the evening news. Did we know we were lying about the drugs? Of course we did."

The Nixon administration did not require evidence that drug use was linked to rising crime, however. And it did not need to prove to the American public that doped-up Blacks were responsible for that crime. It had two facts: drug use was up, and so was violent crime in big cities. Americans would fill in the blank, using the same brutal imagination they always had to rationalize a war on drugs targeting Black Americans.

Alongside its war on drugs, the Nixon administration was engaged in an all-out offensive on Black political leadership. The FBI had been surveilling, threatening, and attempting to discredit Black leaders since as early as 1956 as part of its Counterintelligence Program (COINTELPRO). The FBI sank to new lows under Nixon, however, with its efforts to destroy the Black Panther Party and, according to a bureau memo, "prevent the rise of a Black 'messiah' who could unify and electrify the militant Black nationalist movement."

Hoover had declared the Panthers "the greatest threat to the internal security of the country" in 1968. In the years that followed, the group became the primary focus of COINTELPRO, with the FBI employing surveillance, informants, psychological warfare, legal threats, smear campaigns, and violence in an attempt to "neutralize" the Panthers. The organization, its chapters and leaders, were the target of an estimated 233 authorized actions, according to a later report on COINTELPRO by the Senate Select Committee on Intelligence Activities.

By the end of 1969, five leaders within the Black Panther Party—

Spurgeon Winter, Jr., Bunchy Carter, John Huggins, Alex Rackley, and Bobby Hutton—had been murdered in confrontations with police, rival groups, and other Panthers. Most notably, Fred Hampton and Mark Clark were murdered when Chicago Police Department officers raided Hampton's apartment. Hampton, it would later be revealed, had been marked as a "key militant leader" by the FBI. And on the night of his murder, he'd been sedated by his bodyguard, an FBI informant, who'd slipped a barbiturate into Hampton's drink at dinner.

By 1970, a number of leaders within the Black Panther Party, including Lawrence S. Bell, Bobby Rush, Bobby Seale, George W. Sams, Jr., Geronimo Pratt, Eddie Conway, William Lee Brent, Chip Fitzgerald, Cinque Magee, Albert Nuh Washington, Anthony Bottom, Pete O'Neal, Ed Poindexter, David Rice, Russell Shoatz, the Panther 21, and Angela Davis, were behind bars or facing criminal charges ranging from robbery and inciting a riot to illegal weapons possession, conspiracy, kidnapping, and murder.

Nixon signed the Comprehensive Drug Abuse Prevention and Control Act into law that same year. The law was the opening salvo in the modern war on drugs, and it provided the federal government a legal foundation for its fight. The law had a number of important provisions, but the most significant was Title II, the Controlled Substances Act, which established five "schedules" to categorize substances based on their potential for addiction and their medicinal value.

Substances including heroin, LSD, and marijuana were designated schedule I drugs, meaning the government determined they had high potential for abuse and no accepted medical use. Amphetamines, barbiturates, morphine, and cocaine were among drugs designated schedule II, substances with high potential for abuse but some accepted medical purposes.

With the Comprehensive Drug Abuse Prevention and Control Act on the books, the Nixon administration slowly ramped up its war. Responding to reports that 15 to 25 percent of servicemen in Vietnam were using heroin, Nixon famously declared drug abuse "America's public enemy number one" at a press conference on June 17, 1971. He announced an "all-out offensive," including the creation of a new federal agency dedicated to fighting drugs, the Special Action Office of Drug Abuse Prevention.

To help sell the effort, Nixon argued a connection between drugs and crime. In a special address to Congress issued the same day as his speech, Nixon wrote, "Narcotic addiction is a major contributor to crime. The cost of supplying a narcotic habit can run from $30 a day to $100 a day. This is $210 to $700 a week, or $10,000 a year to over $36,000 a year. Untreated narcotic addicts do not ordinarily hold jobs. Instead, they often turn to shoplifting, mugging, burglary, armed robbery, and so on. They also support themselves by starting other people—young people—on drugs."

In January 1972, following the creation of the Office of Drug Abuse Prevention, Nixon created the Office of Drug Abuse Law Enforcement, with the mission of putting greater emphasis on fighting drugs through the criminal justice system. "Today our balanced, comprehensive attack on drug abuse moves forward in yet another critical area as we institute a major new program to drive drug traffickers and drug pushers off the streets of America," he remarked in his announcement of the new office. "This office will marshal a wide range of government resources, including new authorities granted in the Organized Crime Control Act of 1970, in a concentrated assault on the street-level heroin pusher."

And so it was that in the span of just a few years, the Nixon administration was able to successfully mold its campaign of law and order in response to the civil disobedience of the sixties into a full-fledged war on drugs. And with his insistence on a link between rising crime and drugs—heroin, specifically—Nixon thoroughly racialized his war, making it effectively a war on Black users, Black dealers, Black communities. The Office of Drug Abuse and Law Enforcement performed six thousand drug arrests in its first eighteen months, and the majority of those arrests were carried out on Black people.

Nixon was encouraged by the spread of the drug war to local governments. In January 1973, for example, New York governor Nelson Rockefeller passed the Rockefeller Drug Laws, strict guidelines that mandated prison sentences of fifteen years to life for possession with intent to sell just two ounces or more of heroin, morphine, opium, cocaine, or cannabis. "Rocky can ride this thing for all it's worth," Nixon reportedly joked to his staff after learning of New York's new laws.

Even as the Watergate scandal grew in late 1972 and early 1973, Nixon continued to put emphasis on drug enforcement. Nixon introduced his own proposal soon after. On March 14, 1973, he outlined a plan to increase prison sentences for possession of heroin, including the introduction of mandatory minimums. For a first-time offender caught in possession of less than four ounces of heroin or morphine, Nixon proposed a mandatory sentence between five and fifteen years. More than four ounces would bring a mandatory sentence of ten years to life. For individuals with prior felony drug convictions, he proposed mandatory sentences of ten years to life for less than four ounces and life without the possibility of parole for any more.

Later that year, Nixon merged the Bureau of Narcotics and Dangerous Drugs, the Office of Drug Abuse Law Enforcement, sections of the Bureau of Customs, and other federal offices to create the Drug Enforcement Administration. The new agency was tasked with enforcing federal drug laws both domestically and abroad.

Nixon's agenda would be derailed eventually by the national crisis presented by the Watergate scandal and impeachment proceedings against him, which formally began in February 1974. He announced new federal sentencing guidelines in March but resigned by August, leaving his war on drugs to continue on the state level and to eventually be picked up by future U.S. presidents.

6

—

LENNIE

(1965-72)

LENNIE WOODLEY'S MEMORIES BEGIN in South Central Los Angeles. She was born in Florida, but her dad died when she was just two years old, and she and her mother, Bea, moved to L.A. soon after, to be near Bea's sisters, Doretha and Mozelle.

The young mother and daughter lived first with Aunt Doretha in an apartment near Johnny Pastrami on Crenshaw and Washington. Then they moved into a small home on Second Avenue and Sixty-seventh with Aunt Mozelle and her husband, Archie.

Uncle Archie was among the wave who had migrated to the neighborhood following World War II. He used his benefits to purchase the home on Second Avenue and Sixty-seventh, and a gas station near Seventy-eighth and Central that serviced much of South Central.

The tall, older, light-complected man was a pillar of the community. He was so upstanding that he allowed Bea and Lennie to continue living with him even after Mozelle died suddenly when Lennie was four years old.

It was an odd arrangement—a single woman and her daughter living with her dead sister's husband—but it made all the sense to them. Uncle Archie was older, in his sixties, and had more than enough space. The widower also needed someone to help take care of his home. Lennie's mom had been taking care of people her whole life— her eight siblings and then her husband. Besides, they were family.

The three of them made things work in the house. Uncle Archie was away at his gas station most of the day while Bea kept the house together, cooking and cleaning. Otherwise, she was at church—on Sunday, on Thursday, and any other day she was required for a special service, one ministry or another, or some committee meeting.

Uncle Archie's industriousness afforded Lennie's piecemeal family a comfortable lifestyle. They had a two-bedroom house, with Lennie and her mom sharing the larger bedroom and Uncle Archie sleeping in a back room. There was a small yard in the front and a big backyard with fruit trees—avocado, apricot, peach, lemon, lime, plum, and or- ange. Little Lennie had the best clothes—pretty dresses and frilly socks that made the little dark-skinned girl look like a doll when she and her mom went to church.

Those first few years at Uncle Archie's, the earliest ones that Len- nie could remember, were sweet. She went to church with her mom and sang in the choir. And every now and then, Uncle Archie would bring home greasy cheeseburgers just for Lennie that she'd gleefully scarf down. She liked her school, Hyde Park Elementary, a lot, too. Teachers there said she was gifted and put her in "academically en- riched" classes. Uncle Archie bought her a German shepherd puppy. Lennie named her Dubie, and she became her best friend.

South Central would become infamous in decades to come, but back in the sixties, when Lennie's family arrived, it was still the kind of place Black families wanted to be, full of families from Louisiana, Texas, and Oklahoma.

Many had been forced into abject poverty by racist policies and customs where they came from. Los Angeles wasn't perfect. The city was segregated and used redlining to funnel Blacks south from downtown Los Angeles along Central Avenue all the way to Slauson. Still, it was better than where they'd been, and sometimes better is enough.

South Central provided decent-paying jobs for men at nearby factories and unionized service jobs for women downtown. There were also modest but well-built bungalows, abandoned by whites who fled South Central for other parts of Los Angeles when the Blacks moved in.

But South Central was changing rapidly. Many of the good factory jobs that so many came to Los Angeles for were quietly moving out of the city. People blamed the Watts riots in 1965, but in truth, the trend began much earlier. Between 1963 and 1964, twenty-eight industrial manufacturing firms left South Central and parts of East L.A.—four metal shops, eight furniture factories, one electrical machinery factory, one food processing plant, four textile plants, and two oil refineries.

These were jobs that sustained the local Black community. They made the difference between a Black working-class neighborhood and a ghetto.

By 1965, South Los Angeles—which was more than 80 percent Black—had unemployment rates double those of greater Los Angeles and the entire state of California. One in ten adults in South L.A. was out of work. In 1970, the year Lennie started kindergarten, a quarter of Black Los Angeles lived below the poverty line.

Folks got desperate and from that desperation a new South Central emerged, full of gangbangers, hustlers, and pimps, who moved from the margins of the community to the center.

Bea began tightening the reins on her little girl. Where Lennie had been allowed to play with other kids on the block before, by the time she was in first and second grade, Bea insisted that she play inside and alone. Kids just a little older than Lennie were already getting in trouble, smoking weed and running behind the gangbangers. They were "bad kids," Bea said, and Lennie was meant to be good.

Regardless, little Lennie found a way to be in the mix. She was social by nature, talkative. When Bea wasn't around or watching closely, Lennie would hit the block to play with the neighborhood kids. Because she was the girl with the "mean mama," most of the kids regarded Lennie cautiously. Her only friend was Rudy, a boy who lived on her block. He was a lot like Lennie—talkative and funny. But Rudy had a nice mama, the kind all the neighborhood kids went to when they were too afraid to go to their own.

Meanwhile, Lennie's own mother was only getting meaner. First, it was the rule against playing with the other kids. Then Bea enforced stricter, almost nonsensical rules for a child Lennie's age, and harsher consequences. The smallest infraction—hanging the laundry wrong, taking too long to wash the dishes, "looking funny"—would set Bea off. It started with yelling and almost always ended with a beating. When Bea got mad, she yelled at her daughter, talked down to her, sent her to bed without dinner, and beat her. Not just a few licks with a belt. Bea beat Lennie until her deep brown skin bruised.

One night, Bea was off on a tear. She was mad at Lennie for one thing or the other and started ranting. When Bea let loose, all pretense of godliness fell by the wayside. She was cursing Lennie out. Lennie had learned to just be still, to not say a word until the moment, hopefully, passed. If not, the cursing could turn into beating, which it usually did anyhow. But Bea said something that she couldn't ignore.

"I could tell you shit about your mama and your daddy that would bust your head," she said.

Lennie asked, "Ain't you my mama?"

Bea replied, "I didn't even want you. Your daddy wanted you. If I had my pick, I would have got me a boy. But they wouldn't let me take just the boy, because he was a twin, so I had to get you." That's how Lennie learned, at seven years old, that she was adopted. Not just unwanted by her birth mother, she thought, but by her adopted mother, who settled for her because she couldn't take on twin boys.

It would take years to get the full story, but she'd piece it together from cousins and aunts who knew Bea had married young to get out of her own parents' house. She married a pastor old enough to be her father. They couldn't have children, so they adopted. They found two-year-old Lennie in a Miami orphanage. A short time later, the pastor died suddenly, and Bea was forced to raise her alone.

When the beatings started up, Lennie's sanctuary wasn't church or school but Uncle Archie. He'd console her, cheer her up with a hamburger or a hug. One day, in Uncle Archie's room, he whispered to Lennie, "I'm going to tell you a secret." She was thrilled, of course, to have a confidant and to be confided in. He said, "The secret is I'm your boyfriend, but you can't tell nobody."

From then on, Uncle Archie would coax Lennie to his room whenever her mom was upset or at church, which was often. He would give her little treats before touching her. The treats turned eventually to sips of whiskey. With the help of Johnnie Walker, little Lennie grew accustomed to the routine abuse from Uncle Archie, just as she had to the routine abuse from her mother.

Uncle Archie talked to her like a woman, Lennie thought, and every sip helped her pretend that she was one. She was incubating an alter ego, Linda.

Lennie wanted to crawl out of her skin when Uncle Archie got that look in his eye. Linda learned to take swigs of scotch easily, and how to walk "like a woman" from watching old Mae West movies with Uncle Archie. Nothing fazed Linda. Linda was grown and worldly—sassy, even.

ONE DAY, A SEVEN-YEAR-OLD Lennie was at home with her mom when she heard what sounded like hail coming from the alley behind the house. She knew immediately that some of the older neighborhood kids were "traveling." It was a practice wherein they threw rocks at the backs of houses to see if anyone was home. If no one came to check out the noise, they broke in and stole whatever they could fit in their pockets.

Rudy told Lennie about traveling. He also said that when they came across a house with a dog, they'd throw rocks at the dog to try to force it into its doghouse long enough for them to break in. Lennie heard the rat-tat-tatting getting louder, thought of Dubie pelted into submission, and panicked.

Despite her fear, she told Bea that kids were out back and about to hurt Dubie. She pleaded to bring her dog into the house, where she was never allowed. Bea didn't care. She didn't even move from her seat and check out the noise before saying no.

"No" flipped a switch in Lennie. For the first time, she didn't need a shot of whiskey to become Linda, her defiant defender. Feeling fierce, the girl simply marched into the backyard, retrieved her best friend, and escorted her into the house. Bea was filled with her usual rage when she found the dog inside and she beat Lennie, who was equal parts terrified and emboldened.

Perhaps she was fed up, or else it was a by-product of pretending to be grown for so long, but Lennie decided after the beating that she was better off on her own and that she'd run away from home. She racked her brain for places to go, people nearby who might take her in. Her best shot, she decided, was Fred and Lamont Sanford from the sitcom *Sanford and Son*. They seemed to have plenty of space, and Lennie hoped Lamont might understand what she was going through, seeing that his own father was always calling him names like "big dummy."

That night, when her mother was finally asleep and while Uncle Archie was out, Lennie got dressed. She put on three pairs of pants, two tops, and a jacket. Next, she snuck into Uncle Archie's room and stole the cash he kept in his dresser, three hundred dollars in a tight roll. Then she went to the kitchen and made a few peanut butter and jelly sandwiches for the road. She left Dubie, knowing she couldn't care for both her dog and herself.

Lennie walked the streets of South Central looking for the sign that marked Sanford and Son Salvage. She was afraid out there at night by herself, but she was also excited. Lennie felt like she'd escaped from every awful thing that had defined her short life—from being held captive at home, from her mother and Uncle Archie. She didn't know where she was going, but she liked that every step put space between her and home.

She walked for hours, it seemed, without finding the Sanfords' junkyard. She started to fear it wasn't real. That's when she started to get nervous. She wondered, what would she do if she couldn't find it? She thought maybe she'd made a mistake.

The seven-year-old continued to walk in circles, contemplating her future on the run, until she came across a busy taco stand. Not knowing what else to do, she got in line, ordered two tacos, sat down, and started to cry. A man and woman noticed Lennie sobbing into her tacos. The woman asked her what was wrong, and stories came pouring out—almost everything.

Lennie wailed, describing how the kids were going to throw rocks at Dubie and how her mom wouldn't let her bring the dog in the house. She described the beating she got for bringing Dubie in anyway, and she told them that she'd run away from home. She was out of tears by the end of the story and felt relieved that someone had listened to her.

She was also hopeful that the young couple might save her. Instead, they asked if she had any family they could call besides her mom. It took the wind out of Lennie but, by that point in the night, she'd had enough. She gave them the number for her Uncle Charles, her aunt Doretha's husband, who promptly came to pick her up.

He pulled up in his green Pontiac Firebird. He was enraged. Everybody was looking for her, he said, as he rushed toward the taco stand with a belt in hand. He gave Lennie a few swats and then threw her in the car. Lennie's body dissolved into the Pontiac's plush back seats as he thanked the couple for looking out for her. She was defeated, tired, and completely numb.

7
—
SHAWN
(1967)

JOANNE MCCRAY STAYED INSIDE the day her neighborhood finally got loud and hot. She was as frustrated and as fed up as everyone else, maybe more. But unlike her neighbors, who left the building to loot, Joanne had Shawn to look after. Little white specks of teeth were just starting to break through his gums, and he could finally roll from his back onto his stomach. Some things for the baby or a brand-new radio would have been nice, but she resolved that just as long as people were outside raising hell, she would stay inside with her baby. Safe and sound.

"Inside" was her mother's small apartment on Sixteenth Street in Newark's Central Ward. The place sat atop a bar, but even with the noise that came through the floors, everyone agreed it was a big step up from the Rev. William P. Hayes Homes projects, where they had lived before. Residents of Hayes Homes did their best to get along and look out for one another, but it became abundantly clear in the years since the project was built that families were not meant to live stacked in boxes.

For the few years that they were all together on Sixteenth Street, the McCrays got a little more peace. The apartment was next to a Foodtown, which made it easy to run down for a carton of eggs in the morning or a missing ingredient in time to make dinner. It was also only a few blocks from Central High School. Springfield Avenue, the main drag of the Central Ward's business district, was even closer.

But the apartment on Sixteenth Street got smaller with time. First, Joanne had fallen in love with James Featherstone, a neighborhood boy and Joanne's classmate, who everybody called Bootsie. Then she'd become pregnant, the summer between her sophomore and junior years. On Valentine's Day 1967, she gave birth to Shawn. No more than two months after Joanne brought Shawn home to Sixteenth Street, her sister Denise brought home Otis, her own baby. The small apartment felt as though it might explode with the addition of two babies. Before it could, Newark did.

The story, which spread quickly through the Central Ward, was that a squad car had been double-parked near the corner of Seventh Street and Fifteenth Avenue. A Black taxi driver named John Smith pulled up on it and, seeing that the car wasn't going to move, he'd started to pass. The cops inside stopped the driver before he could get too far. They must have started arguing, because within just a few minutes, those cops were beating Smith. They hit him with their batons, kicked him—all in broad daylight. Then they threw him in the back of the squad car and hauled him off to the Fourth Precinct on Seventeenth Avenue, right across the street from Hayes Homes.

The scene had to have been devastating from the project windows, because word spread that the taxi driver was dead when the officers carried him in. The news traveled from window to window, floor to floor, neighbor to neighbor, and across Newark via two-way radios. By around 8 P.M., a group of Black taxi drivers had formed a line with their cars in front of the precinct, and a crowd had assembled in front of Hayes Homes.

People were more than pissed off; they were fed up. Many had moved to Newark from the South just a few decades prior to escape that kind of brutality. However, they found Newark even segregated its whites. The Irish lived mostly in the Roseville section and filled the ranks of the city's police and fire departments. Italians lived in an area called Seventh Avenue and controlled the construction trades. Newark's Jews were often merchants and lived mostly in Weequahic.

All that was left for Newark's Blacks was the Central Ward, home to some of the worst tenements in all the United States. By 1940, it contained more than sixteen thousand Black residents, many of whom lived in homes that lacked modern heating and indoor plumbing. Barred from trade unions, most made their living as domestics or as janitors, porters, cleaners, or furnace men.

Were they disappointed to learn this was the promised land for which they'd given up everything and everyone they'd ever known? To make things worse, some of them hadn't even set out for Newark. As the folktale goes, some thought they heard "Penn Station, New York" in the unfamiliar accents of northern train conductors, disembarked, and found themselves one stop away from the Big City at Penn Station, *New-ark*.

Their arrival coincided with the creation of the GI Bill and FHA loans that made it easy for Newark's whites to buy homes in the suburbs. Those who had a little money packed up for Vailsburg, Forest Hill, Woodside, and other outlying areas. Working class whites stayed in the city but put distance between themselves and the Central Ward. They moved farther out to Roseville, Clinton Hill, and the Ironbound.

Such neighborhoods were effectively off-limits to Black Newarkers. Realtors refused to show them properties, homeowners wouldn't sell to them, and the banks denied their loans. These policies and practices turned the Central Ward from a run-of-the-mill slum into a Black ghetto in no time. Additional arrivals from the South made it an overcrowded ghetto. The federal government's response to these conditions was *urban renewal,* or as it was called by Blacks back then, "Negro removal." The government would spend millions of dollars to acquire ghetto properties, demolish them, and replace them with new highways and housing projects.

The families displaced by urban renewal could have moved out to some of the housing projects built before the War—Bradley Court, Stephen Crane Village, the Seth Boyden Homes—had they not been reserved for whites. Instead, they had to wait for the construction of Christopher Columbus Homes, Stella Wright Homes, Scudder Homes, and Hayes Homes. The buildings were larger than the white-only projects, high-rises instead of two-to-four-story complexes. They boasted heat, indoor plumbing, and fire-resistant construction. It didn't take but a few years, however, for folks to realize they were not much different from the slums they'd replaced—just vertical.

Time revealed them to be poorly designed and constructed, more warehouses for poor Blacks than neighborhoods.

That was the state of play on the day Newark police officers John DeSimone and Vito Pontrelli decided to lift what looked like a dead Black man out of their squad car and into the doors of the Fourth Precinct, all under the watchful eyes of Hayes Homes residents. The folks who witnessed it had been catching hell for decades. They'd suffered indignity after indignity and refused to accept yet one more.

Newark's rage boiled over during the riots. Folks took off their masks and allowed themselves to be enraged, some for the first time in their lives. In return, the powers that be revealed just how far they'd go to maintain order. The result was both honest and awful.

People can't go back to pretending after something like that. Politicians and community leaders made promises and performed all the niceties, but it did not matter much. The truth was out, and no matter how hard everyone smiled in the street, no one who lived through the riots—white or Black—could forget the things said and done. The spirit of those four days saturated every brick and body in Newark. It informed all that came after.

JOANNE MCCRAY RAISED HER baby boy in a Newark that couldn't shake the riots. Still too young to move out on her own, she stayed with her family in the apartment on Sixteenth Street afterward.

It was there, surrounded by aunts, uncles, and cousins, that Shawn learned to walk and talk. Little pieces of his personality shone through even then.

He did not use a pacifier like other babies but sucked on his fingers instead to soothe himself. And on more than one occasion, Joanne awoke early in the morning to find Shawn had crawled out of bed and teetered into the kitchen, where he attempted to make breakfast for himself. Once, with the help of a chair, he even went so far as to place a pot on the stove.

Joanne and Shawn finally moved into a place of their own some-time after his fourth birthday. Their new home was a two-bedroom apartment near Fifteenth and Morris, just blocks away from the crowded family home on Sixteenth Street. Having lived with so much extended family, Shawn made friends easily. Among the small group of friends he collected were Tony and a brother and sister named Darryl and Nikki. The four played up and down the sidewalks on warm days and sometimes Darryl, who was a few years older, would lead the group on trips to Tip Top's, a neighborhood convenience store. They'd buy cookies and penny candy, and Shawn would occa-sionally see his father, who hung out there.

They made uneasy small talk during these spontaneous reunions, and Shawn would perk up with the attention from his father's friends—Big Rob, Craig, and Harold Boy. The men affectionately called him "Little Bootsie," a nickname that never quite stuck.

When Shawn wasn't playing outside, he was inside with his mother, whom he adored. The two would lie on her bed and watch TV, listen to music, or read. Shawn had his picture books, and Joanne had books with titles like *Dopefiend, Whoreson,* and *Black Gangster* by Donald Goines.

It was time they had together only because Joanne did not work. She accepted odd jobs here and there, but for the most part she and Shawn lived on government assistance and money she sometimes re-ceived from Bootsie. The arrangement kept the young mother scraping by, but it also allowed her to take care of and spend time at home with Shawn, who seemed to grow an inch taller and more spirited by the day.

That small apartment was their cocoon, but it was also expensive. The rent was too high for a young, unemployed mother with little support. Further complicating matters, Joanne found out in the summer of 1973 that she was pregnant again. The financial pressure swelled along with her belly and eventually forced Joanne to do something she never thought she'd have to: move back into Hayes Homes.

The towers were so much a part of the neighborhood landscape that the move did not feel like much of a move at all to Shawn. Hayes Homes loomed in the background while he played outside or walked to the store or back to his grandmother's apartment with his mother. He would come to learn the complexities of his new home as he grew. But all he cared about at the time was what mattered to a six-year-old: that his new home had plenty of open space, filled with an endless supply of new friends waiting to be made.

For many who lived in Newark, Hayes Homes was inextricably linked to memories of the riots and news stories of rising crime. But for residents of Hayes Homes, especially the children, the ten towers spread across more than five acres were a community in every sense of the word. Together the buildings created a square, and in the middle of that square was a neighborhood center that had a gym and classrooms. There were also playgrounds, courtyards, basketball courts, and a senior center. The most important feature, however, was the people.

What did the children care that their neighborhood of high-rises was a recipe for concentrated poverty, that it was already showing signs of neglect? All of that was less important than the fact that their neighbors were also their friends, classmates, and often family. They lived in Hayes Homes together, went to school together, came home together, and played together. They had one another, which felt something like safety.

The McCrays moved into Building 73, unit 9E. They would continue to live in Hayes Homes for the next seventeen years.

Shawn dove headfirst into the childhood comforts of Hayes Homes, starting with the basketball courts at the center of the complex. He had always been tall for his age and he loved to play games, but Shawn learned he was an athlete on those courts. He moved better than other kids, was faster, and could run up and down the court for hours on end without getting tired. Those physical gifts would come to shape the course of Shawn's life, but during those first years in Hayes Homes what mattered most was that they helped him make friends.

He was a good student, too. Having spent so much time reading with his mother at home, Shawn entered school at Cleveland Elementary ahead of the curve. And still a little sore about having dropped out of school herself, Joanne pushed him to do well. Shawn had to start his homework as soon as he got home from school, and under no circumstances could he play outside until it was complete. Such discipline, especially around education, is not often associated with single mothers raising children in the projects, but it was Shawn's norm. As a result, he earned good grades, mostly A's, and was well liked by his teachers.

He also proved a good big brother to Tony, who was born in 1974, and Cheyta, a baby girl born in 1976. He adjusted well to sharing his small room with both his siblings. He looked out for them, especially once he became old enough to babysit. He watched them once a month when Joanne went grocery shopping, or when she'd steal away for a few hours to grab a drink with her girlfriends.

On occasion, Joanne would drag the kids along to her best friend Linda's house on Hayes Street. Shawn played outside while the women socialized over a six-pack, weed, and cigarettes. He made good friends on all those trips to Linda's—Ramone and James, Karriem and Tyrone, Vernon and Cuk. They introduced Shawn to the fine arts of racing old tires down the street and building go-carts that never worked—things kids in the projects did not do.

On Saturdays, the family traveled to Shawn's grandmother's apartment. The trips were special because they meant taking the bus to the Dayton Street projects, where his grandmother had settled along with his aunt Denise, his uncles Mark, Dennis, and Daryl, and his cousins Otis, Bayyinah, Sheronda, Keith, and Darnell. The kids made a playground of the cemetery behind the building and ran amok in a nearby lot. The abandoned cars that filled it became life-size toys that they'd hop in and pretend they were racing.

Those weekend trips to Dayton Street were the only times they took the bus anywhere, practically the only times they left the neighborhood. There were opportunities, of course. Sometimes, parents in Hayes Homes organized field trips for the kids to the movie theater, the skating rink, or even Hershey Park. Shawn, Tony, and Cheyta never went. Joanne did not have many friends in Hayes Homes and wasn't keen on letting the kids out of her sight.

An average day, however, consisted of school, homework, and basketball. For many years, that was Shawn's life. His universe was Hayes Homes and a few other stops in Newark's Central Ward. It was, for the most part, no different than the lives of most American boys coming of age during the 1970s. But there were also regular reminders that he was growing up in one of the nation's most distressed communities, one where the threat of violence accompanied nearly every interaction. One came when two boys tried to jump Shawn during his first year in Hayes Homes.

One of the boys, Terrance Dent, lived in the same building as Shawn but on the fourth floor. Terrance's claim to fame was that he was one of the few kids in Hayes Homes who had a Big Wheel. It was red, yellow, and blue with a huge wheel in front and two small ones in the back. The two boys had bonded over their mutual appreciation for the high-speed hunk of plastic. They'd haul it to the top of the hill near their building and take turns careening into the nearest courtyard. Before they could slide into traffic on Seventeenth Avenue, they would pull the Big Wheel's rear handbrake, which sent it spinning in a small circle.

The other boy who attacked Shawn was Stanley. Shawn did not know him well, but Stanley also lived in the building, and before Shawn moved in, he and Terrance had been pretty tight. All three played together sometimes, but Shawn generally avoided Stanley. He was "bad," Shawn thought. Not one of the worst kids in the neighborhood, but always in the middle of something and taking every opportunity he could to pick fights with the other boys.

All three were in the hallway on the third floor one day when Shawn noticed Terrance and Stanley looking his way and whispering. No sooner had Shawn spotted the mini huddle than Terrance began running full speed toward him.

Perhaps it was all of the kung fu he watched on TV, but something moved Shawn to step quickly to the right and kick Terrance square in the chest, sending his friend flying backward. If he was the fighting type, Shawn might have stayed around to boast, maybe even strike a pose and yell out "Hi-yah!" like Bruce Lee. But he wasn't, so he took off in a sprint up the stairs to the ninth floor.

He ducked Terrance after that, until one day when they bumped into each other in the courtyard. Terrance admitted then that attacking Shawn had been Stanley's idea; he'd just gone along with it. He was sorry, he said. In a way that only makes sense to little boys, the incident only made the two friends closer.

Neither played much with Stanley after that, which didn't matter much, because he was forced to move out of Hayes Homes just a few months later when his grandmother shot and killed his grandfather in their apartment.

Another example of Newark's sharp edges bursting the bubble of Shawn's childhood happened when he was in the second grade. He was walking through Cleveland Elementary's Hunterdon Street entrance when he passed Willie Harris, a boy who lived in Building 65. Willie must've woken up on the wrong side of the bed, because he saw Shawn glance at him as he walked in, which compelled him to ask forcefully, "What you looking at?"

"You!" Shawn replied without stopping.

After a few steps, he turned back to gauge Willie's reaction. What Shawn saw instead was a broken bottle whirling toward his head. But again, he thought fast and threw his left hand up to the block the bottle. It didn't hit him in the face, but it sliced through his hand, leaving a deep cut that required five stitches. Willie was expelled soon after and Shawn spent the next few months learning to write with his right hand.

He slowly built up a resistance to the random violence that plagued Hayes Homes and Newark. The incidents were always upsetting but, like most everyone else in the neighborhood, Shawn learned to keep his head down, to avoid the hotspots and hot people. And he developed skills that kept him out of trouble, like the ability to blend into a crowd when he did not want to stand out or appear bigger when he needed to back someone up off him.

Shawn learned those powers from other boys in the neighborhood, his uncles and cousins. He also learned from the young men who hung out around Building 77. They seemed like grown men then, but they couldn't have been any older than eighteen, nineteen years old.

The guys in Building 77 did not keep the same hours as the other grown-ups. They seemed instead to hang out most of the day, entertaining a near-constant parade of people who'd go in and out of a few apartments on the first floor. Shawn never saw for himself what went on behind closed doors, but he'd read enough Donald Goines novels to guess that the young men were selling drugs.

The closest he ever got to the action was when one of them, usually Tariq, would ask him to run an errand. Shawn would be playing in the courtyard when Tariq would call him over to Building 77. He'd talk Shawn up a little before giving him a five-dollar bill and instructions to "run to the store" for a pack of cigarettes and a soda. It was a windfall for Shawn whenever Tariq said, "Keep the change."

The trips to the store for Tariq often ended in lectures. "Stay out of trouble," he'd warn, or he'd encourage Shawn to keep his focus on his schoolwork. If there was anything ironic about a drug dealer admonishing a kid to stay on the straight and narrow, it was lost on Shawn. The boy reasoned that if anyone knew the perils of street life, Tariq did. More to the point, Tariq was someone he admired. He was confident and seemed to know a little bit about everything. It also did not hurt that he was tall and slim like Shawn and wore his trademark bucket hat tilted on his head just so.

Bootsie was still hanging around the Central Ward at the time, but he did not teach Shawn half of what Tariq did, not even how to ride the ten-speed bike he used for his late-night visits to the apartment. Bootsie had three children with Joanne, none of whom he took the time to get to know. Instead, he crept into the apartment at night to spend time with their mother and was out before morning. Shawn experienced him as a series of entrances and exits, as the faint sound of a bike rolling in and out the door.

8

—

KURT

(1969-78)

ON MAY 19, 1969, members of the New Haven Black Panther Party kidnapped Alex Rackley, a fellow Panther they suspected of being an FBI informant. Over the next two days, Rackley was interrogated and tortured at the chapter's headquarters until he confessed. Three Panthers—Warren Kimbro, Lonnie McLucas, and George Sams, Jr.—then drove Rackley to nearby Middlefield, Connecticut, where they shot and killed him, then dumped his body in the Coginchaug River.

It is still unclear whether Rackley was indeed an informant. However, there's no question the New Haven Panthers were infiltrated by local and federal authorities. Indeed, on the night of Rackley's murder, officers with the New Haven Police Department trailed the car in which he was transported to Middlefield. His body was recovered by state police the very next day.

The authorities essentially allowing the New Haven Panthers to kill Rackley raised suspicions among Panthers and their supporters that the crime was instigated by the FBI as part of its COINTELPRO program. Adding to the suspicion was the behavior of George Sams, a national Panther field marshal who'd come to New Haven to instill discipline in the chapter, and who had orchestrated Rackley's torture and murder.

He was an agent provocateur, some concluded. This assessment was reinforced when Sams began cooperating with police, going so far as to implicate national party chairman Bobby Seale in the murder. Seale had indeed been in New Haven for an appearance at Yale University during the period Rackley was held hostage, but there was no evidence that he ordered the murder, as Sams claimed. Nonetheless, authorities brought charges against nine Panthers, including Seale.

The case became a cause célèbre in the months that followed. Student activists nearby on Yale's campus were galvanized by the case of the New Haven Nine. Members of Yale's Black Student Alliance organized a student strike in the weeks leading up to the trials, scheduled for May 1970. They also planned a May Day rally to address not only the trials but student opposition to the Vietnam War.

Administrators saw the rally as a threat to the campus. It was poised to bring more than twenty thousand demonstrators to campus—Panthers and other so-called radicals who officials feared would instigate violence in the university's hallowed halls. Those concerns came to a head at a faculty meeting on April 23.

More progressive members of the faculty, including Yale's president, Kingman Brewster, Jr., thought the best course was to embrace the rally, to set a table for the protesters and facilitate peaceful demonstrations. However, the university's conservative old guard—a sizable fraction of the faculty—wanted to crack down and bring in authorities to tamp down any demonstrations.

Students assembled and began demonstrating outside of Yale's Sprague Hall as their professors debated inside—all sides growing more restless as the hours ticked by. Just as it seemed the meeting and protest outside might devolve into chaos, members of the faculty moved to allow one student to address the body. That student was Kurt Schmoke, secretary of the class of 1971 and a leader among Black students.

Schmoke entered Sprague Hall and stood before more than nine hundred professors and administrators. He kept his remarks brief. He said, "Many of the students in the group that had gathered outside the meeting are committed to a cause, but there are a great number of students on campus who are confused and many who are frightened. They don't know what to think. You are our teachers. You are the people we respect. We look to you for guidance and moral leadership. On behalf of my fellow students, I beg you to give it to us."

The faculty was so stunned and impressed by Schmoke's measured appeal for counsel that he was given a standing ovation. Subsequently, they voted to approve a plan to suspend "academic expectations" for the rest of the semester so that students, faculty, and staff could assist in preparing the May Day rally. When the day finally came, the campus community offered shelter, food, daycare, and first aid to the estimated fifteen thousand demonstrators who showed up.

The preparations helped prevent any major disruptions. It was an accomplishment put in stark relief just a week later when four students were killed during similar demonstrations at Kent State. Kurt Schmoke was largely credited for making it all possible.

PEOPLE KNEW KURT SCHMOKE was going places long before he quelled an uprising at Yale. Part of his good fortune was the community of people who believed in him. Yet another element was his natural gifts and abilities, which were clear and abundant even to those who met him as a boy.

Schmoke was born in Baltimore in 1949, the son of Murray Schmoke, a civilian chemist for the U.S. Army, and Irene B. Reid, a social worker. He attended integrated public schools on the heels of *Brown v. Board of Education* and showed promise early on. Marion Bascom, the pastor of the Douglas Memorial Community Church, where the Schmokes were active members, remembered him as "a quiet, unassuming boy, but always a boy whom you felt had great depth of mind and spirit."

Schmoke's gifts continued to unfold as he grew into a handsome and strapping young man. He attended the mostly white Baltimore City College, the third oldest high school in the United States, and excelled academically as well as in football and lacrosse. Then, at fourteen, Schmoke was convinced by classmates at City College to join the Lancers Boys Club, an organization founded by Baltimore City Circuit Court Judge Robert Hammerman to instill values like scholarship, service, and leadership in young men.

His intelligence and poise inspired Hammerman, who took Schmoke under his wing. "Right off the bat, I could sense Kurt's intelligence, his warm personality, his natural leadership ability," recalled Hammerman in a 1998 profile of Schmoke in *The New Republic.* "And I told him he was made for a lot more than football. He was meant for leadership."

The judge began meeting regularly with Schmoke, taking him for long lunches at the Johns Hopkins Club and introducing him to Baltimore's most influential lawyers and legislators.

"I wanted him to get exposure to prominent political and legal leaders, both Black and white," said Hammerman . "I've always maintained that, from the time Kurt was fourteen, you could be the grand dragon of the Ku Klux Klan, and if you met Kurt Schmoke, you'd support him for president of the United States. He had that natural, magnetic appeal. You get to know him, you meet him, and you fall in love with him."

That appeal helped Schmoke become president of his junior class and, during his senior year, the first Black student ever elected student body president at City College. All the while, he led the school's football team as quarterback to two undefeated seasons and successive state championships in 1965 and 1966.

"Kurt was probably the hottest thing that had come out of Baltimore in years," recalled Lewis Noonberg, a fellow Lancer. "Public school, Black, bright, good athlete, handsome: He had it all."

Judge Hammerman and others encouraged Schmoke to pursue the Ivy League, and he was finally sold on Yale after the college sent its star running back, Calvin Hill, to Schmoke's home to personally recruit him.

He arrived at Yale in the fall of 1967, in a moment of great challenge and change. Schmoke, a son of Black Baltimore, was there to become what he might—a great leader of his city, of his people. Perhaps more. It was a rare position, one laden with privilege and responsibility, and worlds apart from life in Baltimore, where, the following spring, riots erupted following the assassination of Martin Luther King, Jr.

While the city's Black neighborhoods struggled to rebuild in the days and weeks that followed, Schmoke was struggling to fit in on campus and carry out the unspoken mandate he had as one of the Chosen. He excelled, as he always had. He made light work of being an athlete, a scholar, a leader on campus. Indeed, by 1969, when Schmoke united Yale's faculty and student body behind the Black Panthers, he'd been so excellent for so long it is a wonder that anyone was surprised.

He continued striving, climbing toward his promise in the years that followed. The steps came in rapid succession. First was Oxford, where he studied as a Rhodes Scholar. Then Harvard Law School. Next, he returned to Baltimore and became one of the first Black associates at Piper & Marbury, a silk-stocking law firm. It was a short but expected layover in the private sector. Within a year's time, Schmoke was in D.C., serving as part of the Domestic Policy Council staff during the Carter administration.

But Schmoke's portion was in his hometown. From the time he was fourteen years old and making the rounds with Judge Hammerman, there'd been talk that he'd be the first Black mayor of Baltimore. That prospect seemed not only possible but within reach as the eighties approached. He'd made all the right friends, checked off all the boxes and then some. All that was left was to find a path forward and, of course, remain impeccable.

9

—

AIN'T NO STOPPIN' US NOW
(1979)

A BLACK MIDDLE CLASS has always existed in America, but it was so small as to be insignificant until the 1970s. That changed, in part, because of the Civil Rights and Black Power movements. Those campaigns helped make racial discrimination illegal in America, removing many—though not all—barriers to employment, education, housing, and civic engagement. The result was more opportunity for well-positioned Blacks, and ultimately enough growth in the Black middle class to add a new dimension to Black life.

Just a few years out from the Civil Rights Movement—almost as an answer to the continued stream of complaints coming from the ghetto—Americans quickly turned their attention to the Black middle class. The trend was welcome news for a nation eager to move past reminders of its racism. In a growing Black middle class, those who'd rather not think about the nation's penchant for anti-Black racism finally had something to make them feel good about the American system, evidence that it was fair.

Reports in publications such as *Ebony* and *Black Enterprise* noted how newly middle-class Blacks were savvy and industrious. Most were civil servants, working jobs at various levels of government, but that did not prevent them from being fashionable and enthusiastic consumers of luxury goods. It was also said that for them, "the struggle" was passé. They considered success the best revenge for centuries of oppression and measured that success in salaries, degrees, homes, vacations—totems of middle-class identity.

"To be Black in the U.S. is no longer to be subordinate—not necessarily," declared a 1974 *Time* cover story on the Black middle class. "The national effort to give Blacks a more equitable share of the nation's goods and benefits has had results—uneven but undeniable." The article went on to explain what middle-class status meant to Black Americans, how it came with an immense feeling of being "a useful, functioning part of society—not indispensable perhaps, but not easily dispensed with either."

It was a keen insight, because *expendable* is exactly how the rest of Black America was seen. Starting with the Nixon administration, the federal government adopted a policy of benign neglect regarding issues of race. That left Blacks to navigate post-civil-rights America—all the benefits and backlash—themselves. Efforts to fully integrate the country's schools, neighborhoods, and workplaces withered on the vine. Poverty became concentrated in predominantly Black communities as the Black middle class joined with whites in their flight to the suburbs. From this emerged a Black America with two faces: a community either flourishing or languishing, depending on where the observer was standing.

The percentage of Black people earning at least ten thousand dollars a year more than doubled, from 13 to 30 percent between 1961 and 1971. Along the same timeline, the number of Black people in professional and technical jobs rose 128 percent. The number of Black people in college almost doubled from 370,000 to 727,000 between 1967 and 1971. But even as the Black middle class was expanding, deindustrialization and an economic recession were doing away with meaningful opportunities for work. Ultimately, despite the success of a select few, too many Black people still lived in poverty—nearly a third. After a decade of struggle, riots, and death, those folks had nothing to show for it.

The tension between this beleaguered group and their upwardly mobile counterparts was captured in the *Time* magazine write-up. "Probably the crudest dilemma facing the new middle class is their relationship with Blacks left behind in the ghetto," the article notes. "It is natural enough for the middle class to pull out of the slums once they can afford to—just as other ethnic groups have done. But by leaving, they abandon those who cannot escape the ghetto to its more rapacious elements, aggravating the spread of crime and decay. Small wonder that middle-class Blacks feel some guilt and ambivalence about fleeing to better neighborhoods."

The middle-class Black people interviewed for the story were also said to have expressed their fear of "Black underclass crime" and of other Black people generally. "Their homes in the most luxurious suburbs are equipped with burglar alarms and watchdogs," it said. "Putting so much trust in education, they fear that lower-class Blacks may be a bad influence on their own children."

Despite the growing rift between the groups, middle class and poor Black people worked together to achieve unprecedented success in local politics. The energy of the Civil Rights and Black Power movements was still very much alive in Black America. So Blacks, regardless of class status, mobilized in the 1970s and pooled their resources to elect Black mayors for the first time in a number of big cities, especially in cities that had been rocked by riots in the late sixties.

Kenneth Gibson became mayor of Newark in 1970. In 1973, Tom Bradley and Maynard Jackson were elected in Los Angeles and Atlanta. Oakland got Lionel Wilson in 1977, and Ernest Morial was elected mayor of New Orleans in 1978. Though he was not the district's first Black mayor, Marion Barry was first elected to lead D.C. in 1978, changing forever the political landscape of the district. Each man had his roots in movement politics and ran a campaign to rebuild his city with a focus on Black economic development. Each promised a new age of prosperity through increased cooperation between whites and Blacks.

It may not have been the sweeping change most wanted from the Civil Rights or Black Power movements. Still, the wave of wins was understood as a sign of progress. Having been stagnant for so long and having sacrificed so much, many accepted the forward movement as evidence their time was finally coming.

The moment was given an anthem in the spring of 1979 when R&B duo McFadden & Whitehead released "Ain't No Stoppin' Us Now." The song is a perfect example of Philly soul, a style of music defined by its lush fusion of sounds from across the American social landscape—funk, pop, classical, and soul. "Ain't No Stoppin' Us Now" has all the hallmarks of the genre. It opens with drums and a funky bassline. After a beat, the rhythm gives way to strings fit for a corona-tion. Next up, the refrain of the song, sung in sweet harmony by a chorus of female voices: "Ain't no stoppin' us now. We're on the move. / Ain't no stoppin' us now. We've got the groove."

After "Ain't No Stoppin' Us Now" grooves a bit, Gene McFadden and John Whitehead lay out the thesis. "There's been so many things that's held us down / but now it looks like things are finally comin' around," croons Whitehead at the top of the first verse. McFadden closes it in a powerful baritone, "Don't you let nothin', nothin' stand in your way. / I want y'all to listen, listen to every word I say, every word I say."

The song resonated with many Black Americans as an articulation of their feelings and hopes. It rose quickly to number thirteen on the Billboard Hot 100 and reached number one on the R&B charts, an achievement due in part to the overwhelming embrace of "Ain't No Stoppin' Us Now" as an anthem for post–Civil Rights Movement Black America.

Writer Colson Whitehead paints a picture of the song's popularity in *Sag Harbor,* his semiautobiographical novel about summering in the Black beach community. "At any given moment, someone was playing 'Ain't No Stoppin' Us Now.' It was the Black national anthem. The disco version of 'We Shall Overcome,' courtesy of Mr. McFadden & Mr. Whitehead. It came out of our cars as we drove to the store for last-minute paper plates and ketchup, issued triumphantly from sand-flecked boom boxes on threadbare beach towels, blared out of backyard patios from ancient amps plugged into bright orange extension cords uncoiled for annual duty."

That was the view from the middle of the socioeconomic ladder. But whereas "Ain't No Stoppin' Us Now" operated as an affirmation of achievement for the Black middle class, it was a mission statement for the poor, Black, and aspirational. For them, it captured not that they had made it but their determination to try.

In March 1979, *The New York Times* published a series highlighting the lack of opportunity that existed for Black youth at the time. "The unemployment picture for minority youths, particularly Blacks, is now roughly what it was for the entire nation in the depths of the Great Depression," it noted. "A fourth or more of those who want to work are unable to find jobs."

The article also included a quote from Joseph Cooper, an economist at the National Bureau of Economic Research, who conducted a small poll of jobless youth in Boston. He explained how more than half of the young people he interviewed admitted that they had engaged in illegal activity. "These youths sold marijuana frequently, and some reported that robbery, pickpocketing, burglary and breaking and entering took up most of their time the week prior to the survey week." Cooper added, however, that they all reported wanting full-time permanent jobs.

Just one month later, President Jimmy Carter's chief domestic policy advisor, Stuart Eizenstat, issued a memo to the president on the subject of youth employment. It highlighted that the unemployment rate for Black teenagers had risen from 17 percent to 36 percent between 1954 and 1979, while the unemployment rate remained constant at 13 percent for white teenagers over the same period. Eizenstat echoed the reporting of the *Times,* calling the issue "a critical national problem," important substantively and politically as a "very visible minority issue."

Unbridled ambition requires a vehicle. Without one, it can torture those who have it, perverting their judgment until ambition meets opportunity and is finally satisfied. It seems that's what happened for many young Blacks in the late 1970s determined to let "nothin', nothin'" stand in their way. Cocaine seemed tailor-made for the moment. A stimulant, the substance gets into the bloodstream of users and intoxicates them, making them feel confident, energized, and serene. Those qualities, of course, made cocaine the ideal drug for Black youth at a time when we were either celebrating—or fighting to be one of those who were "movin' on up."

—

JIMMY'S WORLD

IN JUNE 1980, news broke that comedian Richard Pryor had nearly killed himself trying to smoke freebase. According to reports, Pryor was freebasing cocaine and drinking 151-proof rum at home in Los Angeles when either the rum bottle or his pipe exploded. The comedian, engulfed in flames, ran down his street until he was subdued by police and taken to a hospital. Pryor was treated for second- and third-degree burns covering more than half of his body and he spent six weeks in recovery. Later, he revealed that the incident was actually a botched suicide attempt made in a state of drug-induced psychosis.

Days after Pryor's incident, *People* magazine ran a piece on the "dangerous drug craze" behind the tragic accident. It detailed a growing freebase scene among the Hollywood elite. Sly Stone had gone public with his habit, the article noted, and an unnamed "Grammy-winning singer" was so fond of the drug that he had a butane lighter built into his coffee table to make freebasing at home more convenient. "It took something like Pryor to bring all this out in the open," one drug counselor was quoted as saying. "Now the freebase story has broken loose."

Pryor's high-profile accident might have broken the story loose, but the nation still didn't fully grasp freebase's potential for harm outside of Hollywood. Media outlets and public officials were, instead, fretting over heroin and marijuana and focusing almost exclusively on those drugs in their efforts to reduce drug abuse. The best example of these misplaced priorities came in September 1980—three months after Pryor's accident, the year freebase emerged on the scene—when *The Washington Post* published "Jimmy's World," the story of an eight-year-old, third-generation heroin addict from Southeast D.C.

Jimmy, the article said, lived in a heroin shooting gallery with his addict mother and drug-dealing stepfather. He was the product of a rape and had become addicted to heroin at the age of five. His one aspiration in life was to become a drug dealer when he grew up, just like his stepdad. "Jimmy's is a world of hard drugs, fast money and the good life he believes both can bring," the story read. "Every day, junkies casually buy heroin from Ron, his mother's live-in-lover, in the dining room of Jimmy's home. They 'cook' it in the kitchen and 'fire up' in the bedrooms. And every day, Ron or someone else fires up Jimmy, plunging a needle into his bony arm, sending the fourth grader into a hypnotic nod."

The *Post* ran "Jimmy's World" on its front page on Sunday, September 28, 1980. The piece resonated so deeply with readers that they lit up the *Post*'s switchboard almost as soon as the paper hit the streets. Most were incensed and demanded that something be done to help Jimmy.

The Los Angeles Times–Washington Post News Service later syndicated the story to its three hundred client papers, making it a national crisis and even prompting incoming first lady Nancy Reagan to respond. "How terribly sad to read it and to know there are so many others like him out there," she wrote in a letter to a *Post* staffer who covered the First Lady. "I hope with all my heart I can do something to help them. Surely there must be a way." D.C. mayor Marion Barry responded to the story by mobilizing a search party to find Jimmy and his family, whose whereabouts and identities *Post* editors and reporter Janet Cooke refused to share.

There was, however, nothing to share, because the story was a complete fabrication, one that was only exposed after "Jimmy's World" was awarded a Pulitzer Prize for Feature Writing the following year.

But while "Jimmy's World" was fake, it reveals how, at the dawn of the crack epidemic, poor Black communities and drugs existed in a very dark place within the American imagination.

Janet Cooke, the author of "Jimmy's World," began work at *The Washington Post* in January 1980. The twenty-five-year-old reporter, a Black woman, joined the paper at a time when it was still riding high on the prestige of its Watergate reporting. It was also just starting to feel pressure to diversify its historically white newsroom. Ben Bradlee, the *Post*'s famed executive editor, said he circled three things in red pencil when Cooke's résumé came across his desk: her degree from Vassar College and her memberships in Phi Beta Kappa and the National Association of Black Journalists. He passed the résumé on to Bob Woodward, then assistant managing editor at the *Post*, with instructions to snatch Cooke up before a competitor could.

Despite Cooke's impressive résumé—which also boasted two years of experience at the *Toledo Blade*, studies at the Sorbonne, a master's degree from the University of Toledo, and fluency in French and Spanish—she was assigned to the Weekly section. It was a D.C.–focused beat privately referred to as "the Ghetto" by Black staffers who regarded it as a dumping ground. Cooke—charming and attractive, with a penchant for designer clothes—set out immediately to make a name for herself at the *Post* and in D.C. She threw exclusive parties and, according to some, sought out friendships with *Post* staffers she thought might advance her career. Cooke's objective, it seemed, was to rise in the ranks of D.C.'s social scene and on the *Post*'s masthead. Her first step would have to be a promotion off the Weekly desk.

After a few months on the job and having published quite a few stories, Cooke was given an assignment to report out rumors of a new form of heroin. She worked for months reporting the piece but was ultimately unable to confirm its existence. But Vivian Aplin-Brownlee, her editor on the Weekly desk, thought what Cooke had uncovered about heroin use in the district had the makings of a solid piece for the paper's Metro section, which had been running regular reports on heroin in D.C. Aplin-Brownlee turned Cooke and her reporting over to Metro editor Milton Coleman, who agreed.

Coleman reviewed Cooke's reporting and seized on the brief mention of a child addict being treated in a Howard University drug program. Coleman told Cooke that if she could locate the child, the story could land her the front page of the paper, an honor for any young reporter and a surefire path out of "the Ghetto." He also told Cooke that given the delicate nature of the story, she could offer total anonymity to the boy and his family. Cooke took that as an opportunity to write fiction.

"Jimmy's World" went to print without any editor at the *Post* ever asking Cooke to reveal Jimmy's identity or home address. In lieu of photographs, it was paired with original illustrations based on the reporter's description of the boy.

Shortly after the piece ran, Cooke was promoted to the Metro desk. She also received a note from Donald Graham, publisher of *The Washington Post*. "The *Post* has no more important and tougher job than explaining life in the Black community in Washington," the note read in part. "A special burden gets put on Black reporters doing that job, and a double-special burden on Black reporters who try to see life through their own eyes instead of seeing it the way they're told they should. The *Post* seems to have many such reporters. You belong very high up among them."

However, Black staffers at the *Post* began raising concerns about the veracity of "Jimmy's World" as soon as it was published. Vivian Aplin-Brownlee, who had edited Cooke in the Weekly section, was shocked upon reading it. Aplin-Brownlee had been out of the loop during the piece's editing and was deeply disturbed by the unbelievably grotesque account. Moreover, she doubted Cooke's ability to have actually reported it. The young reporter who wore Gucci and Yves St. Laurent fashions in the field wasn't street-savvy enough to get that kind of access, she thought. No dealer would shoot up a child in Cooke's presence. Aplin-Brownlee explained as much to Milton Coleman, but her concerns fell on deaf ears.

Metro reporter Courtland Milloy was also skeptical of Cooke's story. Following the publication of "Jimmy's World," he and Cooke were sent on a reporting trip to find other child addicts and file a follow-up. Milloy said that while driving through Condon Terrace, the tough area Jimmy was supposedly from, Cooke seemed completely unfamiliar with the neighborhood and couldn't locate the boy's house. Like Aplin-Brownlee, Milloy shared his doubts with Coleman, who chalked them up to professional jealousy. In a show of real hubris, *Post* editors then nominated "Jimmy's World" for a Pulitzer Prize in the local news reporting category sometime soon after.

Almost as incredible as the *Post*'s handling of Cooke's story was that of the Pulitzer board. After the News Reporting jury selected another piece over "Jimmy's World," the board awarded Cooke's story the prize for feature writing, unbeknownst to the Features jury, which had selected another piece. The prizes were announced on April 13, 1981, and Cooke made headlines once again as the first Black woman ever to win a Pulitzer in journalism.

Winning the Pulitzer was Cooke's undoing. Proud of their alumna, editors at the *Toledo Blade* went to work preparing a story on her win. They noticed inconsistencies, however, between Cooke's biography as told to the Associated Press wire and their own personnel records. Cooke had not graduated magna cum laude from Vassar College or received a master's degree from the University of Toledo. According to the *Blade*'s records, she'd only attended Vassar for her freshman year before transferring to UT, where she ultimately received a Bachelor of Arts. *Blade* editors alerted the AP to the discrepancies. Within hours of the announcement, both an editor at the AP and the assistant to the president of Vassar were on the phone asking to speak with Ben Bradlee.

The entire affair unraveled by evening. Cooke admitted to lying on her résumé, and after failing for a second time to identify Jimmy's house, she was interrogated in an empty conference room by Woodward, Bradlee, and other editors. After hours of questioning, she finally admitted that the story was made up. Cooke wrote a statement in longhand: "'Jimmy's World' was in essence a fabrication. I never encountered or interviewed an 8-year-old heroin addict. The September 28, 1980, article in *The Washington Post* was a serious misrepresentation which I deeply regret. I apologize to my newspaper, my profession, the Pulitzer board, and all seekers of the truth. Today, in facing up to the truth, I have submitted my resignation." The Pulitzer board withdrew Cooke's prize days later.

"My goal was to create Supernigger," Cooke later said of the lies on her résumé. About the story of an eight-year-old addict, she simply said, "At some point, it dawned on me that I could simply make it all up. I just sat down and wrote it." For its part, the *Post* apologized to its readers in an editorial headed "The End of the 'Jimmy' Story." "This newspaper, which printed Janet Cooke's false account of a meeting with an 8-year-old heroin addict and his family, was itself the victim of a hoax—which we then passed along in a prominent page-one story, taking in the readers as we ourselves had been taken in," read the editorial.

The *Post*'s editors hadn't been taken for a ride, though. They had gone on that ride with Janet Cooke. First, editors pursued the story even though child heroin addicts were impossible to find in D.C. Then the *Post*'s editors made no attempt to confirm that Jimmy or anyone else presented in the story actually existed. According to standard practices for anonymous sourcing, at least Cooke's editor, Milton Coleman, should have known Jimmy's true identity and checked it. Instead, an ambitious young reporter was given carte blanche to publish on the front page of one of the most prominent papers in the country a work of complete fiction.

How could a newsroom that brought down a sitting president using anonymous sourcing be so negligent? How could it nominate such flimsy reporting for the highest prize in journalism? How could "Jimmy's World" win?

Cooke said she never thought it would, but she should have known better. The country's appetite for stories of Black suffering and sickness is well documented, and Black drug addiction is one topic for which Americans have proven ravenous. In "Jimmy's World," Cooke gave her bosses at the *Post* and its readers something they couldn't resist: a story that confirmed all their worst ideas of the ghetto, written by the right kind of Black person. Who needed to fact-check "Jimmy's World" when so many were sure it existed?

In the aftermath of "Jimmy's World," the journalism world debated what lessons the saga held for affirmative action initiatives in the newsroom. It exiled Cooke. The *Post* and the Pulitzer Prizes began gradually repairing their tarnished reputations. Smart people, many concluded, had been duped by a compulsive liar. Their defenses had only been lowered by pressures to integrate. After "Jimmy's World," those defenses were reinforced. There was little to no reevaluation of the story—what it was concocted to convey, and why professionals at the *Post* and the Pulitzers were so eager to accept it.

Meanwhile, the media was failing to devote significant coverage to the real story of drugs in urban America: freebase, the drug spreading out of after-hour clubs and into the streets. What coverage did exist treated the substance like a Hollywood fad. In May 1980, *Rolling Stone* ran a feature on the drug that called it "the top-of-the-line model of the Cadillac of drugs." "Because of the cost, freebase is apparently not a big problem on the street level," the article assured.

In the years that followed, *The New York Times* published stories on the widespread use of freebase in Hollywood and the NFL. *The Washington Post* covered its prevalence in the NBA. Stories on a sharp rise in drug overdoses by the *Post* and the *Times* show that some reporters did make connections to freebase, but even then, they failed to recognize that the nation was in the earliest stages of a drug epidemic.

10

—

LENNIE

(1972-78)

LENNIE HAD ALWAYS ENJOYED LEARNING, but her school life fell apart along with her home life. The two things seemed coordinated to her. Where other kids had been nice and eager to befriend one another before, by the time the abuse at home kicked up, in third and fourth grade, all the kids at school seemed hard and mean. There were boys who bothered her, but the girls teased Lennie the most, usually about her dark skin. If just one girl had been nice to her, or even tried to be a friend, it was lost on Lennie.

There's only so much picking anybody can take, and Lennie had had her fill toward the end of fourth grade. She brought her alter ego, Linda, to school. Instead of ignoring the girls that teased her, Lennie hurled insults right back, using the kind of language her mom used with her. She threatened to fight other kids, sometimes actually coming to blows with them. A fight with a fourth grader was nothing, she thought, compared to the beatings she took at home.

Indeed, Lennie fought so much at Hyde Park that she was kicked out and sent to Fifty-ninth Street School for fifth grade. The new school was just a fifteen-minute walk away from Hyde Park but was worlds away in what it offered. Fifty-ninth Street didn't have a special program for the "academically enriched," for example, and students there didn't go on field trips to museums or other places downtown. Lennie chalked that up to the fact that Hyde Park's principal, Mr. Atwater, was white.

She made a decision before getting to Fifty-ninth Street that she wouldn't let anyone pick on her. Better yet, she decided that she'd bully them before they ever got the chance. Much to Lennie's relief, the tactic worked. The other kids seemed impressed that Lennie had been kicked out of her previous school for fighting—maybe even a little bit afraid.

The fear she instilled in others felt like power to Lennie. She liked that her classmates said things like "You don't wanna mess with her." She liked that there was a group of girls who looked to her for cues, laughing when she laughed and trying not to when she didn't.

She finally had friends, too. They were from her neighborhood but were "from the wrong side of the tracks," as her mom might put it. They ran around in little cliques—each group from one block or the other. Those boundaries were fluid and shifted all the time. What rarely changed, though, was their attitude. Like Lennie, these kids were rough.

Lennie took her new attitude with her to Horace Mann Junior High the following year. She was, by then, what she always wanted to be: one of the cool kids. Lennie cultivated her new status in school, in the neighborhood, like it was the most important thing in the world. To her, it was.

South Central was by then so isolated from the rest of Los Angeles, from the rest of the world, that it might as well have been a desert island. Surviving there meant learning the landscape intimately, knowing who was who and what was what. Thriving meant carving out a place for herself, an identity that people recognized and respected, and a group of allies who might look out for her.

Home for Lennie became everything between La Brea and Western, west to east, Angeles Vista and Florence north to south. The city had official names for the small sections included in the tract—Van Ness, Park Mesa Heights, View Heights, Hyde Park. But to the young people who lived there, it was all the Hood, which consisted of the Bacc Hood; the Front Hood; the Dime; and the Avenues, where Lennie lived—on Second and Sixty-seventh.

These new names signaled a shift in the neighborhood from a place under the authority of the City of Los Angeles to a place under the control of residents. Their values became the law. Their hustles became the economy.

The neighborhood could also be separated into different kinds of people. There were the working people, of course: folks who clocked in every day, were looking for work, or went to school. There was also a fair share of hustlers, gangsters, and gangbangers. Everyone coexisted in a shared ecosystem in which a working person's son might be a hustler or a gangbanger, and gangsters had kids who went to school.

Because everyone was connected in one way or another, it was easy to think nothing of the illicit activities. Lennie didn't think of drug dealers, for example, as scary guys in back alleys trying to hook young kids on poison. They were people like her neighbor Joe Rat, who used the money he made selling drugs to help pay his mom's rent. In her mind, what Joe Rat and the rest did—the pimping, robbing, gambling—was a means to an end: money, security.

It was only natural, then, that Lennie fell in with the kids from "the wrong side of the tracks." She felt like they had something in common, and the young gangbangers and hustlers accepted her easily, liked her for her boldness, her sense of humor, and the fearlessness she projected.

Lennie could talk shit, smoke, and drink with the best of them. Before long, she was a fixture in the neighborhood, someone people looked forward to seeing and catching up with. She craved the attention, the free drinks she got when hanging out, and the occasional five or ten dollars she'd get when somebody "hit a lick" and felt generous.

Whether they knew it or not, Lennie needed the money. Her mother's cruelty had evolved over the years from physical and verbal abuse into withholding things. It started off with dinner but grew to other meals, and essentials like deodorant, pads, and soap. Getting new clothes that fit her developing body was also out of the question, so Lennie used the little money people in the neighborhood gave her for those, too.

Lennie tried like hell to find odd jobs as a preteen, but she was too young and a girl in a time when jobs like bagging groceries, delivering papers, and mowing lawns were mostly reserved for boys. Still, she applied for any job she heard about until finally, the summer after seventh grade, she got lucky and was hired to work as a teaching assistant at the L.A. School of Gymnastics. Lennie didn't know the first thing about gymnastics, but thankfully she didn't have to. The job was simple—some basic tumbling, making sure toddlers didn't break their necks while jumping on trampolines and in ball pits. It was daycare for rich kids, she thought.

The gym was out in Culver City, home to Sony Pictures and MGM Studios. Lennie took a couple of buses to get there, the 209 to Leimert Park then the 105. The ride was nice, the change of pace and place, even though it took an hour each way. It gave her time to think. Houses got bigger and cars nicer as she moved from one neighborhood to the other. Plus, people at the gym and elsewhere in Culver City were curious about Lennie. A Black girl from South Central was an oddity there. Parents of kids at the gym liked chatting her up, especially the dads. A rush came over her when someone, usually a man, stopped in his tracks to talk to her.

Lennie didn't put much mind toward her developing body, but men sure seemed to. There was suddenly something in their eyes when they talked to her. It was the same look Uncle Archie had. The look scared her, but it also made her feel powerful and special. What's more, the men seemed nice. They smiled big and asked her questions about school and her job. Some of the men in Culver City even offered her rides when they saw her waiting at the bus stop and gave her their business cards when she'd decline. Just a month into the summer, Lennie had an impressive collection of cards from executives and producers.

She felt empowered by the newfound attention, from the men in her neighborhood and the ones in Culver City. The only person she had to talk to about it was Uncle Archie, who encouraged Lennie to get whatever she could from the men—free meals, money, gifts. She did exactly that and used the money random men gave her to buy things her mother never would—jelly sandals, handbags, form-fitting clothes that made Lennie feel less like the "little Black bitch" her mom liked to call her.

Lennie still didn't look a day over fifteen once she was all dressed up, but she felt like her transformation to Linda was complete. She felt different in her deep-brown skin. Her thick, dark hair and eyes that almost disappeared when she smiled were of a source of pride, not embarrassment, as men ogled her. She must be something, she thought, if those men wanted her.

One day, Lennie was waiting for the bus home from Culver City when a man pulled up to the stop and asked her if she wanted a ride instead. The man seemed nice, so she got in. Once on the road, he asked all the usual questions—where she was from, what she was doing out in Culver City. He seemed interested in everything except how old she was.

Out of nowhere, the man asked her if she wanted to go to a hotel. Lennie had been doing her best to seem cool and grown-up during the conversation. Still, the question spooked her a bit. However, something came over Lennie. She was reminded of everything Uncle Archie had said and done to her over the years. She felt numb, which made it easier to say yes.

The whole experience didn't last more than thirty minutes or so. It didn't seem real to Lennie at first. It was almost like she wasn't there as the man booked the room, led her in, then proceeded to have sex with her. When he was done, he gave Lennie eighty-six dollars and dropped her back off at the nearest bus stop.

Lennie sat stunned. On one hand, she was excited to have eighty-six dollars and impressed with herself for not acting like a little girl. But she was also sad. Hot tears started to pour from Lennie's eyes and she was sobbing before she knew it. She tried to stop but couldn't. One bus passed, then another, and Lennie was still crying.

Most people walked right past Lennie. They stole curious glances but didn't stop, except for one neatly dressed older Black man. He asked her if she was okay and why she was crying. Between deep breaths, Lennie explained what had happened. To her surprise, the man didn't berate her or pull away in disgust. Instead, he reached into his pocket and pulled out a bag of white powder. He put a small dab of it on the back of Lennie's hand and told her to sniff it. "It'll help you get over that," he said.

ACT

III

—

OUTBREAK

11

—

SUPERDRUG

IT'S A WONDER THAT the coca plant ever caught anyone's eye. It isn't showy like the poppy, a plant with long stalks and colorful flowers that shoot up from earth in lush fields. The opium-producing poppy practically calls out for harvest. Coca, on the other hand, is unremarkable on its face.

Erythroxylum coca, its scientific name, grows in shrubs, the kind someone might line a yard with if they don't have the patience to tend to something more delicate but still want curb appeal. Its branches sprout leaves resembling the common bay leaf, and tiny red berries. If you didn't know better, you might mistake it for a bush of Christmas holly.

It was the indigenous people of the Andes who took note of coca and began cultivating it thousands of years ago. Throughout western South America—in Bolivia, Colombia, and Peru, where it grows— native people chewed coca leaves to increase their energy and endurance. They also used it for medicinal and religious purposes.

When the Spanish began their conquest of the Andes in the 1500s, they paid little mind at first to Incan claims that the plant was the gift of the gods. In fact, Spanish officials banned coca as "an evil agent of the devil" until they saw how it made the Incas, whom they'd enslaved, more productive. After that, the Spaniards began doling it out to the Incas three to four times a day to energize them for work in the mines and fields.

Coca eventually made its way to Europe, and over the next few hundred years, European scientists experimented with the plant in attempts to isolate the part of it responsible for the benefits noted by the Incas. In 1860, German chemist Albert Niemann finally succeeded in isolating the chemical compound, an alkaloid he named "cocaine" from "coca," which was what the Incas called the plant in their language, and the Latin suffix "-ine," which means "made from."

Cocaine became popular throughout Europe and the United States in no time. It was administered in powdered form by doctors, as an anesthetic and to treat everything from fatigue and flatulence to morphine addiction. Sigmund Freud was a vocal proponent of cocaine. He experimented with it himself at the beginning of his career and in 1884 published a paper titled "Über Coca" based on his experiences. Freud described the work as a "song of praise to this magical substance."

Cocaine was also used recreationally. Powder cocaine was available for sale at pharmacies across the country and often mixed into sodas and cocktails at bars. Most notably, John Stith Pemberton's 1886 recipe for Coca-Cola called for five ounces of coca leaf per gallon of syrup. It's estimated that a glass of the original Coca-Cola contained around nine milligrams of cocaine.

Cocaine consumption increased fivefold between 1890 and 1903, according to some estimates, with nonmedical use accounting for much of the increase. As it became more accessible, the population of those who consumed cocaine grew to include the working poor, including Black laborers.

A 1902 article titled "Negro Cocaine Fiends" in the medical weekly *Medical News* claimed that cocaine made Black people stronger, increased our endurance, and made us "impervious to the extremes of heat and cold." Cocaine began replacing coffee and whiskey anywhere hard labor and grueling conditions existed—on docks and levee construction sites along the Mississippi, in mines in the West, on plantations and railroad construction camps throughout the South. "Use of the drug among negroes is growing to an alarming extent," *The Atlanta Constitution* reported in 1901. It was this association with the American underclass, with Blacks, that first turned Americans against cocaine.

Newspapers began running stories of brutal crimes committed by cocaine-crazed Negroes. It was said that cocaine use by Black people caused spikes in violent crime, including white America's age-old anxiety: the rape of white women by Black men. These reports stoked the hostilities of racist whites already resentful of signs of Black progress and paranoid about violent crime.

States across the country soon enacted restrictions on the sale and distribution of cocaine. Even Coca-Cola was forced to change its formula just after the turn of the century to include cocaine-free coca leaf extract. But these changes did little to quell the growing hysteria regarding Black people and cocaine.

Tensions came to a head in Atlanta, the home of Coca-Cola, on September 22, 1906. That afternoon, city newspapers reported four separate alleged incidents of white women being raped by Black men, presumably under the influence of cocaine. Incensed, white men and boys assembled into mobs.

Historians say between ten thousand and fifteen thousand white people gathered in the Five Points area of downtown Atlanta by nightfall. In roving gangs, they attacked Black men, women, and children on streetcars, in the post office and hotels. According to reports, Black men were hung from lampposts; others were shot or stabbed to death.

Street by street, the mobs ransacked Black-owned businesses, focusing much of their destruction on Decatur Street, where a majority of Black-owned restaurants and bars were located. They then moved on to Black neighborhoods near downtown Atlanta, destroying more businesses and homes until, like a sporting event, the riot was brought to an end by heavy rain.

The massacre's final death toll is disputed, but the most conservative estimate is that twenty-five Black Atlantans were killed that night. Hundreds more were injured and incalculable damage was done to Black Atlanta's economy. The city's mayor, James G. Woodward, concluded in a statement to *The New York Times,* "As long as the Black brutes assault our white women, just so long will they be unceremoniously dealt with."

It wasn't just mobs of murderous whites in Atlanta. Much of the scientific community in the United States was at the time thoroughly convinced that cocaine triggered something in Black men that made us rape white women.

Hamilton Wright, a physician and pathologist who served in the State Department as United States Opium Commissioner under President Theodore Roosevelt, wrote in a 1910 report, "It has been authoritatively stated that cocaine is often the direct incentive to the crime of rape by the Negroes of the South and other sections of the country." In a 1914 congressional hearing on drugs, Christopher Koch, a physician serving on the State Pharmacy Board of Pennsylvania, echoed that judgment. "Most of the attacks upon the white women of the South are the direct result of a cocaine-crazed Negro brain," Koch testified.

Later that year, New York physician Edward Huntington Williams published an article in *The New York Times* entitled "Negro Cocaine 'Fiends' Are a New Southern Menace: Murder and Insanity Increasing Among Lower-Class Blacks Because They Have Taken to 'Sniffing' Because Deprived of Whisky by Prohibition." Williams argued that just a few sniffs of cocaine led to lifelong addiction in Black people, rendering the addict a constant menace until he was "eliminated." For added effect, the doctor claimed cocaine had the double-whammy effect of making Black people both better marksmen and somehow impervious to gunshots, even when vital organs were hit.

With hysteria at a fever pitch, Congress passed the Harrison Narcotics Tax Act on December 17, 1914. It was the first-ever federal anti-drug law. It did not prohibit the possession of drugs, however. Rather, the act imposed a special tax on the production, importation, and distribution of opiates and coca products in the United States. The result was that it became more expensive for retailers to keep cocaine-laced products on the shelves, thereby making it harder for consumers to access them.

The Harrison Act proved effective at stemming the consumption of cocaine in the United States. Use of the substance declined steadily year by year after the law was enacted. By the 1950s and 1960s, cocaine and the Negro fiends supposedly created by it were considered a danger of a bygone era. Americans moved on to new threats, marijuana and heroin—substances that had come to be associated with Mexican immigrants and Black people, thus with crime and violence.

In response to a sharp rise in marijuana-related arrests in the 1960s—from 18,815 in 1965 to 61,843 in 1967—President Lyndon Johnson consolidated the Treasury's Federal Bureau of Narcotics and the Food and Drug Administration's Bureau of Drug Abuse Control into the Bureau of Narcotics and Dangerous Drugs in 1968 and placed the new agency under the control of the Department of Justice. America's anti-drug apparatus was coming into shape. Its philosophy would soon follow.

On September 21, 1969, the U.S. Customs Service initiated Operation Intercept. It was one of the relatively few actions taken under the next president, Richard Nixon, to combat marijuana in the United States. The operation put pressure on traffickers by having customs agents conduct inspections, mandated to last at least three minutes, of every vehicle crossing into the United States from Mexico. The operation lasted twenty days, effectively halting the smuggling of marijuana across the border during the period.

However, one *Wall Street Journal* report on Intercept noted, "Far from rejoicing at the marijuana shortage, some narcotics officials are now afraid that pot smokers may switch to other, more dangerous routes to euphoria." "Youthful drug experimenters, if they can't get one kind of drug, will look for something else," William Durkin, head of the New York Bureau of Narcotics and Dangerous Drugs, told the *Journal*. Indeed, cocaine use increased in the years that followed. Among Americans eighteen to twenty-five years old, it rose from just over 9.1 percent in 1972 to 12.7 percent in 1974. By 1977, 19.1 percent of young Americans had used cocaine.

This period marked the birth of America's racial double standard on drugs. While previous generations believed that drugs had a special impact on Blacks, they were simultaneously puritanical about drug use in whites. In the 1970s, however, Americans developed two minds regarding drugs. They continued to believe in the Black drug fiend but also came to accept "experimentation" in whites as a hallmark of youth. At the absolute worst, addiction in whites was considered a sickness, a tragedy.

Cocaine illustrates this point more than any other drug. While other drugs were targets of government campaigns and bad press throughout the 1960s and 1970s, cocaine was normalized. It was given a pass, the kind bestowed in this society only on something found sufficiently white.

"Among hostesses in the smart sets of Los Angeles and New York, a little cocaine, like Dom Perignon and Beluga caviar, is now de rigueur at dinners. Some partygivers pass it around along with the canapés on silver trays," read a May 1977 story in *Newsweek* magazine. The same year, the National Institute on Drug Abuse published a report simply titled "Cocaine: 1977." It detailed the rapid rise of cocaine in the United States during the 1970s and outlined the history of the drug and its pharmacology. "It produces a euphoria, a sense of intense stimulation and of psychic and physical well-being accompanied by reduced fatigue," the report explained. "It is also ranked high in desirability because of its convenience of use, rapid onset of action and its exotic qualities. At least part of its appeal is its rarity, high price and use by celebrities, musicians and other folk heroes."

Also included in the report was a brief warning that would prove prophetic: "While the evidence accumulated thus far does not justify the claim that the American public is now suffering greatly as a consequence of cocaine use, it is evident that much more needs to be known before any actions are taken that might result in a wider availability at lower cost."

Cocaine's heightened profile meant increased demand and ultimately more opportunity for drug traffickers. At the time, it cost about five thousand dollars to process and smuggle a kilo of cocaine, which sold in the United States for as much as seventy thousand dollars. That kind of profit made the cocaine trade incredibly lucrative. With Mexican cartels still scrambling from attacks on their business by the U.S. government, Colombian traffickers—having become the top suppliers of marijuana in the United States—readjusted their operations to focus on cocaine.

A dominant cartel emerged in Medellín, Colombia, led by Pablo Escobar. Escobar entered Medellín's criminal underworld as a teen, forging lottery tickets and stealing cars. He advanced in his early twenties from petty crimes to the drug trade. Not yet a kingpin himself, Escobar worked as a courier for more established traffickers, running coca paste from farms in the Andes to laboratories in Medellín. The coca paste, a crude product made from mashed coca leaves, kerosene, and other chemicals, underwent another chemical process once in Medellín. It was converted there into pure cocaine hydrochloride, the white powder taking the United States by storm.

With a leaf-to-powder understanding of the cocaine business and some money to invest, Escobar created his own cartel—a collection of coca producers, couriers, and smugglers. Within a few years, the Medellín cartel would dominate the international drug trade by streamlining its cocaine production process and protecting its business with violence.

The cartel also took advantage of the U.S. government's failure to monitor drug trafficking by air. Escobar had the daring idea to fly small planes loaded with cocaine into the United States from Colombia. Bales of pure cocaine would be loaded onto the cartel's planes in Medellín, then flown to and offloaded at remote U.S. airstrips, or dropped offshore, where they were recovered by couriers on high-speed motorboats. At an average of four hundred kilos per shipment, the cartel could net $20 million in a single run, making Escobar and his partners very rich men as they flooded American cities like Miami, New York, and Los Angeles with high-quality cocaine in the process.

"Previously, cocaine had trickled into the U.S. in relatively small consignments. Smugglers like Escobar transformed it into a professional business, exporting cocaine by the plane-load," explained economist Tom Wainwright, author of *Narconomics*. "Economies of scale reduced their costs. And the sheer amount of product flowing into the United States meant that prices fell, as supply outpaced demand."

Meanwhile, Black communities across the country were disaffected and dispossessed. The 1970s had marked a period of "benign neglect" on behalf of the government, as Daniel Patrick Moynihan, then a Nixon advisor, put it. Black Americans found themselves further isolated in ghettos as whites fled to the suburbs in response to integration efforts. Deindustrialization and an economic recession also did away with a number of meaningful opportunities for work, causing the Black unemployment rate to double from 7 percent to 14 percent during the decade.

As the 1980s approached, it seemed America was a nation unwilling to make social, political, and economic room for its Black citizens. Their backs were against the wall and their neighborhoods were ready to explode. All it would take was a catalyst, and cocaine seemed tailor-made for the moment. The stimulant was associated with pleasure and escape. It flooded the brain with dopamine, leaving users feeling euphoric. It was the ideal drug for a grief-stricken people.

According to one government report, the price of cocaine dropped by as much as 80 percent over the same period. There was so much, and it was so cheap, that dealers began experimenting with it. Powder cocaine was mixed with chemicals to produce a smokable and therefore more potent form of the drug. It was dubbed "freebase" after the complex chemical process by which the cocaine alkaloid was "freed" from its powder base.

The trouble with freebasing, however, was that it was incredibly difficult to do and the process involved volatile chemicals such as ammonia and ether. Both making it and smoking it often ended in explosions. Because freebase acquired a reputation for being dangerous, it never took off.

What came next is the stuff of legend. There is no agreed-upon account of exactly how the knowledge made its way to the streets of California, but dealers and users discovered at some point in the late seventies that smokable cocaine could be made with common baking soda instead of volatile chemicals.

Tootie Reese, a South Central L.A. drug kingpin during the 1960s and 1970s, says he learned the process as early as 1976 from Bay Area chemistry students—"white guys at Cal Berkeley." That was the same year a small book publisher in Berkeley released *The Pleasures of Cocaine*. The book was written under the pseudonym Adam Gottlieb by a Bay Area writer and drug enthusiast named John Mann. Sold primarily in head shops, the book was a primer and how-to guide for users and dealers that included a simple recipe for making freebase with baking soda.

The still-young war on drugs was at that time focused on marijuana and heroin, so freebase cocaine grew in popularity without much government intervention.

A few years later, in 1980, Congress held a hearing before the Select Committee on Narcotics Abuse and Control on drug paraphernalia. Along with roach clips, bongs, rolling papers, and coke spoons, the committee was interested in learning more about cocaine conversion systems, kits sold by a number of manufacturers that included everything needed to make freebase. During the hearing, a California physician named Franklin Sher described in detail the process and ease of cooking the drug. "A saucer, a glass, a paper towel and Arm & Hammer baking soda are about all that is needed."

12

—

SHAWN
(1978-80)

THE YEARS TICKED BY for the McCrays in Building 73, unit 9E. As he approached adolescence, Shawn grew tall and slim—traits he inherited from Joanne's side of the family. His love for reading grew as well, first with a collection of books by Richard Wright that Joanne brought home. After devouring those, he moved on to other books and *The Star-Ledger*. Shawn also became closely acquainted with the family's set of the *Encyclopedia Britannica*. He was directed to the thick books whenever he had a question. "Look it up," Joanne would tell him, followed by a reminder of how much she was paying to have them in the house.

Her efforts at home paid off. Shawn did so well in school that in the fall of 1978, when it came time for sixth grade, he was placed in Ms. Barnett's class. Ms. Barnett was a tall older woman with gray hair and glasses, believed by students to be the meanest at Cleveland Elementary. School administrators, on the other hand, thought she was the best and therefore assigned her students they believed to have potential.

Shawn did not appreciate it at first. Ms. Barnett had a reputation for giving fifty-question quizzes, and if a student performed especially badly on one, she'd read his or her grade aloud for the whole class to hear. Ms. Barnett also kept a chair near her desk reserved for students who misbehaved. They'd be made to sit in that chair until lunch, at which point she ate her usual, a cold-cut sandwich with extra onions, and lectured you up close and personal.

Regardless, being placed in Ms. Barnett's class meant that he'd get better instruction and would learn alongside the highest performing sixth graders. Shawn learned of another great benefit toward the end of the school year.

That April, Joanne received a letter in the mail from Ms. Barnett asking her to attend a meeting at the school. Just the thought of the letter made Shawn sweat. When most kids got a letter from the teacher, a beating soon followed. But this one did not suggest he was in any trouble. It simply asked that Joanne stop by after school the following day to meet with representatives from something called the Victoria Foundation.

The next day, after Shawn returned from school, Joanne told him to stay home with Tony and Cheyta. She rushed to the school, just as curious about the letter as Shawn. A few stomach-churning hours passed before she burst back into the apartment with the biggest smile on her face Shawn had ever seen. She was so happy that he forgot about the meeting for a moment and wondered whether she hit the Pick-It.

Joanne rushed over to Shawn, hugged him, and announced with great pride that he was one of five sixth graders hand-picked by Ms. Barnett to attend St. Rocco's School in the fall. It was a great opportunity, she explained. St. Rocco's was a Catholic elementary school, and the Victoria Foundation was an organization that helped "inner-city" kids who did well in public schools get a better education. They'd cover the full cost of Shawn's tuition and even provide him with bus fare so he could get across town to St. Rocco's. All Joanne had to do was get ahold of a few uniforms.

As far as Shawn knew, everyone went from Cleveland Elementary to West Kinney Junior High, then to Central High School. St. Rocco's? He'd never even heard of it. Now, all of a sudden, he was expected to take a bus to this strange place and sit in class with who knows. The thought was so unsettling that his stomach went sour.

Ms. Barnett must've made a mistake, he reasoned. But before letting the words leave his mouth, his eyes met his mother's and he registered again just how happy the words "free Catholic school" made her. That's when Shawn realized that he'd have no choice. It was school, after all, and if attending St. Rocco's was anything like doing his homework, it was nonnegotiable.

He found out the next day in class which other students would be joining him. Laverne Ward, Sean Lewis, Rhonda Seeley, and Michael Turner had also been picked. They were all what the Victoria Foundation had called "inner-city youth," but like Shawn, Laverne and Rhonda lived in Hayes Homes. Shawn had by then some basic understanding of the ways people thought about kids from the projects. Laverne and Rhonda joining him at St. Rocco's was a good thing, he thought. He wouldn't be the only one.

Ms. Barnett began that day with an announcement to the class meant especially for Shawn and the others she'd picked. She was going to make them work even harder as the final days of school approached. "You will not embarrass Ms. Barnett or Cleveland Elementary," she said.

A similar message came from a source Shawn did not expect: Tariq, the neighborhood dealer. Shawn had known Tariq all his life; he was a fixture in the community. Shawn would update him on his life and ask Tariq about his. On his way home that day, Shawn saw Tariq in his usual spot outside Building 77. Curious what he might think, Shawn shared the news that he was going to a Catholic school. He half-complained about not getting to be with his friends at West Kinney and having to take a bus across town. Tariq shook his hand to congratulate him.

"Don't let that school change you," he told Shawn. "There are going to be kids in there who don't come from the same environment as you. Make them accept you; don't try and be accepted." He explained that guys like them, people from the projects, were not supposed to make it out. "This is all set up for us to fail," Tariq said. Shawn would have to prove everybody wrong.

Despite being in the top of their class at Cleveland, Shawn and the others were made to attend summer school at St. Rocco's ahead of the new school year. That gave him just a week or so of freedom before he was in the school uniform of white collared shirt, blue slacks, cardigan, and clip-on tie. Joanne had to travel to Irvington to buy the "dress clothes" for Shawn, the first he ever owned.

Shawn was skeptical about St. Rocco's from the start. The building was much smaller than Cleveland's. St. Rocco's modest three-story building looked like a daycare center compared to Cleveland's thirty-seven-room, six-story complex. Where each floor of Cleveland had a series of hallways that twisted and turned, St. Rocco's was built like a sawed-off shotgun, with short halls on each floor. Shawn was also surprised to learn that the school's gym doubled as its auditorium. Catholic school, Shawn thought, might not be the big deal it was made out to be by the adults around him.

He was also unimpressed with the teachers. Shawn was assigned just two classes for summer school, and each had its own instructor. For math, he had Ms. Mattia. She wore jeans practically every day of summer—jeans so tight that they quickly became the subject of conversation among the prepubescent boys in Shawn's class. It was something he could never even imagine Ms. Barnett doing.

Then there was Mr. Droz, who taught English. He was a thin white man, probably in his twenties, and was also the coach of the boys' basketball team. Shawn was told by administrators upon entering that he should get to know Droz in hopes of joining the team, but the teacher seemed bothered by Shawn whenever he tried talking to him. Shawn had had tough teachers before. Mr. Carroll, his third-grade teacher, was a surly older Black man with a bald head who wore a suit to school every day. Whenever a student misbehaved, Mr. Carroll would call him or her up to his desk, have them put their hands out, and smack them with a ruler exactly five times. Droz wasn't tough like Mr. Carroll. He was something else a young Shawn couldn't quite name.

Things became clearer just a few weeks into summer school when someone vandalized Droz's car. Shawn learned about it the day after, when he was called downstairs to the office by Mr. D., the school's principal. Someone had scratched "I hate you Droz" onto the hood of the teacher's car, and Mr. D. wanted to know if Shawn had done it or what he knew.

The question took Shawn completely off guard. In a matter of weeks, he'd gone from a "good" kid at Cleveland to a suspect at St. Rocco's. If he'd been older, he might have been able to articulate the injustice, but all he could do at the time was state the obvious: he didn't do it. He did not know what kind of car Droz drove or where he parked. He didn't hate the man; he barely knew him.

The incident made an impression on Shawn. He couldn't understand why they'd think he had it out for Droz, or that he was capable of vandalism. He had his suspicions, however, remembering Tariq's warning about how the outside world viewed project kids like him: "This is all set up for us to fail." Shawn felt a coldness from the adults at St. Rocco's over the next few days, then a sudden thaw. He figured they must've found the culprit, though no one said so or apologized.

The rest of summer school went by without a hitch, but Shawn was put on notice by what happened. The moment was brief, probably forgotten by Mr. D. and Droz no sooner than the scratches were buffed out of the car, but it confirmed the twelve-year-old's fear that he did not belong at St. Rocco's. It was a sentiment he expected from other students. It never occurred to him that it might also come from teachers, too.

Nevertheless, Shawn was excited to start his seventh-grade year when fall finally came. He was going to officially be a junior high school student, and if he played his cards right, he might even get to join St. Rocco's basketball team. Even more clutch was that he had made a handful of friends among the eighth graders who attended summer school. Being a seventh grader who could hoop with eighth-grade friends added up to one thing: he'd be The Man at St. Rocco's.

SHAWN'S FIRST OFFICIAL DAY at St. Rocco's began as his days of summer school had. He woke up early to eat breakfast and put on his uniform. To get to school on time, he had to leave the house by 7:15. From there, he walked quickly down Hunterdon and cut through Cleveland's playground to Bergen Street. Sean Lewis and Michael Turner, the other two boys with Victoria Foundation scholarships, lived nearby. Their groggy presence at the corner of Eighteenth Avenue and Bergen signaled that Shawn was right on time to catch the 7:30 A.M. number 5 bus.

Shawn was anxious, but his nerves were steadied by Sean and Michael. When they arrived at St. Rocco's, all the students were assembled in the school's small playground waiting to be herded into their respective homerooms. Without saying a word, Shawn, Sean, and Michael agreed to huddle together in the crowd.

Students at St. Rocco's ranged from kindergarten to eighth grade. There was just one class for each grade level. They all seemed to know each other, Shawn thought as he watched the other students laugh and chase each other around. They'd been attending Catholic school together for years. Some were brothers and sisters whose parents had enough money to send the whole family to places like St. Rocco's. They looked like regular kids, not too different from his friends at home. But they must be special, Shawn thought.

The students were told after a while to line up by grade level and were brought into the school. There were just twenty or so students in Shawn's grade, a fact that shocked him. And he only had two teachers. Ms. Mattia was back in her skin-tight jeans to teach math, science, and art. But Droz wasn't returning to St. Rocco's, Shawn learned. There was a new teacher in his place named Mr. Baskerville, a Black man with a medium build and a deep voice who wore thick glasses. A small rush of excitement coursed through Shawn when he learned that Mr. Baskerville would be his primary instructor for the seventh grade, responsible for teaching English, social studies, and music.

On the very first day of class, during English, Mr. Baskerville explained that seventh graders would be reading a number of books, including *The Outsider* by Richard Wright. Hearing that made Shawn sit upright. It was his favorite of all the books his mother kept on the bookshelf at home. Shawn raised his hand when Mr. Baskerville was finished.

The Outsider was a "good book," he announced, expecting to be congratulated for his maturity and worldliness. Instead, Mr. Baskerville asked how Shawn knew it. "Because I read it," Shawn explained. Without missing a beat, Mr. Baskerville accused Shawn of lying. "You're from Cleveland Elementary," he said. "I know they don't read those types of books."

Shawn had never mouthed off to a teacher before. He had always been too afraid at Cleveland and, quite frankly, never had a reason. But something came over him that day. He felt insulted for sure, but there were other upsets—being uprooted from his neighborhood, accused of vandalizing Droz's car, forced to attend summer school he did not need just to assure the folks at St. Rocco's that he was good enough to learn from them.

Without thinking, Shawn blurted out, "You're right. I didn't read it at Cleveland; I read it at home." Time seemed to stand still as a hush fell over the class. Apparently, no one ever talked back to a teacher at St. Rocco's or even considered it. Stunned, the students looked back and forth between Shawn and Mr. Baskerville, eager to see the next act in the drama unfold.

Mr. Baskerville didn't demand that he move to a seat near his desk. Nor did he rap on his knuckles with a ruler. In fact, Mr. Baskerville didn't seem angry at all. He was incredulous, which was somehow worse.

He asked Shawn to describe the book, which he did happily. *The Outsider* by Richard Wright was about a Black man named Cross Damon, he explained. Damon is unhappy. He wants more out of life but can't get it. After surviving a train accident, Damon fakes his death and tries to start over as someone new. But he ends up just as unhappy in his new life as he was in the old one. Damon continues, miserable, until he's killed.

If Mr. Baskerville was impressed with Shawn's recitation, he didn't let on. He offered neither praise nor apology. And instead of addressing his mistake, he simply moved on to the next item on the syllabus. Shawn accepted that as a point for him against St. Rocco's.

Mr. Baskerville would continue to talk down to other students—sometimes outright insulting them—but he never tried it again with Shawn. He did, however, make a practice of directing questions the rest of the class couldn't answer Shawn's way. Shawn didn't always have the right answer, but he did often enough that the ritual became something of an unspoken competition in his mind.

While he was battling with Mr. Baskerville in class, the rest of Shawn's experience at St. Rocco's was rather easy. He'd grown six feet tall by the time school started, which meant that he could pass as an eighth grader. That was important when it came to impressing girls, something Shawn was increasingly desperate to do.

And without trying much, he made friends with a group of cool kids at St. Rocco's—Kenny Johnson, Ricky Singleton, Jeffery Montague, Craig Sampson, Derek Peterson, and Christopher Spruill. From this group, he got the encouragement he needed to try out for the basketball team. The team was pretty good, they said, plus guys on varsity "got girls."

Tryouts began on a Saturday at 8 A.M. that November and were held in the gym. Shawn arrived early and was joined by what looked like every boy in the seventh and eighth grades. Another teacher, Mr. Smith, had replaced Mr. Droz as coach. He was no-nonsense and began drilling the boys at the stroke of eight o'clock. They were drills Shawn had never done in his life, and he hated them. After so many years of pickup games at Hayes Homes, he just wanted to play. Nevertheless, he ran the laps, did the suicides, and sprinted back and forth from half-court like a boy possessed.

Somewhere between deciding to try out and the last set of suicides, Shawn fell in love with the idea of being on the basketball team.
He started fantasizing about the uniform, the games, and the girls
he'd get. He returned home that first day of tryouts, and again the
second day, soaked in sweat and hopeful that he made a good impression on Coach Smith.

Shawn got to school earlier than usual that Monday morning and
was let into the building by Mr. Baskerville, who had the list of the
twelve boys who made the team. Not only was Shawn picked but he
was put on varsity.

He didn't know it then, but it was a turning point in his life. Before
making the team, Shawn had been just another project kid. That designation put him on a path that led most often to disappointment or
devastation. Attending St. Rocco's altered that some. On paper, a
Catholic school education led to greater opportunities. Basketball
went beyond that. It came with opportunities but also a new identity:
student athlete.

How Shawn would take to that new identity was one matter. The
tremendous impact it had on the people around him was another. He
went from outsider at St. Rocco's to mascot, from interloper to ambassador. That was the power of sports, he learned. Playing could
transform the player in the imaginations of those around him and
endear him to them.

13

—

LENNIE

(1978)

LENNIE WAS GRATEFUL FOR THE "BUMP," as the man had called it. It not only made her stop crying but made her feel safe and confident—so confident, in fact, that she didn't tense up at all when he told her that he was a pimp named Rooster.

But unlike with most other men, Lennie didn't see anything wild in his eyes when Rooster looked at her—just concern. So the two just sat there at the bus stop talking until she figured out where she would go next. Before parting ways, he gave Lennie some advice: always use a condom.

Lennie took her eighty-six dollars to the Fox Hills Mall and bought a bottle of perfume. Still buzzing from the cocaine, she started to feel that she had done something impressive and glamorous. She was a "money maker," she told herself, and she'd never have to ask her mother or Uncle Archie for anything again.

From that moment on, Lennie had two lives. There was her life in South Central—going to school and hanging out as she always had—but then, whenever she needed something, Lennie made her way over to Culver City and waited for a man to find her.

It was too easy. For one thing, the police didn't bother her. It was like she was invisible to them—and most everyone else except the men who wanted her. And Lennie didn't have to do anything to get their attention beyond dressing up in her school clothes and sitting at a bus stop. Within half an hour of when she sat down, one would pull up to ask where she was going and if she wanted a ride.

Not even the sex was difficult, not when she closed her eyes and thought about other stuff, or if she pretended that she was someone else. Besides, the sex was just a brief part of the experience, she told herself. She didn't even have to ask for money after. Like clockwork, they'd go into their wallets, pull out a crisp hundred-dollar bill, and hand it to her.

The hard part was keeping it a secret, because as much as Lennie liked the attention and loved the money, she didn't want anyone to think of her as a ho. She didn't think of herself like that. To her, it was just something she did every now and then, no better or worse than how the hustlers of her neighborhood made money, or what she did with Uncle Archie.

Lennie would sneak over to Culver City a few times a month after her job at the gymnastics school ended. She still went to school, though, and maintained a presence in the neighborhood. And because she held on to her old life, she never had to focus entirely on what she was doing in Culver City. It was "over there" to her, a stage that only existed when she was on it—and so it stayed for the better part of a year.

Whiskey helped calm her nerves on the days she went out. By then, Lennie had grown from taking shots and the occasional drink at a party to drinking cupfuls of Uncle Archie's Johnnie Walker before and after school. She drank so much that she would have to refill the bottles with water, carefully calibrating the mix to maintain the amber color.

The drinks helped drown out any worry Lennie had that she might get caught. It made it easier for her to transition between her two lives, too. With a drink, it was nothing to go from class to the bus stop and back home.

DURING THIS TIME—LENNIE'S EIGHTH-GRADE year—she met Jay (not his real name). He was tall and dark. And even though he was just two years older than Lennie, he seemed grown-up to her. Jay was also running the streets, but he had an easy way about him, and a smooth baritone that made Lennie's heart beat a little faster whenever he was around.

Jay went to Horace Mann, too, and lived near the school. They never officially met but sort of gravitated toward each other, the way schoolkids do. Before Lennie knew it, they were talking in-between classes or at lunch. Then he started walking her home, which gave them even more time to talk. Lennie loved those talks and the sound of Jay's voice.

She called herself dating other boys before, but that was just something to do. Back then, the kids said they were boyfriend and girlfriend, but it usually didn't mean anything beyond telling other people that they "go together" and maybe kissing. It was different with Jay. Lennie knew right from the start that she loved him.

After a few months, Lennie was sure that Jay loved her, too. The very thought thrilled and terrified her. She was still catching the bus over to Culver City. Like everyone else in the neighborhood, he had no idea, and Lennie was gripped by fear that he might find out. She thought about quitting, just stopping altogether and moving on like it had never happened. But then she would run low on money, need something, and be back at it.

Lennie could feel herself changing inside. It was different than when she had played at being Linda to keep from being scared. She felt like she finally was Linda, that she was grown. Lennie had lost her innocence. She didn't care for school anymore, going only because her mom would kill her if she didn't. Lennie would show up drunk most days and sneak out early. If teachers noticed, they never did any-thing. Lennie also started using the money she made to get her hair done and buy "grown-up" clothing—heels and clothes that were short or tight, sometimes both.

The only thing in Lennie's life that made her feel like a thirteen-year-old was her hopeless devotion to Dubie, her dog. That hadn't changed. Neither had her relationship with her mom, who was still beating her whenever she got mad enough.

Those beatings reached their most brutal during Lennie's eighth-grade year. It was like Bea could sense the change in her daughter and felt even more of a need to terrorize her. On more than one occasion, she choked Lennie until she almost passed out. People saw the bruises, but no one ever intervened.

One day, Lennie was at home in the kitchen with her mother when Bea started fussing. She was going on and on about something and getting herself riled up. Lennie knew better than to move or to say anything, so she sat quietly in the breakfast nook, watching Bea, which only seemed to agitate her more.

Bea grabbed a pot and put it on the stove, ranting and raving the whole while. Lennie tried to focus on how happy she'd be when she was finally eighteen years old and could move out. Her mother poured in water first, then she poured in a few cups of sugar. Lennie watched her as the water boiled. Her mother was crazy, Lennie thought, carrying on like a lunatic and cooking God knows what. That's when Bea came at her with the pot.

By some grace, Lennie was able to get up from her seat before the scalding-hot syrup came flying across the kitchen. She was stunned at first as she tried to make sense of what had happened. Then it clicked that her own mother had tried to douse her with homemade napalm. As soon as that registered, the thirteen-year-old snapped. Lennie took off after Bea, screaming, "You bitch! I'm gonna kill you!"

Bea dropped the pot and ran away from Lennie, through the kitchen and toward the back door, but her steps were slick from the syrup and she fell before she could get away. Lennie, in a rage unlike anything she'd ever felt, stood over her mother ready to strike. Everything in Lennie wanted to get back at Bea, to slap her or choke her, but she couldn't. She saw her mother scurrying and afraid and felt pity. Instead of dealing with Bea the way she might have dealt with her, Lennie simply said, "See, Mama, God don't like ugly," and walked out the back door. Bea never raised a hand against her after that day.

14

—

KURT

(1978~84)

THE ROAD TO BALTIMORE'S City Hall was a relatively short but winding one for Kurt Schmoke. He navigated it carefully—seizing just the right opportunities, turning on a dime when he had to, and avoiding the pitfalls that had taken out countless bright and talented men who'd traveled the path before him.

His first step was a big one—leaving his job in the Carter White House. Schmoke oversaw Black-focused programs for the Small Business Administration and the Department of Transportation. Stuart Eizenstat, Carter's chief domestic policy advisor and Schmoke's boss, was confounded when the twenty-nine-year-old broke the news that he was leaving.

"You meet with Cabinet officers, even the president of the United States," said Eizenstat. "Don't you find the job interesting?"

"Of course."

"Then why leave?"

"I want to go back to Baltimore," said Schmoke.

Eizenstat told *The Washington Post* years later that he considered Schmoke "well dressed, always polite, never overly assertive," perfect to play the background in D.C. Unspoken in that assessment was the fact that Schmoke was Black and, despite his impressiveness, still considered a long shot for elected office.

His ticket back was being appointed an assistant United States attorney in Baltimore, and in 1978 he and his new wife, Patricia, returned to the city.

The time-honored trajectory had been to join one of the neighborhood political clubs that dominated politics in Baltimore. The clubs picked their favorite sons and elevated them first within a ward and then within the city. But that system had never worked for a Black politician. Schmoke knew that if he was to become mayor, he'd have to forge his own path from the outside in. The job of federal prosecutor was an unusual launching pad, but it was perfect for Schmoke.

For someone with his education, training, and background, it made sense that he entered public life as a prosecutor. Such a job allowed him to serve while also earning a good reputation on crime, an increasingly important issue in Baltimore. It also had the effect of inoculating him, a Black man and a Democrat, against charges that he might be soft on crime and drugs—that is to say, on other Blacks.

A few years into the job, Schmoke and his allies began looking around Baltimore's political landscape and seeing openings. A major one was the Baltimore City state's attorney's office. Milton B. Allen was elected the first Black state's attorney in 1970 but lost the job in the following election to William Swisher, a tough-on-crime attorney who ran television ads calling Baltimore a jungle. Swisher was reelected in 1978, but a few years later, Schmoke decided he was vulnerable.

Swisher had strong support among the city's working-class whites but was weak with more affluent and educated whites and with Blacks, who made up the majority of the city's residents. Another Black lawyer, Dwight Pettit, had run against Swisher in 1978 and based his campaign on blasting Swisher's alarmist rhetoric. Pettit reminded voters of the "jungle" comment. Swisher had also encouraged crime-wary voters to "shoot first and ask questions later." Pettit and others interpreted these messages and others as dog whistles to racist white voters who perceived the city as being overrun by Blacks and crime. It was a valid criticism but it failed to inspire the multiracial coalition Pettit needed to win.

"Kurt had a better sense of the times," says U.S. congressman Kweisi Mfume, who had a spot on the Baltimore City Council in 1978, "and a better sense of the process of healing."

When he ran against Swisher in 1982, Schmoke focused on Swisher's record, arguing that his office had a practice of abusive plea bargaining and wasn't aggressive enough on drugs. "The issue is leadership," Schmoke told *The Washington Post*. "Who's going to be the most effective in getting the most out of that office? The answer is me."

"Mr. Schmoke is a go-getter and an achiever who has done everything he set out to do, and done it well," *The Baltimore Sun* noted with approval in its endorsement of Schmoke.

His strategy was to pull together the "enlightened good-government liberals," as he called them, and Black folks from across the city—the impoverished Black communities in East Baltimore and the upwardly mobile West Baltimore. The plan paid off, and in September the thirty-two-year-old Schmoke beat Swisher in a landslide—100,611 votes to Swisher's 58,829.

BALTIMORE DIDN'T HAVE MUCH of a drug market before the 1960s. Indeed, it was so small that the Baltimore City Police Department's narcotics unit, established in 1951, was said to maintain a detailed file on every dealer and addict in town, mostly musicians and other "hipster" types. The quaint practice became increasingly difficult in the mid-sixties as heroin took off in the city and others across the country.

The rise of heroin in Baltimore can be attributed to a few factors. Chief among them was the ascent of the French Connection, a Mafia-controlled drug network that smuggled Turkish heroin into the United States through Marseille, France. The French Connection pumped up to five thousand pounds of heroin into the United States annually, making the substance readily available in places like Baltimore, where it had previously been scarce.

Young people in Baltimore were in a special kind of despair, a state of collective depression brought on when their expectations for progress were abruptly dashed. To cope with unemployment and underemployment, poor housing, and few signs that things would get better, many turned to heroin to fill the gap between their hopes and realities. It was the situation all around the country, but the trend was especially pronounced in Baltimore, where use of heroin began surging around 1963 and peaked in 1971.

The Baltimore Police Department's response throughout the seventies was to target the kingpins of major local drug rings. Police arrested or ran them off one after the other: James Wesley "Bighead Brother" Carter, Frank "Black Caesar" Matthews, John Edward "Liddy" Jones, and Charlie Burman.

With each arrest, a few things became clearer. First, it became apparent that, as long as the drug market existed, there would be new kingpins ready to replace old ones. Second, the constant arrests of kingpins destabilized the streets, creating a musical-chairs effect as rival groups vied for dominance. As a result, Baltimore's drug market only became more treacherous and violent.

In Schmoke's early years as a prosecutor, he thought, like most everyone else in law enforcement, that he could arrest Baltimore out of its drug problem. He figured drugs were illegal and therefore the drug problem was a crime problem, to be responded to like all other crimes: with police, prosecutors, and prisons. He was a drug warrior, a very aggressive and successful one.

Schmoke created a full-time narcotics unit within his office to handle drug prosecutions, a sign of just how seriously his administration took the problem. Arrest numbers were up in no time, along with the office's conviction rates and drug seizures. Schmoke would eventually attain the highest drug-offender conviction rate in the city's history and seize so many vehicles from drug dealers that folks in law enforcement joked that he was the largest used car dealer in Baltimore.

Several drug kingpins were locked up during this flurry of prosecutions, including Walter "Gangster" Webster, Ancel "Tucky" Holland, Maurice "Peanut" King, Melvin Stanford, Clarence Meredith, and "Little" Melvin Williams.

A detective named Marcellus "Marty" Ward was at the center of a number of the cases. Ward, a Black man born in Baltimore, joined the force in 1971 after serving as a marine in Vietnam. In no time, the handsome and outgoing rookie became a rising star within the department, earning a string of commendations, including a nomination for Policeman of the Year in 1980 and two bronze stars.

Ward could "get next to anybody," his partner, Gary Childs, told *The Baltimore Sun*. "He could go out on the streets and be just like he'd grown up in the projects for the last 20 years."

That knack for infiltration, his zeal for the job, and, frankly, the color of his skin led Ward into undercover work, first in the BPD's Criminal Investigations Division—the department's main drug-fighting force—and later in the Drug Enforcement Administration's Baltimore district office task force.

As an undercover officer, he was a part of an eight-month investigation that put an end to Maurice "Peanut" King's $50 million heroin operation in 1982. Just two years later, he helped bring down five major drug rings with a combined yearly gross estimated at more than $25 million.

But by 1984, Ward was getting too well known on the streets. His superiors thought it best that he rotate out of the DEA task force and back into regular police work, but Ward had some unfinished business. He and his partner, Gary Childs, were at the tail end of an investigation into the Southwest Baltimore drug gang run by Mark Walker and Lascell Simmons. They weren't the biggest fish in Baltimore, but Walker was the lead suspect in an open murder case, and after two successful buys, Ward had duped the two into revealing the location of their stash: a second-floor apartment above a candy store at 1829 Frederick Avenue.

So, after being granted a three-week extension to close the case, on December 3, 1984, Ward strapped on a wire and met with Simmons at the apartment. The two talked for more than an hour while Walker stepped out to meet Ward's purported business partner. Of course, there was no partner, and Walker was met instead by police officers, who placed him under arrest. Once he was in custody, Ward received a coded phone call telling him that a raid was pending. He was supposed to leave right away but didn't.

The raid team had to get through three doors to get into the apartment—first a door that opened from the street, then another that led to a stairwell, and finally the door to the apartment. Ward was still sitting on a couch, just a few feet from Simmons, when they burst through the first door. The tense moments that came next were captured on his wire.

Simmons: I heard a sound in the yard.
Ward: Is that right?
[Boom sound in the background]
Simmons: What was that? What the fuck was that . . .
     Sit down.
[Shot one. Shot two.]
Ward: Oh, shit.
[Shot three.]
Ward: Ohhhh, shit.
[Shot four.]
[Moans, gasps.]

In all the commotion, Simmons had confused the police officers busting into his apartment for a stick-up crew. Ward, it was later determined, had tried to disarm the dealer and, for his heroism, received four bullets to the chest from a .357 Magnum.

Ward lay bleeding as Simmons negotiated through the door with

Ward's distraught partner. Simmons gave himself up only after Childs threw his police ID into the room. Marty Ward took his last breath a few minutes later. He was just thirty-six years old and left behind a wife, two sons, and countless devastated colleagues.

As state attorney, Kurt Schmoke knew Ward well. He prosecuted Ward's cases and considered him a fine officer. As another Black man climbing the ranks of law enforcement in Baltimore, he thought of Ward also as a comrade in arms. Naturally, Schmoke was devastated by the news of the detective's death. His grief was made worse as he prepared the case against Ward's killer and was forced to replay over and over his final anguished moments, captured by the wire.

In the end, what Schmoke heard on that tape changed him. He pursued the death penalty against Simmons, settling for life in prison, but he also started to think about the drug war differently. Listening to Simmons—the fear in his voice, his insistence that the officers raiding his apartment were there to rob him—Schmoke concluded that the problem wasn't just addicts hooked on drugs but dealers hooked on drug money. Simmons, he thought, cared more about his stash than he did Marty Ward's life.

Schmoke started to wonder if maybe the way to kill the three-headed monster of crime, addiction, and now AIDS in Baltimore was to take the profit out of distributing drugs at the street level. Just maybe, he thought, the answer wasn't law enforcement but decriminalization.

15

—

ELGIN

(1975-86)

SOME PEOPLE CALL YONKERS the sixth borough. It's just that close to the city, located directly north of the Bronx and eight stops away from Harlem on the Metro-North. It feels similar, too—a small but dense village spanning twenty or so hilly square miles filled with old tenements and distinct ethnic communities: Irish, Slavs, Puerto Ricans, and Blacks who moved north during the Great Migration.

That's where Elgin Swift grew up, far enough from New York City to be denied its prestige but close enough to share in its way of life. Like Yonkers itself, he was mixed—a combination of Portuguese on his mom's side and different kinds of white on his dad's—Polish, German. The result was a tall and slim kid, light but not pale, with sandy brown hair. As far as anyone in the neighborhood cared, he looked Puerto Rican, or "Spanish," as they put it.

His mom died before he could know her, when he was just one year old. She shot herself, he was told. Elgin didn't have siblings, so that left him and his dad alone together as he grew up. Elgin's dad, Stephen, was a busy man. He got up early every morning for treatment at a nearby methadone clinic. The rest of his time was spent on one hustle or another—driving a cab for a while, odd jobs, whatever he could do legally to make the most money for the least amount of work.

From what Elgin could tell, his dad was smart. In fact, Elgin's grandmother—the only other family he had around—bragged often that her son had a genius-level IQ. That intellect was most evident in his encyclopedic knowledge of handguns and mastery of all things electrical. When Elgin was about seven years old, Stephen brought home a ColecoVision and an Atari 5200. In the early 1980s, before most people knew what a computer was, Stephen also had a Commodore 64 that he and Elgin played games on. He even showed his son how to call up other computers to trade software.

The systems were so expensive then it was a wonder they had them in their small apartment in one of the poorest areas in the city. And to protect them, Stephen had a strict rule against guests. Whenever Elgin would ask to invite a friend over, the answer was always no. "I don't want nobody knowing what we have," Stephen would say. Consequently, Elgin spent much of his time at home with his father or, more commonly, alone in their apartment. As he grew, so did his fascination with the world outside their second-story windows, the one his dad disappeared into.

Yonkers became poorer, more isolated, and more dangerous throughout Elgin's childhood in the seventies and eighties. Still, for city kids like him, the streets were the only place to be. They were where all the fun was—block parties, games of stickball and manhunt. The streets were also where the people were, making them incredibly attractive to Elgin, who loved to be in the mix.

Elgin's pent-up energy came bursting out at school. He was a smart kid, that much was clear, but he was mischievous, a bit of a troublemaker. He talked back to teachers, got into fights, always with a plan to finesse his way out of trouble—behavior he perhaps learned from his dad.

His third-grade teacher was Ms. Bailey, a tall and sturdy woman who Elgin called Battle Cat for her long fingernails. He wanted to be a break-dancer back then, and central to that dream was looking the part, including wearing spiked bracelets like Shabba Doo in *Breakin'*. According to Ms. Bailey, that was against dress code. "You can have it back at the end of the year," she said after taking it. But when the last day of school came, Ms. Bailey claimed she couldn't find the bracelet. All hell broke loose. Elgin threw a fit, and a chair, at Ms. Bailey. That was his last day at PS 27.

The Board of Education placed him at PS 32 the next fall. He was emboldened by then and took to doing silly things like flipping over his desk or stealing food from the cafeteria just to see what would happen. What happened was he got kicked out of that school, too, then got passed on to PS 29, where he eventually finished fifth grade.

It wasn't until he arrived at the Enrico Fermi School that Elgin met his match, a teacher who wouldn't just pass him on to the next. His name was Mr. Green. He was a stocky old Black man with gray hair and a goatee. Mr. Green didn't take any shit. In a time when teachers could still put their hands on students, he'd invite quarrelsome boys outside when they got rowdy in class. That usually helped cooler heads prevail.

He was constantly trying to get through to Elgin, who by then had traded in violent outbursts for skipping school altogether. He'd remind him that he "wasn't a bad kid, just doing bad shit." Elgin respected Mr. Green, and he liked him. Mr. Green gave him the attention and care he didn't know he needed. Still, Elgin ran the streets.

His best friends at the time were boys from his neighborhood, Jab and White Boy Rob. Jab was a tall, light-skinned boy who lived around the corner on Valentine Lane. He was probably six-three or six-four at just twelve years old. Rob was a short Italian kid with an even shorter temper. His family had money, or at least there was always enough cash around the house for Rob to go on adventures.

Elgin and Jab would skip school together just to catch the train to Brooklyn or Queens. He and Rob would skip and hit up arcades, parks, and comic book stores along Central Park Avenue. Or they'd shoplift spray paint and markers from Broadway Hardware to make graffiti. Elgin loved every second of it, including the small moments waiting for his friends at the train station and watching the midday people go about their lives.

Doing what he wanted to do—instead of what he was supposed to—made him feel alive. That electric feeling would last the train ride, and the walk home, all the way up to his block. Sometimes, he'd visit neighbors to keep it going. Dabney was always down to kick it, or White Boy Petey, or Junito, who lived upstairs in his building. Visits with Junito were especially nice because his mom cooked every night. That guaranteed Elgin at least a plate of rice and beans, which he loved.

His most consistent company at home was the stereo. Back then, his dad had an eight-track tape player, a turntable, and music by Bob Dylan, Elvis Presley, and James Brown. Elgin listened to a lot of his dad's old stuff until hip hop came along. The first rap song he heard was 1984's "Jam on It" by Newcleus. He didn't know what the sound was at the time, but he knew that he liked it. From then on, it was Kiss-FM and WBLS on Fridays and Saturdays.

Those were the easy years, Elgin's "good ol' days." Things weren't perfect—not by any means—but for that brief moment in time, he felt safe. There was an invisible hand that seemed to order his life, his block, all of Yonkers. The hand would disappear in the years to come. Everything around him would be upended by drugs. His family of two would be torn apart. But as he listened to the radio and practiced his backspins, everything seemed right.

16

—

SHAWN

(1980-85)

THE EARLY 1980S INTRODUCED "stranger danger" into the lexicon. The murders of Black kids in Atlanta were just starting to make the headlines, and pictures of missing children started to appear on milk cartons after a white boy disappeared in New York. An urban legend emerged among children in Newark during this period. In whispers, they talked about a group of killer clowns that rode through the city in a black van snatching up children. The hysteria reached such a level that the teachers at St. Rocco's began warning students to travel to and from school together if they could.

More than ever, Joanne wanted Shawn indoors when he wasn't at school or playing basketball. Even his friends would remind him to watch himself as he moved about—especially if he was going to an area where he didn't have family and friends. Doing that—being in the wrong place without someone to vouch for you—was like asking to get robbed, or worse.

Shawn traveled in a group even before stories of the black van circulated. His second year at St. Rocco's, he walked home with three other boys—Sean Lewis, Michael Turner, and Terrance, a neighborhood friend who'd received a scholarship to St. Rocco's the year after Shawn. The group had an after-school routine. They sold their bus tickets to buy day-old pastries from the bakery at the corner of South Orange Avenue and Tenth Street. Then they walked for twenty-five sugar-fueled minutes back to Hayes Homes.

One day, the boys were scarfing down donuts on their usual route when they noticed two older boys in the distance with a German shepherd on a chain. Shawn's Spidey sense hadn't gone off much since the time Willie Harris threw the bottle at him, but it was activated as the mysterious duo and the dog approached.

Terrance must have spotted some malice in their gait, because he immediately made a run for it. It was too late by the time the danger registered for the rest. By then, the older boys were just the length of a leash from them and the dog was growling. The boy wielding the beast warned them that he'd sic his dog on them if they tried to run, and then he asked if they were wearing watches. None were. Disappointed but undeterred, the boys made Shawn and his friends empty their pockets.

The assailants got away with no more than three dollars. Shawn made his money back the next day when he sold his bus tickets again, but the incident shook him up. It was the first fissure in the better, safer world he supposedly entered when he enrolled at St. Rocco's. He, Sean, Michael, and Terrance continued to walk to and from school, but they never again traveled that route. Perhaps as practice, they also took to playing a game where one or the other would shout, "the black van," and they'd all take off running.

Despite the trouble all around him, or maybe because of it, Shawn doubled down on his efforts at school. He continued to excel in class and once again made the varsity basketball team. The team won more games that year than it did the year before. St. Rocco's went 32–5 that season, with Shawn as a starter knocking down jump shots from the corner.

The larger world of basketball started to open to Shawn when St. Rocco's got a new gym teacher named Paul McPleasant. Paul, as he allowed the kids to call him, was a basketball fanatic and had season tickets for the Nets. He took Shawn and other members of the team to games. He also introduced them to the Pony Classic Christmas Tournament up in Orange. The best high school teams in the state competed in the Pony Classic, and the games were packed with rowdy fans cheering for players like Camden High's Billy Thompson, Milt Wagner, and Kevin Walls, who all played like pros.

When St. Rocco's season was over, Paul helped Shawn enter tournaments throughout the state, and when the school year finally ended, he presented him with an award to attend an all-paid week at the Pocono Invitational Basketball Camp. There was more good news for Shawn in the form of a letter from the Victoria Foundation announcing that it would continue to pay for his education if he went to a Catholic high school. This time around, Joanne let Shawn pick from the handful in the city. He settled on St. Benedict's Prep, an all-boys school, because it was within walking distance of Hayes Homes and didn't require a uniform.

As much as Shawn hadn't wanted to attend St. Rocco's at first, he dreaded leaving when the time came. It had become a second home to him over the years, an oasis in the desert that was Newark.

THE HIGH SCHOOL YEARS are hard for most kids, and Shawn was no exception. He was practically allergic to the culture of St. Benedict's, which emphasized excellence and discipline.

The epitome of this was the school's mandatory weeklong orientation program. Overnight, as it was called, began with a few words from Father Ed, a slim and clean-shaven young white man, who introduced himself as the headmaster, a term that reminded Shawn of slavery. The next speaker was Mr. DiPiano. He put so much emphasis on the rules at St. Benedict's that it was easy to miss the fact that he was the school's wrestling coach. Last up was Mr. Greene, a burly Black man who held the title "Dean of Discipline." He puffed out his chest while making his introduction and made it clear that he and the rest of the staff wouldn't hesitate to correct any boy who got out of line.

The culture of St. Benedict's no doubt helped guide many young men on paths toward success, but it was the last thing Shawn needed. He had spent most of his short life learning to be unfazed by threats. That was how he responded to the posturing of Father Ed and the rest.

He was already someone, he thought. He had a way of being in the world, and the last thing he was going to do was check it at the door because a group of strangers said so. It didn't help that the group of strangers were mostly white men. From their mouths, the word "discipline" sounded like "subdue," and Shawn would not be subdued. He went through the motions during Overnight, reciting the songs and mottos. But in the back of his head, he told himself that the whole thing was corny.

Others weren't as stealthy as Shawn. Probably feeling as Shawn did, one boy joked around during Overnight, didn't complete assignments, and bickered with the upperclassmen who helped run the program. A few decades later, the boy might have been diagnosed with a behavioral disorder, but it was 1980 and the administrators at St. Benedict's were not having it. They deemed him a problem student and decided to make an example of him. It started with push-ups, but by the end of the week, the boy had been beaten with a Wiffle ball bat, had a clipboard cracked over his head, and been humiliated by being wrapped head to toe in toilet paper—all in front of the other students.

There were other things that bothered Shawn about this new school. He didn't like that the upperclassmen who helped run Overnight had a tradition of dropping books on the freshmen while they slept. He thought the school song was wack, along with the motto, "Benedict hates a quitter." But more than anything, he despised the example they had made of the other boy, the problem student. It was flat-out wrong, he thought, and if that was the St. Benedict's way, then St. Benedict's was foul.

As soon as he got home, Shawn asked Joanne to transfer him to another high school, Seton Hall or Essex Catholic, but it was too late. She informed him that the deadline to register for those schools had passed and he'd have to make the best of things at St. Benedict's. No surprise that he never felt safe at the school after that. He decided it was hostile territory, a judgment that only intensified as he matriculated.

Shawn, who had always enjoyed school, started to hate it. He disliked the curriculum, resented being assigned books like *Adventures of Huckleberry Finn* and *The Scarlet Letter.* It didn't help that history was taught at St. Benedict's by Mr. DiPiano from Overnight.

It was the beginning of a tug of war inside of Shawn. He was pulled on one end by the person he had been—the smart boy with potential, the student athlete poised to earn his way out of the projects. Yanking him in the other direction was the person everyone feared he'd become: a failure, a thug, a statistic. Unsure of which way to go, Shawn played in the middle. He did just enough schoolwork to move from class to class and spent the rest of his time cultivating his armor, a veneer of steely indifference.

The middle seemed to work until one day well into his freshman year when Father Ed and Mr. Greene showed up on his doorstep. From his bedroom, Shawn heard them tell his mother that they were there to talk about his grades and basketball.

Inside the apartment, Father Ed explained that Shawn had a 0.9 grade point average and was failing six of his classes. Shawn might flunk out of St. Benedict's if he kept it up, he said. In the short term, he was at risk of not being eligible to play basketball for the school. Joanne was surprised but maintained her composure. Shawn had never had issues in school, she explained, and she'd had no idea he was struggling.

The adults came to his bedroom after a while. Father Ed and Mr. Greene gave speeches about how important his education was, how great an opportunity he had at St. Benedict's. Joanne was uncharacteristically reserved given the news. She didn't raise her voice or go flying across the room at Shawn, as he thought she might. She simply nodded in agreement with Father Ed and Mr. Greene, never taking her eyes off her son.

Joanne assured the men that Shawn's performance would improve before showing them to the door. Then she returned to his bedroom with just one thing to say: she wasn't going to pull him from St. Benedict's, no matter what kind of stunt he pulled.

The end of his first year at St. Benedict's came as a huge relief to Shawn. Summer meant more freedom, less responsibility, and the chance to be a part of the action in his neighborhood again. Much to his delight, Joanne was finally beginning to loosen the reins, despite his poor performance in school.

Shawn's main hangout that summer was the basketball court at the New Community Corporation, a nearby housing project.

One day, Shawn was sitting courtside and waiting to play when he struck up a conversation with a boy named Quill. The two exchanged niceties—where they were from, who they knew, comments about the game—before Quill remarked that Shawn sort of resembled Quill's father. "My dad's name is James," said Quill. Shawn thought maybe it was a coincidence until Quill described his dad and said his nickname: Bootsie.

Shawn hurried home after the game to tell his mother what he had learned. Joanne confirmed the news. Bootsie had a lot of children, she said, at least six besides Shawn, Tony, and Cheyta. She knew the whereabouts of some: two of Bootsie's boys lived near Weequahic Park, another two lived in New Community Corporation, where Shawn played basketball. Quill, whom Shawn had met, lived on Thirteenth Street across from West Side Park with two sisters and his mother, Bootsie's wife.

It hit Shawn that moment why his father had been distant all those years: he was married, it turned out, and carrying on an affair with Shawn's mother. Shawn, Tony, and Cheyta were the products of that affair. Bootsie sank in his estimation, but what upset him even more was that, unbeknownst to him, he'd probably crossed paths hundreds of times with his brothers and sister—at the store, on the bus, on playgrounds and basketball courts.

It never occurred to Shawn that he could question Joanne about her relationship with his father, or that he might confront Bootsie during one of his late-night visits to the apartment. That was not the way children engaged adults back then, at least not in his family or any other that he knew. So instead of getting his questions answered or being consoled, Shawn was left quietly devastated. He spent the rest of the summer practicing his game, all the while hoping to run into his long-lost siblings.

He began acting out as soon as the school year began. At first, it was stealing lunches from his classmates' lockers. That quickly graduated to swiping pastrami sandwiches from the cafeteria when the lunch lady wasn't looking. Shawn didn't need the food, but he enjoyed the thrill of breaking the rules and getting away with it. It made him feel like an outlaw.

Before he knew it, Shawn was in a cycle: He was acting out, which everyone at St. Benedict's expected of a kid from the projects. In turn, his classmates and teachers treated him like a problem child. That only made him want to act out more. He relished his new reputation but simultaneously resented his better-off classmates for thinking so little of him. Naturally, then, Shawn took great delight in the fact that guys he knew from Hayes Homes had gone up to St. Benedict's on more than one occasion to rob his bougie classmates for their new jackets, sneakers, and jewelry, even their bus cards.

Because everyone knew that Shawn and Terrance lived in the projects, the pair were called into Father Ed's office and grilled about the robberies. For Shawn, the suggestion that he was involved rubbed him where he was the sorest. He got his revenge by putting hits out on classmates, telling the stick-up kids from his neighborhood when one had new gear.

Shawn's resentment also bubbled up to the surface one day in math class when he was bickering with another student, named Douglas Biggs. Douglas was a freshman from East Orange, preppy and light-skinned with curly hair. The two went back and forth trading petty insults until Shawn reached a breaking point. He told Douglas, "Say something else and I'm going to punch you in the face." Douglas said something else and laughed. A rage engulfed Shawn. He walked over to where Douglas was seated and punched him as hard as he could in the nose, leaving Douglas doubled over and leaking.

The incident resulted in Shawn's first suspension from school and the basketball team. It upset his mother, but he didn't care, because the fight was all anyone talked about when he returned to school. He'd grown in status by punching out Douglas. He was considered a tough guy, which wasn't worth much in actuality but meant everything to Shawn.

With that, the tug of war was over. Whatever was holding the pieces of him together finally gave way and Shawn was split in two. He was at once a student athlete, the pride of Building 73, and a budding juvenile delinquent. A seed had been planted—the realization that there was a way through life other than the one prescribed by his mother and teachers. It thrilled Shawn, the way one might be thrilled to suddenly learn he had superpowers.

The rest of Shawn McCray's high school years were full of ups and downs. He got into petty theft sometime between sophomore and junior years, held guns for friends, even tried his hand at robbery. All the while, he was just skating by in his classes, earning whatever grades were required to play basketball. He was anchored, it seemed, to the person he had been, but drifting nonetheless into the streets.

BEFORE SHAWN COULD DRIFT ENTIRELY, he received terrible news: his mother was sick. Shawn had witnessed her health declining: occasional coughing had become nearly constant. Still, it came as a shock when Joanne was diagnosed with tuberculosis, a potentially deadly disease. Losing her—his only parent and the person closest to him in the world—was unthinkable for Shawn. The road ahead was also unimaginable. According to doctors, she could make a full recovery, but only if she was hospitalized, leaving her children without their mother for months.

The family scrambled to prepare. Aunt Denise stepped in to pay the bills at the apartment and moved Tony and Cheyta into her already crowded place in Georgia King Village. That left seventeen-year-old Shawn alone in Hayes Homes the summer between his junior and senior years.

If he was inclined to take advantage of having the house to himself, that desire went away when he saw his mother in the hospital. She was laid up in bed, almost lifeless, with tubes and wires connecting her to machines. The sight brought Shawn, tough as he wanted to be, to tears. Seeing his mom like that shifted something inside him. He returned home from the hospital determined to get his act together—as if staying out of trouble would help heal Joanne and bring her home sooner.

Shawn settled into a routine over the next few months. He woke himself early in the morning, read the newspaper, and stuffed any mail that came to the house in his backpack before setting off for summer school at St. Benedict's. After school, he walked straight to the University of Medicine and Dentistry of New Jersey, where Joanne was being treated. There, he gave his mother the mail and updated her on things at home and school. After that, it was off to visit Tony and Cheyta. On most days, Aunt Denise sent him home with a little cash or food stamps, which he used to buy snacks and TV dinners.

Joanne returned a shrunken version of her former self: gaunt, less energetic, and in need of more help from Shawn. He obliged, helping his mother out in every way he could and staying close to Hayes Homes in case of an emergency.

His renewed enthusiasm for the straight and narrow lasted into the school year. It was Shawn's senior year, after all, his last shot at setting things right and getting into college. He hadn't put much thought into that fact before, but suddenly the moment was upon him and pressing, thanks to Joanne's health scare.

Shawn had what it took to play college ball, and there had been word among his coaches that a few schools were interested in offering him a scholarship. His grades were lousy, however, and that made it nearly impossible for most schools to take him seriously. He hoped decent SAT scores might sway recruiters—that and the strength of his private school background. But before Shawn could put his plan into motion, he received devastating news.

It was a month or so into the school year and he was hanging out with friends in the cafeteria when Father Ed walked in. "McCray, what are you doing?" he asked. Shawn explained that he had a free period, which prompted Father Ed to ask why he wasn't doing home-work. Shawn replied that he didn't have any. That's when the priest dropped a bomb. He said, "You know you're not graduating." Shawn didn't know.

Once he got over the initial shock and embarrassment, Father Ed explained to Shawn that all his slacking over the years had left him a few credits short of what he needed to graduate. He would have to stay another year if he wanted a diploma from St. Benedict's.

There was no way Shawn was giving the school a fifth year, so when the day was done, he rushed home to tell Joanne what he learned and pleaded for a transfer out. Still on the mend, she listened to Shawn as he explained how humiliating it would be to get held back, how he couldn't stand another year of high school. Much to his surprise, Joanne conceded. She wouldn't keep him at St. Benedict's if he didn't want to be there.

Shawn and Joanne took the bus to St. Benedict's together the next morning. They met with Father Ed in his office and informed him that Shawn would be transferring to Central High School, the public high school closest to Hayes Homes, Joanne's alma mater. He tried to talk them out of it, even promised to schedule more basketball games for the next year's season, but Shawn's mind was made up.

After the meeting with Father Ed, they took another bus to Central, where they met with Mr. Adler, the school's guidance counselor. It turned out that while Shawn might not have had enough credits—four in each subject—to graduate from St. Benedict's, he already had more than enough to graduate from a Newark public school. Mr. Adler glanced briefly at Shawn's transcript before approving the transfer. And just like that, he was a student at Newark's Central High School. All that was left for him to do was to pass the state Minimum Basic Skills test, busy himself with electives, and get through the school year.

17

—

LENNIE

(1978–80)

FROM THE MOMENT LENNIE stood over her mother, she was committed to not taking shit from anyone anymore, and that included Uncle Archie. It was like a dam had burst open in the thirteen-year-old and all the anger she'd suppressed throughout her short life was starting to rise in her like flood water. Her temper was quick now, and she knew how powerful it could be when harnessed.

She was at home one day when her cousin called to say that Lennie's aunt Doretha had passed away after a long fight with cancer. Lennie had loved her aunt Do. She hated crying but she allowed her tears to roll out as tribute. Lennie forgot that Uncle Archie was in his room. He'd apparently heard the surprise in Lennie's voice when she was on the phone and came out to ask what happened. Still in tears, she explained that Do was dead. His response was to unzip his pants and pull out his penis. He said, "Look, Lennie. Look."

The shock, then rage, that filled Lennie must've read on her face, because he quickly put it away and returned to his room. Still, Lennie was furious. She went to the kitchen, into the drawer where they kept tools, and retrieved a hammer. Lennie intended to go into the room and bash Uncle Archie's skull in, but he'd locked her out. She started hammering at the door.

She thought about the inside of that room and all the times she'd been abused behind that big wood door as she pounded away with the hammer. She hammered and screamed, "I'm going to kill you!" over and over again until she was exhausted. Then she sat back down and finished crying. Uncle Archie didn't dare come out until Bea came home, and then neither he nor Lennie said a word to Bea. They just pretended like nothing happened despite the banged-up door.

As odd as it may seem, Lennie only had the confidence to stand up to Uncle Archie and to her mother because of drinking, smoking weed, running with gangbangers, and even selling her body. It all made her feel powerful, or at the very least like she was in control. Lennie finally felt free of them.

She went to school when she had to—meaning if a letter came to the house. Otherwise, she was hanging out with Jay, or making money. The next two or three years were a cycle of just that—some school, drinking, hanging out, drinking, dodging the truant officer, drinking, making money at the bus stop in Culver City.

Lennie started venturing out to other neighborhoods, and she started to meet all types of characters. The sex industry was everywhere in Los Angeles, and full of young women like her who needed fast money. In 1978, it was also full of pimps. Lennie vowed to never have a pimp—she didn't want anyone controlling her ever again. Still, she liked talking to them. They were interesting to her. They talked slick and liked to have a good time.

She met one pimp named Teddy Bear at a liquor store on Crenshaw and Fifty-seventh. He bought Lennie a bottle of whiskey and invited her to come home with him. Back at his place, Teddy put on records and talked the usual pimp shit while Lennie sipped. He usually only dealt with white girls, he said, but he wanted Lennie. Lennie, meanwhile, only wanted a drink, maybe to smoke some weed, and to go home buzzed.

Two or three drinks in, Teddy left the room and came back with a large device made of glass. Lennie had snorted powder a few times since Rooster gave her the bump. She'd even smoked a few primos—joints laced with cocaine—with some friends. What Teddy showed her was completely different: little white rocks that he put into the glass.

Teddy hit the pipe first, and when he did, a huge plume of thick white smoke filled the glass then disappeared into his mouth. It was gorgeous, Lennie thought. He handed the pipe to her next. Without a moment's pause, she took a puff while Teddy held a butane torch to the little white rocks, just a few inches from her nose. She felt the rush almost instantly, like peace was entering her body as she inhaled. Then he showed her how to make it.

Teddy mixed a tiny bit of powder and some water into a jar. Then he grabbed a bottle of ammonia from under the sink and started adding it, too, drip by drip. Like magic, little white droplets formed inside the glass. Lennie sat enthralled as he finished the process.

Teddy went and got another clear liquid next. He poured a dash of it into the jar, screwed on a lid, and started to shake it. He put the jar down and, after about a minute, there was a thin layer of what looked like milk floating on top of the water. Teddy used an eyedropper to carefully pull the liquid off the water, then squeezed it out onto a mirror to dry. "This is what we smoked," he said. "Freebase."

Lennie had not heard about freebase before then, and she was delighted when Teddy explained that it was a more sophisticated way of doing coke. It was "[upper] echelon," he said. Within weeks, Lennie had her own pipe and was smoking freebase daily.

Paired together, always together, with her trusty Johnnie Walker, freebase made Lennie feel good—better than she'd ever felt her whole life. She soared in the brief moments after taking a hit—high above South Central, above her family, above all the men she dealt with, high above even herself.

Cocaine was still relatively expensive at the time, but Lennie managed. If she was lucky, she scored some from a trick. She got it for free other times from her neighbor Joe Rat. Plus, Teddy's little lesson made Lennie one of very few people in the neighborhood who could make freebase, a service she was happy to provide in exchange for some of the finished product.

Freebase turned Lennie's life into one big party. She was high every chance she got, floating on a thick white cloud from the neighborhood to Culver City, sometimes stopping by school in between. Lennie became the girl who went to every party, the girl who loved to get high. There wasn't a whole lot of shame in that. The seventies were all about partying, and other kids as young as Lennie were already into PCP, angel dust, pills. Practically everyone she knew smoked weed. Plenty of people sold it. Then freebase took over.

It trickled in through the hustlers and pimps who were already dabbling with coke, then to their friends and associates. Overnight, it went from something nobody had ever heard of to the hot new thing to try or sell. There was probably no better place than South Central to sell freebase. The area's economy had been devastated for years, and by the late seventies there was a whole generation of young men coming of age and eager for an opportunity to make money.

The gangs were another major factor. To be sure, Los Angeles had been a hotbed for gang activity as early as the 1920s, but the late 1960s and early 1970s saw the founding of the city's two most powerful Black gangs: the Crips in 1969 and the Bloods in 1972. Each gang's territory grew over the years, getting closer and closer to Lennie's neighborhood.

Simultaneously, the small cliques that had always existed in the Hood started linking up—through school, or relatives who lived on other blocks. With gangbanging on the rise, those loose networks firmed up into real alliances, which were critical to protecting oneself against being beat up by strangers, robbed, or otherwise taken advantage of.

Sometime in the mid-seventies, the guys in Lennie's neighborhood wanted to make it official. They put in a bid with Crip leadership to officially become a "set." They called themselves the Rollin' 60s Neighborhood Crips, taking their name from the numbered streets at the heart of the Hood between Slauson and Florence Avenues.

The Rollin' 60s were known to be enterprising, with members busy in a number of hustles. Freebase only intensified things. A few of them saw the opportunity the drug presented early on and helped their set get in on the ground floor.

The next few years in the Hood saw freebase's boom. Money was pouring in, and people could finally afford the things they needed. They bought cars, paid down their bills, and gave their moms money. Celebrations became more regular, card parties and cookouts. All the while, people from all over Los Angeles began flowing into the Hood to buy freebase, weed, whatever their thing was.

Those early years, when the 60s first started rollin' and freebase was on the ascent, were some of the happiest in Lennie's young life. She'd broken free of her family and created, she thought, a place for herself in the world. Still a child, Lennie figured she knew all she needed to be a woman—most important of which was how to separate men from their money. Lennie had that, and she had freebase. She thought she had it all.

ACT

IV

–

EXPANSION

18

—

READY ROCK

COCAINE WAS EXTREMELY PROFITABLE for anyone who could get his or her hands on enough to sell. The barrier for entry was about $150, the wholesale price for an "eight ball." That eight ball could then be divided into smaller amounts and sold at a small profit, especially if "cut" with another, cheaper stimulant like caffeine powder. Once cut, the product was less pure but the difference was undetectable to the average user.

Richard Donnell Ross didn't know there was that much money to be made from cocaine when he made his first sale. All Ross knew was that the small bindle of powder given to him by an old friend was supposed to be worth fifty dollars. He would learn in no time, however, just how lucrative the drug business was, as he earned millions of dollars within just a few years, changing the American sociopolitical landscape in the process.

Ross was part of the Second Great Migration, a mass exodus of five million Blacks from the South to the North, Midwest, and West between 1940 and 1970. He and his mother moved to South Central Los Angeles from Troup, Texas, in 1963, when he was three. Ross's mother supported them on what she earned cleaning offices and landscaping. The two struggled despite her hard work and spent much of Ross's childhood receiving government assistance.

He grew up ashamed of his family's poverty. He was embarrassed, for example, that they were so poor they had scavenged canned goods from busted-up stores after the Watts Riots, so he started hustling as a child. He cut lawns, pumped gas for tips, ran errands for neighbors to earn extra money. Making money was his main objective, so he didn't hesitate when, while playing roller derby with friends in a neighborhood park, a man offered him an opportunity to win a quarter for every tennis ball he could hit into a box.

The man was Richard Williams. Not to be confused with the father of Venus and Serena, this Williams was also a prominent tennis coach in Compton with a reputation for finding and developing athletic talent in South Central through his California Tennis Association for Underprivileged Youth. Williams saw potential in Ross and took the boy under his wing. By ninth grade, Ross was so good that Williams recruited him to join the tennis team at Susan Miller Dorsey High School, where Williams helped run the tennis program.

Ross advanced as a player at Dorsey, making it to the semifinals in a few tournaments and even earning the attention of a recruiter at Cal State Long Beach his senior year. A scholarship to Cal State was a clear path out of poverty. The one holdup, however, was his academic performance.

Ross had been skating in school, it turned out, passed from grade to grade even though he could barely read or write. The Cal State recruiter backed off when he learned that Ross might not graduate, let alone score high enough on the SATs to qualify for admission. Discouraged, Ross dropped out of high school in 1979, at the age of nineteen.

Not ready to give up tennis or school, he enrolled at Los Angeles Trade Technical College, where he learned to bind books and reupholster car seats and continued to play tennis as part of the L.A. Trade-Tech tennis team. Ross quickly came to the realization that trade school wasn't going to launch him into professional sports or out of South Central. He was devastated. It didn't take long for him to turn to crime.

Led by his love of lowriders, Ross fell in with a small group of car thieves. He was arrested for the first time in 1982 and charged with possession of stolen auto parts. While awaiting trial, he received a call from Michael McLaurin, a childhood friend who had left South Central on a football scholarship to San Jose State University. McLaurin had something to show him and wanted to meet up. Ross ventured north to the West Adams section of L.A., where McLaurin was staying in a guesthouse. Inside, McLaurin showed him a plastic bag filled with small paper bindles. Each package contained about half a gram of cocaine, or fifty dollars' worth.

Ross had never seen the white powder in real life and knew very little about it outside of what he'd seen in movies like *Super Fly.* Nevertheless, he agreed to sell it, for a small cut.

Along with a friend named Ollie "Big Loc" Newell, Ross went to the Algin Sutton Recreation Center at Eighty-eighth and Hoover, just blocks away from their old middle school. There, they ran into a customer, a pimp named Martin who was known around the neighborhood. Martin produced a small kit and demonstrated for Ross and Newell how to cook the powder into a rock, which he proceeded to smoke. Without their product or payment for it, Newell and Ross returned home wondering what to do and what they would tell McLaurin. While they were still searching for an answer, Martin pulled up in front of Ross's home. He had one hundred dollars and wanted to buy more.

It was the beginning of Ross's career as a drug dealer. He worked as a low-level cocaine dealer for McLaurin for a short period but struck out on his own once he met an auto upholstery instructor at the Venice Skills Center who could connect him to a wholesale cocaine supplier. The instructor introduced him to Henry Corrales, a Nicaraguan trafficker who began selling to Ross and Newell. Through Corrales, Ross met Danilo Blandón, another Nicaraguan who could secure even more weight. Little by little, they assembled a small crew of dealers to help sell the product and graduated from ounces to kilos.

By 1982, just three years after dropping out of high school, Ross was a major dealer selling cocaine primarily to wealthy customers across L.A. Business was booming but customers were starting to ask for what he'd seen Martin the pimp make: freebase. To keep business going, Ross paid Martin the pimp to cook his cocaine until he finally mastered the process himself. In a move of marketing genius, he called the product "ready rock" and sold it in twenty-dollar hits. He taught the recipe to every new recruit on his growing team of dealers.

Freebase was identical to the powder from which it was derived on a molecular level. It was the rapid onset of the substance's high and its low cost that made it popular, especially in poor communities that did not previously have access to cocaine. News of an easier, cheaper method for consuming the nation's most in-vogue drug spread rapidly by word of mouth. It started first with a small group of dealers and wealthy individuals and expanded out to their associates, and eventually reached the streets. In L.A., that meant the street gangs.

A gang culture had always existed in Los Angeles and some gangs sold drugs—PCP, marijuana, amphetamines. A gang's primary purpose, however, was to protect the young men who joined it from other gangs of young men across the city. But the culture shifted in the late sixties as the gangs started to consolidate. Members of gangs associated with two South Central high schools came together in 1969 to form the Crips. According to legend, the name was a reference to the walking sticks members used to style themselves. Just four years later, in 1972, a handful of other gangs from nearby Compton combined to combat the Crips. They called themselves the Bloods, as in "blood brothers."

Growing up in South Central in the sixties and seventies, Rick Ross had a front-row seat to the birth of the Bloods and Crips, gangs whose memberships swelled into the thousands by the time he started dealing. Ross leveraged his childhood friendships with Crip and Blood leaders to become a major supplier to the gangs. Through the Crips and Bloods, he established a distribution network so powerful that it brought down the wholesale price of cocaine even further, a savings he passed on to dealers and ultimately to users.

For his central role in the rise of crack, "Freeway" Rick Ross is often miscredited as its inventor. That dubious distinction probably belongs to the mysterious Bay Area college students and hippies who experimented with cocaine throughout the sixties and seventies. Ross, however, is the man who popularized the substance by help-ing make cocaine, freebase in particular, ubiquitous in Los Angeles. Where cocaine had been a substance reserved for the elite, Ross used his unique connections to both Nicaraguan traffickers and L.A.'s street gangs to create a drug enterprise that made cocaine cheap, widely available, and easy to consume. With ready rock, Ricky Ross did for cocaine what McDonald's did for beef.

19

—

FROM PAUPERS TO PRINCES

FREEBASE GAINED A FOOTHOLD mostly in urban centers, sites of divestment in the 1980s. In them was a market of eager users and dealers that didn't exist elsewhere. Scholar William Julius Wilson called them the "truly disadvantaged." *Faces at the Bottom of the Well* was how Derrick Bell put it. In the 1980s, these disaffected folks were looking to either feel good or make money.

According to ethnographies, freebase crept into communities through after-hours clubs in L.A., New York City, and Miami. These establishments, as their name suggests, stayed open past the legal hours of operation for bars and nightclubs. Descended from the juke joints Black people created in the South under Jim Crow, they were places in Black communities where residents could eat, grab cheap drinks, listen to the latest music, and dance. As unregulated party spaces, they were also sites for drug sales and use. As early as 1980, after-hours clubs were known as places where one could buy freebase and where it was even sometimes made.

But freebase isn't a discreet substance. To make it, one needs equipment and chemicals. Using it also creates a scene—pipes, open flames, smoke. Given its complicated nature, freebase had to eventually move from after-hours clubs to spaces where dealers could cook and sell it and where users could smoke it openly.

From after-hours clubs, it moved to "freebase parlors" in the early eighties. These spaces were often the homes of dealers, equipped with everything needed to make freebase—stoves, pots for boiling, scales—and stocked with water, baking soda, and cocaine. Just like at opium dens a century earlier, users paid admission at freebase parlors, around three dollars, and fees to rent pipes and butane torches.

This ended in the mid-eighties as many first wave users began to descend into addiction and dealers became less inclined to operate freebase parlors in their own homes. They could be evicted if landlords or neighbors found out what they were doing, and the volatile chemicals that were sometimes used could cause fires. To solve the problem, some dealers moved their operations to properties rented for the sole purpose of selling freebase.

But then crack, safer and easier to produce, quickly eliminated the market for other forms of freebase. Users brought crack markets home through deals with dealers where they set up shop in their homes in exchange for crack.

These crack houses fostered unseen levels of violence and disorder. There was violence in the drug trade, casual violence among users, and sexual violence around the sex trade that existed in and around crack houses. Crack houses often caught fire. People were killed in and around them, exciting an aggressive police presence.

Out of the clubs and in homes, crack spread rapidly. Use expanded from L.A. up the West Coast as more people became aware of its high quality and low cost, and as competition pushed dealers into untapped markets.

Word hit Oakland and Sacramento first. Then it traveled across state lines to Portland, Seattle, Reno, Las Vegas, Salt Lake City, Denver, Minneapolis, Omaha, Phoenix, Tucson, Shreveport, Oklahoma City, Kansas City, and St. Louis. And just as freebase was spreading out from the West, it started to appear in Miami and New York City.

From those cities, also major destinations for South American cocaine, it permeated the Eastern Seaboard.

Whereas Bloods and Crips had been major distributors on the West Coast, the cocaine trade grew out East and in parts of the South thanks in part to Jamaican gangs known on the street as "posses." The posses, alongside Dominican and Haitian drug networks, helped spread freebase from Miami to Atlanta and into cities in North Carolina and Virginia. From New York City, they spread freebase upstate and across state lines into Newark and other parts of New Jersey, Philadelphia, Baltimore, D.C., and Boston. When all was said and done, their operations extended as far into the country as Detroit, Cleveland, Columbus, and Minneapolis.

It was during freebase's expansion period, between 1981 and 1985, that several notorious drug dealers emerged. Rayful Edmond, Cornell Jones, Michael "Fray" Salters, and Tony Lewis began selling in D.C.; Darryl Reed in Oakland; Jemeker Thompson, Thelma Wright, Brian "Waterhead Bo" Bennett, and Michael "Harry-O" Harris operated alongside Ricky Ross in Los Angeles; Santiago Luis Polanco-Rodríguez, Kenneth "Supreme" McGriff, Brian "Glaze" Gibbs, Howard "Pappy" Mason, Lorenzo "Fat Cat" Nichols, Sam "Baby Sam" Edmonson, John "Bloody Hatchet" Hatcher, Alpo Martinez, Rich Porter, and Azie Faison in New York City. The period also saw the proliferation of several drug syndicates—the Chambers Brothers and Black Mafia Family in Detroit; the Philadelphia Black Mafia; the Supreme Team, Bebos, and the Rugby Boys in New York City.

For Black and Latino youth in particular, the drug trade and the rise of freebase was an unprecedented economic opportunity. It was as though they'd struck gold in land thought to be barren. To the one, the biggest kingpins grew up in extreme poverty in some of America's most devastated communities. Like generations of Americans before them, these young prospectors were willing to take on extreme risks and skirt the law in pursuit of their fortunes. The advent of freebase was their Gold Rush, their Homestead Act, their Prohibition.

Almost overnight, young men and women who had walked holes in their shoes as children could afford homes, cars, and luxury goods. More often than not, they showed off their new wealth through clothing brands that symbolized the American middle-class lifestyle: Polo Ralph Lauren, Nike, Adidas, Kangol, Izod, Lacoste, Levi's. For many young dealers, selling drugs was about acquiring these totems of the American Dream.

And who could blame them? Popular culture was obsessed in the 1980s with wealth and upward mobility. Black children were presented almost exclusively with media that encouraged them to transcend the ghetto and reach toward whiteness.

On NBC, *Diff'rent Strokes* followed two Black boys from Harlem as they adjusted to the high life on New York's Upper East Side after being adopted by a wealthy white businessman. *Gimme a Break!* was about a Black housekeeper taking care of white children in a California suburb after their mother died. On ABC, *Benson* followed a wisecracking Black butler who lived and worked in a mansion owned by a very wealthy and very dysfunctional white family. The titular character on *Webster* was a Black child adopted by a well-off white family. *The Jeffersons,* which ran until 1985, on CBS and *The Cosby Show,* which first aired in 1984, on NBC both centered on upwardly mobile Black families.

Those were just the sitcoms. In music, there was a new crop of Black artists who were talented for sure, but were promoted by record labels due in part to their ability to "cross over": Prince, Janet Jackson, Whitney Houston. During this period, even Michael Jackson, Aretha Franklin, Patti LaBelle, Lionel Richie, and other soul and funk artists adjusted their sound to attract white audiences and pop success.

The one major alternative to this deluge of whitewashed culture was hip hop, which emerged from the ghetto alongside freebase. It was a subculture defined by four creative elements: emceeing, DJing, breakdancing, and graffiti writing. Hip hop was pioneered by the exact type of people who pioneered freebase. They were young, mostly Black and Latino, poor, and lived in the cities. Emcees in particular used hip hop music as a vehicle to tell stories about ghetto life, including drugs.

It was in hip hop culture that young people in urban centers found a vehicle for authentic expression. Not yet commercialized or popular, hip hop music existed on the margins. Emceeing put a premium on autobiography and the telling of stories to which the average listener could relate. Early hip hop music was in that sense more committed than news media, television, and other genres of music to amplifying the voices of young people living in America's ghettos.

Hip hop's first anti-drug hit was released on Sugar Hill Records in 1983. "White Lines (Don't Don't Do It)" by emcee Melle Mel, one of Grandmaster Flash's Furious Five, presented a cautionary tale about the dangers of cocaine, including freebase. "A million magic crystals painted pure and white / A multi-million dollars almost overnight," Melle Mel rhymes. "Twice as sweet as sugar, twice as bitter as salt / And if you get hooked, baby, it's nobody else's fault / so don't do it!"

Where government and media failed to flag the threat of freebase, hip hop stepped up. "White Lines" didn't reach as wide an audience as *Diff'rent Strokes* or *The Cosby Show.* Still, for many young people it sounded the alarm. When Melle Mel chanted, "Something like a phenomenon," he confirmed that the events unfolding around them were part of something greater.

The phenomenon was evident in the young men who had turned from paupers to princes overnight. It was also evident in the rapid deterioration of users. Freebase's powerful but short high drove addiction. As with any other drug, some users were able to remain highly functional. The lives of a great many fell apart, however. They were financially drained by addiction. Careers were ended and relationships strained. Even the appearance and behavior of some users changed as they lost weight and became withdrawn and erratic.

According to the National Institute on Drug Abuse, cocaine was in 1981 the "fastest-growing source of serious drug-related medical problems." One Bay Area epidemiologist explained to *The New York*

Times that the number of people showing up at his clinic for help with cocaine addiction doubled from the last half of 1980 to the first half of 1981.

Rates of overdose were also on the rise. In New York, cocaine overdoses increased 36 percent; Boston, 46.4 percent; New Orleans, 52.9 percent; Miami, 71.5 percent; Philadelphia, 83 percent; and Los Angeles, 90.4 percent.

"We're seeing a definite shift to a more vicious type of cocaine abuse," noted Gene R. Haislip, the DEA's director of enforcement. "There is a clear upward nationwide trend to mainlining and freebasing the drug that is an obvious change for the worse."

A 1983 survey conducted by researchers at Fair Oaks Hospital in Summit, New Jersey, identified some of the ways freebase was negatively impacting the lives of those who used it. It found that the average freebase user was twenty-five years old, college educated, had an average annual income in excess of $25,000, and spent $820 a week on the drug. Three-quarters of respondents said they preferred freebase to food, family, and sex.

20

—

LENNIE

(1980-82)

BY THE TIME LENNIE WAS FIFTEEN, freebase had evolved into "ready rock," crack. It was even more popular than base had been, because just about anyone could cook it without fear of blowing themselves up. Ready rock became almost mythical on the streets as word spread of its pleasures, such as the magical bell users heard ringing in their ears as the high set in. The crackling sound of a heated rock breaking down gave the substance a name that would stick: crack.

The wide availability of cheap cocaine and the ease of cooking crack pulled guys who might not have otherwise sold drugs into the trade. Its rock-bottom price seduced unexpected users, too. Where there had been distinct differences among gangsters, gangbangers, hustlers, pimps, and ballers, crack made the lines between them disappear as everyone got in on the act. Before long, practically everyone in the Rollin' 60s was selling crack, as well as other South Central gangs like the Eight Tray Gangster Crips, the Van Ness Gangster Brims, the Harvard Park Brims, and the Inglewood Family Gangster Bloods.

Crack made them serious money—tens of thousands, sometimes millions of dollars. That surge of cash created some of L.A. gangland's highest moments but also some of its lowest. It changed the people who had it, just as crack began changing the people who used it. All were under crack's spell.

Crack turned grown men into lackeys who hung around dealers day and night, eager to run errands in exchange for a few rocks. Women who would never think about prostitution offered up their bodies freely for a hit. Lennie saw this, the power crack had to elevate some and reduce others, and was unnerved. Nevertheless, she kept smoking it.

She was still dating Jay at the time, and he was still clueless about where she went when she left the neighborhood. Seemingly satisfied with whatever little pieces of herself Lennie gave him, he never asked. Maybe because they were just kids. Maybe because he didn't care to know her better.

The two had been seeing each other for a few years, and even though they were having sex, things were still casual. They had sex unprotected a few times. That was about the depth of Lennie and Jay's intimacy. He never officially asked her to be his girlfriend, and she didn't pressure him. Jay was probably seeing other girls, she figured, and that made it easier to keep secrets from him.

One day, Lennie was finishing up with a trick in Culver City near Hayden and Higuera. He was dropping her off when two guys from the neighborhood, Nate Dog and Sylvester, spotted her getting out of the car. The car was a Bentley, and the driver was white. Lennie knew the moment she saw them watching her and smiling that she'd been found out.

Nate and Sylvester didn't let Lennie forget what they saw. They made little comments whenever they ran into her around the neighborhood, and on more than one occasion threatened to tell Jay. Lennie was afraid of what might happen, what people would say and think, if her secret got out. That only made her want to smoke more, which sent her back out into the streets for money.

Relief finally came when Lennie learned that Jay had been ar-rested for murder. A part of her was sad to see him go, but another was looking forward to it.

That spring, Lennie attended her cousin Andrea's graduation. It was a warm day in Southern California, beautiful outside, but some-thing felt off from the moment she woke up. The feeling didn't let up as Lennie sat through the ceremony. She was uncomfortable, tired, and dizzy at moments. She felt at one point like she might vomit. She didn't need a doctor to tell her; Lennie knew then that she was preg-nant.

The first thing Lennie did was tell her mother, who promptly cursed her out and, despite being a holy roller, told Lennie to "kill it." Lennie waited for Jay to call from prison to give him the news. She didn't know what to expect when she picked up the phone, but a part of her held out hope that he'd be excited. She hoped that for once someone, when presented with the option to hurt her, would choose not to. Jay was her first, after all, the first person she'd wanted to have sex with, and he'd talked a big game about wanting to be together in letters after getting locked up. Lennie hoped that meant something.

He listened quietly as she told the story of getting sick at Andrea's graduation. When Lennie was done, Jay announced that the baby wasn't his.

The two argued. Lennie was sleeping with other people, he said, and he threatened to have her beat up. Jay was a big name in the neighborhood, and Lennie knew that he probably meant what he said. Still, she felt hurt and insulted. She said, "Fuck you," and "You're going to need me and my child before we need you," before hang-ing up.

THE NEXT FEW WEEKS WERE HELL. Lennie argued with her mother and with Jay. She cried in between the arguing and contem-plated what she might do. One of her neighbors, an older lady who lived on the block, saw Lennie crying in her backyard one day and came over to ask what was wrong. Lennie said she was pregnant. "Well, baby, the time for crying is over," said the woman.

The words didn't point a path forward, but they were a comfort to Lennie nonetheless. "The time for crying is over." Hearing that shored up something in Lennie. The woman was right, she thought, and she wanted to keep her baby. She'd love it no matter what and do everything she could to give it a better life then she had.

Lennie got out of Uncle Archie's house, moving in with her next-door neighbor Rich Rollin' Rudy's mom for the remainder of her pregnancy. Most important, she stopped working the streets, stopped smoking crack, drinking, and everything else. She also went back to school.

During those months, it was like the universe was conspiring to help Lennie. Ms. Hayden, an administrator at Crenshaw High, put together a program to help her catch up academically. Lennie also found a women's clinic on Crenshaw where the doctor was kind enough to sponsor her Lamaze classes.

Still, the pregnancy wasn't without challenges. Lennie remained at odds with Jay, who had a new girlfriend and had her convinced that Lennie was lying about being pregnant by him. The girl threatened to beat Lennie up. Lennie was scared, sometimes so afraid that she didn't want to leave the house, but she did. She went to school and to her doctor's appointments. The time for crying was over.

Months later, in January 1982, Lennie gave birth to a baby boy. He was healthy—seven pounds, nine ounces, twenty-two inches—and cute as a button. He had her eyes and his father's nose. Lennie named him Jamal. Looking at him, she was filled with a sense of accomplishment. He was here. She'd done what she had to do. Lennie wanted nothing more than to celebrate by getting high.

Lennie's mother fell in love with the baby boy instantly, allowing her to bring him home. In fact, Lennie had never seen Bea so pleased about anything. She doted on Jamal, ran out to stores to buy him clothes and toys, whatever caught her eye. He was her baby, Bea would say proudly.

Lennie also got help here and there from the neighborhood. The dope boys and ballers gave her money for the baby and rides when she needed them. Joe Rat and Let Loose would even let her drive their cars. With support at home, Lennie had time enough to go back to her old ways.

Despite her pledge to do whatever she could for Jamal, Lennie more or less left raising him to her mother. She was more concerned with getting high than with what might happen to her baby in the care of a woman who had abused her. Lennie wouldn't admit that then, however. She told herself instead that her mom loved Jamal too much to do anything like that to him.

The streets were different when Lennie started smoking again. People were robbing and killing each other over drugs and money. Drug use itself got scary, too. Users disappeared from their families for days at a time, sometimes weeks. People lost their homes and started living in crack houses or on the street. Children went without food. Lennie once witnessed a mother smoking crack with her thirteen-year-old son. She wanted to stop them, but she herself was too high to do anything. Despite the devastation around her, Lennie continued to smoke crack over the next few years, drifting further away from her baby and into the streets.

Lennie lost friends, as people in the Hood began distancing themselves from her and other users, calling them baseheads, smokers, crackheads. It seemed to her that the worst of the treatment was reserved for women who smoked crack. They became objects of abuse and ridicule from men who saw them as both suddenly attainable and beneath them.

It wasn't just dealers who abused addicts. It came from practically every direction. Once during this period, Lennie found herself with Jamal in the heart of the Hood, near the train tracks off Van Ness. She was out there trying to buy crack. It would be a quick stop, she told herself, then she'd get the baby home. An LAPD cruiser swooped in before she could get what she came for.

The officer got out and asked Lennie what she was up to. She replied that she was just headed home. It was an honest answer, she thought, because she didn't yet have drugs on her. Lennie expected she'd be sent on her way, but the officer instead handcuffed her and put her and Jamal in the back seat of his car.

At eighteen, Lennie was having her first real run-in with the law. She was scared and confused about what would happen next, especially to Jamal. But before she could ask any questions, the officer opened the door to the back seat, got in beside Lennie, and proceeded to pull her pants down, inches from her baby. There was nothing she could do.

21

—

HYPE

(1981-86)

THE OFFICIAL RESPONSE TO the epidemic was slow in the early years, at least on the part of the federal government. On the campaign trail, Ronald Reagan had made few comments on drug use in America—curious given the political points the issue had scored for Nixon just a few years prior. Instead, the "moral leadership" proposed by the Reagan campaign promised a "spiritual revival" with few specifics. The issue of drugs seems to have only come into focus for Reagan after he was elected.

In March 1981, spurred by a question from a reporter during a press conference, Reagan articulated the approach he intended to take. He argued that it was "virtually impossible" to block the smuggling of drugs into the United States given our porous borders. "It's like carrying water in a sieve," he said. Instead of focusing on the supply side of the drug problem, Reagan said he believed the more effective approach was to focus on demand. In other words, instead of going after international cartels bringing drugs into the United States, he wanted to go after users.

By targeting young people specifically with an anti-drug education campaign, Reagan thought it was possible to win the war on
drugs. "It's far more effective if you take the customers away than if
you try to take the drugs away from those who want to be customers," he said.

Later that year, in July, Reagan appointed Carlton E. Turner his
senior policy advisor for drugs. Turner, who would more or less determine drug policy for the Reagan administration, had a curious
background. He was an organic chemist by education and spent the
early part of his career studying drugs, primarily marijuana. That
work led him to a role as director of the University of Mississippi's
Research Institute of Pharmaceutical Sciences. From his post at Ole
Miss, Turner became involved in training narcotics agents on the federal, state, and local levels. It was through trainings and consultancy
that he met Ross Perot, the Texas millionaire and politico who ultimately introduced him to the Reagan White House.

Turner was an anti-drug zealot, especially when it came to marijuana. He dedicated much of his career to opposing the drug, believ-
ing it to be a major destructive force in American society, tied to the
civil unrest of the sixties and seventies. In an October 1982 profile in
Government Executive magazine, Turner identified marijuana as a pillar of "the counterculture" and called its use a "plague" that "tagged
along during the present young-adult generation's involvement in
anti-military, anti-nuclear power, anti-big business, anti-authority
demonstrations; of people from a myriad of different racial, religious
or otherwise persuasions demanding rights or entitlements politically
while refusing to accept corollary civic responsibility."

Equipped with this set of beliefs, he entered the Reagan administration with three stated objectives: to increase anti-drug enforcement efforts, to shift the government's attention away from heroin to
marijuana and cocaine, and to establish a national education and prevention program.

Almost immediately, First Lady Nancy Reagan emerged as the

public face of the administration's efforts. Perhaps inspired by the reporting in "Jimmy's World," she took on the mantle of spreading the anti-drug message to America's youth.

In a campaign coordinated by Turner, Mrs. Reagan traveled to schools across the country to talk to children about drugs. It was during a 1982 visit to Longfellow Elementary School in Oakland, California, that the First Lady happened upon a slogan for her campaign. When asked by a girl what to do if she was offered drugs, Mrs. Reagan responded plainly, "Just say no."

Later in 1982, the administration expanded its efforts beyond public awareness to actual policy. On June 24, 1982, President Reagan signed Executive Order 12368. Conceived largely by Carlton E. Turner, the order assigned much of the White House's drug policy to the director of drug abuse policy, a title Reagan had given to Turner in March of that year.

For the signing of the order, Reagan was joined by the heads of eighteen federal agencies, the vice president, military leaders, and the commissioner of the IRS to the White House. "We're rejecting the helpless attitude that drug use is so rampant that we are defenseless to do anything about it," he announced. "We're taking down the surrender flag that has flown over so many drug efforts; we're running up the battle flag."

It was indeed more than just a simple shift in bureaucracy. In prior administrations, White House drug policy had been made by a number of offices handling both enforcement and public-health concerns. Under Reagan, however, all drug policy would be directed by one office, led by a man who believed the federal government could arrest and propagandize its way to a drug-free America. What followed was an all-out offensive the likes of which might have made former president Nixon proud.

White House officials were insistent that the anti-drug campaign wasn't a political issue, but starting in the spring of 1983, a year before the president would be up for reelection, First Lady Nancy Reagan flooded television with anti-drug media appearances. First, she put her experience as a Hollywood actress to use when she guest starred as herself on a March 1983 episode of *Diff'rent Strokes* that focused on child drug and alcohol abuse. Later that year, Mrs. Reagan sat in as a co-host of *Good Morning America,* ABC's two-hour talk show, for an entire program dedicated to the topic. She also acted as narrator for 1983's "The Chemical People," a two-part special on drug and alcohol abuse shown across three hundred public television stations.

As former entertainers, the Reagans recognized the tremendous potential of weaponizing television and other media in the war on drugs. Leveraging President Reagan's connections as former president of the Screen Actors Guild, the White House also coordinated loosely with a number of media organizations to advance its message. The Reagan administration worked with the Academy of Television Arts and Sciences, the National Association of Broadcasters, and the newly created Partnership for a Drug-Free America. These three organizations launched massive campaigns in the early eighties to infuse television programs with anti-drug messaging and produced a number of public service announcements.

The programs and advertisements created during the period often blurred the line between fact and fiction. Most portrayed the physical effects of drugs inaccurately in an effort to scare young people. Their basic message was that drug use, from marijuana to heroin and cocaine, led immediately to a life of desperate addiction or death. The people who sold drugs were usually portrayed as predators, shadowy figures who lurked in the dark looking for children to corrupt.

The year 1983 also marked the launch of the Drug Abuse Resistance Education program in Los Angeles. DARE was the brainchild of Los Angeles Police Chief Daryl Gates, who also pioneered the concept of special weapons and tactics (SWAT) units within the LAPD, spurring their creation in police departments across the United States. Gates also infamously defended police chokehold maneuvers in 1982, when he argued that a physiological deficiency made them deadly to

Blacks. He was quoted in the *Los Angeles Times* as saying, "We may be finding that in some Blacks when it is applied, the veins or arteries do not open up as fast as they do in normal people."

Gates's LAPD partnered with the Los Angeles Unified School District to send officers into classrooms to talk with young people about the dangers of drug use. In DARE, many police chiefs and politicians saw an easily replicated "community policing" initiative. It was an irresistible model that spread like wildfire across the country.

ON OCTOBER 12, 1984, the federal government made a huge leap forward in its war on drugs when the United States Congress passed the Comprehensive Crime Control Act. The act was the first broad revision of the U.S. criminal code since the early 1900s. Among other things, it reinstituted the federal death penalty; abolished federal parole; and increased federal penalties for the cultivation, possession, and transfer of marijuana. It also enhanced penalties for possession of firearms for violent felons; created a special Department of Justice fund for law enforcement agencies to retain the proceeds from asset forfeitures; and established the United States Sentencing Commission, which streamlined sentencing in federal courts through official guidelines.

After consulting with a New York City ad agency, Nancy Reagan also launched her "Just Say No" campaign in earnest in 1984. According to the Reagan Library, in that year alone, the First Lady made 110 appearances and fourteen anti-drug speeches. In the years to come, she visited sixty-five U.S. cities, thirty-three states, and nine foreign countries to promote the program, which became an unavoidable part of popular culture during the eighties.

Perhaps as a result of the Reagan administration's near-constant talk of drugs, the media finally began covering the spread of freebase as an epidemic.

Beginning in November 1985, *The New York Times* assigned a reporter to cover illegal drugs full-time. From there, coverage continued to snowball, with magazines, newspapers, and television programs all over the country introducing Americans to crack.

America got an up-close and personal look at the then-raging crack epidemic in February 1986, when *Spin* magazine published an in-depth feature story by a young writer named Barry Michael Cooper. Living in Harlem, Cooper had heard stories about the crack houses being set up along 145th Street. Curious, he reported the word on the street. What resulted was a sensational, nearly five-thousand-word exposé on crack and the people using it.

"These white pellets of prepackaged freebase (cocaine in its purest form) are extremely frightening. Frequent users—peer-pressured 13-year-olds to 60-plus grandparents—don't associate its use with the savage addiction of heroin or the hallucinogenic insanity of angel dust, its two predecessors in Harlem's crippling drug trilogy," Cooper wrote. "But in the last year, crack has become the drug of choice; the exhilarating rush of its 5-to-15-minute high brings a distorted sense of power, a king-of-the-hill nirvana. Like Huxley's 'soma' in *Brave New World,* crack is, for many, escape, booster, stabilizer, and status quo."

Cooper interviewed detectives with the NYPD bereft over the young, rich white kids flooding Harlem in BMWs, Mercedes, and Volvos to buy crack. He went into crack houses and detailed their operations. "Inside the more active ones there are usually four men: two at the door and two in the middle of the room, watching everyone and everything, armed with Berettas, Uzis, and MAC 10s," he wrote. "The room is stripped bare except for a long rectangular table, which has numbers written on top from one to five. Behind each number are rows of vials of crack. Scattered around the basehouse are chairs and card tables, each with a pipe and torch on top. Admission to the basehouse is $3, as is separate rental of a pipe and torch. The crack ranges from $10–$50 a bottle (hence the markings on the table). Sitting time is 15 minutes. To stay longer is to pay another $9. To try to take a bottle of crack without paying is to be chopped and grated by rounds of automatic fire."

The centerpiece of the feature was Gary Martin, a husband and father of two who worked as a youth counselor on Staten Island by day but used and sold crack by night. Through Martin, Cooper took readers on a tour of a crack-struck Harlem. He also outlined the many ways the man's life had devolved in just a few short years of using crack. "It's a heavy habit, because you start neglecting your essential needs. Like rent, food, clothing, your kids, your family," Martin explained. "Somebody's gonna starve to have that glass dick stuck in your mouth."

Just as it seemed the crack story couldn't get any bigger, it catapulted from concern to crisis on the morning of June 19, 1986, when it was reported that basketball player Len Bias had died of a cocaine overdose.

Bias, a first-team All-American at the University of Maryland, had been selected by the Boston Celtics as the second overall pick in the NBA draft just two days earlier. He was on top of the world, fielding comparisons to Michael Jordan and looking forward to a $1.6 million endorsement deal with Reebok, when he called friends over to his dorm room during the early hours of June 19.

Bias, some teammates, and his longtime friend Brian Tribble reportedly did lines of cocaine and celebrated over the next few hours. Sometime around 6:30 A.M., Bias got up to use the bathroom. He stumbled, then sat back down on his bed, where he lapsed into a seizure. Tribble called Bias's mother and then 911, but by the time paramedics found Bias he was already unconscious and had stopped breathing. Attempts to revive him were unsuccessful and Bias was pronounced dead at 8:55 A.M. of cardiac arrhythmia induced by a cocaine overdose. No other drugs or alcohol were found in his system.

News of the tragedy broke within hours and the nation was stunned. It seemed unthinkable that one of the country's top athletes— a six-foot-seven, 221-pound man with no history of heart disease— could suddenly die from a cocaine overdose. Because such a high concentration of the drug—6.5 milligrams per liter—was found in Bias's blood, the medical examiner who performed his autopsy concluded that Bias had consumed the freebase form of the drug.

The conclusion flew in the face of statements from the friends who were with Bias that morning. It also conflicted with reports that police found eight grams of powder cocaine in Bias's car and recovered straws containing cocaine residue from a garbage can behind his dorm.

In the tragic story of the promising athlete's death, elected officials, journalists, and members of law enforcement had a cautionary tale about the dangers of crack. Perhaps more than any speech the Reagans could give, any PSA or article, the death of Len Bias galvanized the nation, drafting many into the war on drugs. In years to come, he would remain the prime example of how a young person could lose it all, even his or her life, experimenting with drugs.

22

—

SHAWN

(1985~86)

SHAWN EASED INTO LIFE AT CENTRAL. It was heaven, he thought, with a pretty girl or a familiar face around every corner. The curriculum wasn't as rigorous as St. Benedict's, and he got along with his teachers and enjoyed his classmates. He fit in—especially once basketball season got underway.

Shawn spent years honing his skills—pickup games, neighborhood tournaments, competing in the Catholic school league. It was all preparation for his arrival at Central, he thought. Shawn was ready to test his mettle against Newark's best players, the boys in the public school league.

He soldiered through intense tryouts, and after a week, when the smoke cleared, he'd made the cut, beating out a hundred or so other boys for a spot on varsity. The rest of the team consisted of Big Naim, J.C., Tariq Brown, Sean West, Big Butts, Norris Colson, Safee, Delvin Wilson, Tyrone Ousley, Mike Rooks, and Shawn "Mad Dog" Jones, who became Shawn's best friend.

Their first game of the season was against St. Anthony High School, coached at that time by the inimitable Bob Hurley. He wasn't yet a coaching legend, but Hurley would go on to amass twenty-six state championships at St. Anthony, five with undefeated teams. Central lost the game but proved formidable, scoring fifty-five points to St. Anthony's fifty-eight. Shawn remembered the comment Hurley gave to the newspaper afterward: "Newark Central has talent to burn."

Shawn made his mark during that game. The new guy on the team, he played like he had something to prove and managed to score points against some of St. Anthony's best players. There was a short older man in the stands rooting for Central. After a few plays, he started calling Shawn "Sam Perkins," the name of the University of North Carolina's star center.

Shawn's classmates were also taking note. The following day, they talked him up in the halls between classes. That was how he met Bertina Moore, Sheryle Washington, and Vonnie Jones—girls he began dating soon after.

All the attention sent Shawn's ego through the roof. It was like a dream, the opposite of the nightmare he'd experienced at St. Benedict's. Everything was a struggle there. At Central, he fell easily into a role that no one questioned.

He also had a fast friend in Mad Dog. He and Shawn hit it off right away. They, of course, had basketball in common, but they also shared a sense of humor and a laid-back sensibility. At a time when most guys their age were trying to act hard, Shawn appreciated that Mad Dog kept a smile on his face and could take a joke. After a couple of weeks of school, you couldn't see one without the other.

Mad Dog always picked Shawn to guard in practice. He was a hell of a defensive player, and Shawn would complain. He'd say, "I thought I was your boy. Pick on somebody else." Mad Dog would laugh and say, "You are my boy. Nobody is going to work you harder than me."

After St. Anthony's, Central's next big game was against Malcolm X Shabazz High School. While Shawn and his teammates were earning a reputation in the Newark public school league, Shabazz already had one, and star players, including future NBA power forward Anthony Avent. On top of that, the game was set to be televised on Channel 3.

That the game was televised was lost on neither team. Each was on fire, keeping the score tight throughout the first half. Some especially enthusiastic Central supporters arrived during the third quarter. Shawn, who loved the reaction of the crowd more than anything, got an extra boost from the *oohs* and *ahhs* as they got louder and louder. He played his heart out for the remaining minutes of the game, helping to lead the team to victory with nineteen points and eleven rebounds. Shawn was picked as MVP of the game and he did an interview with Cablevision afterward. His moment had come, he thought, finally.

Maybe if he had been close with someone who'd gone to college, he could have better appreciated how temporary his problems at St. Benedict's were. He might have buckled down and spent his time at Central planning for college and finding a path toward college ball. Instead, Shawn luxuriated in his hoop dreams.

For four years, the only thing Shawn had thought about besides basketball was getting out of St. Benedict's. It was a fantasy that organized his greatest desires to be accepted, celebrated even. That's what motivated him, but that year at Central was as far into the future as Shawn had imagined. After it was over, he found that he'd put himself in a trick bag: he wanted to continue playing college ball, but his transcript, grades earned largely while resenting St. Benedict's, made that new dream nearly impossible.

All those years in Catholic school had instilled in Shawn some expectation that he'd get out of Newark's Central Ward and make something of himself. He wouldn't admit it, but Shawn was waiting for another break. Just as the Victoria Foundation had swooped in to take him to St. Rocco's, he expected someone to notice his skills on the court, to discover him, and show him the next step. It was a ridiculous expectation given all that was stacked against him. But what are teenagers if not ridiculous?

Just a few weeks before the last day of school, right as Shawn was ready to give up, he got lucky. Mr. Daniels, the boys' basketball coach, came to him and asked if he'd ever heard of Keystone Junior College. He explained that it was a small school located in the mountains just ten miles outside of Scranton, Pennsylvania. It was mostly white, "nothing like Newark," he said, but they had a basketball program, and the coach was interested in players from Central.

Shawn jumped at the opportunity and immediately got in contact with the coach at Keystone, a man named Dennis Mishko. The two talked briefly, and afterward Shawn had the guidance counselor at Central fax his transcript over to Mishko's office. Just a few weeks later, sometime after graduation, he was in a car with Mr. Daniels headed toward La Plume, Pennsylvania, to officially tour the campus.

Shawn expected Keystone to be small but wasn't prepared for exactly how quaint the school would look in person. The buildings were no more than a few stories each, and the grounds were so covered with trees that the campus seemed tucked into a forest. Just looking up at the giant trees with their canopies of red, green, and yellow made Shawn homesick for Hayes Homes and the bricks of Newark.

Coach Mishko met Shawn and Mr. Daniels near the entrance to campus. He was shorter than Shawn had expected but also nicer, with an easy smile that softened his already round face. He was happy to see Shawn, he said, and was eager to sell him on Keystone.

Mishko gave the grand tour. He showed Shawn the boys' dorm, which was equipped with a washer and dryer and a lounge to watch TV. Then the student center, which had a cafeteria, a game room, and a deli. The tour ended with a stop at the gym, an old barn that had been retrofitted to house both a stage for the theater program and a basketball court.

After they'd seen the campus, Mishko took Shawn and Mr. Daniels to a nearby Burger King where they talked specifics. Shawn's tuition, room, and board would be covered if he played for Keystone, Mishko explained. All he had to do was pick a major, keep his grades up, and help the team beat Keystone's rival, Lackawanna Junior College. He was building a team, Mishko added, big guys from all over the Northeast—Philly, D.C., Newark, Baltimore.

Mr. Daniels and Mishko continued to talk while Shawn finished his food and slipped into a daydream. He imagined himself at Keystone, in classes and around campus. He didn't look anything like the students on the brochures he picked up in the student center, but the more he imagined the more it felt right. Going would give him a break from Newark, he thought, and he could even make good on all those years of Catholic school by becoming the first person in his family to graduate from college. Maybe if he did it, Tony and Cheyta would follow behind him.

On the way back to Newark, Shawn thanked Mr. Daniels for taking him to see Keystone. It was above and beyond anything he'd expected from a coach, especially given that he'd been at Central for just a year. Mr. Daniels told Shawn that he should accept the offer from Mishko. It was his only option for college, Mr. Daniels explained, and the best option for his life.

WHEN THE TIME CAME to finally pack for Keystone, Shawn was filled with a mix of excitement and dread. His going away was a good thing, everyone said, including Mad Dog and Bertina, whom he was still dating. Still, he couldn't help but feel like he was on shaky ground leaving his neighborhood.

Joanne was the happiest, happier than she'd been the day she learned he was going to St. Rocco's. And the news spread quickly once Joanne knew. Shawn was soon the pride of Hayes Homes as neighbors took turns congratulating him, only the second person from Building 73 to go to college.

Mr. Daniels gave Shawn a ride to Penn Station. Once he arrived, he hurried to the Trailways counter and spent eleven dollars on a one-way ticket to Scranton. The bus was relatively empty when it arrived, and Shawn carted on all of his worldly possessions—two bags, and a large suitcase full of clothes and a few things Joanne was able to buy for his dorm. With that, he was on his way to begin a new chapter.

Coach Mishko had a big smile on his face when Shawn stepped off the bus in Scranton. "Kids always say they'll attend your school, and sometimes they never show up," he said. Shawn lugged his bags to Mishko's car, and the two made the short drive to campus. On the way, Mishko explained that he'd been back and forth to the bus station all day picking up recruits. The news lifted a weight that Shawn didn't know was there. "Other kids from the city are on their way," he thought. And they were also taking the bus.

Keystone was the same small school it had been when Shawn visited, but with students now on campus and walking around, it felt alive. His dorm room looked bigger, and Shawn was all of a sudden impressed with the new digs—a sizable room with two beds, two desks, and two closets on the first floor of Tewksbury Hall, right next to the lounge.

Other students moved about outside as Shawn made quick work of unpacking his things. The students were mostly white, just as he had been told. The few Black students he saw were guys, big and tall. Probably athletes like him, he thought. Whenever he heard female voices approaching the walkway near his window, he said a silent prayer that one might come from a Black woman and was disappointed every time. Still, the white girls at Keystone were cute, he thought. And much to his surprise, they weren't all rail thin like the ones on TV.

Shawn met the rest of the team later that day. They were still months away from the start of the season, but Coach Mishko thought it best that everyone get acquainted early. Also at the meeting was the assistant coach, Doug Walsh. He said he was from Scranton, looked to be in his late twenties, and came off to Shawn like the kind of hard-nosed white boy who was used to earning the respect of young Black players, which wasn't easy.

As the players went around the room introducing themselves, Shawn noticed that only a few of the freshmen were from Jersey and

New York. The majority were from Philly. There were just three sophomores on the team—Steve Truitt from Baltimore, Rick Eubanks from D.C., and Kimmey Doney from Trenton. Eubanks had yet to arrive on campus, but from the way Mishko and Walsh talked about him, it was clear that he was the star of the team. But even in his absence, the team looked strong—focused and athletic. Just standing there among them got Shawn amped for the season to come.

The very next day, he got up early to meet with his guidance counselor and schedule his classes for the semester. Shawn settled on human services as a major. He had never heard of it before, but the course catalog explained that the field dealt mostly with understanding and helping people. Shawn got along easily with most people, so he picked the major hoping that whatever he needed to learn would come just as easy.

He was still shaken, it turned out, from his experience at St. Benedict's. His indifference toward school had nearly derailed his life by ruining his chance at playing college ball. Shawn wanted to hedge his bets this time around, so after he was done in the guidance counselor's office, he went directly to Coach Mishko. He explained to him that the only reason he'd gone to Keystone, to college even, was to play basketball. He couldn't imagine sticking around if he found himself ineligible. He wanted the bottom-line word on what he had to do to stay on the court.

Mishko was both taken aback and amused. "I respect and appreciate your honesty," he told Shawn. Then he explained that all he had to do to remain eligible was maintain a 2.0 grade point average and earn twelve credits a semester. Then he asked Shawn a question no one ever had: "What's your five-year plan?" Shawn didn't have one and didn't know he was supposed to. Mishko took a breath and looked at Shawn with genuine concern.

"Don't let basketball use you," he said. "You have to use it. Take advantage of the opportunity you've been given. If basketball is what motivated you to go to college, take it as far as you can. If it takes you to the NBA, let it. If it takes you to a college degree, let it. Either way, you're a winner." He paused before continuing. "People are expecting you to fail," he said. "You have to prove them wrong."

For the second time in his life, Shawn was reminded that life was set up for him to fail—first by a young neighborhood dealer and now by an old white basketball coach. It was a heavy message, but he took it as a sign that Mishko was good people and that he'd done the right thing by attending Keystone.

He returned to his guidance counselor's office immediately after the talk to add another six credits to his schedule. He would do more than remain eligible, Shawn decided; he would give college a college try.

Shawn attended his classes, took notes, and studied hard. There wasn't much else to do in La Plume, Pennsylvania. When he wasn't in class or practice, he was working. Thanks to Coach Mishko, he had a work-study job manning the front desk in Moffat Hall, the girl's dorm on campus. It provided, along with the twenty-five dollars Joanne sent him every other week, enough to take care of his basic needs.

True to form, Shawn befriended the girls in Moffat. He also became friendly with their boyfriends, every now and then letting them stick around past visiting hours. In return, the girls in Moffat showed him how to raid the vending machine in the lobby using a wire hanger. Mostly white girls from the area, they had never met anyone like Shawn. They were enamored with him, not least of all because he was tall, good-looking, and on the basketball team.

Shawn loved his status as a big man on campus, the attention it came with and the occasional ride or free meal he'd get. He started enjoying himself even more once the season got underway.

The Keystone Giants started with a bang, knocking off teams one after the other—Penn State Hazleton, Baptist Bible College, the University of Scranton. The team was 5–0 until they played Princeton. It was the JV squad, but they were strong and big. In the end, Keystone lost by ten points and got chewed out by Mishko for letting "a bunch of white boys" beat them. The team lost another game after that but they became closer along the way, learning one another's strengths and weaknesses. Shawn emerged as a player to watch, something he learned one weekend when Joanne called him on campus to share that there was a story about him in *The Star-Ledger.*

The headline read, "Giants McCray Deadly Shooter." "Keystone Junior College men's basketball team expects the spirited play of freshman Shawn 'Scooter' McCray to be a factor in the Giants' future success," opened the piece. It went on to detail Shawn's contribution to the team's 5–2 season and had a quote from Mishko: "Scooter is without a doubt the deadliest outside shooter on the team," he said. "With his size, he can do many different things, and combined with Rick Eubanks and Dexter Whitfield, we have three guys who can perform consistently in all facets of the game." Hearing the pride in Joanne's voice as she read each passage over the phone felt good. It made all the work he was putting in worth it.

The team continued to win from then on, and they celebrated their victories most weekends by partying. When there wasn't a party off campus, practically the entire team would congregate in one player's room. One Saturday night, a bunch of guys were in a dorm, along with a couple of sophomores Shawn hadn't met before. The alcohol was flowing, and go-go music was playing from a boom box. Someone decided to roll a joint. Before it was sealed, he pulled out a plastic bag with a white substance inside. Shawn must've looked shocked, because people started laughing. "This is what all the young guys do in D.C.," said the guy with the joint. "This stuff right here stops your heart for a few seconds."

Drugs were all over Newark, but Shawn had never seen them up close and personal, at least not anything more serious than weed. Now, at a college in the mountains of Pennsylvania, he was watching people smoke cocaine. He could have left the room at that moment. He probably should have. But instead, when the joint came around, he put it to his lips and gave it a puff. He didn't feel anything afterward except uneasiness about the situation. Shawn stayed long enough to not draw attention then went back to his room. Shawn never hung out with those guys again.

That moment in the dorm room was just the beginning. When Shawn went home for winter break, drugs were everywhere. All of Newark seemed to be smoking, snorting, or selling cocaine, and he couldn't understand how so much had changed so fast in his neighborhood. His family and friends were doing all right; drugs had never been their thing. But people seemed different across the Central Ward. They were in their own little worlds, on one-man missions to either get high or get money.

The game against Lackawanna Junior College was one of the first Keystone games played after winter break. Having been on something of a winning streak, Shawn and the others approached it like any other. They paid for their arrogance as Lackawanna wiped the floor with them in front of a packed gym. Afterward, Mishko ripped the team for getting too comfortable, and Shawn was reminded of what Mishko had said to him when they first met: that the only win he expected from the team was against Lackawanna, its rival.

Everyone was on edge at the next practice. They'd never heard Mishko shout the way he had after the loss, and they expected he'd work them extra hard as punishment. But Mishko never showed up. Instead, the team had to deal with Coach Walsh. Still hoarse from the game, Walsh whispered a stream of expletives at the players and laid out the weaknesses in each of their games. He was disappointed, yes, but also just pissed off. Lackawanna didn't beat them because they were a better team, he said, but because they played smarter.

Shawn and the others filed out of the gym a little sore, but each knew Walsh was right. They'd been lazy and disorganized, floating from game to game like they were at home playing pickups. The reality, however, was that they were all at a junior college trying to salvage their hoop dreams. Doing well at Keystone was their only path to playing at a Division I school, and they were blowing it. It rallied the team. Each man was determined to play harder and smarter from there on out.

The second game against Lackawanna came with all the excitement of an NBA championship. It was held at Keystone, and thanks to heavy coverage from the local papers, residents of La Plume and Scranton packed the gym. For their part, professors at Keystone offered extra credit to students who attended. It all made for an electric atmosphere.

Shawn was the sixth man at the start of the game and was anxious to get in. He shot up and ran onto the court when Mishko finally called his name. Dexter always knew how to set Shawn up for a shot and he did just that, driving hard into the paint then kicking the ball out to Shawn, waiting in the corner. They'd run that play so often that it was like second nature to them both. Shawn pulled up with ease and sank the ball into the net. It was on after that. Keystone played well for the rest of the game and won by a hefty margin.

It's impossible to convey the amount of pride and satisfaction Shawn felt after the game. Mishko and Walsh heaped praise on the team for its remarkable comeback, and so did the entire community around Keystone. But it was deeper than attention and praise. The win against Lackawanna was the first time Shawn had set his heart on something and made it happen. It was his first victory, one made sweeter weeks later when he received his final grades. He hadn't set academia on fire, but he was more than eligible to play his sophomore year. The coach was excited when he got the news but pushed Shawn for more. He had a good season, Mishko said, but he'd have to work harder on and off the court next year. He'd need sixty credits to graduate, and for acceptance at a Division I school. And he needed to wow recruiters, not just at some games, but at all of them.

Then Mishko reached into a drawer in his desk and pulled out a stack of mail. They were letters from colleges looking to recruit Shawn, schools including Saint Peter's, Loyola, and UC Berkeley. Others were interested, too, Mishko said. He had another stack of letters from Fort Hays State University in Kansas, St. Thomas Aquinas College, and Monmouth University. Shawn took the image of Mishko holding the stack back with him to Newark. It became an anchor for him, and he'd return to the thought throughout the summer when things got hard, or when the call of the streets got too loud.

Back in Newark, guys were making money hand over fist. Haneef was in control of Building 61-65, with three boys working for him. Bobby Evans and another guy named Shawn were hustling out of Building 41-45, Pee Wee and Gerald out of 84-88. Over where Tariq used to deal had been taken over by Papo, Dollar Bill, and Steph. Building 338-342 was run by the Gregorys, Fats, June Bug, Hass Moody, Ant Man, Craig White, and Craig's brother Derrick.

Shawn put the thought of how much money he could make out of his mind and focused, as he always had, on basketball. There were fewer and fewer guys making time for pickup games, but Mad Dog, his old buddy from Central, was still around. The two of them would go over to New Community to play, or down to the Eighteenth Avenue School, which also had a court. Afterward, they'd see what was happening in Fairview Homes and strike up a game of pitty pat with their friends there if they could.

A regular schedule of basketball and card games made for an uneventful summer, which was exactly what Shawn wanted. Only one thing interrupted the lull. It occurred hundreds of miles away but might as well have happened in the Central Ward. It was June and Shawn was sitting in Zeke's Barber Shop on Irvine Turner Boulevard. The shop was loud with the usual cacophony—a clash of buzzing clippers, dudes lying, and music blaring. Then, suddenly, the song on the radio stopped and the DJ came on. He announced that Len Bias had died of heart failure.

The entire shop was rendered silent for once. Shawn especially was stunned. The news felt personal, and even closer to home when it was later revealed that Bias's heart failure was caused by a cocaine overdose, possibly from smoking it.

The tragedy dominated the rest of that summer. It cast a pall over everything. Shawn and Mad Dog talked constantly about it. It was impossible not to. You couldn't watch the news, read a paper, or pass a magazine stand without seeing an update on the investigation into Bias's friends that soon followed.

What happened to Len Bias brought the story of crack into the mainstream, but it also raised the stakes for Shawn and his friends. The drugs taking over their neighborhood were deadly. That much was evident. However, it was also clear that the drug trade was incredibly lucrative.

When Shawn and Mad Dog talked, the conversation usually touched on who was "smokin' that shit" and who was "gettin' money." Shawn tried to remember that he had a reason to stay on the straight and narrow. But he also wanted in.

ACT

V

–

SURGE

23

—

LENNIE

LENNIE SPENT ALMOST EVERY dime she made on whiskey and crack. She spent the money she made on the street, the AFDC check she got from the state, the money she continued to steal from Uncle Archie. Nearly every night, Lennie was taking two or three hundred dollars to Johnny, a dope man who lived nearby.

By then, there were very few people in Los Angeles just experimenting with crack. The oldest users—those who'd transitioned from powder to freebase—were now addicts, the occasional users were on their way, and most folks who might otherwise try it saw enough to know better. Lennie was among the first group, an addict and a heavy user at that.

Five weeks out from her high school graduation, she had four F's and a D. But she went in, talked to a few teachers and administrators, and convinced them to pull together some work for her. She studied hard, finished the schoolwork, and cleared her graduation requirements by the skin of her teeth.

Aside from that one goal, Lennie was completely disconnected from the events around her and the passage of time. There were moments of clarity when she wouldn't smoke, or sometimes right after, when she asked herself if it was worth it. It wasn't, but she didn't know how to stop. She had surrendered herself to addiction. Years passed in a blur of tricks, smoke, and drink.

Then one day she was at home with Jamal, who was just two years old. She had just finished smoking and was combing the carpet for any crumbs of crack she might have dropped. Her baby, still with a pacifier in his mouth, got on his hands and knees to join her. He started handing Lennie little white pieces of lint. That was when Lennie knew she had to stop.

She scoured the yellow pages until she came across a number for House of Uhuru, a rehab facility near Watts. With trademark candor, Lennie explained over the phone that she was addicted to crack and needed help. She was lucky. A bed was open, and the man on the line said she could come immediately.

Lennie went to Bea next. Despite their differences, it was still hard to say what she knew she had to, so Lennie just came out with it. She held her crack pipe in her mother's face and said, "This is what I'm doing." She told Bea that she wanted to go to treatment and asked her to take care of Jamal while she was away. To Lennie's surprise, Bea agreed to help.

Lennie liked the House of Uhuru. The program was housed in a large building and run by what felt like real people. She'd learn later that many staffers and counselors had been addicts themselves and otherwise involved in street life. Their backgrounds gave them an edge, and they ran the program with a Scared Straight approach. Women and men were segregated. Women couldn't wear long nails or makeup. Men's heads were shaved.

Lennie tried her best to fit in, but from the moment she arrived, she stood out. Her manner, her style, the way she thought were all guided by principles she'd learned on the streets. It was a "hood mentality," counselors told her, and she'd have to drop it to get clean.

She knew that she needed a new way of life, but it never occurred to Lennie that a new way meant a new her. Lennie's personality was hard won. It had saved her from her mother and Uncle Archie and kept her safe all those years in the streets. Lennie listened to what she was told, but something inside of her rejected the idea.

Instead of trying to change, she walked around in high heels every day, like she did when she was working. She changed outfits constantly. The thing that bothered the staff most, though, was Lennie's walk, a swishy saunter that she'd mastered while walking the streets. She couldn't turn it off even if she tried.

Lennie was constantly at odds with the staff for what they considered bringing the streets into the facility and what she considered just being herself. When she wasn't on the phone with a friend from back home, she was either joking around with other patients or arguing with them. After four months, the folks at House of Uhuru had finally had enough and kicked Lennie out of the program. She just wasn't ready for treatment, they said.

A kind older woman counselor who'd grown fond of Lennie cried while she packed her things to leave. Lennie held her head high as she walked out of the facility and made declarations that she'd stay clean. She believed it at that moment. Perhaps the counselor was crying because she knew better.

Lennie's old friend Rudy came with his girlfriend, Francine, to pick her up from rehab. She asked him to stop by a dealer friend of hers no sooner than they left the parking lot. But Rudy was proud of Lennie and wanted to see her sober again. He said no. He went further and took Lennie to his place in the Jungles, an infamous apartment complex about three miles away from their old neighborhood.

He left her there with Francine in hopes she'd come to her senses. But Rudy couldn't keep her there forever. She did eventually go home, and when she did, Lennie went back to using.

24

—

KURT

(1984–88)

HEROIN MAINTAINED ITS HOLD on Baltimore well into the 1980s. Indeed, while crack was becoming a major presence in other cities as early as 1983, it wasn't until the late eighties that authorities saw an influx in Baltimore. They found suppliers, mostly Dominican groups from New York, bringing cocaine into the city in cars and on buses via I-95, or if they knew enough to avoid detection, via U.S. Route 13 to U.S. Route 50 and then I-97. Once the product arrived, it was distributed to homegrown dealers or Jamaican drug posses.

Baltimore's drug culture had revolved for so long around heroin that dealers saw little reason to sell crack at first. Users were reluctant, too. In fact, intravenous drug use was so much a part of Baltimore's drug culture that most cocaine users preferred to inject the substance. But the low price of crack and the near-immediate high were irresistible. Little by little, the market for crack got stronger, the product got better, and the idea of smoking it became more accepted.

Before long, users were not only smoking crack but mixing it and heroin into speedballs, one part heroin and one part crack mixed with water and an acid—lemon juice or vinegar, usually—then cooked on a spoon until it all melted into a smooth, injectable liquid. A speedball, it was said, gave users a balanced high: a combination of a stimulant in cocaine and a depressant in heroin that offered the thrill of crack without the jitters and nerves that usually accompany the substance.

In Baltimore, a symbiotic relationship formed between crack and heroin. Many users consumed both drugs, and the addictions fed each other—crack to perk up and heroin to mellow out. In no time, both were widely available in the city, with most dealers selling both "boy" (heroin) and "girl" (cocaine).

BY 1987, BALTIMORE WAS REBRANDING. Its longtime mayor, William Schaefer (he served from 1971 to 1987), had redeveloped the city's downtown before running for Maryland governor and being elected at the tail end of his fourth term. He left his office to Clarence Henry "Du" Burns, Jr., then council president.

Burns, a Black man born in Baltimore in 1918, had climbed the ladder of the city's politics starting at the bottom rung. He hadn't attended college but worked for twenty-two years at Dunbar High School as a locker room attendant, picking up wet towels and washing uniforms. During that period, Burns created his own political club, the Eastside Democratic Organization. It grew in size and influence over the years, and as president of the club, Burns grew in stature.

He was finally elected to city council in 1971 and became Baltimore's first Black council president in 1986. His focus had always been the development of Baltimore, his beloved Eastside in particular; however, Burns's efforts in Baltimore's political establishment would backfire, because while downtown's renewal was celebrated in some circles, it was a point of contention in others.

Baltimore, the nation's eleventh-largest city, was open for business and primed for tourism, but it was still one of the nation's poorest cities. It had declining employment (blue-collar jobs especially), an underfunded and underperforming school system, among the high-

est teenage pregnancy and infant mortality rates in the country, and a
low-income-housing crisis. It was also suffering from crack and heroin epidemics. The city's Black residents, 55 percent of Baltimore's
total population, felt these issues most acutely, and they wanted a
change of the guard.

Kurt Schmoke saw his opportunity and seized it. He hired Larry
Gibson, a seasoned Black political operative who knew the lay of the
land in Baltimore, and the two went to work building a campaign
against Burns. Schmoke's 1987 mayoral campaign pledged to build
on the economic momentum created by Schaefer while also improv-
ing the city's social services—"people programs," as Schmoke called
them.

His agenda, though vague, was a hit. A poll by *The Baltimore Sun*
taken in mid-April 1987 showed Schmoke leading Burns 60 percent to
26 percent among Democrats who were "most likely to vote." Burns
was able to close the gap some, but not enough, and on Primary Day
1987, Schmoke brought in a total of 79,529 votes to Burns's 74,070.
After sailing through the general election, thirty-seven-year-old
Schmoke became the first elected Black mayor of Baltimore.

Historically, Baltimore had been prosperous. Indeed, it had been
an important port and an industrial hub until the mid-twentieth century. That changed in the 1960s with the rise of deindustrialization
and the elimination of manufacturing jobs. (Bethlehem Steel's Spar-
rows Point mill, for example, employed more than thirty thousand
workers at its peak in 1959 but had shrunk its workforce to just eight
thousand by the 1980s.)

Job losses, desegregation, and resentment over the 1968 riots all
fueled a mass exodus of whites to the suburbs, further eroding the
city's tax base. (Between 1950 and 2010, Baltimore lost approximately
one-third of its population and 70 percent of its white residents.) Having assumed office in 1971 during the downturn, Schaefer tried to reverse the city's fortunes by encouraging the development of the
downtown and tirelessly promoting the city's Inner Harbor, in hopes
that Baltimore would survive with a shift toward tourism. But tour-

ism dollars never really materialized. The result was three distinct Baltimores, says historian Marc V. Levine: the Renaissance City, represented by downtown and the Inner Harbor; the Suburbs, neighborhoods located outside city limits in Baltimore County; and the Underclass City, comprised of West Baltimore and other neighborhoods like Fairfield, Dundalk, the Monument Street area.

When Schmoke entered office, he set his sights on redeveloping the Underclass City. He was fond of saying, "The ingenuity, courage, and money that built the waterfront can now build the home front." It was wishful thinking. After all, downtown Baltimore's renaissance had been made possible by a mix of private money and federal aid. But the business community wasn't interested in redeveloping the ghetto, and federal aid to cities was drying up.

Schmoke wanted Baltimore to be known as "the city that reads," as the slogan of his literacy initiative would have it. He was a scholar, after all, and truly believed that quality public education was one key to addressing the poverty, joblessness, and devastation that plagued the city. He wanted to improve the city's schools, public libraries, and Baltimore City Community College. He had an aggressive plan to do it. But just five months into the job, Schmoke's agenda was redirected.

He was asked to address a gathering of big-city mayors and police chiefs at the U.S. Conference of Mayors in Washington, D.C. Given his record as a prosecutor, organizers placed Schmoke on a conference committee tasked with studying the HIV/AIDS crisis and the potential value of needle-exchange programs. They also asked him to deliver remarks on the impact of the war on drugs in Baltimore. Schmoke accepted the opportunity, and in doing so forever altered the trajectory of his administration, life, and legacy.

The night before he was set to present, he tore up the speech that had been prepared for him. "I had two speechwriters, and Howard Lavine wrote a pretty good overview of the city and some of the issues we were facing related to substance abuse," Schmoke later told *Baltimore* magazine. "But I thought, 'No, this is a unique opportunity, with the police chiefs and mayors in the same room.' I had one night to rewrite it, and I didn't show it to anyone, including my chief of staff, because I did not want to be talked out of it."

When Schmoke opened his mouth on that April day in 1988, what came out was revolutionary. In his trademark even tone, he criticized U.S. drug policy and proposed that the mayors of America's big cities and their police chiefs consider decriminalization. "Have we failed to consider the lessons of the Prohibition era?" Schmoke asked the leaders. "Now is the time to fight on the only terms the drug underground empire respects—money. Let's take the profit out of drug trafficking."

"We didn't seem to be getting anywhere," Schmoke said later. "Law enforcement would make a show of the drugs and money they seized, but the problem persisted. Marty Ward and all that was floating around in my head before the mayors' meeting in D.C. This group will be engaged, I thought. Hopefully, it will start a discussion." Instead, the speech was met with deafening silence.

When he returned to Baltimore and City Hall later that afternoon, Schmoke learned that the Associated Press was already working on a story about the speech, one saying that he was in favor of drug *legalization*. That, of course, wasn't the case. He had called for mayors to consider *decriminalization*—the loosening of criminal penalties imposed for minor drug possession—while the manufacturing and sale of drugs would remain illegal. Legalization, on the other hand, would mean completely overturning laws banning drugs, thereby making way for manufacturing and sales. It was a distinction completely lost on the press and many of Schmoke's peers.

Suddenly, the new mayor was thrust into the national spotlight and forced to defend his idea to incredulous audiences. He made his case in countless print and radio interviews and in appearances on *Nightline* with Ted Koppel, with Morley Safer on CBS, *The Phil Donahue Show*, PBS, and elsewhere.

Practically everywhere he went, Schmoke was blasted as inexperienced, naïve, and misguided. In a scathing editorial for *The New York*

Times just a month after Schmoke's speech, Democratic congressman Charlie Rangel called him "promising" but his ideas off-base. "Those who tout legalization remind me of fans sitting in the cheap seats at the ballpark" wrote Rangel. "They may have played the game, and they may think they know all the rules, but from where they're sitting they can't judge the action." Rangel concluded the piece by encouraging lawmakers to "take this legalization issue and put it where it belongs—amid idle chit-chat as cocktail glasses knock together at social events."

To his credit, Schmoke refused to back down in the face of criticism. To the contrary, when he was asked months later by Rangel to testify before the House Select Committee on Narcotics Abuse and Control, he again presented a case for decriminalization. "We have spent nearly seventy-five years and untold billions of dollars trying to square the circle, and inevitably we have failed," he said. Instead of a law-enforcement response to drug use, Schmoke proposed "a measured and carefully implemented program of drug decriminalization."

He outlined three initial steps. The first was to eliminate all criminal penalties for marijuana possession. Step two was to build on existing methadone treatment programs for heroin users by allowing public-health professionals to administer heroin and cocaine to addicts "as part of supervised maintenance or treatment programs." Finally, Schmoke wanted the government to explore broader decriminalization through a commission that would "study substance abuse, including tobacco and alcohol, and make recommendations on how they should be regulated based upon their potential for harm." The entire program, he suggested, could be funded with money otherwise spent on law enforcement and interdiction.

"Providing legal access to currently illicit substances carries with it the chance—although by no means the certainty—that the number of people using and abusing drugs will increase," Schmoke conceded. "But addiction, for all of its attendant medical, social, and moral problems, is but one evil associated with drugs. Moreover, the criminalization of narcotics, cocaine, and marijuana has not solved the problem of their use."

Other mayors called to testify before the committee—including Marion Barry, mayor of D.C., and Donald C. Master, mayor of Charles Town, West Virginia—agreed with Schmoke that the war on drugs had been an expensive failure. They also conceded, to varying degrees, that some drug addictions should be treated as medical problems. Still, committee members were unmoved, most insisting that a program to treat addiction as a public-health issue was an inadequate response—to the threat of crack, in particular.

"What kinds of drugs would be legalized? Would we not have to legalize the killer crack?" asked committee chairman Charlie Rangel in his prepared statement. New York congressman Benjamin A. Gilman echoed Rangel's concern over the substance. "Does anyone really think that, under legalization, the crack addict is going to go into a twenty-four-hour-a-day drug supermarket, pick up a 'legal' dosage of crack, and then stay out of trouble?" he asked. "I don't think so."

Others on the committee simply condemned Schmoke's proposal as a "surrender" in the war on drugs and urged yet more escalation instead. "We just sent a spaceship up into space today," said Congressman E. Clay Shaw, Jr., of Florida, "and we can from space . . . pinpoint where every cocaine leaf is on the face of this earth that is growing out in the sunshine. We can do it." And if countries like Colombia and Bolivia didn't cooperate with the U.S. government's efforts, Shaw said, "take them out, period."

Schmoke meant for his speech before the U.S. Conference of Mayors to start a dialogue among elected officials. He thought it was possible to, at the very least, debate the merits and drawbacks of decriminalization. But by the time of his testimony before Congress, it was abundantly clear that substantive debate was out of the question. Positions on drugs had hardened too much in Washington, especially as they related to crack.

In retrospect, the hearing felt to Schmoke like an ambush. His initial remarks, though controversial, had made some noise around the country, and a few key people were coming out in support, including conservative political commentator William F. Buckley, free-market economist Milton Friedman, astronomer Carl Sagan, federal judge Robert W. Sweet, and David Boaz, executive vice president of the Cato Institute. It seemed the committee did everything to bury such voices, stacking the hearing instead with speeches from each congressman on how unthinkable the idea of decriminalization was.

Merely suggesting there was another way to address the issue of drugs in urban America cost Schmoke much of the credibility and political capital he'd been building since he was fourteen years old. Within less than a year, he'd been transformed in the public imagination from a brilliant young politician with proven leadership on urban crime to a naïve idealist who was in over his head in Baltimore, "a brilliant spokesman for a bad idea," as New York mayor Ed Koch described him. Indeed, the rebuke was so immediate and intense that Schmoke began jokingly introducing himself when speaking publicly as "the young man people say used to have a political future."

SCHMOKE BECAME MAYOR OF BALTIMORE at perhaps the worst time to become mayor of a major city. Everyone, including Schmoke, hoped that he could work some magic and bring together the multiracial, cross-economic coalition that backed him to direct its powers toward the city. But while the new mayor was talented and charismatic, he was no magician.

Once in office, Schmoke proved himself to be quite ordinary— a run-of-the-mill administrator. He was soft-spoken and brainy and embraced official procedures. To that end, one of his first big stumbles as mayor was hiring five executive assistants to serve as point people for each of the five major agencies within city government. When the heads of those agencies eventually complained to the press that they couldn't get through to the mayor, the assistants were reassigned to other jobs in City Hall and their roles consolidated into a single chief of staff.

Feeling the limitations of his office in the early years of his administration, Schmoke called for regionalism, or greater cooperation among the city of Baltimore, its suburbs in greater Baltimore County, and the state of Maryland. On his watch, the state assumed financial responsibility for Baltimore City Community College. Schmoke suggested it also be responsible for the city jail, the circuit court, the state's attorney's office, and the sheriff's office.

Schmoke tried to make good on his campaign promises. He raised starting salaries for teachers and increased school funding by 47 percent, steps toward making Baltimore "the city that reads." He also replaced the police department's revolvers with 9mm semiautomatics and in 1990 alone filled thirty thousand potholes, a record in Baltimore. They were meager initiatives—just about all he could afford with the city's limited resources—but voters appreciated the gestures and reelected him in 1991 by a larger margin than he'd won with in 1987.

Schmoke was reelected during Baltimore's darkest days. According to the Maryland Alcohol and Drug Abuse Administration, the number of crack addicts admitted to drug treatment programs grew by 60 percent in 1990. This increase accompanied a spike in violent crime, including homicides. Baltimore experienced 234 homicides in 1988. That number rose steadily, to 262 in 1989 and 305 in 1990, stayed level at 304 in 1991, and rose again to 333 in 1992.

The rise in killings, most by gunfire, could be attributed to the drug trade. Authorities noted at the time a trend of "younger, tougher drug traffickers" coming into Baltimore from New York. "They are much more transient and independent," said Captain Michael Andrew, commander of Baltimore's drug enforcement unit, in an interview with The Washington Post. And instead of the .22- and .38-caliber revolvers dealers had used for decades, the new guys were equipped with 9mm automatic and semiautomatic handguns with up to eighteen bullets to a clip. The result was more turf wars and deadlier shootings.

Perhaps still feeling the sting of his failed proposal years earlier, Schmoke made a pivot toward law enforcement. He told reporters in January 1992 that "community-oriented policing will help combat crime," adding, however, that "no one should assume that there is a magic-wand solution to this complex problem."

The period marked a distinct shift in Schmoke's approach to the drug war. Where he'd insisted before that law enforcement had failed and decriminalization was the answer, he started to compromise and began advocating for treatment for drug users in addition to stiff penalties for dealers. At best, the shift was a response to Baltimore's devastation. A more cynical reading is that Schmoke capitulated to his critics and folded in the face of backlash.

Still, he never stopped his fight for a public-health response to addiction, even tweaking his message to emphasize "medicalization," a term he hoped would cut through the confusion regarding decriminalization versus legalization. Schmoke continued to attend conferences, forums, and other convenings to give talks on the topic. Instead of arguing, he'd ask questions: Do you think we are winning the war on drugs? Do you think more of the same will make a difference? And if not, are you willing to consider something else?

His persistence and new common-sense approach yielded modest gains. In Baltimore especially, the mayor's detractors got used to the mayor's ideas, and their heated outrage eased eventually into a cool skepticism. Whereas Schmoke had received hate mail regarding his position on drugs early on, in his second term the general tone became, "You're wrong, but let's see."

25

—

SHAWN

(1987)

SHAWN RETURNED TO KEYSTONE that fall, but he couldn't quite shake what he'd seen back home. He was plenty busy with basketball practice, his work-study job, and an eighteen-credit schedule. But he wondered if it all was a waste of time. The sad truth was that he'd seen drug dealing do more for guys than he'd ever seen basketball or college do. He worried he was missing out on something big, maybe the opportunity of a lifetime.

Shawn found out during a weekend back home that Terrance, his very first friend in Hayes Homes, and Mad Dog, his best friend, were selling drugs. Shawn's in finally came one day when he and Mad Dog were hanging out. Mad Dog asked him if there was anyone at his school who sold weed. He wasn't sure, he said, but there were people on campus who smoked it, especially the white boys.

The following Monday, they went together to Penn Station and boarded a bus to Scranton with $1,200 worth of weed in tow. Shawn didn't yet have a roommate that semester, so the plan was for Mad Dog to hustle out of his room and stay for as long as it took to sell out. It was an incredibly stupid idea, and if Shawn had thought twice about the possible consequences, he would have said no. He didn't think twice about it, though. He hadn't even struck up a deal with Mad Dog. All he'd considered was how much money his friend stood to make and all the fun they could have in the meantime.

Shawn was in a rush to show his friend the campus and introduce him to his school friends. Surprisingly, Mad Dog fit right in. He hit it off with Dexter and the rest of the team, even joining them for a few practices. Coach Mishko liked Mad Dog and was so impressed by his skills on the court that he tried to recruit him.

Mad Dog had other plans. While he was making friends, he was also finding customers. Shawn introduced him to one of the biggest potheads on campus, and it was on from there. The pothead told a friend who told a friend, and Mad Dog was the man on campus in a matter of days. He sold out in the span of a week, charging twice what he would have back home and making nearly $2,400 in the process.

Shawn hated to see his friend leave but was pleased that everything had gone to plan. Mad Dog thanked him with a brand new minifridge, groceries, and four hundred dollars. It was the worst thing that could have happened to Shawn. He tried his best to focus on school after that, but it was too late; he was instantly hooked on the fast, easy money.

He passed all his classes that fall, but he was finding it harder and harder to stay focused. Then he learned during winter break that Hayes Homes was being closed. Some combination of that news and a busy basketball schedule made things worse. His grades started to slip, and by the school year's end he was failing a class in statistics, one he needed to graduate. It was like St. Benedict's all over again.

He met with Coach Mishko, who made things plain: Shawn was three credits short of the requirement for his associate degree. He could make them up in summer school, but his scholarship wouldn't cover that, so he'd need to come up with a thousand dollars out of pocket. Shawn had already spent the money Mad Dog gave him on sneakers, silk shirts, and a pair of leather pants.

Shawn didn't have enough credits to graduate from Keystone or transfer to Loyola or UC Berkeley, schools that had reached out to Mishko about him the year before. St. Thomas Aquinas was interested, but Shawn was unimpressed by the Division III school. Even if he'd flunked away his shot at playing D-I ball, Shawn still thought he was too good to play D-III.

Mishko got back to him a few days later with one last option: Caldwell College in Caldwell, New Jersey. It was small like Keystone, Mishko explained, and it was looking to fill its roster. Shawn had never heard of it or of Caldwell, New Jersey, but he was interested. He got the phone number of the new coach, Rich Marshall, and gave him a call.

Caldwell was a Catholic women's college that had just gone coed in 1986, Marshall explained over the phone. He was creating the men's basketball program from the ground up, and he wanted to do it with a strong team that included experienced players. Marshall pointed out that Caldwell wasn't an NCAA Division I school. It was, however, D-I in the National Association of Intercollegiate Athletics and its schedule would allow Shawn to compete against players for six NCAA Division I schools. Best of all, Caldwell was only a twenty-minute drive from Newark.

Shawn had heard from coaches as far back as high school that he should never commit to a school before visiting in person, but the closeness to home sold him. He was so desperate to stay close to home that he accepted Marshall's offer then and there, over the phone.

He was back home and in the thick of things within weeks. The drug activity aside, Hayes Homes had changed. There was a time when residents took pride in maintaining their building. There were even competitions for the most beautiful lobby and courtyard. All that ended when the Housing Authority decided to close Hayes Homes. Almost overnight, the agency slowed down on collecting trash and making repairs, so Shawn returned to a building that was filthy and falling apart. Light fixtures hadn't been repaired, so the halls and stairways were dark at all times of the day, and there were bags of garbage piled up in the lobby.

It threw residents into a quiet crisis. They talked about it nonstop, the way small towns in other parts of the country might buzz about tornado season, the threat of drought, and other natural disasters. Reasons aside, it was something happening to their community, and all they had to hang their futures on were promises made in official notices. The most persistent residents got a few details when they could get through to some bureaucrat on the phone.

The decline of Hayes Homes was mirrored in the degradation of the community that made it up. Something had shifted from just the summer before, Shawn thought. More drug deals were happening on the street instead of in cars and behind closed doors. People were also smoking crack out in the open. They were selling their possessions for it—their kids' bikes and video games. Some of the neighborhood's finest ladies—friends, moms, sisters, daughters, crushes—were selling their bodies for a few measly rocks.

The frenzy around crack scared Shawn off selling hard drugs. There was too much competition among dealers, and crack seemed to change almost everyone that touched it into the worst version of themselves. But weed didn't scare Shawn. More people smoked it. The dealers were low-key and the smokers weren't desperate.

He asked around and found out that a guy who used to live in his building was selling weed in East Orange. They hadn't been super close, but Shawn reached out, and the guy was happy to do someone from his building a favor. The business was simple: he bought nickel bags from a Jamaican guy in Harlem and sold them as dimes in the neighborhood. Shawn got started with the little money he saved from a school refund check.

The business was good and safe. Shawn built up a clientele among his neighbors, mostly older folks who had known him growing up. Before long, he was taking trips to Harlem by himself—just two PATH trains across the Hudson River into Manhattan, then a subway ride up to Edgecombe and 145th Street, where he met the Jamaican.

To keep a low profile, Shawn always dressed like he was going to hoop, in basketball shorts and a backpack. Sometimes he carried a ball. Shawn made the trip twice a week and never had an incident, except one time.

They were right at the end of a transaction and about to leave the Jamaican's apartment. Shawn went to open the door that led to the hallway. That's when all hell broke loose. The Jamaican pulled a gun from his waistband and began screaming in patois. Two men came out of a room with guns drawn. "Who is this guy?" asked the Jamaican, with a gun to Shawn's head. Shawn was in shock and unable to speak.

Thankfully, Shawn's friend stayed calm. He yelled, "He didn't know! He didn't know!" The Jamaican stood there with a gun to Shawn's head. His eyes were wild as he searched Shawn's for any sign of malice. The fury fell away when he didn't find any, revealing a mix of anger and relief as he lowered his gun. "Get the fuck out" was all the Jamaican could muster.

On the way home, with Shawn's heart still beating out of his chest, he learned that you never open the door in a drug dealer's place of business. "Doing that make them think you're letting in stickup men, or the police," his friend said. Shawn never did it again, not with the connect in Harlem or anyone else.

Outside of almost getting Shawn killed, the weed business was reliable, and it allowed him to provide for himself that summer. But he was nowhere close to getting the kind of money his friends were from selling cocaine. So, despite the devastation he saw in the Central Ward and the legal danger he knew existed, Shawn started to consider the idea of selling crack, too. He was already selling an illegal substance and risking jail time, he reasoned. And so far, he'd survived dealings with some menacing dudes. If he wasn't selling it, somebody else would. Everyone else would. Shawn used these arguments to justify selling crack, and it slowly seemed more an inevitability than a choice.

Shawn didn't know much about street dealing, but he had seen enough to know that locking down the right territory was critical. Fights broke out over who had the right to sell where, and sometimes worse. Shawn wanted to avoid all of that. He wanted his business to be safe and uncomplicated. He decided to sell out of his own building, where there wasn't anyone hustling yet, and recruited a neighbor named Rich who was also interested in hustling out of Building 73. Instead of competing with him for the building, Shawn decided to team up.

The two pooled together fifty dollars and took it over to Hucka-buck, a guy in Building 61-65 who everyone knew sold cocaine. He sold Shawn and Rich about $50 worth of coke, just enough to get started. The two didn't have a scale, so they decided to split it eight ways and pack it into little envelopes made of aluminum foil. Selling them at $25 apiece, they stood to make $150 profit to split between the two of them.

Their first few shifts were at night because neither wanted to be seen selling drugs, not by the cops but by Miss Ann or Miss Dent, who saw it as their duty to sit in their windows and reprimand drug dealers. They'd known Shawn, Rich, and the rest their whole lives, and Shawn's biggest fear was Miss Ann or Miss Dent catching him and calling his mother.

The nights were quiet as Shawn and Rich built their clientele, usually users on their way to another block. In fact, those first few days were so slow that other dealers seeing them standing there without customers would try to give them tips. The most common recommendation was a better location. They held out, however, and things eventually picked up after a series of shootings in other buildings. Even drug addicts were leery of that kind of scene, and one by one they migrated over to Building 73.

Shawn and Rich graduated from fifty-dollar pieces to half an eight ball. Before long, they were re-upping three to four times a night. Terrance, a wholesaler by then, saw how well the two were doing and offered to replace Huckabuck as their plug. It was a no-brainer. He was from their building, after all, and he had fish scale—an almost pure grade of cocaine named for its flaky and iridescent appearance.

The operation became seamless with Terrance in place. Shawn and Rich bought from him, bagged up in Rich's bedroom, then sold right in front of their building. When they needed a re-up, they just yelled up to Terrance's window and he'd drop down more coke. The cycle repeated five to six times a night until about 6 A.M. That's when Rich and Shawn would finally clock out and head over to Boaz, a restaurant on Irvine Turner and West Kinney, to eat and count the wads of cash they'd collected.

Shawn had earned a few thousand dollars by the end of summer. It was a fortune to him, someone whose family barely got by on public assistance, and he was in a rush to spend it. It was too late to buy the Lee or Levi's jeans, Izod sweaters, and Lacoste polos he'd wanted as a teen. Instead, Shawn splurged on sneakers, designer clothes, and lots of gold—chains, rings, and caps for his teeth. These were the new symbols of success where he came from, ways of advertising one's style and status in the hood.

Another opportunity to make a statement came that summer when the Def Jam tour hit Madison Square Garden. All of Hayes Homes wanted to go, including the thirty or so guys who were hustling out of the buildings. Eric B. & Rakim, Public Enemy, KRS-One, and LL Cool J were all part of the lineup, making it easily the most talked about show of the year. Anybody who was anybody had to be there, and they had to be fresh to death.

To prepare, Shawn and Rich made a trip downtown to a shop on Washington Street run by a guy named Emmanuel. He was Newark's answer to Harlem's Dapper Dan and was even said to have worked for a while under the legendary clothier. Emmanuel made them each a custom velour sweatsuit with Gucci monogram trim. Shawn's was light gray with red trimming that went around the collar and down the sides of his jacket and his pants. Rich's was green on green. Monogrammed on the back of Shawn's jacket was his nickname, $SCOOTER$. Rich's read, $RICHIE RICH$.

But it wasn't enough just to look good. They also wanted to arrive in style. A couple of the guys in the neighborhood had the bright idea to rent stretch limousines—then the epitome of wealth, celebrity, and class. Shawn loved it and pitched in about a hundred dollars to take part in the spectacle. On the day of the show, five limos came rolling down Seventeenth Avenue. The entire neighborhood looked on in amazement as Shawn and the others stepped out of the projects in custom outfits, dripping in gold, and boarded the luxury vehicles. Someone had the idea that they should ride around the projects a little before taking off, so the caravan cruised for a while, with guys hanging out the windows and sunroof.

The caravan circled around the projects once before taking off. They went down Boyd Street, then down West Kinney, crossing both Springfield and Morris. Kids ran alongside the cars the whole time, hoping to get a look at who was inside. Neighbors who weren't as fortunate waved from the street and cheered the caravan as it made its way through the Central Ward. They were cruising toward New Community and loving every second of it when the cars came to an abrupt stop near the Clinton Milk Company. It was unclear what was going on from Shawn's vantage point in the back of the caravan. The situation came into focus, however, when a door to his limo opened and the men outside identified themselves as police officers. They were looking for Lil' Nick, Murph, and Muhammad, some youngins from Building 61-65.

Not one of them was in the caravan, so after a few minutes of searching and questioning, the police let everyone go on their way. They breathed a sigh of relief in Shawn's limo and laughed about how the cops were looking for three kids when they had major hustlers right there in front of them. Shawn laughed along, but he was also shaken. The stop was a sign, he thought. If the police weren't on to them before, they certainly would be going forward.

Nevertheless, Shawn was on a cloud after the concert. The moment he and his friends created, more than the concert itself, put a battery in his back. He felt like he and his friends had arrived. They were no longer project kids but something more: winners. Shawn committed himself to hustling even harder to maintain his new status. He embraced the drug trade as his industry, complete with competitors, peers, gossip about bad moves and innovations. He considered himself a professional.

It was a good feeling until one night, while he was working late, Shawn saw a figure moving toward him through the projects. As the person got closer, he realized it was his father. Bootsie stopped at a distance. Shawn, not knowing what to do, didn't do or say anything. He just stared at the man. "I just finished talking to your mother, and she told me you're out here selling drugs," Bootsie said, as though they'd last talked at the dinner table.

Shawn tried to look cool as he processed both his father's presence and the news that his mother knew he was selling drugs. Shawn was too proud to lose his composure, though—not in front of Bootsie, at least. He just continued to stare into his father's face.

"How much money you making?" Bootsie asked. "I'm doing all right," Shawn replied. He braced himself for a lecture about how he was throwing his life away and jeopardizing what could be a promising basketball career. Instead, Bootsie simply said, "Be careful out here," and walked away. Shawn hadn't realized he had any respect for his father until that moment, when the last shreds left his body.

He left the block soon after and returned home, where his mother was up and waiting on him. She asked, "Did you see your father?" Shawn replied simply that he had and retired to his bedroom.

26

—

ELGIN

(1987-89)

ELGIN WAS COMPLETELY IN LOVE with hip hop by the time he was twelve. It was almost as if rappers stepped in to raise him. Thankful, he hung on their every word for life lessons and advice on how to make it in an increasingly complicated world.

In someone like KRS-One, Elgin finally had a role model who talked like him, a superstar fluent in the language of the streets who told stories that applied to life in the city. From *Criminal Minded*, KRS-One's first album, Elgin learned the importance of being "real" instead of a "sucker MC."

Public Enemy's *It Takes a Nation of Millions to Hold Us Back* affirmed his identity as a rebel. Elgin, of course, wasn't a part of the "us" Chuck D rapped about. Still, he identified with the rapper's critique of the system that created the ghetto where he lived. He imagined himself as the one escaping from the state pen in Chuck D's rhyme on "Black Steel in the Hour of Chaos."

Chuck D and KRS-One made Elgin want to build and sharpen his knowledge. He sought out books like *Message to the Blackman in Amer-*

ica and *How to Eat to Live* by Elijah Muhammad. He read them from cover to cover because his favorite rappers rhymed about them.

But while Elgin had KRS-One and Chuck D in his ear, he also had other, more immediate influences. He lived down the way from a group home called Leake and Watts Services, which was home to a lot of kids from Brooklyn. Although they were older and troubled, Elgin started hanging with the kids from Leake and Watts and learning their hustles.

They taught him how to not get caught hopping turnstiles at the train station, how to pick pockets in a crowd. He got a crash course in classic New York hustles like three-card monte and selling fake gold chains to tourists. One guy, a Puerto Rican kid named Ramon who went by the alias Kid Nice, taught Elgin how to steal car radios and rims and where to sell them.

Elgin approached each new deed with enthusiasm, not because he wanted to steal or needed the money but because he got to spend time with the older boys. Inevitably, they'd be impressed with his skill and fearlessness, and that only emboldened him to go further the next time. It didn't take long for him to get arrested.

Getting busted by the cops scared Elgin at first, but he learned quickly that there wasn't much they could do to him as a minor, at least not back then. He'd just be charged and eventually sent home with a stern warning to stay out of trouble. Once, Elgin was arrested twice in one day. The officers at the precinct said, "We can't wait until you're sixteen," each time he was released. "Once you turn sixteen, it's over for you."

All those run-ins acquainted him with the fine men of the Yonkers Police Department. There was one officer named John Hayes, another who everyone called Blondie. One cop called Stewart drove a blue Caprice and would pretend to be a taxi driver looking for drugs. It was a little ridiculous, Elgin thought, because everyone in the neighborhood knew he was a cop. But he supposed that was Stewart's thing—pretending to be a cabbie—just like breaking into cars was his.

The cops in Elgin's neighborhood weren't yet focused on stop-

and-frisk. Instead, they used their discretion to sort kids behaving badly from the bad kids. That fell by the wayside over time, however, as crack swept through Yonkers and police cast a dragnet over the city. Before 1987, Elgin had only ever heard of crack on songs like Boogie Down Productions' "Remix for P Is Free" and "Monster Crack" by Kool Moe Dee. Then some of the guys from Leake and Watts started talking about smoking woolas—joints laced with crack. That trend lasted only a short while and ended promptly once the boys got their first look at crackheads, people who were seriously addicted to the drug.

These had been people who might have given Elgin fifty cents to run to the corner store. Then, suddenly, they were looking bad—thin, tired, and unkempt. A lot of his neighbors ended up like that. There was one guy who scared Elgin. He had been cool, would hang out on the block and tell the kids how they "didn't know shit." Sometimes, he dropped a few jewels on them. But after crack he was like a zombie, a walking corpse focused on one thing: getting high.

Guys from the neighborhood took to abusing the crackheads who'd once been their neighbors. Elgin heard stories of women and girls he knew from the neighborhood selling their bodies for crack. Rumor had it a friend's mother had sex with a pit bull in exchange for crack. Elgin didn't know whether it was the truth or a sick joke, but it made him deathly afraid of the drug, and he knew then that he'd never try it.

During this scourge, things got better at home when Elgin's dad met and started dating a woman named Naomi. She was short, with short hair, and kind of looked like Madonna, Elgin thought, and she was nice. He liked her, especially after she bought him a pair of Air Jordan IVs, the black-and-white colorway with cement-gray details. Plus, his dad seemed to want a life with Naomi, which kept him home more. The two of them would hang out at the house, and after Naomi left, Stephen would talk about the plans they were making to start businesses and move together into a better neighborhood.

The two of them carried on like that for a couple of years, and things were all good. Then one day Elgin was sitting on the toilet and flipping through a magazine when he came across an ad featuring Mike Tyson. Elgin was struck by the image—Tyson looking formidable, with the words "Iron Mike Tyson" in large metallic letters. He was admiring the ad when he noticed a trace of white powder on it.

He didn't say anything at the time, but he'd seen enough after-school specials to suspect it was cocaine. Naomi was using coke, he figured, and probably his dad, too. He tried to put the thought out of his head. It wasn't so bad, he thought. But every time he was alone in the bathroom, he felt compelled to open the magazine to the ad, almost to see if it was still true. The subtle hint of powder faded but never completely went away.

It must've affected Elgin more than he knew, because he was arguing with his dad one day about something he'd done and his dad said, "You know, I'm only doing this because I care about you." Without thinking, Elgin fired back, "You don't care about me. All you care about is getting high." Stephen acted confused. He said, "You don't know what you're talking about," but the look of shock and shame on his face told another story.

After a while, Stephen and Naomi started arguing. Things would get so tense that she didn't come by the apartment for days at a time. Then a week went by without Elgin seeing her, then weeks, until she was gone altogether.

Sometime soon after, Elgin was hanging out with Alex, a kid who lived on the first floor of his building. Alex was older, tall and light-skinned, with a nose ring and Caesar haircut. Alex mostly kept him around to help break into cars and so he had someone to pick on. They were standing in the hallway that led into their building and talking shit when out of nowhere Alex said, "You know your dad smoke crack, right?"

Elgin turned bright red. He figured Alex was picking at him again, so he tried to stand up for himself. He said, "No, my dad don't do crack. My dad does coke." Alex shook his head. He said, "I been in your apartment with your dad and your dad smoke crack." Then he explained in detail where Stephen kept his pipe—in a small wooden box on his dresser. Elgin tried to dismiss it with "Yeah, whatever," but as soon as the two were done talking, he hurried home to check. Sure enough, on his dad's dresser was a wooden box, and inside of it was a charred glass pipe.

All he could think at that moment was, "Damn, my dad is a crack-head." He was angry with his father for smoking crack, angry with Alex for telling him, and angry with himself for looking.

That moment marked a decline in Elgin's relationship with his dad. Stephen had never been Cliff Huxtable, but his son still respected him. That was impossible to do once he knew his dad smoked crack. It changed the way Elgin thought about him, for sure, but crack also changed Stephen. He stopped getting his hair cut and otherwise keeping himself up. The little time he was home, he was holed up in his bedroom with the door closed. He'd come out sweaty and wild-eyed, then leave suddenly on another mission.

His dad's sudden descent into addiction hurt Elgin more than he could explain. He felt betrayed, abandoned by the only family he had. Things only seemed to get worse from then on. Stephen began steal-ing Elgin's stuff. It began with a Nintendo system he'd given him. Stephen said he had a friend whose son was in the hospital dying of an incurable disease and needed something to do to pass the time. Elgin knew it was a lie, but he couldn't say no. Of course, he never saw the Nintendo again.

Then other things started disappearing from the house, and after a while his dad stopped buying groceries. Finding something, any-thing, to eat became Elgin's daily struggle. He foraged through the kitchen for something edible—bread, peanut butter, raw tomatoes with salt. He'd buy a slice of pizza or a wedge for dinner if he came across a couple of dollars. Square meals were so few and far between that Elgin went from slim to scrawny over the course of a year.

He knew it wasn't right or even okay, what his dad was doing, but he had no one to turn to. That's when Elgin, who hadn't been to church since communion, turned to God. Every night, he'd get on his knees at the foot of his bed and ask for a way out. He'd say, "I don't want to live like this. I want to live a normal life, like what I see on TV." He didn't have a lot of hope, but he figured maybe if he asked, God would hear him and guide him through whatever was to come.

27
—
WAR
(1986-88)

AS CRIME RATES CONTINUED to rise in the 1980s, the public's interest in the topic heightened and the issue became an animating force in American politics. Voters began once again evaluating candidates for public office based largely on how tough they were willing to be on crime. In return, Republicans and Democrats alike intensified their rhetoric, often overstating and oversimplifying the threat of crime in America. They took more hard-line positions, advocating with increased fervor for harsher and harsher penalties for even the most minor of offenses.

This new attitude congealed into the "broken windows" theory of policing, which held that any visible disorder in a neighborhood, symbolized by actual broken windows, contributed to the perception that the neighborhood was open for crime. As a result, more crimes were committed—including serious violent offenses. Criminologist George L. Kelling and sociologist James Q. Wilson, who came up with the theory, hypothesized that arrests for minor offenses like vandalism, jaywalking, and public intoxication could bring down rates of other crimes, like murder. In collaboration with mayors and other elected officials, police departments in many cities took up broken windows and other zero-tolerance policies.

The theory had plenty of critics from its inception, but mayors and police chiefs embraced the theory to justify their inclinations toward more draconian anti-crime measures.

Rates of crime, including violent crimes—murder, robbery, rape—had been going up since 1960. In 1960, for example, 161 violent crimes were committed for every hundred thousand Americans. That number more than tripled to 364 by 1970. By 1980, it had ballooned to 597 violent crimes for every hundred thousand Americans, and the rate continued to grow throughout the decade. Facing those numbers, authorities decided to cast a dragnet over American cities.

In America, drugs had long been associated with immorality and a criminal lifestyle—especially when used by Blacks and Latinos. In the eighties, the use or sale of illegal drugs started to stand in for all crimes. Drugs were murder. They were robbery, rape, assault, and theft. Consequently, drug users and dealers became murderers, robbers, rapists, thieves in the American imagination. It was Nixon's war on drugs in a new form, with renewed strength and purpose.

When Len Bias died of a cocaine overdose in 1986, he brought decades of frustrations with crime, new concerns about crack, and the nation's eagerness to get tough to a head. Lawmakers, many of whom had followed Bias's basketball career as he grew up in the D.C.-Maryland area, homed in on the tragedy as an event that could rally the nation's collective will.

According to reports, the Democratic speaker of the House, Thomas "Tip" O'Neill, held a meeting with the chairmen of eleven House committees a month after Bias's death to call for a bipartisan effort to develop a comprehensive drug law that could be brought to the floor by September, a month before the 1986 midterm elections. *The New York Times* reported that House Democratic leader Jim Wright, the legislator designated to lead the effort, wanted to act before Republicans could claim the issue as their own. Wright said his most pressing concern was that Congress "act before television lost interest in the drug story."

Congress had the wind at its back. A *New York Times*/CBS News poll from September 1986 found that 13 percent of Americans believed drugs were the nation's most important problem. Only two percent had given that response in April of that year, before Bias's death. A whopping 50 percent of those polled also stated that increased drug use reflected a "fundamental breakdown" in morals, and two-thirds said they were willing to pay more taxes to jail drug dealers. Another poll by Gallup asked Americans which drug they believed posed the most serious threat. At 42 percent, "crack" and "other forms of cocaine" was the most common response.

"Right now, you could put an amendment through to hang, draw and quarter," said Claude Pepper, a Florida Democratic congressman, in an interview with *The New York Times*. "That's what happens when you get on an emotional issue like this." Leon Panetta, then a California Democratic congressman, explained, "It's so easy from a political point of view. There is no downside on drugs."

Meanwhile, the Reagan White House noticed the flurry of activity from Democrats. "The Democratic Party had finally found its legs and was prepared to take some measures—we couldn't let them take the issue," Mitch Daniels, a former political director of the Reagan White House, would later say.

To get a piece of the action, the Reagans took to the airwaves on September 14, 1986, for a special address on drugs. Masters of the TV medium, the president and first lady gave the address from the Executive Residence instead of the more formal West Wing. Sitting side by side on a small sofa, they spoke to the audience "not simply as fellow citizens, but as fellow parents and grandparents and as concerned neighbors."

"Despite our best efforts, illegal cocaine is coming into our country at alarming levels and four to five million people regularly use it," President Reagan announced. "Today there's a new epidemic: smokable cocaine, otherwise known as crack. It is an explosively destructive and often lethal substance which is crushing its users. It is an uncontrolled fire."

The first lady amplified the alarm with the story of Paul, an infant exposed to cocaine in the womb, who suffered two strokes after birth and spent his first month of life in an incubator. "Our job is never easy, because drug criminals are ingenious. They work every day to plot a new and better way to steal our children's lives, just as they've done by developing this new drug, crack," she warned. "For every door that we close, they open a new door to death. They prosper on our unwillingness to act. So we must be smarter and stronger and tougher than they are."

President Reagan previewed some of what his administration had in mind. He promised a drug-free America, and proposed a $3 billion commitment to the effort, including treatment. He also enlisted every American to do their part. "There's no moral middle ground. Indifference is not an option," he warned. "We want you to help us create an outspoken intolerance for drug use. For the sake of our children, I implore each of you to be unyielding and inflexible in your opposition to drugs."

Later in September, the effort got another boost when both NBC News and CBS News aired specials on cocaine. For its program, "48 Hours on Crack Street," CBS dispatched eighteen camera crews, twenty-five producers, and ten correspondents across New York City over the course of one weekend. Nearly fifteen million American households tuned in. The hit spawned a follow-up special and a new franchise for the network, *48 Hours*.

As the ninety-ninth Congress drew to a close, some members worried that they were rushing the new crime bill. Despite their concerns, most voted for it anyway, and all told the bill passed in the House 378 to 16 on October 17, 1986.

Democratic congressman Mike Lowry of Washington was one of the few who voted against it, calling the bill "legislation by political panic." Chuck Schumer, then a Democratic congressman, voted for the bill but later expressed his dismay with it and the process by which it was created. "Maybe we had the wrong solutions but not the wrong problem," he noted. "What happens is that this occurs in one seismic jump instead of a rational buildup. The down side is that you come up with policies too quickly and that the policies are aimed at looking good rather than solving the problem."

Ten days later, on October 27, President Reagan signed the Anti-Drug Abuse Act of 1986 into law. The sweeping legislation added $1.7 billion in federal funds to the $2.2 billion already spent each year on law enforcement, drug treatment, and education programs. Just as the Comprehensive Crime Control Act of 1984 had, the Anti-Drug Abuse Act increased the number of drug offenses with mandatory minimum sentences.

It established a mandatory minimum sentence of five years without parole for possession of five grams of crack cocaine—the same minimum sentence mandated for possession of five hundred grams of the exact same drug in powder form.

It was a seismic shift in drug policy. These laws treated crack users and dealers as a different class of criminal, punishing them with sentences that would soon swell America's jails and prisons.

Assembled with Reagan in the East Room of the White House for the signing ceremony were congressional leaders in both parties, schoolchildren, professional athletes, the first lady, and others. "The American people want their government to get tough and go on the offensive, and that's exactly what we intend, with more ferocity than ever before," he said before putting pen to paper.

For good measure, Reagan signed a proclamation on October 31 retroactively designating October 1986 Crack/Cocaine Awareness Month. When asked about the delay, a spokesman for the Federal Register said, "The president didn't get around to signing it until then because of the campaign," meaning that year's midterm elections.

The Anti-Drug Abuse Act of 1986 drew criticism no sooner than it was signed. Analysts kicking the tires found it didn't exactly live up to its promises regarding drug education and treatment, or the president's vow that the law wasn't intended to fill prisons and jails with drug users. Just 12 percent of the $1.7 billion provided by the law was allocated to drug education programs. In fact, most of the funds were set aside for criminal justice efforts—$1.1 billion for local, state, and federal law enforcement agencies and $96.5 million for new federal prisons, for example.

Behind the scenes, the Reagan administration was unsure of how to dole out the money. After the bill had been signed, all the pens had been handed out, and the midterms were over, the logistics of the Anti-Drug Abuse Act were left to bean counters in the Office of Management and Budget. "It was an administration without adult supervision," Deborah Steelman, a former associate director of the OMB, told *The New York Times*. "Overall, the details were left to implement themselves."

Meanwhile, cocaine was at its most accessible as prices fell to historic lows. Dealers broke their "dime" and "twenty" vials down into "nickels," which contained up to one-quarter of a gram of crack and sold for five dollars. Some dealers sold two nickels for nine dollars. Others broke nickels down into even smaller rocks that sold for as little as fifty cents.

By this point in the epidemic, casual users were few and far between, leaving the addicts in a desperate scene that often turned violent. The open-air markets of the streets were more volatile than the freebase parlors and crack houses that preceded them. The new environment filtered out the gentlemen dealers of the sixties and seventies and replaced them with dealers who were willing to use force to claim and maintain turf. Drug dealing quickly became a vocation for hardened criminals and adolescents too naïve to understand the risks of what they were getting into, or desperate to make money despite the danger.

They were freelancers who dipped in and out of dealing whenever they needed a quick influx of cash. These dealers would set up shop on an empty block and sell out as soon as they could, sometimes never to return. Such an atmosphere naturally bred competition and violence. Dealers fought other dealers over turf. They fought with users and were often robbed by stickup kids.

As police officers noted the shift to open-air markets, they intensified their patrols of high-traffic areas. This led sometimes to violent confrontations between cops and dealers, and often to the harassment of innocent residents. Even arrests of dealers, something one might assume to be a net win, had the effect of increasing turnover on the street, which led to more volatility in the market and ultimately more violence.

One interesting exception to the lawless street dealing of the period was what scholars have dubbed "crack seller co-ops," a designation given mostly to crack markets based in public housing projects. Ironically, the common design of housing projects made for ideal drug markets. They were isolated communities, usually with only a few exits and entrances. Resident dealers, many with lifelong relationships, would also coordinate their efforts to monopolize sales. They also had a better lay of the land than police, and residents warned one another about police presence before officers could step foot in a complex.

Despite the growing frenzy around crack, these markets became fixtures in America's ghettos. They blighted the landscape in many communities, and community members—the vast majority of whom had no connection to crack—were left to navigate them and the violence they generated.

On December 9, 1987, officials with the National Drug Policy Board testified before the House Select Committee on Narcotics Abuse and Control and admitted that the federal government had made little progress in the year since the Anti-Drug Abuse Act was passed. They acknowledged that demand for drugs was still high among the estimated twenty-three million Americans thought to be routine users, and that the nation's borders remained "largely a sieve."

"Anytime you have one out of ten Americans using or abusing drugs, you have a problem that won't be solved overnight," said Frank Keating, one of the board members.

The one area where the government had made headway was incarceration. Federal prisons with a capacity of 28,000 already held 33,135 prisoners in 1986. By 1987, their population had grown to 48,300. The population of state prisons was 470,659 in 1986. It grew to 533,309 by 1987. That year, the Justice Department estimated that at least half the individuals entering America's prisons would be drug offenders by the end of the decade. It was the acceleration of a maddening dynamic, one wherein Black communities were overpoliced and overincarcerated but still underprotected.

The dynamic was compounded the following year when Congress passed the Anti-Drug Abuse Act of 1988. The follow-up bill upped the ante of the 1986 law by imposing a sentence of life without parole for offenders with two or more prior convictions. It also allowed the death penalty for murders committed in the course of drug-related crimes. Lastly, it denied a number of federal benefits to individuals convicted of drug crimes, including public housing, student loans and grants, and other federal loans and licenses. The law also mandated a minimum sentence of one year for simple possession of crack, making it the only illegal substance for which a first possession offense triggered a mandatory minimum penalty.

The second Anti-Drug Abuse Act also established the Office of National Drug Control Policy, with a national director of drug policy, known colloquially as the "drug czar." The post elevated the Drug Abuse Policy Office, created by Reagan in 1982, from a department within the White House's Office of Policy Development to an executive-level office in its own right, on par with the National Security Council.

In the last year of his presidency, Ronald Reagan declared his efforts in the war on drugs "an untold American success story." The use of illegal drugs had, he said, "already gone out of style in the United States." It was an assessment completely divorced from reality. Most experts agreed, to the contrary, that Reagan's anti-drug campaigns had failed. "We're not winning the war on cocaine," Coast Guard admiral Paul Yost admitted to *The Washington Post* in February 1988. Indeed, according to the National Narcotics Intelligence Consumers Committee report, inventories were high, wholesale prices were the lowest ever recorded, cocaine sold on the street had never been purer, and the substance was readily available throughout all areas of the United States.

But while Reagan had failed to create a drug-free America, he'd succeeded wildly in drug politics. He did so by conflating the nation's legitimate fear of rising crime with its anxieties about increased drug use. The undercurrent to both, of course, seemed to be lingering hostility toward people and communities of color. At least that's what was borne out in the anti-drug messaging of the period—drug users were damned, especially crack addicts, and dealers were heartless monsters. The Reagan administration, with the help of a Democratic Congress, declared war on dealers and users alike. It handled them like enemy combatants, not American citizens swept up in an epidemic. Taxpayers happily footed the bill for this war on drugs and rewarded its architects with reelection.

An extra price was paid by Americans living in neighborhoods hit hard by the crack epidemic, mostly Black and Latino Americans. They suffered not just the ravages of the crack epidemic but the damage inflicted by the government's war on drugs. They had to navigate both drug-related violence and police harassment. They saw loved ones lose their lives to both addiction and incarceration. All that remained after their communities were ransacked by the epidemic and the war was grief, trauma, and shame.

VI

–

PEAK

28

—

SHAWN

(1988)

SHAWN COULDN'T CARE LESS about Caldwell by the start of the school year. First, he learned that not all his credits from Keystone would transfer to Caldwell, so he entered the college as a sophomore instead of a junior. Then he discovered in practice that he didn't like his teammates. They were nice guys, sure, but Shawn didn't think they could play worth a damn. Those with some skills were weak, undisciplined, and ball hogs.

Shawn's disappointment sent him headfirst back into selling drugs, something only made easier by Caldwell's closeness to Newark. It was nothing that first semester for Shawn to simply catch a bus from Caldwell back to Hayes Homes just to hit the block. Once he got bored with hustling or made enough money for the things he wanted, he was back on the bus to campus. It became such a routine that Shawn memorized the schedules for buses that ran between Caldwell and Newark.

Sometime that fall, Joanne received a letter from the Housing Authority telling her it was time to finally move. After seventeen years in Hayes Homes, the family had been assigned housing in the new townhouses on Chadwick Avenue, right behind the Bergen Street School. Their new place was a four-bedroom apartment with three floors, two bathrooms, and a washer and dryer hookup.

Joanne, Tony, and Cheyta loved the new apartment, but it took Shawn some getting used to. The streets on the block were cobblestone—some of the last in the city. To Shawn, they were odd. Years of apartment-dwelling also made him uncomfortable living so close to the street. It didn't seem right that he could just walk out of their front door and have only a sidewalk, no courtyard, between him and the rest of the world. It seemed the only thing Shawn did like was the shower in the new place. Nobody in the projects had one, just bathtubs, and Shawn had grown to love the feel of hot showers based on all the time he'd spent in locker rooms over the years.

The draw of the projects was strong, however, and Shawn constantly found himself back in front of Building 73, hustling into the early hours of the morning. He would buy half an ounce of cocaine, bag it up at home on Chadwick, then hop in a cab to what was left of Hayes Homes. He didn't think things could get any worse over there, but they did once the last families moved out of the projects. With almost all the residents gone, the complex was only used for selling drugs.

It was around this time that turf wars started to kick off around Hayes Homes. An old-school hustler named Akbar Pray was pushing out the young guys getting money in the Central Ward. He had a young enforcer working for him who went around the project forcing dealers to either buy their product from Pray at a markup or move off the block.

One night, Shawn was standing in front of Building 73 with Phil Martin, a neighbor who hustled out of the building sometimes while Shawn was away. A black two-door Benz pulled into the parking lot along Seventeenth Avenue. Out came a guy with a Jheri curl and black leather gloves.

"Who is this dude?" Shawn asked.

Phil said it was Pray's enforcer. He ran most of the guys who sold for Terrance away from Hayes Homes, Phil explained, and even shot at him once.

The tough guy walked over to Building 77 and just stood there staring in Shawn and Phil's direction. They'd served a couple of customers before one who was on his way to another dealer saw Shawn and made a beeline. It was one of Shawn's old customers, but the enforcer flipped out. He was yelling, "I told y'all niggas about short-stoppin'." Then he shouted, "Min-Mu, bring down my nine."

Too naïve to know what was happening, Shawn continued to serve the buyer as the enforcer stormed over with a 9mm handgun. He pointed it at Shawn's left knee and demanded to know whose cocaine he was selling. By then, both Phil and the customer had scurried off, but Shawn wasn't shaken. He'd been around enough real gangsters to know the gun was for show and this guy was a clown who didn't really want to use it. "Who did you buy the shit from?" he asked again.

Shawn was quick on his toes and instead of telling the truth, that he'd bought the cocaine from Terrance, he said, "Mad Dog."

Apparently, his old friend had some pull, because the guy put his gun away and walked back to his car. Before driving off, he made a point of saying, "Don't let it happen again."

That confrontation marked the beginning of the end of Shawn's dealing in Hayes Homes. He hustled out in front of Building 73 a few more times, but things were never the same again.

It was the end of one era but the beginning of another. With Hayes Homes done, Shawn had to find new turf. That wasn't as easy as just planting a flag on a city block, though. He needed a convenient spot, one where he'd have friends to watch his back. He could think of no better place than his new block on Chadwick Avenue. Hayes Homes may have been taken apart piece by piece, but enough of the pieces—friends and families from Hayes Homes, Scudder Homes, and the Dayton Street projects—had been displaced to Shawn's new street.

Shawn linked back up with Rich and Terrance, who were by that time living in apartments near Seventeenth Street and Avon Avenue. Together, they took stock of the activity in the neighborhood. They noted that the nearest dealers, some guys just a few blocks away on Clinton Avenue, were selling heroin and dimes of cocaine in small vials. Shawn and his friends weren't interested in heroin. They figured they could compete when it came to cocaine, so they set up shop.

They originally wanted to do as they had in Hayes Homes and package their product in tiny aluminum envelopes, but that wouldn't play on Chadwick. The transactions were out in the open, which didn't allow time to open the envelopes and show customers the product. They adapted and moved to vials, too, but went up a size from what the boys on Clinton Avenue had. Packing the tiny glass tubes left Shawn's thumbs sore, but the hard work eventually paid off.

Business picked up once word got out about the bigger vials of quality product. In no time, Shawn was back to making the kind of money he made in the projects. To shore up the business, his crew established a few rules. There was no serving pregnant women or serving in front of kids. High-school-age dealers weren't allowed to work during school hours. Running up to cars was also forbidden.

Another major rule was that if anyone on the block had beef, they had to notify the rest of the block. Last but certainly not least, they had to tell each other where their stashes were hidden at all times. It was a way of looking after each other's product. It was also a precaution against the police who, if they did a raid, would pin a stash to the closest man.

He should have been doubling down his energies in school and on basketball, but Shawn's focus was on making money and hanging out on Chadwick. For what it was worth, he liked his classes at Caldwell more than he had the ones at Keystone. He was settling into his major, sociology, and even picked up a minor in criminal justice by then. The coursework was interesting but, to Shawn, school was a diversion from his real life.

That didn't stop him from making a few friends on campus. He even had a campus girlfriend, a petite, light-skinned girl from the suburbs named Perla. Shawn had written off most of his teammates, however, and Coach Marshall. They weren't worth his time, he figured. In the end, the Caldwell Cougars finished their season 14–19. It should have been a major disappointment to Shawn, but he barely cared. Summer was approaching.

SHAWN EMBRACED THE SUMMER MONTHS. He could dive all the way into hustling and wouldn't miss a thing because he had a game, a test, or had to be in class. He finally bought a car that summer, a red Dodge Omni that he paid for with cash. He tricked it out with fifteen-inch speakers, an amplifier, tweeters, and a brand-new radio from the electronics store down on Market Street. The car helped him better run the streets with Terrance, who had an all-white four-door Benz that he called the Ghost.

The two would ride out to Harlem some nights and cruise down Eighth Avenue. Harlem was like another world, Shawn thought. The women were beautiful, and everyone seemed to be getting money. He and Terrance would usually end up at a club called the Rooftop, where they parked outside and waited for it to let out. The women who trickled out were usually down to hang and grab something quick to eat with "the guys from Jersey."

Around this time, the cocaine business was moving from dimes to nickels, which exploded the market. Shawn and his crew responded by breaking down their product into smaller vials and selling them two for five dollars. After that, money poured in from all directions.

Shawn was pushing up to a kilo each day. He'd end up with stacks of bills in each pocket, and sometimes there were so many customers that he'd have to send them to somebody else in the crew—Terrance, Phil, Lamar, or Frank. Shawn took home about $1,000 at the end of each day, sometimes with product to spare. To hide the money and the drugs, he paid a neighborhood handyman to come by one day when his mother was away and install a fake pipe that ran from the washing machine to the wall. The only other people who knew about it were Terrance and Tony.

All the money flowing on Chadwick attracted dealers who wanted in, women interested in dating guys with money, and the police. One day, Shawn and some friends were sitting on the block when a group of five or six men came walking up. They stopped where Shawn was and introduced themselves as officers with the Essex County Sheriff's Bureau of Narcotics.

One of the cops, an older Black man, asked them their names. Shawn cooperated, figuring they would have already arrested him if that's why they were there. He told them his name, and so did his friends. That's when the man in charge told them that he was responding to a complaint that drugs were being sold on the block. He asked if anyone knew anything about it. Shawn and the rest shrugged and looked around like it was the most ridiculous thing they'd ever heard.

The officers seemed satisfied and started to walk away. Then the older Black officer stopped and, to everyone's surprise, asked, "Where's Terrance?" Shawn tried his best not to let on how shaken he was. He replied, "Terrance doesn't live over here." The officer gave a knowing look before turning again to walk away.

Shawn didn't know what was going on, but he was more cautious after that. He used his stash spot more often instead of keeping drugs on him or in his car. He and the crew also came up with a nickname for the police, "Mistic," after a fruit juice that was popular at the time. Whenever a cop car was in the area, marked or unmarked, everyone would holler out, "Mistic," and the whole block would tighten up.

It made Shawn miss the good old days at Hayes Homes when they didn't have to worry about the cops. If police so much as approached the projects, everyone ran into their buildings, and put sticks in the doors to keep them from coming in. Inside, you could take off up the stairs and lose them after about three to four flights.

All the precautions seemed to work for a while. Business went on as usual until sometime around Martin Luther King Day. Shawn had practice earlier that day but decided to rush home to make some quick money on the block. After selling the little product he had, he called Terrance for a re-up. It was Big Monday, and Shawn watched the game between Georgetown and Duke while he waited what seemed longer than usual. Finally, the doorbell rang. It was Frank with the package. Shawn paid him $1,400 and Frank left. Easy.

The plan had been to bottle it up right away, hit the block, and sell out in time to get back to campus. But Shawn couldn't take his eyes off the game. He waited for a time-out to run upstairs and stash it in his bedroom, in his top dresser drawer. He was back in front of the television thirty minutes later when he heard a loud knock on the door, then a voice, "Police! Police!"

Shawn froze for a moment but jumped into action when they started to knock louder. "Police! Police!" He ran up the stairs to retrieve the coke. Once he had it, he made a dash to the bathroom, where he ripped through the bags and poured it into the toilet. The officers kicked down the door and were on their way up the stairs, but it was too late; Shawn had already flushed it.

Shawn walked calmly out of the bathroom with his hands in the air. The first cop up the stairs put his gun in Shawn's face and started screaming, "Get on the ground! Get on the ground!" Another yelled, "He flushed it!" The next thing Shawn knew, he was on the ground, having taken a punch to the face.

They started asking questions once he was back on his feet. By that time, Joanne, who'd been in her bedroom, made her way out to investigate the commotion. She and Shawn were herded down to the living room while the officers continued to search the house. Shawn knew they wouldn't find anything but about $3,500 that he kept in a cheap safe in his bedroom. That, he figured, could be explained away easily as money he'd saved from a school refund check. There was another $9,000 stashed in the laundry room, but they'd never find that, he thought. And they didn't. One officer did, however, find a single vial half-filled with cocaine in Shawn's bedroom. He thought for a moment that the vial had been planted but remembered how the last time he bagged up, he'd skipped vacuuming his carpet, which he usually did.

The officers emptied Shawn's pockets and gave the contents, some money and a pager, to Joanne. She stood there shaking her head in disbelief as Shawn was led out of the house and into a police car.

Shawn was arrested for possession and held at Essex County Jail. He'd heard stories about the county jail and was nervous but not especially afraid. Shawn wasn't afraid of being around people others considered dangerous. He'd grown up in Newark, after all, one of the country's most dangerous cities, and in that city's most infamous projects. So, while he didn't expect jail to be a walk in the park, he was confident that he could handle it.

Shawn was booked that Monday but told he'd have to wait until Friday to see a judge. Shawn had never heard of anyone being held without bail, not for a minor drug charge. It seemed wrong, he thought, unfair. Still, he was in jail and there was little he could do outside of complaining, so he settled in for the stay.

As Shawn expected, he knew more than a few of the guys there from around the way. Salaam Craig was there, as was Raheem Boyd's younger brother, whom Shawn only knew as Raheem Boyd's Younger Brother. Both were from Hayes Homes and greeted Shawn warmly.

They gave him the rundown on how things operated in the jail— who was who, and who to look out for. Raheem Boyd's Younger Brother, who was in jail on a murder charge, was kind enough to share his commissary. All he asked in return was that Shawn put something on his books when he got out.

When Friday finally rolled around, Shawn learned that he'd been assigned Judge Clifford Minor. That was a good thing, the other men told him, because Minor was a Black man and had a soft spot for first-time offenders. He might be inclined to look kindly on Shawn, they said.

The public defender Shawn was assigned explained to the judge how his client had never been in trouble, that he was, in fact, a college student. Sure enough, that defense worked on Judge Minor. He looked down from his bench and saw, probably, some misguided version of himself. He could have thrown the book at Shawn but instead gave him the kind of lecture that had always been wasted on him.

The judge tried to impress upon him the importance of good choices. He warned that Shawn might not be so lucky in the future, then released him on his own recognizance with the hope that something stuck. Shawn had no clue what those words meant, "his own recognizance," but he offered a polite "Thank you" to the judge anyway. He wished he'd said more when his lawyer later explained that he could go home without putting up bail.

Joanne was cool, almost withdrawn, when Shawn returned home. It had become her way. She didn't scream and fuss about having her door busted, or being pushed around by the police. She just shook her head in disapproval. Then she told Shawn what was obvious, what everyone else was telling him: that he was going to ruin his life if he didn't quit running the streets.

It was the first time Joanne had acknowledged her son's drug dealing directly, and hearing the words from her mouth made him feel ashamed, like a boy who'd been caught with his hand in the cookie jar. He couldn't say anything but "I'm sorry" and "I know."

The first thing he did after talking to his mother was check his room for the cash he'd left in his safe. It was gone; seized by the police. Then he checked the laundry room stash and found his $9,000 nest egg still there. It only occurred to him after he checked on his money that the entire apartment was spotless, including his room. Apparently, Joanne had spent the week literally cleaning up the mess her son created.

Shawn went to see Terrance later that day to discuss the raid. Neither could make sense of what happened. How'd the police know about the re-up? they wondered. Why hit Shawn of all people? He was doing well, for sure, but he wasn't the biggest hustler in Newark, on Chadwick even.

Whatever the reason, it was clear to them both that police were watching the block, and an investigation was likely on. They'd have to be more careful, Terrance resolved. Shawn agreed and, going a step further, decided to fall completely back from hustling. He was heeding his mom's and Judge Minor's warnings.

29

—

ELGIN

(1989-92)

LIVING THE WAY HE did made Elgin obsessed with money, and rightfully so. He needed it for food and other basic things his father failed to provide. But more than that, he wanted money to buy material things—gold chains and outfits matched perfectly to brand-new sneakers. None of it could change Elgin's circumstances. But who cared as long as he was "fresh"? It was a logic that compelled not just Elgin but many other young guys in his neighborhood, most of whom were also desperately poor and keeping up appearances.

Elgin finally got a chance to make some money when an older guy from the neighborhood named Bruce gave him and White Boy Rob some crack to sell. Within minutes of having it in hand, he saw Tony D., a neighborhood "crackhead," walking down the street. It was his chance, Elgin thought. He said, "Yo, I got crack. What's up?" and opened his hand to show Tony D. the product. Tony looked at the rocks, then at Elgin, and said, "Okay, my friend is gonna buy it for me, but I need to take it to him." Naïve, Elgin agreed and handed it over. "Wow! This is easy," he thought.

Elgin waited outside Tony's friend's apartment for a long while before Tony D. came back down. He handed the rocks back to Elgin, saying, "My friend don't wanna buy any today." Elgin said okay and thought nothing of it. He stood on the block and after a few minutes found someone else to buy it. The guy came back five minutes later, furious. He said, "What the fuck are you doing? This is baking soda, not crack."

Being scammed by one crackhead and reprimanded by another was embarrassing but Elgin learned from it. His first lesson was to always get the money up front. The second was that he could sell crack without actually having any. With that, he gave the disgruntled customer back his money and took the baking powder to another neighborhood. He sold it there to someone he'd never seen and got away as soon as possible.

The incident birthed his career as a nickel-and-dime dealer. He started by selling bits of soap or baking soda until friends fronted him real crack. It was an on-and-off thing, something he only did when he needed food, bus fare, clothes, etcetera. He got the hang of it within a few years. He learned how to pick up on who was buying and who wasn't. He found a plug. Elgin also grew accustomed to fast money.

The ease with which Elgin took to selling drugs was a testament to crack's ubiquity then. His dad was using it. So were his neighbors. And nearly everyone he grew up with was selling, either full-time or nickel-and-diming like him. The shows Elgin watched on TV— *Growing Pains, The Cosby Show, Family Ties, Silver Spoons*—may as well have been set on a distant planet. Elgin's world consisted of a few blocks in Yonkers, and its lifeblood was crack.

He'd stepped his game up by the time he was sixteen. Instead of selling for friends here and there and getting a little kicked back, he went into business for himself. It was as easy as saving some money and taking it down to West Harlem.

There was a restaurant on 143rd and Broadway that sold coke to just about anyone. The guys behind the counter would ask, "What you need, papi?" All Elgin had to say was how much money he had.

"One hundred," or "three hundred." It was as simple as ordering rice and beans, which they included in every order to make it look legit.

There was a newsstand that sold empty vials just a few blocks away at 145th and Broadway. KB Con, a sneaker store, was right next to that. Together, the three businesses formed a drug-dealer supermarket.

Elgin bought as much as he could on his trips to the Heights, usually about a hundred dollars' worth. Sold at five dollars a vial, the investment would earn him about two hundred, three hundred dollars in profit. Sometimes, he switched up his business based on trends. If he heard buyers say they had good crack from a guy whose vials had purple tops, he switched to purple tops. When other dealers started to sell two smaller vials for five dollars, so did Elgin.

He had friends who tried to be big-time and take more weight. Others increased their profits by traveling out of state, to Connecticut or Massachusetts, where a vial's worth of crack could be repackaged in plastic wrap and sold for $20. Elgin thought both approaches were too risky. Instead, he waited for the first or fifteenth of each month, when local users would spend their entire welfare checks with him. He even took food stamps, seventy cents on the dollar.

He made good money for someone in high school, about $200 a day on the days he decided to work, and he spent it all to craft the perception he wasn't struggling. He bought Air Force 1s and New Balance 696s—popular sneakers among hustlers. Guys who were really getting money might go to Dapper Dan in Harlem for a custom jacket. Elgin was cool with his Pelle Pelle and Knicks Starter jackets. He took major risks to get them. But it was worth it in the end, as Elgin developed something of a reputation for being fresh. It offset the other reputation he had for being the son of a crackhead.

But street dealing was a solitary, turf-based business. Dealers didn't hang out with other dealers when they were on the block, and people who weren't selling drugs weren't very likely to post up while he conducted business. Moreover, to keep things safe and simple, Elgin usually worked nights when all the other hustlers were out at

Skate Key or Arthur's or Brown Eyes. It could be lonely but he preferred it to going home.

One day in the spring of 1991, Stephen went to Elgin and said
there were some guys, dealers, who wanted to set up shop in their
apartment. He asked if it was cool, as though Elgin had any real say
in the matter. Elgin knew better than anyone that Stephen would do
whatever his addiction commanded, so he agreed. He said, "Fuck it.
Whatever. Do what you're gonna do."

Four "friends" of his father's moved in soon after. They were
from Brooklyn, Elgin learned, and the guy in charge was called
Unique. They weren't much older than Elgin at the time, between
eighteen and twenty-three years old, and they were surprisingly cool,
but the anxiety caused by their presence was impossible to ignore. Yet
everyone, including Elgin, behaved as though it were a normal situation, like they all were just friends hanging out and not locked in a
scary, shameful arrangement. Elgin's home was becoming a place he
avoided, one where all his worldly possessions were secured by a padlock on his bedroom door.

About six months after the dealers moved in, Elgin was holed up
in his bedroom one night when he heard what sounded like people
busting through the front door. That sound was followed by a commotion in the apartment. His dad was saying, "No, don't do this."
Then Elgin heard footsteps moving closer to his room. His dad yelled,
"It's just my son in there. Do whatever you gotta do but leave him
alone." The footsteps retreated and he was left to listen.

Elgin pressed his body against a wall, making himself as small as
he could in case bullets started flying. He heard the robbers demand
money, and he heard them moving through the apartment looking
for anything else of value. Then they were gone, and it was quiet. He
crept out of his room eventually and found the apartment in disarray.
His father and the dealers were similarly undone.

Not being home also came with risks. For example, Elgin stayed
at his friend Petey's on New Year's Eve that year. When he came
home the next day, the first thing his dad said was, "I didn't touch any-

thing." Naturally, Elgin was confused—that is, until he saw that the padlock on his bedroom door was broken.

He never played the tough guy—in fact, he didn't like confrontation at all—but seeing the empty closet where his clothes were supposed to be sent him into a frenzy. He stormed through the apartment shouting, "Who took my shit?" Stephen was stuttering as he tried to calm Elgin down and come up with an excuse. Unique and his crew were quiet, watching Elgin to see what he might do next. That made him angrier. When Elgin couldn't take the stonewalling anymore, he said, "Look: I don't know who got my stuff. But I'm getting ready to leave. I'm going to get a gun. And I'm coming back, and if somebody don't have my shit, it's gonna be a problem."

True to his word, he left to see a friend across town who he knew kept guns. He returned about three hours later, ready for whatever. He didn't need the gun, however, because there was a trash bag smack dab in the middle of the living room with his things in it. It wasn't all of it, but enough to calm Elgin down. One of the dealers explained that Stephen, who was nowhere to be found, had broken into his room and taken his stuff. He'd sold pieces off to the dealers in the house and others around Yonkers.

Elgin spent the next six hours going block to block asking dealers, friends in some cases, if his dad had sold them his clothes. He got a few more items back, but a lot of his stuff was gone. On the surface, he felt disrespected by what his father had done. Under that, he felt violated and embarrassed. Elgin had things in lieu of a family and a normal home life. Stephen seemed to respect that, even in the worst moments of his addiction. They had an unspoken agreement, Elgin thought, and it was broken in an instant.

The incident was a turning point for Elgin. He didn't realize it before, but he'd been quietly holding out hope that his dad would get better, praying that he would. The nickel-and-dime dealing, running the streets, it was all something to do while he waited for his life to change. After Stephen did the unthinkable, Elgin stopped hoping and stopped waiting.

30

—

CZAR

(1 9 8 9 – 9 0)

GEORGE H. W. BUSH was already a seasoned drug warrior by the time he entered the Oval Office in 1989. He had served as Reagan's vice president and in that role had an active hand in the administration's anti-drug efforts. Bush also proved himself adept at the politics of crime when, during the 1988 presidential race, his campaign ran its "Revolving Door" attack ad. The television ad blasted Bush's opponent, Massachusetts governor Michael Dukakis, for supporting a weekend furlough program for prisoners. Some used the opportunity to reoffend, most notably a convicted murderer named William Horton, who raped a woman and brutally assaulted her fiancé while on furlough.

Dukakis attempted to counter with an attack ad of his own. It told the story of a heroin dealer named Angel Medrano who raped and killed a pregnant mother of two after escaping from a halfway house run by the federal government. The Democratic candidate's attempt to wield the threat of drugs and crime was too little too late, however. A CBS News/*New York Times* poll found that of all the 1988 political ads, "Revolving Door" had the greatest impact. It caused the percentage of Americans who felt Bush was "tough enough" on crime to surge from 23 to 61 percent just before the election. Bush won the election by more than seven million votes and nearly eight percentage points.

Coming into office, Bush had a literal mandate on drugs. The Anti-Drug Abuse Act of 1988 required that the new president appoint a national director of drug policy who would, within six months of his confirmation by Congress, present a report to Congress outlining the new administration's national drug strategy. Bush tapped William J. Bennett for the job of director. Bennett was a former educator who'd served as education secretary in the Reagan administration and as head of the National Endowment for the Humanities. Ambitious and a rising star in Washington, he reportedly volunteered for the job after it was turned down by others.

Despite having no expertise regarding drugs, public health, or law enforcement, Bennett was charged with not only developing a plan to win the drug war once and for all but coordinating efforts between thirty federal agencies involved in anti-drug efforts, including the DEA, the FBI, Customs, and the Bureau of Alcohol, Tobacco, and Firearms. He was confirmed by the Senate in a 97–2 vote in March 1989 and quickly went to work.

After just a month on the job, Bennett announced that his office would make Washington, D.C., a test case for its work. He unveiled a nearly $100 million plan that included the construction of new pretrial detention and prison facilities, efforts to rid public housing of drug users and dealers, and a campaign that would throw the full weight of the federal government's law-enforcement resources at the district.

Drug-related murder cases would be investigated by the FBI; intelligence experts at the Pentagon would monitor activity at airports, bus terminals, and hotels; DEA agents were tasked with infiltrating drug rings. The Justice Department estimated that Bennett's Metropolitan Area Task Force, as he called it, would arrest and incarcerate five hundred drug traffickers over an eighteen-month period—about as many as federal prisons could accommodate.

But the Drug Crime Emergency Assistance Program for the Washington Metropolitan Area lacked both stated goals and an overall strategy. On paper, it consisted of just four pages that listed the various programs to be undertaken, the agencies involved, and a budget. More than half, $57 million, of the nearly $100 million in authorized funds was to go toward the creation of new facilities. An additional $7.9 million was to go to the DEA and the FBI. Just over $4.1 million was to be spent on drug treatment and prevention.

The District of Columbia, run at the time by Mayor Marion Barry, would receive no direct funding. Bennett had met with Barry just before his plan for D.C. was completed. The mayor reportedly explained that a law-enforcement campaign that had already been undertaken by local police had depleted the district's coffers without producing much change. Following the meeting, district officials sent a sixty-page report to Bennett's office outlining more than $100 million in needs: police radios, surveillance vans, recreation programs, treatment centers. Bennett never responded, according to reports, but called a press conference to unveil his plan ten days later. District officials were not invited.

"I've said this as frankly as possible: the local government has not acted in as responsible a way as it should," Bennett explained when announcing the program. "The plain fact is that, for too long and in too many respects, the D.C. government has failed to serve its citizens."

Beyond Bennett and beyond just D.C., many placed the blame for the crack epidemic and its accompanying violence at the feet of big-city mayors, the majority of whom were Black Democrats. New York City, Newark, Philadelphia, D.C., Detroit, L.A., Oakland, New Orleans, and Atlanta had been hit the hardest by the epidemic and were struggling to recover. They all also happened to have Black mayors. Despite the hard-line measures most took, they were still perceived as insufficiently tough on drugs and crime, either because they were Democrats or because they were Black.

Barry, as mayor of the nation's capital, came to symbolize this group of city leaders. He was an outsider figure and his path to politics had been through activism. Such had also been the case for others, like Andrew Young in Atlanta, Coleman Young in Detroit, Tom Bradley in L.A., and Wilson Goode in Philadelphia.

And like his contemporaries, Barry had gone to great lengths to combat drugs and crime in his city, on top of managing other significant issues in employment, housing, and development brought on by the economic challenges of the period. In fact, by the time Barry met with Bennett to discuss the Drug Crime Emergency Assistance Program for the Washington Metropolitan Area, his administration had already launched its own enforcement campaign called Operation Clean Sweep. Starting in 1986, Clean Sweep sent squads of police officers into the district's known drug markets. Over the next two and a half years, the Metropolitan Police Department made around forty-seven thousand arrests, one of the highest rates per capita in any American city. Regardless, the drug trade continued to expand, and D.C.'s murder rate continued to rise.

Whether or not the federal government ever believed in the Barry administration's capacity to bring order to the streets of D.C., doubts were certainly exacerbated by rumors that Barry himself used crack. The rumors became a real cause for concern in early 1989 when authorities began investigating a man named Charles Lewis, a dealer who turned out to have connections to Barry. That investigation would eventually lead to a sting to catch Barry in possession of cocaine, and to Barry's arrest on January 18, 1990.

Elsewhere, Bennett was pitching his ideas for anti-drug measures to anyone who would listen. In a July 1989 speech before the American Legislative Exchange Council, he encouraged state governments to deny driver's licenses to and seize the cars of convicted drug offenders. Bennett also called on states to adopt a five-point plan that included building more prisons and hiring more police, judges, and prosecutors. He promoted state laws that would require state agencies and anyone doing business with the state to penalize employees caught using drugs on the job. Bennett proposed that states explore military-style "boot camps" and mandated community service for drug crimes. He also demanded stricter oversight of drug treatment programs, his only proposal related at all to treatment.

Next, Bennett unveiled his national anti-drug plan in August 1989, meeting a deadline set by Congress. "We should be tough on drugs," the plan read, "much tougher than we are now. Our badly imbalanced criminal justice system, already groaning under the weight of current drug cases, should be rationalized and significantly expanded."

Bennett's plans for D.C. and the nation converged during the summer of 1989, when President Bush and White House aides met to discuss how best to present the administration's anti-drug program to a national television audience. According to reports, Bush was given a draft of his speech that included the idea of holding up a bag of crack bought in Lafayette Square, the small park directly opposite the White House. "He liked the prop," one aide told *The Washington Post*. "It drove the point home."

But getting their hands on crack was more difficult than members of the administration imagined. White House communications director David Demarest reached out to the Justice Department about procuring crack but was informed that very little was actually sold in areas near the White House. Officials with the Justice Department then contacted officials with the DEA to inquire about busts pending in the area. There was nothing planned near the White House, but undercover agents with the DEA's Washington field office agreed to set something up.

Keith Jackson, the dealer who ultimately sold crack to the president of the United States, didn't seem to know what the White House was, let alone where it was. When undercover DEA agents phoned him to meet at a park near the White House, he reportedly replied, "Oh, you mean where Reagan lives." The eighteen-year-old eventually found his way there and, on September 1, 1989, exchanged three ounces of crack for $2,400.

Just four days later, on September 5, 1989, Bush was in the Oval Office holding up a bag of crack for the cameras. "This is crack cocaine, seized a few days ago by drug enforcement agents in a park just across the street from the White House," he said in his first televised address. "It's as innocent-looking as candy, but it's turning our cities into battle zones, and it's murdering our children. Let there be no mistake: this stuff is poison."

Bush used the address to announce his administration's plan to get even tougher on drugs. "To win the war against addictive drugs like crack will take more than just a federal strategy," he added. "It will take a national strategy, one that reaches into every school, every workplace, involving every family." Later in the speech, he outlined Bennett's plan to "enlarge our criminal justice system across the board—at the local, state, and federal levels alike."

Bennett seemed, in the fall of 1989, thrilled about the optics. In talking with a reporter for *Rolling Stone,* he likened the war on drugs to "an old western with Henry Fonda, or Clint Eastwood." The "cowboy in the capital," as *Rolling Stone* dubbed him, was said to be mulling a run at the presidency as he made television appearances and accepted opportunities to be profiled in glossy magazines.

He had no right to be so cavalier. Bennett's Drug Crime Emergency Assistance Program had some success, but overall it failed to make a dent in D.C.'s violent drug trade. While the rate of adults arrested with cocaine in their systems dropped between 1989 and 1990, violent crime was still increasing in D.C. at alarmingly high rates. Homicides, for example, rose from 434 homicides in 1989 to 483 in 1990, making the district the nation's murder capital for a second consecutive year, a trend that would continue until 1992.

Bennett appeared before a Senate panel in February 1990 to discuss where his program had fallen short and somehow managed to put the blame on district officials. The Barry administration had failed to demonstrate a commitment to controlling drug abuse, he said, pointing to Barry's arrest a month before as evidence. "We have done everything we committed to do," Bennett told the panel. "But the federal responsibility cannot replace local responsibility." He added, "We're tired of being flogged for a problem that is not of our making."

A September 1990 article in *The New York Times Magazine* entitled "D.C.'s War on Drugs: Why Bennett Is Losing" concluded, however, that "by excluding local officials, Bennett's working group lost the chance to benefit from the district's own drug-fighting efforts." What Bennett would have likely learned from the Barry administration was that arrests and incarcerations would prove futile as long as the drug trade provided economic opportunity, and as long as treatment needs went unmet.

Bennett announced that he would step down as the nation's first drug czar just a month after the *Times* published its feature, on November 9, 1990. He went out with a bang, again blaming his failures in D.C. on Marion Barry and calling the nation's capital a "basket case."

In accepting Bennett's resignation, President Bush thanked him for putting the country "on the road to victory." A more appropriate postscript for Bennett's tenure came in a statement from Marion Barry. It read: "Bill Bennett has joined the parade of people who are using me as an excuse for our nation's failure to deal adequately with a problem that is both an illness that affects millions and at the same time is a multibillion-dollar trade that is spawning violence in every urban area of our nation."

31

—

SHAWN

(1990)

SHAWN SHIFTED HIS ATTENTION back to school in the months that followed his arrest. He started sleeping in the dorm room he'd been assigned and got to know his roommate, a funny Italian kid named Ken who took one look at Shawn and nicknamed him "Dirty Money."

Then, in mid-April 1989, Shawn was in his dorm room when his pager started to vibrate. It was near 5:00 A.M. and the buzzing wouldn't stop. He picked it up after the fourth page and the bottom fell out of his stomach when he saw the calls were coming from home.

Shawn rushed to a nearby phone booth to return the call and, much to his relief, his mom answered. She, Tony, and Cheyta were okay, she said, but the police had been back to the house. They said he was wanted for conspiracy. The officers weren't still there, but she'd given them the name of his school, and they were on the way.

Almost as soon as Shawn hung up, there was a knock on the side of the phone booth. He glanced over, and standing to his right was a large white man wearing a green jacket that read DEA. "Are you Shawn McCray?" the man asked as Shawn opened the door. His mouth had gone completely dry and his heart was beating out of his chest, but Shawn was somehow able to mutter, "Yes."

The agent took him back to his dorm room, where Shawn was allowed to put on proper clothes and shoes. Ken and Shawn's resident advisor looked on in a state of total shock. Then Shawn was led outside, handcuffed, and placed in the back of a van.

The whole process couldn't have taken more than thirty minutes, and unlike the dramatic raid at Shawn's home, it was relatively quiet. In fact, the only thing to alert the students of Caldwell that anything was amiss was the helicopter that hovered above campus for a moment and then disappeared into the night sky as swiftly as it came.

The drama came later, as Shawn sat on the floor of the van. The group of five agents, all of them big and white, started to go in. "You fucked up now," one said, barely able to hold back his glee. "You're never coming home," said another. "You went to college for nothing." It went on like that for twenty minutes that felt like forever.

Finally, the van stopped, and Shawn was led out to what looked like an old courthouse. They took him inside, down a flight of steps, and into a room. Cheers erupted as he walked through the door. "We got another one," said a new white man.

After being processed, Shawn was led into another room for interrogation. He recognized one of the men questioning him as the cop who had punched him during the raid. Shawn expected what came next: they told him that he was in a lot of trouble and needed to "help himself."

"How?" asked Shawn, though he already knew what they meant.

"Give us some information about what's going on in the streets, like who's selling guns. Give us a murder. Give us something to help your situation," said the cop who'd punched him.

Instead of cooperating, Shawn asked, "What am I being charged with?"

"Are you going to talk?" the cop replied.

Shawn, feeling himself by then, said he had nothing to talk about but his charge. "I don't know anything," he added coyly. "I'm in college. That's where you picked me up from." The officer called Shawn a stupid motherfucker before having him taken out of the room.

The holding cell where he was eventually placed contained familiar faces, all friends and associates of Terrance. Frank was there, J.J. and his brother Rock, and Samaad from Nineteenth Street— everybody except Lamar and Terrance himself. The group made small talk but inevitably drifted into an awkward, brooding silence as the night wore on. Each was thinking, no doubt, about the predicament he was in and all he stood to lose. That was certainly what was on Shawn's mind.

They were transported to court the next morning and went before the judge one by one. Frank, who was just about eighteen years old and had no criminal record, went first. He got a $35,000 cash bail without the option to put up just 10 percent to a bondsman. The judge meant business, Shawn thought. J.J. was next. and his bail was $150,000, no 10 percent option. Then it was Shawn's turn.

The public defender they'd all been assigned spoke on his behalf. He acknowledged that Shawn had an open charge for possession of cocaine but made it a point to highlight his enrollment at Caldwell. The judge looked at Shawn as if to assess whether he looked like a college student. After having a good look, he said "Fifty thousand cash bail with no ten-percent option."

Shawn sat in jail, pissed and growing angrier with every minute that passed. The police hadn't told him any more about the so-called conspiracy he was caught up in, and he was sure it was bullshit. He'd straightened up since the raid at his house, he reasoned, and hadn't gone anywhere near the block. The thing had something to do with Terrance. That much was clear from the people in the cell. But what? Then Shawn looked over at Frank, and it all started to make sense: the charge was actually connected to the raid.

He'd called Terrance the day of the raid, something he almost never did, because they lived so close. Usually, if Shawn needed to talk, he just walked the five doors down. But Frank was running late with the delivery that day, and Shawn called to check up on him. Terrance's phone was tapped, Shawn figured. The other guys there were always calling Terrance about one thing or another, but that one call was the only proof of Shawn's involvement. That's how they knew about the re-up. That's how they got him.

There were by then only four weeks left in the semester, and Shawn was suddenly worried that he'd miss his finals. The thought echoed through his mind as he was transported back to Essex County Jail. It got louder as he changed into an orange jumpsuit and was placed in a cell with Rock, Frank, Benny, Samaad, and Case from Twenty-first Street.

He wasn't ready to give up, and he got to work on getting released as soon as he was settled. He called home the first chance he got and, after letting Joanne know what was happening, asked her to reach out to one of his coaches, a guy named Bruce Bartlett who'd been an assistant under Coach Marshall. They weren't especially close, but Bartlett was a lawyer out of Rutherford and Shawn hoped he might be inclined to help. And that's all he could do—hope while he waited to hear back.

While Shawn was making moves to be released, everyone else seemed to be getting comfortable. Back then, the jail allowed prisoners to wear their own clothes while incarcerated, and the guys he came in with were having outfits sent up in addition to underwear, socks, and other basics. They were playing cards, reading, listening to music—finding ways to pass the time. Shawn wanted no part of it and stayed to himself, in his orange jumpsuit, almost in protest. He was in jail, he thought, but not for long.

He waited patiently as one day passed, then two, then three. He was just minding his business on the fourth day when he overheard an old head explaining to someone how anyone could request a bail reduction after thirteen days inside. Shawn called his mom later that night with what he'd learned.

She'd been in touch with Coach Bartlett, the lawyer, she said. He hadn't made any promises but said he'd try his best to help Shawn. She said she'd ask about trying to get the bail lowered.

Shawn was finally released from jail after two weeks of being locked up. His former coach, it turned out, did care enough to help, and he had filed a motion for a bail reduction on Shawn's behalf. His bail was subsequently dropped to $2,500, which Shawn covered easily with the money from his stash spot. Shawn called to thank him after his release and Bartlett said his staying out of trouble would be thanks enough. The administrators at Caldwell were similarly gracious, allowing Shawn time to retake the finals he'd missed. He was, however, banned from living on campus.

Before long, he received an offer from the prosecutor: a few months in prison for the possession charge. It was a decent offer. Bartlett said so, but Shawn turned it down.

He was in denial, convinced that all he had to do to avoid jail was the right thing—work his job, go to school, stay off the block. It was magical thinking for sure, but Shawn was right, in a way. The police and prosecutors on the case eventually got tired of him and made another offer: one year of probation and a $1,000 fine. Shawn didn't press his luck that time, and he accepted the deal. Then, like magic, his conspiracy charge was dropped due to insufficient evidence.

When all was said and done, Shawn had survived many people's worst nightmare and was no worse for the wear. It was a moment of incredibly good fortune, of unearned grace, for which he was grateful. He showed his gratitude by recommitting to staying out of trouble.

Shawn decided to finally get a nine-to-five job—his first. Luckily for him, that was back when businesses hired primarily through HELP WANTED signs in their windows, and one day, while he was driving home from Caldwell, he saw that the Budget Rent a Car a few blocks from campus was hiring. He walked in and struck up a conversation with the manager, a pretty Italian woman named Sue.

The job was cleaning cars, she said, which was no problem for Shawn. All that mattered to him was that the job paid and would keep him far away from the trouble on Chadwick Avenue. There was the matter of an interview with the general manager, a guy named Larry, but the job was as good as his after Shawn mentioned that he was a student at Caldwell.

The rest of Shawn's summer was devoted to cleaning cars at Budget. It was a full-time job that kept him busy from 7:30 A.M. to 6 P.M., sometimes working extra hours. It left no time for nonsense.

When he wasn't at work, Shawn was avoiding home by hanging over near Felix Fuld Court, which everyone called Little Bricks. He kept up that schedule in the months that followed, through to the fall then the winter and spring. In that time, he also helped some friends from Chadwick get their first jobs at Budget—first Andre, then Gene and Shelton.

All told, probation might have been the best thing for Shawn. It kept him focused through his senior year of college, and by the time it was almost done, he was ready to graduate.

The odds had been against him, but Shawn actually walked across the stage at Caldwell College in May 1990, less than a year after being arrested. He accepted his degree, a Bachelor of Arts in sociology, in front of his mother, grandmother, Tony, and Cheyta, Mad Dog, and a few other friends from the neighborhood. It was a great moment, one he'd never forget but that he eventually set aside.

THERE WAS SOMETHING ABOUT the spring and summer months that brought out the worst in Shawn—out of his whole neighborhood, really. The temperature would rise, and like clockwork, people would trickle back out of their homes and into the streets: girls in less clothing, addicts looking to get high, hustlers looking to make money from the addicts to spend on the girls.

Shawn's will to do the right thing and avoid the streets broke during the summer of 1990 along with the weather. It was like he was pulled back to the block by an unseen force.

He had a college education, something that was supposed to change his life, but selling drugs afforded him more than a bachelor's degree in sociology. The block also came with a group of people he'd known his entire life who would assist, promote, and protect him. Community like that was rare in a legitimate workplace, especially for a young Black man.

He started selling drugs again but was smarter this time around. He held on to his day job at Budget, which kept him from getting too deep into the streets. And he stopped selling directly to users. They were too unpredictable, he thought, and too numerous. With each one he served, new customers especially, he felt more exposed to scams and maybe even to police. Instead, he made his money by selling to other dealers. He dealt in clips, packs of ten vials that usually went for five dollars each on the street. Shawn sold a clip at wholesale prices, for thirty-five dollars.

Consequently, he had loyal customers from all over Newark. Dealers from Bergen Street bought from him, Big Ish from New Community, Rah from Clinton Avenue, Ali from Fairview. Even Gene was buying clips from Shawn to sell up at Caldwell. Everybody wanted to see the Big Man, and with that kind of clientele, Shawn was back to making serious money within just a few months.

Shawn, like many guys who sold drugs during that period, did so to afford a basic middle-class life, not to get rich. Hustling filled the gap between the low-income lifestyle they were born into and the one they believed they deserved.

Hence, Shawn used the proceeds of his second job to buy a new car, a black Jeep Wrangler that he outfitted with rims, a gray soft top, and a car phone—state-of-the-art technology in 1990. Fresh clothes and shoes were another necessary expense. Shawn had every style and color of Timberland boots, a couple of Pelle Pelle jackets, stacks of jeans and shirts. He only wore them to go out—never on the block—but just being able to buy them made him feel good. He also gave his mom money for things she needed around the house, and for Tony and Cheyta.

Every now and then, Shawn blew money betting on games of pitty pat or on the occasional trip to Harlem, where he'd catch amateur night at the Apollo and get a bite at Willie's Burgers. Still, he didn't carry on like a high roller, and he never missed a day of work at Budget. Working there was also easy money for him. Plus, cleaning cars gave him time to think. It was a much-needed break from the near-constant traffic and chaos of the block.

His basketball career officially over, he also started playing in the neighborhood leagues. One was called the Hole, and its games were played at Jesse Allen Park on Muhammad Ali Avenue, across from the Stella Wright projects. Shawn entered as part of a team put together by Mad Dog. They called themselves the Jazz at first, but later N.W.A., after the rap group. It included Shawn, Mad Dog, and Big Na—all former teammates from Central—along with guys Mad Dog played with in the Salvation Army League.

Being back on the court helped to center Shawn. Basketball did that for him. It was a stabilizing force that helped align his mind with his body and organize his thoughts. He loved basketball. He'd known that all along, but it became abundantly clear once he was back to playing for the fun of it. It also didn't hurt that the Hole had something of a profile in Newark, with teams from different neighborhoods and housing projects around the city. That gave real stakes to the competition, Shawn thought.

These were good times for Shawn and his friends. Everyone was young and free and getting money. And for whatever reason, the police weren't bothering them. It was at this point that Shawn and the rest of the guys from Chadwick became known as the Zoo Crew. It all started one day on the block. Quan and Barry B. were planning a weekly party at Skate 22, a popular rink in Union Township. They wanted a name to promote it, something catchy and cool. As a joke, someone suggested Zoo Crew since the police and politicians were always calling guys like them animals. They laughed, but the name stuck.

Quan used it to promote the party at Skate 22. Then he got T-shirts made and gave them out to everyone. People saw those shirts on some of the coolest, toughest, most successful guys in the neighborhood, and they wanted to be down. Zoo Crew would become a name brand in Newark, like Nike or Adidas.

The city, it seemed, was waiting for something of which it could be proud, something that represented a new, post-projects Brick City. Despite being associated with drugs, the Zoo Crew became just that. Then it took on a life of its own. Guys from all over Newark started claiming that they were Zoo Crew. Shawn was as surprised as anyone to witness it happening. He was still working at Budget, after all.

Things got more hectic about a year into the Zoo Crew craze when Dre, Red, M.J., and Quan started hanging in East Orange. That spread the name even farther and created a connection between the Zoo Crew and Illtown, as East Orange was called. At that time, the pride of Illtown was Naughty by Nature, and Treach, one of the group's members, started hanging with the guys on Chadwick.

His presence solidified the fact that the Zoo Crew had arrived, and Shawn and his friends attained a measure of status and success that none of them had imagined growing up in the projects. The icing on the cake came the next summer, when N.W.A. won the Hole's championship. That year, they had Ira "Mae Mae" Bowman and Eric Williams on the team, both of whom went on to play in the NBA. N.W.A. ripped through the tournament that year and was the talk of Newark for weeks.

Sometime soon after, Shawn was at his favorite late-night spot, Tom's Chicken Shack on Clinton Avenue, when he ran into Bertina Moore. He hadn't seen her since his freshman year at Keystone, and the two caught up while she waited for her food. At that moment, Shawn was reminded of how sweet Bertina had always been. She still looked good, too, he thought. The two exchanged numbers and got together a few weeks later. Within months, they rekindled what they'd had as teenagers and became a couple again. He told her about everything he'd been through in the years since they lost contact— about everything except the drugs.

It became harder to keep them a secret the bigger the Zoo Crew got. The notoriety also came with unwanted attention from the cops. Before long, there were regular patrols up and down Chadwick again. Two cops, Chip and Joe, would roll up in an unmarked car. They made the occasional arrest, but they mostly just watched—sometimes from a house on Bergen Street, rumor had it, and even from the Bergen Street School. There was another team of officers named Walt and Burtchek. Walt was the cool type and never said much. Burtchek was the talker of the two and he always meant business. He wouldn't chase a guy down for an arrest. Instead, he'd find his stash and hold it until he saw him again. Then he'd cuff him.

But by far the most despised pair of officers were Fletch and Dave. They'd do anything to catch somebody selling drugs—hide behind houses, jump out from behind bushes. They would even stand on the corner at night and act like they were selling drugs themselves, just to get the jump on someone. It was a marvel that one or both of them never got shot.

Because Shawn worked a day job, he had few run-ins with police. There was one incident, however, in the spring of 1992. He was bagging up in his bedroom when he heard a commotion outside. He rushed to the sidewalk to see what was going on and found officers chasing Jabu, who was beating them in a foot race between and around houses on the block.

Shawn was watching it all go down when he was snatched up by a young Black cop from the neighborhood. He was another one that nobody liked, mostly because he'd roll down Chadwick mean-mugging everyone, making threats and cracks. Like all the other guys on the block, Shawn jokingly referred to the officer as "Super Cop."

Super Cop hemmed up Shawn and proceeded to search his pockets. When he didn't find drugs, he took his keys and opened his mailbox. Shawn sometimes hid his stash there. That told Shawn he was probably under surveillance. The stash wasn't there, though, not this time. Super Cop eventually had to let him go.

A year later, Shawn was with Terrance and Frank playing ball at the playground on Madison Avenue when someone from Chadwick ran over and said the police were raiding houses on the block. They were told the entire street was taped off and police were handcuffing and running background checks on anyone outside and over eighteen. Shawn, Terrance, and Frank were anxious to see what was going on at home but decided it was best to wait out the police. Then someone else came to the playground to tell them that both Shawn's and Terrance's mothers had been arrested at their homes.

Shawn stayed away from Chadwick Avenue and spent the rest of the night at a friend's. On one hand, he wanted to run straight into the police station and demand his mother be released, but he also didn't know what, if anything, they might have on him.

He worked up the nerve to call out of work and return home the next morning. He was met outside by his aunt Denise, who saw him and flew into a rage. She was yelling, "Have you lost your mind?" and "You better get my sister out of jail!"

He hurried past her to his bedroom and started putting the pieces together. It had been ransacked for sure, but amazingly, the cocaine was still sitting in his hamper. He searched further and noted that $6,000 was missing from the top of his closet, but he still had $12,000 in his other bedroom stash. He thought the police couldn't have a case if the drugs were still there. So against the advice of every nerve in his body, he went downtown to see about his mother.

Shawn walked into the station on Franklin Street. He told the officer at the front desk that his house had been raided and his mother had been arrested. He said he would own up to whatever was found. The officer asked his name and his mother's and ran the information through the system. After looking for a while, he informed Shawn there was no warrant for his arrest, but Joanne had been charged with possession of cocaine.

Shawn again said that whatever they found was his and offered to trade places with his mother. The officer explained that it didn't work like that. Joanne had already been processed and would go to court within forty-eight hours. Shawn was headed out when another officer, one he guessed was working on the case, started yelling at him.

"You piece of shit!" he said. "You're going to leave your mother in jail? You're a fucking coward," he yelled.

Shawn tried not to let what the officer said get to him as he walked out of the station, but on some level, he felt they were right. He couldn't imagine anything worse than his mother locked up for something he did. He consoled himself with the thought that at least she was locked up with Niecy, Terrance's mom, who was more street-smart.

Joanne's hearing was two days later, not nearly soon enough for Shawn. Her bail was set at $5,000, and he paid as soon as he could. Then he left home, a little afraid of what her reaction might be when she saw him. When he finally came back later that day, Joanne was sitting at the dining room table. She looked up when she heard him come in the door. She said, "I hope you learned your lesson." That was the last time they ever talked about what happened, and the charges were eventually dropped.

If Shawn had to guess, he'd say the police had an informant who said there would be drugs in his house or Terrance's. That's why there weren't any arrest warrants. The plan had been to rush in, arrest whoever was home, and find the drugs later. But the police couldn't find the drugs. "Idiots," Shawn thought. The only upside was they'd made such a mess that whatever investigation they had going was probably off. At least that was how he reasoned that it was okay to keep running with the Zoo Crew.

And what other choice did he have? Zoo Crew wasn't an affiliation that he could just drop. It was made up of people he'd known most of his life. Sure, Shawn could quit selling drugs. But was he supposed to just stop going outside, stop talking to his friends, move and never look back? That was out of the question. Shawn's home was Hayes Homes, Chadwick Avenue, the Central Ward. His family was the Zoo Crew.

The police raid and the arrests were meant to break them up, but it only brought the group closer. If anything, the attention from police—throwing Terrance and Shawn's moms in jail—made them feel persecuted. From then on, it was the Zoo Crew versus the police. And with every overzealous police interaction that followed, the Zoo Crew was further cast as a symbol for Newark's least and left out.

They were at once victims of Newark's neglect and agents of harm in the city. The police were attempting to disrupt the flow of drugs in the city but abusing people in the process, something they had a history of in Newark. In an environment like that, it was hard to distinguish the good guys from the bad guys.

It got even harder after Terrance opened a few businesses in the neighborhood. He had Zoo Sportswear, a small clothing store on Bergen Avenue. There was also Zoo Flowers, a florist shop; Boney's Place, a takeout restaurant; and an auto parts store called Get Wise. The businesses were fronts for the Zoo Crew's drug trade, but they also represented development the likes of which the Central Ward hadn't seen in decades.

Shawn was on top of the world by the spring of 1994. As unlikely as it seemed, he felt like he'd finally struck a balance between his straight life and his street life. Things were going well with Bertina. He was still living at home with his family, but only to be near the block. He was saving money, too—about $20,000 he kept split between a savings account and stashes around the house.

He would have stopped time if he could and lived in that moment forever. It wasn't perfect, but he had everything he ever wanted: a girl, friends, his family, and the means to take care of himself. It was messy, Shawn's version of the American Dream.

It came to an abrupt end the day after Memorial Day, 1994. Shawn got a call at work. It was Big Na on the phone. He said Mad Dog had been shot and was in surgery. A chill ran through Shawn's body, but he tried to stay cool. A lot of guys from around the way got shot but survived, he thought. Mad Dog was as tough as any one of them. "Mad Dog will be all right," he said. He kept telling himself that after hanging up. But the phone rang a short while later, and it was Big Na again. He said, "He's gone, Scooter."

Shawn had never lost anyone as close to him as Mad Dog, and he was in a state of utter shock at the news. It was as if he had left his own body for a moment. His brain seemed to stop, and all his senses were gone. When he finally came to, he burst into tears. It was one of the few times Shawn ever allowed himself to cry.

Shawn tried to piece together what had happened over the next few days. He learned from talking with a few people that Mad Dog had been standing around a dice game when an argument broke out. He broke it up. Mad Dog didn't know that one of the guys fighting, a sixteen- or seventeen-year-old kid named Shahiem from Upper Clinton Hill, ran home to get a gun.

Shahiem came back and lit up the block, shooting one other person in the foot and Mad Dog in the groin. The bullet hit a main artery. Doctors at the hospital tried to stop the bleeding but couldn't. Just like that, Shawn's best friend was gone. No goodbye, no nothing. Mad Dog was taken away suddenly from a family that loved him, including a baby boy, his namesake. Mad Dog was just twenty-seven years old.

32

—

THE LIFE

THE NEWS MEDIA BECAME consumed eventually by crack and created characters to tell the drug's story. There was a seemingly endless stream of stories about drug-dealing gangs and crack kingpins. Missing from much of the coverage, however, were portraits of people like Lennie: the users.

Even stories about so-called crack babies managed to brush past the lives of their mothers. The brief attention paid was usually focused on the irresponsibility of them getting pregnant. The question of *how* addicts became addicted was an afterthought. It was as though their lives had no purpose or meaning beyond the presumed burden they placed on society.

Women users, Black women in particular, fell to the absolute lowest rung on the nation's social ladder. As such, their stories and their insights reveal the depth of the crack epidemic—just how bad things got and what damage was done.

The very nature of crack, its intense but brief high, demanded that addicts used constantly to stay high. But constant use costs money, and a lot of it. Men addicted to crack were able to steal and rob to get high. Sometimes, dealers and other people gave them odd jobs like mowing lawns and running errands. Women, however, had fewer avenues for income and were often steered into sex work, if they weren't sex workers already.

Lennie had been selling her body since she was thirteen years old. She wasn't proud of that fact, but to her sex work was a means to an end. It was risky, for sure, but it was dependable. She could get paid what she thought was decent money and, for the most part, both she and the tricks abided by the unwritten rules of the trade.

All of that went out the window as the crack years rolled on. Toward the mid-eighties, the streets became flooded with women suddenly "in the life" due to their addiction. Like Lennie, they engaged in sex work primarily to support their habits. With that, crack became almost synonymous with prostitution, and the addition of crack only made the sex trade more desperate.

The going rate for sex decreased and expectations from the tricks rose. Women were expected to do anything for five or ten dollars, or just another hit. High-risk sexual behavior became more common. For the women in this world, it was a dangerous race to the bottom.

Many of the women who became addicted to crack had histories of childhood sexual trauma and sexual assault. For them, there was already little difference between sex and abuse. But the line became so blurred during the crack years that it might as well have not existed.

In the minds of many, women like Lennie were no longer people. They were strawberries, crack hos, skeezers—women who'd fallen even lower in esteem than their male counterparts because they'd abdicated their duties as mothers, wives, sisters, and daughters to get high.

In a time when crack still cast a dark shadow over entire communities, people sought to elevate themselves by humiliating and outright abusing crack addicts, women especially. Crack houses became houses of horror where women were routinely raped, gang-raped, beaten, and battered by men, who were often under the influence of crack as well. Sadly, the crack house was the only place for some women to go. Such was true for many women as their addictions advanced and crack took its toll on their lives and bodies, and they became less desirable in the traditional sex trade.

Women who smoked crack, especially if they traded sex for crack, lived with the constant fear of being attacked or killed. Crack made them sick, destroyed their lungs, destroyed their families. It wore them out. It was their poison until they were high. Then it was an antidote for all that ailed them.

Lennie never got too close to other users, but sometimes she learned their stories. Many of the women she met had been abused growing up, like her. They'd experienced abandonment, violation, deprivation, or sudden loss and had substance abuse modeled for them by relatives. A psychologist might say these women, including Lennie, were depressed and suffering from PTSD. There weren't, however, many psychologists around to make those observations, so they were characterized within their communities as moody or crazy. The way they coped, with drugs and alcohol, was dismissed as a habit they could break if they weren't so irresponsible.

It was a life rife with stigma, one in which the women constantly battled perceptions of themselves as useless. Many were ashamed of what they did for drugs and money, and they had to navigate the disdain directed at them for being both crackheads and prostitutes. The worst was when a woman started to believe what she was told about herself. It was the path of least resistance, but also the beginning of a descent that made recovery nearly impossible.

And the longer a woman remained in the life, the more likely she was to experience additional trauma. It was a devastating cycle: smoking crack to relieve depression or PTSD and feelings of worthlessness, being retraumatized in efforts to obtain crack, and smoking more crack to relieve the new trauma.

ACT

VII

–

DECLINE

33

—

WAR II

(1990-94)

TWO DECADES AFTER NIXON originally launched the war on drugs, the issue had come to define both parties. Despite the many other national concerns that cropped up, domestic and international, Republicans and Democrats migrated back to crime and drugs every election season, each party desperate to prove it could be tougher.

Having claimed so much of the issue under Reagan, Bush and the Republicans were unwilling to admit that the course they had taken was wrong. The government couldn't arrest its way to a drug-free America. That much was made abundantly clear with the failure of drug czar Bill Bennett. Still, Bush decided to stay the course. Instead of shifting his anti-drug efforts to focus on, say, drug education and treatment—areas that had largely gone neglected—Bush upped the ante on enforcement and incarceration.

The drug politics of the nineties would prove more complicated than they had been in the eighties. After watching the Dukakis campaign implode around crime, Democrats were resolved to never again appear weak on the issue. The party had a plan to wrestle the war on drugs away from Republicans, and that meant beating them at their own game. Leading that effort was Democrat Joe Biden, then a senator from Delaware.

There was no Democrat better for the job. Biden, it turns out, had fingerprints on every major piece of crime legislation during the Reagan years. He served as Democratic floor manager for the successful passage of the 1984 Comprehensive Crime Control Act. He was one of sixteen Democrats who co-sponsored the Anti-Drug Abuse Act of 1986, and he was instrumental in crafting the 1988 Anti-Drug Abuse Act. In fact, it was Biden who reportedly coined the term "drug czar," the shorthand used for the director of the Office of National Drug Control Policy.

As the nineties approached, the parties became locked in a bitter custody battle for the war on drugs marked by one-upmanship. Republicans, led by Bush, proposed more prisons and funding for law enforcement. Democrats, led by Biden, came back with even bigger numbers. It was a race to the bottom, with very little distinguishing progressives from conservatives besides small differences on guns and the death penalty. And by the late eighties, those two items were just about all that was left to legislate.

Bush initiated debate over use of the death penalty in the fall of 1989 when he proposed that Congress allow for the execution of "drug kingpins," however loosely defined. His proposal was bolder than the 1988 Anti-Drug Abuse Act, which already allowed for the execution of so-called kingpins whose criminal activities led to another's death. Bush sought, in effect, to make the distribution of drugs, in and of itself, a capital offense.

Congressional Republicans responded to Bush's call with the Comprehensive Crime Control Act of 1989. The legislation expanded the death penalty, as Bush had proposed. It also sought to limit appeals of death sentences and provide even more funding for law enforcement and incarceration. Not to be outdone, the Democrats put forward legislation of their own, the Crime Control Act of 1990. Introduced by Joe Biden, the bill increased Bush's request for aid to local police from $350 million to $600 million and more than tripled Bush's request for new FBI agents from three hundred to one thousand.

The Democrats' bill was slightly more progressive than the one put forward by Republicans, though not by much. It proposed expanding the death penalty but exempted juveniles and the intellectually disabled. Where the Bush-backed legislation limited the window for appeals of death sentences to just a year, Biden's bill limited them to eighteen months. And while the Bush bill offered stiffer penalties for the use of semiautomatic weapons in crimes, Biden's bill added a ban on the six most-used semiautomatics.

On a trip to Kansas City to meet with local law enforcement and visit a former crack house, Bush called Biden's bill a "Trojan horse." "It looks like a real crime bill. It sounds like a real crime bill. But in actuality, it will be tougher on law enforcement than on criminals," he said. Biden, ever the drug warrior, responded in a statement: "Well, the Trojan horse was filled with soldiers who won their war, and my crime bill is loaded with money for more police and drug agents—soldiers we need to fight the war on crime today."

After months of intense debate and maneuvering in Congress, Biden came out on top when legislators agreed to a stripped-down version of his bill. Gone were the provisions regarding the death penalty and guns. In the end, the major provisions of the final Crime Control Act of 1990 merely increased penalties for child abuse and approved yet more funding for law enforcement—the politically easy stuff. Signing the bill into law, Bush expressed his disappointment over the absent provisions. "The American people deserve tough, new laws to help us prevail in the fight against drugs and crime," he said.

The fight for a big, comprehensive crime bill continued in March 1991 when Biden introduced the Violent Crime Control Act of 1991 into Congress. It authorized the death penalty for forty-four federal offenses, restricted habeas corpus petitions, banned assault weapons, increased penalties for firearm offenses, and reaffirmed existing law that prohibited the use of illegally seized evidence at trial.

The bill also authorized $1 billion in aid to local law-enforcement agencies and required that death row prisoners have adequate counsel as a condition to the limits on habeas corpus. It also allowed individuals sentenced to death to argue that their sentences were the result of bias by producing statistical evidence that people of their race in a given jurisdiction were more likely than others to be charged with murder or sentenced to die. It contained provisions relating to terrorism, drive-by shootings, youth violence, rural crime and drugs, drunk driving, and victims' rights. For extra measure, Biden even included the Brady Bill, legislation that would impose a waiting period on the purchase of handguns.

The Bush administration countered in mid-March with the Comprehensive Violent Crime Control Act of 1991. Like Biden's bill, it sought to expand the death penalty, but to forty offenses—four fewer than the Democrats proposed. It limited habeas corpus petitions and stiffened penalties for firearms offenses. The Bush-backed bill also included provisions relating to juvenile offenders, gangs, terrorism, victims' rights, sexual violence, and child abuse. In fact, the only provisions that really set it apart from Biden's bill were removal of the racial justice provision and its approach to illegally seized evidence. (Bush wanted to make it permissible at trial through a "good faith" exception.)

Biden's bill would pass the Senate, and the Republican bill would pass both the Senate and the House. Still, neither became law. Months of debate altered both considerably and, in the end, Bush insisted that not even the Republican bill went far enough to restrict appeals and relax evidentiary rules. He refused to sign it, putting the fight over crime on hold until 1992, a presidential election year.

Bush rekindled debate months later, during his 1992 State of the Union address. "Congress, pass my comprehensive crime bill," he pleaded. "It is tough on criminals and supportive of police, and it has been languishing in these hallowed halls for years now. Pass it. Help your country." That would never come to pass.

His failure to advance his party's agenda in 1990 and 1991 proved that Bush wasn't half the drug warrior his predecessor had been. Reagan had used stagecraft and the power of television to create urgency around the subject of drugs in 1984. When Len Bias died of an overdose in 1986, Reagan rode the wave of that tragedy to even greater success. Bush had no stagecraft, no high-profile tragedy to corral Congress around his proposals, which were even tougher measures than Reagan signed into law. Bush also had stiff competition in a new generation of Democrats. Those New Democrats were determined to win back the White House and willing to use the tactics of the Republican Party against its weakened leader.

After twelve years of being denied access to the White House, Democrats figured if they couldn't beat Republicans, they would join them. The party underwent a transformation that included rebranding, realignment on the issues, and the prioritization of candidates who reflected the voters Democrats lost in the 1960s—white men from the South, the heartland, and the blue-collar Northeast. A star emerged from this shift in Democratic politics: Arkansas governor Bill Clinton.

Clinton ran for president in 1992 arguing primarily that Republicans had tanked the economy. The national debt had ballooned, the income gap had widened, and unemployment was up. Encouraging Americans to "vote Democratic for a change," Clinton promised new jobs, affordable healthcare, and a middle-class tax cut. He also promised that he and his vice presidential running mate, Al Gore, were part of a new generation of Democrats who supported the death penalty and would end welfare. It was a nod to conservative voters who appreciated the war on drugs and Reagan's denunciations of "welfare queens," a coded phrase used to describe Black women who abused public assistance.

Clinton's resolve was tested in January 1992 with the execution of an Arkansas man named Ricky Ray Rector. Rector was on death row after being found guilty of murdering one man and then a police officer in the process of turning himself in for the initial crime. After killing the officer, Rector shot himself in the head. Despite putting a bullet through his frontal lobe, Rector survived—though with significant mental impairment. A judge ruled that he was competent enough to stand trial, and a jury ultimately convicted Rector of murder. He was sentenced to death.

By 1992, Rector's appeals were exhausted. His only hope was clemency from Governor Clinton, who was already on the campaign trail playing the part of crime fighter. Against strong objections from many, including the National Coalition to Abolish the Death Penalty and the NAACP Legal Defense Fund, Clinton allowed the execution to go forward as scheduled. He even flew to Arkansas to attend the event despite the fact that no law required the governor to be present. Clinton reportedly remarked after it was over, "I can be nicked a lot, but no one can say I'm soft on crime."

It was a defining moment for Clinton and the New Democrats. In the previous presidential election, Michael Dukakis had not only been buried by the "Revolving Door" commercial featuring Willie Horton but famously failed to support the death penalty—even in a hypothetical situation in which his own wife was raped and murdered. "I don't see any evidence [the death penalty] is a deterrent," was Dukakis's response to that odd question during a debate. "I think there are better and more effective ways to deal with violent crime." Clinton inoculated his campaign from any such test by overseeing the Rector execution. But he didn't stop there.

Still looking to establish himself as a serious candidate and shore up his tough-on-crime bona fides, Clinton traveled to the outskirts of Atlanta on the eve of Super Tuesday, 1992. There he visited a small prison boot camp at the foot of Stone Mountain, a 1,686-foot monadnock that was the site of the founding of the second Ku Klux Klan in 1915. The mountain became a Confederate memorial in 1972 when the likenesses of Stonewall Jackson, Robert E. Lee, and Jefferson Davis were carved on its north face.

At the facility, Clinton was joined by prominent Georgia Democrats—Governor Zell Miller, Senator Sam Nunn, and Congressman Ben Jones. The four men said a few words about Georgia's anti-crime efforts and Clinton's proposals and stood for photos. The backdrop was Stone Mountain, yes, but also a phalanx of uniform-clad prisoners who'd been lined up behind Clinton for the press conference. Almost all were Black men.

Photos from the event appeared in newspapers across the country the next day, including *The New York Times*. They elicited outrage from many, including Clinton's chief primary opponent, Jerry Brown, who described the scene as "a bunch of Willie Hortons" with "white guys standing in front of them like colonial masters." Clinton defended the optics, however, claiming he had visited the facility and arranged the photo opportunity to demonstrate his commitment to incarceration alternatives.

That kind of messaging was key to Clinton's political viability. In one breath, he'd argue for policies that disproportionately harmed communities of color. In the next, he'd express concern for those same communities and indignation over how they'd fared under Republican leadership. His hat trick: because crime victims were disproportionately Black, Clinton was able to pass off proposals that would hurt them more as ones intended to help. Clinton's proposals, especially pertaining to crime, were white-facing solutions to Black-facing problems.

This subtext of the 1992 election became explicit on the afternoon of April 29, 1992, when four white police officers were acquitted on charges related to their brutal attack on a Black man named Rodney King. The assault on King had been captured in an eight-minute video by a bystander just a year before. It showed a group of uniformed Los Angeles Police Department officers surrounding him on the ground and taking turns punching, kicking, and beating him with batons. One of the first examples of police brutality broadcast across the country, the King video called attention to a culture of police violence that reached a fever pitch during the war on drugs. It stunned and angered many Americans—feelings that boiled over when the officers got away with it.

Rioting erupted within hours of the verdict. It's estimated that thousands of people participated as the uprising spread from South Central Los Angeles into other areas of the city. The events lasted six days, during which a thousand properties were damaged, 63 people were killed, and 2,383 others were injured. Among the seriously injured was a white truck driver named Reginald Denny, whose route took him through South Central during the uprising. Denny was stopped by men at the intersection of Florence and Normandie Avenues, pulled out of his truck, and beaten nearly to death in a scene that mirrored Rodney King's assault.

In the wake of the L.A. Uprising, a prominent activist, author, and rapper named Sister Souljah was asked by a reporter for *The Washington Post* whether the "Black-on-white" crime that occurred that day was "wise." Sister Souljah replied: "I mean, if Black people kill Black people every day, why not have a week and kill white people? . . . Do you think that somebody thinks that white people are better, are above and beyond dying, when they would kill their own kind?" The remarks were taken by many as an endorsement of Black violence against whites, including by Bill Clinton. Or at least that was the way he made it seem during an appearance at Jesse Jackson's 1992 Rainbow Coalition Conference.

According to reports, Clinton's campaign staff had been locked in debate about how to best distance the candidate from Jackson prior to the event. Sister Souljah's presence at the conference a day before gave them an opening. At the tail end of his address, Clinton departed from his usual stump speech to blast Sister Souljah, comparing her to David Duke and calling her statements to the *Post* hate filled. The event would go down in political history as the "Sister Souljah moment," a term later applied to any public repudiation of a controversial person, group, or idea associated with one's politics.

Jackson later expressed his dismay with the candidate's surprise attack. "He was invited to our house as a guest, and he used the platform to . . . embarrass us," he complained to *The Washington Post*. "I invited him to promote unity, but he came to establish distance." Regardless of the reverend's hurt feelings, the tactic worked. The "Sister Souljah moment" marked an upturn in Clinton's popularity. After that, he moved quickly from third place in the polls to first.

Overseeing Ricky Ray Rector's execution, the stunt at Stone Mountain, the "Sister Souljah moment"—all helped put Clinton on the offensive when it came to crime. Those moments assured white voters of where Clinton stood concerning Blacks, drugs, and crime. He was at home standing before rows of Black prisoners in the shadow of the Klan and the Confederacy. He wasn't beholden to the Jesse Jacksons and Sister Souljahs of the Democratic Party. He was willing to confront them, even expose them as the real racists. He wasn't some bleeding-heart liberal who'd let a Willie Horton get away with raping his wife, or theirs.

Clinton came out fighting in the summer of 1992. In July, he made a campaign stop in Houston, Bush's adopted hometown, where he attacked the president's record on crime. Flanked by police officers at the steps of City Hall, Clinton argued that Bush was failing law enforcement by not signing the Brady Bill. "We cannot take our country back until we take our neighborhoods back," he said. "Four years ago, this crime issue was used to divide America. I want to use it to unite America. I want to be tough on crime and good for civil rights. You can't have civil justice without order and safety."

During the speech, Clinton discussed his proposal for a program that would create a pipeline from the military to police departments. He also shared his vision for military-style "boot camps" across the country for nonviolent first-time offenders. These measures, along with a ban on some automatic weapons and, of course, more funding for police and prisons, rounded out Clinton's big ideas to "take our neighborhoods back."

Throughout the campaign and during the presidential debates, Clinton would press Bush on drugs and crime, but there was largely no need. In less than a year, he'd successfully articulated what a Democratic war on drugs and crime might look like and proved he was the drug warrior the country needed, among other things. In the end, Clinton outperformed Bush with white working-class voters, turning

Arkansas, Georgia, Kentucky, Louisiana, Missouri, and Tennessee Democratic in the process. His election with 370 electoral votes ended twelve consecutive years of Republican Party control of the White House.

Clinton's campaign promises dictated that the Democratic president ramp up the war, and passing a crime bill became a major priority of the Clinton administration. "The crime bill is a means to a further end," wrote senior Clinton advisor Rahm Emanuel in a January 1994 strategy memo. "The crime bill is also a vehicle to communicate to the public a set of strongly-held values that the President embraces, as well as the President's tough stance on crime and criminals."

Black community leaders were planning preemptive opposition. January 8, 1994, marked the last day of a three-day conference on crime held by Jesse Jackson's National Rainbow Coalition. The conference pulled together Black elected officials, ministers, and business leaders and produced proposals for both government action and community programs to ease crime in Black communities.

Included in the Rainbow Coalition plan was a challenge to one hundred churches to provide mentors for at least ten young men each. The organization also proposed a youth march on Washington, on the twenty-sixth anniversary of Martin Luther King, Jr.'s assassination, to demand a coherent urban policy and a meaningful jobs bill. Last but not least, the plan called for lobbying efforts in opposition to any crime bill that might be put forward. Some present were in favor of a crime bill but many others were not.

"The crime bill should be supported by us," said Baltimore mayor Kurt Schmoke. "We do need to send a signal throughout our communities that certain types of activities will not be tolerated, that people will be held accountable, and that, if there is evil manifested by actions taken by individuals who choose to prey upon our residents, that that evil will be responded to quickly and correctly."

"I look at our crime bill as one more expense," said Clinton's surgeon general, Joycelyn Elders, who favored enhanced early-childhood educational support. "I don't see the great investment in prevention."

Congressman Kweisi Mfume of Maryland, chairman of the Congressional Black Caucus, argued the crime bill would not reduce crime, but that it would "find better ways to incarcerate people, to be tougher on those who [commit] crime, and to give us a sense that we are more secure as a result of the new prisons and the tougher sentences."

Meanwhile, the Democrat-controlled Congress had been hard at work drafting legislation for the new president to sign since the fall of 1993. House Judiciary Committee chairman Jack Brooks of Texas and Joe Biden, Judiciary Committee chairman in the Senate, both introduced bills reflecting the policies Clinton campaigned on—more cops and prisons, new death penalties, an overhaul of the death row appeals process, and a ban on assault weapons. While the Brooks bill faced challenges in the House, Biden took his bill straight to the floor and senators agreed in November 1993 to his $22.3 billion bill.

When House members returned in 1994, they decided to craft a more comprehensive response to the Senate package. In April, they voted for a $28 billion crime bill that was similar to the Senate measure but included more than twice as much money for social programs to prevent crime and excluded an assault weapons ban. It also contained the Democrats' long-sought provision to allow defendants to use sentencing statistics to challenge their death sentences as racially discriminatory.

"Politically, I think the Democrats have recaptured this issue," Chuck Schumer told *The Washington Post* after the House bill passed. "In campaign after campaign, the Republicans would attack Democrats as soft, mushy-headed, and uninterested in fighting crime. After this bill, they can't."

On July 28, the two bodies settled on a $30.2 billion version of the bill that jettisoned the House provision regarding racial bias in death penalty sentencing but agreed to keep the assault weapons ban. The measure funded hiring one hundred thousand new police officers, banned nineteen types of assault weapons, extended the death penalty to an additional sixty crimes, and provided new funding for crime prevention and prisons.

At a ceremony at the Justice Department featuring hundreds of uniformed police officers, Clinton called the legislation "the toughest, largest, smartest federal attack on crime in the history of our country." He said, "This is one of the reasons that I ran for president."

Today, the 1994 crime bill is often misremembered as a piece of legislation for which there was broad consensus, but that's not the truth. On August 12, 1994, the House actually shelved the bill on a procedural vote due to opposition to the assault-weapon ban by gun proponents and concern over the death penalty provisions. Most vocally troubled about expanding the death penalty were members of the Congressional Black Caucus, including John Lewis, Charlie Rangel, and Cleo Fields.

"I grew up with strong feelings against capital punishment," Lewis told *The New York Times*. "I think it's barbaric and should have been outlawed many years ago. It represents a period of our past and is not worthy of a great nation."

Clinton met with Lewis and other caucus members. He applied pressure to get their support. "He was selling his presidency, the party and the fact that we will not get a better bill than this," said Charlie Rangel, one of the congressmen present for the meeting. Rangel, Lewis, and others would ultimately relent and vote to bring the bill to the floor.

With a considerable number of Democrats conflicted about the legislation, it took the support of House Republicans to pass it. To secure that support, Democrats agreed to shift funds from crime-prevention programs, which Republicans dismissed as "pork" and wasteful "social programs," to more police and prisons. All told, 46 Republicans joined 188 Democrats and one independent to pass the bill. It was enough to offset the 64 Democrats who voted in opposition to the bill, the new president, and their party.

The Violent Crime Control and Law Enforcement Act of 1994 passed the Democrat-controlled House 235–195. Included in the yeas were Chuck Schumer, Nancy Pelosi, Bernie Sanders, Kweisi Mfume, Corrine Brown, Sanford Bishop, Bobby Rush, and Jim Clyburn. Twelve of the 64 Democratic nays came from members of the Congressional Black Caucus: William Clay, John Conyers, Charlie Rangel, Bobby Scott, Louis Stokes, John Lewis, Earl Hillard, Mel Watt, Don Payne, Cleo Fields, Maxine Waters, and Ron Dellums.

The bill passed the Senate 95–4. The only Democratic senators to vote against the 1994 Crime Act were Russ Feingold of Wisconsin and Paul Simon of Illinois. Among the Democrats who voted for it were stars of the party: Ted Kennedy, Robert Byrd, Joe Biden, Pat Moynihan, Dianne Feinstein, John Glenn, John Kerry, Harry Reid, Carol Moseley Braun, and Barbara Boxer.

Senate majority leader George Mitchell rightfully claimed the crime bill for his party. "This is a Democratic bill. The principal author of the bill is a Democrat. The principal supporter for this bill is a Democratic president," he boasted.

"Today the bickering stops," said President Clinton at a White House signing ceremony attended by police officials, big-city mayors, members of Congress, and relatives of homicide victims. "The era of excuses is over; the law-abiding citizens of our country have made their voices heard. Never again should Washington put politics and party above law and order."

Congresswoman Cynthia McKinney of Georgia, a Congressional Black Caucus member, said the final bill contained "an ounce of prevention, a pound of punishment, and a ton of politics." Still, it hobbled into the Senate the week of August 22, 1994. Debate lasted three days, and on August 25, just before 11 p.m., the bill cleared both houses of Congress.

As passed, the 1994 Crime Act authorized $8.8 billion over six years to support the hiring of one hundred thousand new police officers across the country. It provided another $7.9 billion in grants to the states for the construction of new prisons and boot camps. Of that, half was set aside for states that adopted "truth-in-sentencing" laws, which required repeat violent offenders to serve at least 85 percent of their sentences. Another $1.8 billion was authorized to reimburse states for the incarceration of undocumented immigrants.

The bill did provide $6.9 billion in funding for crime-prevention programs, including $1.6 billion in grants for programs designed to reduce crimes against women and $1 billion for drug courts as an incarceration alternative for first-time or nonviolent drug offenders. The lion's share of the funding authorized by the bill, $30.2 billion, would be held in a general "crime trust fund" and used to pay for any programs authorized by the legislation.

In terms of new laws, it banned for ten years the manufacture, sale, or possession of nineteen different types of assault weapons as well as ammunition-feeding devices that held more than ten rounds. It authorized the death penalty for dozens of federal crimes, including treason, kidnappings resulting in death, and murder of a federal law-enforcement official. Notably, it mandated life imprisonment for a third violent felony, commonly known as the "three strikes" provision.

The 1994 Crime Act also included some particularly callous provisions aimed, it seemed, at cruelty for the sake of tough-on-crime politics. It allowed juveniles as young as thirteen to be tried as adults in federal court for certain violent crimes and crimes involving guns. It also ended college funding for the incarcerated by making them ineligible for Pell grants. The last measure even drew the ire of conservative *Washington Post* columnist George Will, who called the elimination of Pell grants for prisoners an act of "grandstanding and chest-thumping" by "Sheriff Clinton" and a Congress full of "would-be Wyatt Earps hot to be deputized."

34

—

KURT

(1992-96)

IT APPEARED TO MANY that Kurt Schmoke was out of steam by 1992. He'd been mayor for five years and was in the middle of his second term, and newspapers were already speculating about the end of his career. "It's Not Easy Being Mayor," declared *The Washington Post*. The profile of Schmoke questioned whether he'd someday be a Maryland senator or governor and, if that was what he wanted, why he'd picked a stepping-stone as precarious as mayor of Baltimore.

Local and national press frequently described him as "cerebral" and "aloof," more of a thinker than a doer. It was true that he hadn't put up many points on the board, big shiny wins he could point to as successes of his administration. However, the nineties brought with them the potential to change that. After twelve years of Republican control of the White House, political winds were finally shifting, and it just so happened that Schmoke's Ivy League background would help him navigate them.

As Bill Clinton's star rose, Schmoke, who'd befriended Hillary Clinton when both were at Yale, found he had a potential ally headed to the White House. Schmoke became an early and key supporter of

Clinton's. He campaigned for him in Maryland and in New York state, and called on other mayors around the country to endorse the candidate. Schmoke also helped draft the campaign's urban policy position, which Clinton unveiled during a visit to West Baltimore.

From the pulpit of Douglas Memorial Community Church, Clinton promised "not just a deal but a solemn agreement to create new opportunity" in urban centers. Schmoke spoke in identical terms months later as he addressed the crowd at the Democratic National Convention (he also had the distinction of being the only mayor of a major city appointed to the convention's platform-drafting committee). In his speech, he accused the Bush administration of "trashing cities and the people who live in them" and said Clinton would bring a "new covenant"—investment in children, higher education, job training, healthcare, infrastructure, and the environment.

Schmoke was in Little Rock with Clinton on Election Day and was overjoyed when his candidate won. His name was being floated for a spot in the president-elect's cabinet, but Schmoke saw the election as even more reason to stick things out in Baltimore. He would finally get the chance to be a mayor with access to funds, a real opportunity to bring about change.

How he and voters in Baltimore would be rewarded for their support was still unclear. In their personal conversations, Clinton explained to Schmoke that there would still be fiscal constraints under his administration. And Schmoke, of course, respected that Clinton couldn't just throw billions at cities. Nevertheless, he believed that the new president's agenda aligned with Baltimore's needs, and that Clinton would do what he could to help the city.

"I liked that he recognized that federal government was not going to be able to give us a lot and that we needed to do it in other ways," Schmoke told *The Baltimore Sun*. "He understood that we need more flexibility in spending the money we are already getting, in being able to cut bureaucratic red tape. He was supportive of programs initiated at the neighborhood level up rather than federal government down."

Schmoke worked to advance his refined vision of medicalization for addicts and law enforcement for dealers. In 1992, he installed a young doctor named Peter Beilenson as Baltimore City Health Commissioner and, anticipating that some federal funding might eventually materialize, the pair got to work on making Baltimore a model city for medicalization.

In many ways, the 1992 presidential election was a restart for Schmoke. Getting in early on the Clinton campaign paid off. It gave him a friend in the White House, a powerful ally who owed him favors. It also helped restore some confidence in his administration, which had been plagued for years by talk that the mayor lacked the killer instinct it took to get things done. Heading into 1993, Schmoke had some of his political capital back, and he wouldn't hesitate to spend it.

In the spring of 1993, Schmoke created the Mayor's Working Group on Drug Policy. He charged its seventeen members—addiction specialists, public-health researchers, experts in law enforcement, and local political operatives—with studying Baltimore's drug problem and developing strategies to address it. Members included Beilenson; Judge Robert Bell of the Maryland Court of Appeals; Arnold S. Trebach, president of the Drug Policy Foundation; and David M. Altshuler, a research scientist at the Johns Hopkins Institute for Policy Studies, as group moderator.

At the group's first meeting, Schmoke's only directive was that they feel free to go wherever the best ideas led. With that, he left them to their own devices. Following the mayor's directive, they started with the long shots: legalization, needle exchanges, amphetamines to help wean cocaine addicts off the substance. All ideas were considered, but in the end, the group agreed to limit their proposals to those that had a chance of being implemented.

The group pushed and prodded the ideas in subsequent meetings. They questioned the risks involved with each—legal challenges, the potential impact on hospitals and the courts. They even weighed public opinion on certain ideas and the political implications of recommending them. The group also discussed European harm-reduction models—legalized marijuana in the Netherlands, what made Amsterdam's methadone clinics a success, and the failure of a needle-exchange program in Zurich.

Ultimately, the group whittled their ideas down to a set of practical proposals that the City of Baltimore could implement without a change in federal law or a vote in the state legislature. Their report, released in September 1993, recommended the expansion of methadone programs, a needle-exchange program, and a shift in law-enforcement priorities from nonviolent drug users to drug traffickers. It also called for the creation of a "drug court" to steer nonviolent users into treatment, and training for doctors, nurses, and pharmacists so they might better recognize and treat addiction.

"Some people would view this report as being radical," Schmoke told *The Baltimore Sun*. "I view it as calling for reform rather than revolution and incremental change rather than a radical reversal of policy."

Truly, what the Mayor's Working Group on Drug Policy put forward went a long way to reduce the harm associated with addiction. It showed, for example, that crime decreased where methadone was readily available. And that, with between ten thousand and thirteen thousand of Baltimore's thirty-five thousand intravenous drug users carrying the HIV/AIDS virus, a needle-exchange program had tremendous potential to reduce the rate of transmission in the city. Finally, with 57 percent of drug arrests in 1992 for mere possession, the creation of a drug court could free up resources and allow law enforcement to focus on drug dealers.

Nonetheless, the report was the target of criticism from all over. First were the opponents of methadone maintenance, who argued that the programs only transfer a heroin addict's dependency from one substance to another. A number of people were also against needle exchanges. Both Baltimore's state's attorney Stuart O. Simms and Mike Gimbel, director of the Baltimore County Office of Substance Abuse, expressed their doubts publicly. "Our ultimate goal should be to make people drug-free," Gimbel said. Simms said he had "very significant concerns" about the impact of needle-exchange programs in particular. "Are we exchanging the possibility of lower AIDS infection rates for longer addiction cycles?" he asked.

Maryland governor William Schaefer was yet another critic. Even before reading the report, a representative for his office expressed skepticism. "[Addiction] should be treated as a legal problem," said Page Boinest, the governor's press secretary. "He thinks you shouldn't change the priority simply to drug dealers, but you have to keep pressure on all segments of drug use, from the kingpin down to the single user." Schaefer vowed to oppose any change in state law that would permit needle-exchange programs outside of "a limited, strictly controlled pilot program."

Even if the report had been favorably received, there was still the matter of money. Baltimore had very little to spare, and its lack of resources presented perhaps the biggest hurdle to expanding drug treatment services. In 1993, Baltimore spent just over $150,000 on drug treatment programs, and with no new revenue on the horizon, the only immediate option for funding the working group's proposals was raising taxes.

Just as Schmoke's vision for medicalization was taking shape, so was the Clinton administration's anti-drug policy. In April 1993, shortly after Schmoke's working group met for the first time, Clinton unveiled a $13.04 billion anti-drug budget that barely deviated from those of his Republican predecessors. It designated $8.30 billion for law enforcement and $4.74 billion for rehabilitation and education—a proportional split of 63.66 percent to 36.34 percent—about 1 percent more for demand reduction than Bush had included in his last drug budget. Overall, the Clinton budget proposal increased the funding of anti-drug enforcement efforts to four times what they had been under Reagan.

Weeks later, Clinton named Lee P. Brown, the former New York City police commissioner, director of the Office of National Drug Control Policy, an office Clinton elevated to the cabinet level while simultaneously slashing its funding from $17.3 billion to $5.8 billion and reducing the staff from 146 to just 25. Announcing the appointment, Clinton said, "It's time to turn our attention home," and pledged to shift away from interdiction programs to focus more on community policing.

Rightfully, the budget and the hiring of Brown made many reformers skeptical of Clinton's commitment to turning the tide in the nation's war on drugs. The skepticism was affirmed that fall, in October 1993, when Brown finally shared the White House's anti-drug plan, which was an echo of the budget—both of them miles away from the dream of treatment on demand that Clinton sold when he was campaigning.

People speculated that Clinton's resolve had evaporated or was never there from the start. Schmoke, however, was undeterred, and on November 24, 1993, he wrote the president a letter asking him to rethink his approach: "I think it is imperative that we view substance abuse as a public-health problem and treat it as such by reversing the current balance of funding related to illicit drugs from 70 percent for law enforcement and 30 percent for treatment/prevention."

If Clinton was considering Schmoke's letter, he stopped in December 1993, when Surgeon General Joycelyn Elders, in an appearance before the National Press Club, recommended that the federal government study the idea of legalizing drugs.

"I do feel that we would markedly reduce our crime rate if drugs were legalized," Elders said in response to a question. "But I don't know all of the ramifications of this. I do feel that we need to do some studies. And some of the countries that have legalized drugs and made it legal, they certainly have shown that there has been a reduction in their crime rate and there has been no increase in their drug use rate."

Mirroring what happened to Schmoke in 1988, opponents of the Clinton administration swarmed on the remarks. "Americans must be wondering if the surgeon general is hazardous to our health," said Senator Bob Dole of Kansas, then the minority leader. Clinton, succumbing to the pressure, reportedly censured Elders in private and publicly distanced himself from her. "The president is firmly against legalizing drugs, and he is not inclined in this case to even study the issue," said White House spokeswoman Dee Dee Myers. (Within a year, Elders would be forced to resign from her post.)

In February 1994, the Clinton administration surprised many when it revised its anti-drug budget, allocating more money for drug treatment and programs to prevent drug abuse. Though Clinton did not accept Schmoke's 70/30 formula, he came close, budgeting a 60/40 split between law enforcement and treatment/prevention. "I think the strategy moves in the right direction," Schmoke told *The Baltimore Sun*.

The mayor named the needle-exchange bill a top priority moving forward. He even discussed with his health commissioner, Peter Beilenson, the possibility of simply launching the program and forcing Governor Schaefer to send state police to shut it down. Before it got to that, he and Beilenson lobbied legislators and Schaefer's secretary of health. They impressed representatives from Baltimore with the sheer number of HIV/AIDS cases in the city and representatives from outside the city with how much money could be saved by reducing rates of infection.

The arguments were persuasive. Opposition to the bill never materialized, and by the time Schmoke and Beilenson testified at hearings, legislators were sharing their own connections to the diseases. Elijah Cummings, then a delegate in the Maryland House, spoke of the funerals he attended at his church almost weekly. Representative Ruth Kirk spoke emotionally of her own brothers, who had died from AIDS contracted from drug use.

When the vote was finally called, the bill passed 83–57 in the State House and squeaked by in the Senate 24–23. Governor Schaefer signed the legislation, which allowed a three-year pilot program, into law May 2, 1994. He said it was a bill "I do not favor [and] do not like," but in signing it, noted that it was time to try something new.

On the morning of August 12, 1994, a cream-colored Winnebago parked on North Caroline Street slid open its door and staffers with the Baltimore Health Department began collecting and distributing syringes. For each needle turned in, participants in the program were given a clean needle marked with a barcode. Staffers also talked to participants, whom they also tested and treated for HIV, tuberculosis, and syphilis.

1994 was the height of Schmoke's success in creating a more humane response to drugs in Baltimore. It was far from what he envisioned when he first floated the idea of broad decriminalization before the Conference of Mayors, but it was also the most he could achieve with limited funds and limited supports.

He established Baltimore's needle-exchange program in August, but earlier in the year also launched the city's drug-treatment court to steer addicts away from jail and toward treatment and other social services. Paid for with $2.3 million in federal grants, the court was created to serve six hundred defendants, thereby reducing caseloads in criminal court and, ideally, prison populations.

PEOPLE SPECULATED FOR YEARS that Kurt Schmoke would run for higher office, either governor or U.S. Senate. 1994 would have been the year to make a move, but ultimately he didn't. Instead, Schmoke vowed to finish the work he started in Baltimore and ran for a third term as mayor.

The race would become a referendum on his leadership and so much of what he represented. There were concerns over how Schmoke had handled Baltimore's public schools. And, as mayor, he held the bag for the continued decline of the city—population and job losses, rising crime, and the rest. On a much deeper level, there were also plenty of people who simply felt as though the era of the Black mayor was over, that Schmoke and others had had their shot and it was time to move on.

It made sense, then, that Schmoke's opponent in the 1995 mayoral race would be city council president Mary Pat Clarke, a white populist and former schoolteacher who fashioned herself a "doer"—in contrast to Schmoke, a thinker.

Clarke was known throughout her time on the council as someone who *didn't* look before she leapt, who made bold declarations that weren't always thought out but who tried to troubleshoot the everyday problems residents faced. In that sense, she was in the mold of William Schaefer, Schmoke's predecessor, known for driving around Baltimore looking for potholes to fill.

Clarke sometimes proposed legislation without considering the cost, attempted to rush bills through council without the necessary support, and generally made promises she couldn't keep. For this, she earned her fair share of detractors—but also supporters, who saw her as a regular person trying everything she could.

She became an avatar for the frustrations that residents had with the state of things in Baltimore, and Clarke placed every grievance, each complaint, at the feet of Kurt Schmoke. He was a good guy, she said, but had failed to turn the city around—a feat she thought possible with more forceful, common-sense leadership. She was Baltimore's Great White Hope.

For all the energy Clarke's campaign created, including an endorsement from the *Sun,* Schmoke was characteristically unfazed— even when polls showed them in a statistical dead heat. An August 1995 profile of the mayor described him as "tranquil" while facing both the challenges presented by his difficult job and the Clarke campaign.

"In Schmokespace things might be bad but not that bad," the story read. "Not so bad that they cannot be helped by this program or that grant. The mayor has an answer, or he's researching an answer or he's awaiting a report or he's blowing up a high-rise and putting up something new. In the rubble he finds hope, in the dust he plots a new course. One step at a time."

Schmoke had reason to be confident. He was an incumbent. He had the support of Maryland's new governor, Parris Glendening, and

President Clinton. With $1.3 million raised for his campaign, he could also outspend Clarke on TV and radio ads, mailers, and other campaign materials. Schmoke had also never lost anything. His path from class president at Baltimore City College to the mayor's office had been marked with one win after the other. But could Kurt Schmoke win yet again?

When he first ran for mayor, his Ivy League background, experience as a prosecutor, and progressive ideas made Schmoke a candidate everyone could get behind. He received high-profile support from key figures in Baltimore, Black and white. He also won the endorsement of *The Baltimore Sun*. It all came together to de-racialize Schmoke, to make him the first man elected mayor of Baltimore who happened to be Black.

But more than seven years of handling issues like crime, budgets, education, and housing in a big city steeped him in Blackness. He was the Black mayor of an increasingly Black city plagued by problems many associated with Black people.

Schmoke had never received more than 25 percent of the city's white vote, and with every swipe Clarke took at him for being out of touch, she threatened to also peel away the support of frustrated Black voters. The Schmoke campaign, led again by Larry Gibson, read the racial politics of the moment and decided not to ignore but to engage them. For the first time ever, Schmoke geared his campaign explicitly toward Black voters, white resentment be damned.

The campaign secured the endorsement of Baltimore's Black newspaper, the *Afro-American*. It took to the streets blaring a recorded message from actor Charles Dutton (star of the Fox sitcom *Roc*). It also distributed red, black, and green bumper stickers and posters with the slogan SCHMOKE MAKES US PROUD, a pan-African reminder to folks that they were at risk of losing their Black mayor, as other cities had.

The bold appeal infuriated some who accused Schmoke of "playing the race card," but his campaign insisted that the message merely summed up the general sentiment around the mayor. "I'm not apologetic at all," Schmoke told the *Sun* when questioned about his tactics. "For the majority population of this city, those colors have traditionally been symbols of pride and empowerment, not division."

Once again, his calculations paid off. The race was supposed to be a squeaker. Polls had Schmoke and Clarke neck and neck in the final days of the campaign. He beat her by a landslide—59 to 39 percent.

Schmoke took the oath of office for a third time on December 7, 1996. The ceremony was a celebration of the "spirit of Baltimore," as Schmoke put it. The event also went to great lengths to highlight the city's diversity, with performances by groups ranging from a troupe of Irish step dancers to a choir from Morgan State University, a nearby historically Black college.

"Our city is going to get stronger and stronger," Schmoke told attendees. "We'll have a diverse economy that provides jobs for people who will work hard to get themselves trained. We'll have fewer vacant houses and more home ownership to stabilize the city, and this is going to be a cleaner and safer city."

35

—

SHAWN

(1994)

THE FOLLOWING MONTHS WERE a blur for Shawn as he just sort of drifted from day to day. Bertina did her best to keep his spirits high, but it was hard for Shawn to get happy again after Mad Dog died. He'd be just minding his business and, without warning, be reminded of what happened. He stopped going to parties, stopped hanging on the block, stopped doing most things except going to work at Budget.

He'd done so well by then that he was asked to become a manager in charge of three locations. Shawn had already helped his boy Andre get a job there, and once he became a manager, he helped others get on, including his brother, Tony. The job came with a company car and a decent salary, enough for him to quit hustling altogether, which he promptly did, for good this time.

As Shawn fell back, the Zoo Crew continued to blow up. Naughty by Nature had a song on their album *Poverty's Paradise* where they said, "Zoo Crew niggas are the craziest." Queen Latifah wore a Zoo Crew jersey on an episode of her sitcom *Living Single*. Celebrities like Chi-Ali, Biz Markie, Ol' Dirty Bastard, and Chris Webber would visit members of the infamous crew when they were in Newark. It was bittersweet for Shawn, but not even celebrity status was enough to keep him in the streets after what happened to Mad Dog.

He was complaining to a friend one day about the tournament system in Newark when the friend asked why he didn't start his own program. Shawn had played on teams for most of his life at that point, and that had never occurred to him. To his credit, he didn't just let the words go in one ear and out the other but did some research into what it might take. It turned out not much. After a trip to the New Jersey Department of the Treasury, the Zoo Crew Basketball Program was born in March 1996.

Shawn pulled together a team from kids in the neighborhood. They weren't unlike him when he was younger, hanging out around basketball courts in search of anything to do with their time. Some he knew from around the way.

The first tournament was put on by the Amateur Athletic Union and held at St. Mary High School in Rutherford, New Jersey. The winner would advance to a regional tournament in Akron, Ohio—a big deal for the kids, most of whom had never been outside of the Central Ward.

The competition was tough, but the Zoo Crew team worked its way through the tournament, all the way to the championship. They played better than Shawn could have imagined in the final game, keeping the score tight. They trailed by three points in the last few minutes of the game, but then they got a steal and a layup, which cut the other team's lead down to one point. With less than thirty seconds remaining, a Zoo Crew player stole the ball. There was no one between him and the hoop. He could have driven toward it for a wide-open layup, but he didn't. Instead, he made an abrupt stop at the three-point line and let the ball fly. The next few seconds felt like minutes as Shawn watched the ball come down and sink through the net. The boy turned to him and yelled, "I got it! I got it!" It was the happiest Shawn had been in a very long time.

Shawn put up the money for the team to compete in Ohio. He paid everyone's entry fees, rented a fifteen-passenger van, and secured the hotel rooms. It wasn't cheap, but he couldn't have cared less. He wasn't even upset when his team lost all four of its games. Coaching had lifted him out of his depression.

Shawn was headed home from a practice one night and stopped at a light. He looked over to the sidewalk and saw two boys fighting. Both looked to be no older than twelve. A woman was trying to pull one of the boys away, but he was having none of it. "Get the fuck off me," he yelled as he swung wildly. Then Shawn saw another woman run toward the melee. She shouted, "Eman, that's your mother!"

"His mother?" Shawn thought. Something came over him, and he hopped out of the car, ran over, and snatched the boy up. Away from the fight, he tried to talk some sense into him. The boy huffed and puffed, but he listened, or at the very least he stopped cursing for a second. Once he was calm, Shawn returned him to his mother and got back in his car. Shawn was driving again a few months later when he saw the boy walking across Bergen Street with a radio in his hand. Shawn pulled over and asked where he was headed. "To school," the boy said. Shawn knew he was lying, because it was already past 9:00 A.M., and the nearest school was in the opposite direction. He told the boy to get in the car, that he'd take him to school.

On the way, they started talking. The boy, Eman, went to Camden Middle. Shawn asked whether he was allowed to bring a radio to school. The kid replied with a smile, "I'm Eman; I do what I want." Shawn didn't know why, but he found the kid charming. Eman had some behavior issues—that much was obvious—but also seemed self-aware, like he was in on the joke. Plus, the kid said he was nice on the court.

Before Eman got out of the car, Shawn invited him to come by the Bergen Street playground to practice with his team. Eman said he'd think about it, which was as good as Shawn could hope for.

Sure enough, Eman showed up that Saturday, late and with a much smaller boy in tow. His name was Des, Eman said. Des was eight years old and wanted to play, too. At the time, the youngest boys on Shawn's team were eleven years old, but it was clear by the look on Eman's face that they were a package deal. He was loyal, Shawn thought. That made him like Eman more.

Once practice got going, Shawn could see that Eman did have some skills, but he needed the discipline that could only come from proper coaching. He loved to play, for instance, but would inevitably lose his temper when the game got serious. He'd miss a shot or catch a foul and be ready to fight.

Shawn took Eman under his wing after that. He coached him like all the other kids but would also visit him at home every now and then. He would take him to get something to eat or drive him over to Jersey City to cruise the strip—anything to change his environment for a few hours. They had the kind of conversations Shawn had had with Tariq when he was a kid, the kind he wished he'd had with his dad.

What Eman lacked on the court he made up for in influence. It turned out that he was something like the Man among the boys in the neighborhood. And once he started coming to practice, the rest followed. He brought his cousins Bap, Do-Do, Huggy, and Butter, along with his friends Keshawn and Ramon. Before long, most of the boys who lived on Avon Avenue were playing in Shawn's program.

Running the basketball program kept him so busy that there was no time for the other stuff. He quit his job at Budget to focus on it and opted instead to manage Zoo Sportswear part-time for Terrance. But even that eventually took a back seat to practices, games, and trips to play in different tournaments. One day, Shawn looked up and was no longer a drug dealer but a full-time coach.

From there, the Zoo Crew Basketball team entered tournaments in Ohio and Rhode Island. Shawn also created *Zoo Sporting Newz*, a biweekly newspaper that covered youth sports in the city and was given out at local high schools. The paper, the tournaments, all of it was funded with money the kids themselves earned by selling candy bars. Indeed, the boys in the program lived up to their namesake as they quickly mastered the art of street sales.

Shawn's life had come full circle. Basketball had been his life raft growing up. It kept him afloat no matter what trouble came. It afforded him a private school education, got him into and pulled him through college. It might have even kept him out of prison on more than one occasion. Now he was passing it on, in the same way coaches had done for him.

IT WAS JUNE 8, 1997, and Shawn was with Terrance at Sultan's house on South Tenth Street. It had been a beautiful day as they played cards and Sultan set up for a get-together that he was hosting that night. Before that could happen, though, they got word that there was a big disturbance involving the police near the corner store on Clinton and Chadwick. As far as they knew, whatever was going on didn't involve the Zoo Crew, but it was happening in their neighborhood, so Shawn, Terrance, and Sultan left to go check it out.

It was pandemonium when they got there. People were screaming and crying. Police and ambulances were everywhere, and what looked like an unmarked police car was wrecked in front of the store. The story, Shawn learned, was that Shitty, a thirteen-year-old kid from the block, was walking out of the store when a woman asked him for some change. The woman was Dannette Daniels, a neighborhood addict everyone knew as Strawberry. Shitty gave her a quarter, but the two cops who apparently saw it all go down thought he was serving her crack.

Shitty took off running, and one of the cops gave chase. The other threw Strawberry, who happened to be pregnant, against a car. People said he roughed her up trying to put handcuffs on her bony wrists. Eventually, he gave up and tossed her in the back seat of his unmarked car so he could help his partner with Shitty, who was by then in cuffs. He hadn't remembered, however, that his keys were still in the ignition.

Strawberry tried to get away by climbing into the driver's seat and putting the car in reverse. The cop saw it happening and dove into the driver's-side window to stop her. The two tussled as the car raced backward across Clinton Avenue. Then there was a gunshot and a crash. When the smoke cleared, Strawberry was dead from a bullet to the neck.

The police tried to cover the car, with her body still inside, to block the view, but it was too late. Word of what happened had spread through the neighborhood, and a crowd had formed on the scene. Then things got ugly. People started hurling insults at the police. A few guys went around slashing the tires on the squad cars. It would have turned into an all-out riot had it not been for Amiri Baraka and his son Ras, who came on the scene to keep the peace.

Shawn wasn't familiar with Amiri Baraka, the Newark-born writer and activist who initiated the powerful Black Arts Movement, but he'd heard about Ras. At the time, Ras was leading an organization called the Black Nia FORCE. It was a community group that, among other things, went around the city passing out *Know Your Rights* pamphlets focused on police misconduct and abuse.

After getting the crowd to disperse, the Barakas came by Chadwick to talk. They said they wanted to put together a protest and needed the Zoo Crew to join them. Shawn had never participated in anything like a march or rally, but he liked the Barakas immediately, especially the elder Baraka, who had a way of talking to young people.

The first protest occurred about a week after Strawberry was killed. It started with a march from Zoo Sportswear down Clinton Avenue to Broad Street, right to the steps of City Hall, where Mayor Sharpe James was holding a press conference. Shawn was amazed to see the protest grow bigger and bigger as they passed through the city and chanted, "No justice, no peace! We're tired of crooked-ass police!" The crowd was nearly three hundred deep by the time it reached City Hall.

The mayor was there doing damage control. Investigations were underway, he said, but in the meantime Robert Leaks, the officer who killed Strawberry, would be suspended without pay. Then Terrance was invited to make a statement as an organizer of the protest. In his remarks, he complained about the abuses of Newark police and promised to march on City Hall every week until Officer Leaks was arrested. He closed by saying, "If I see the police officer, I will arrest him my damn self."

His comments put a target on the Zoo Crew. Newark's finest were so upset with the protest that they organized their own. They had T-shirts made that read BLUE CREW on the front. On the back, they had the words ZOO CREW, behind bars.

Clifford Minor, the older Black judge who had gone light on Shawn after his first arrest, was by then the Essex County prosecutor, and he was sending word to Terrance that he wanted any further protests called off. When Terrance failed to respond, Minor's office subpoenaed him to come in. It was all an effort, it seemed, to intimidate the Zoo Crew and keep them from causing more trouble. Terrance buckled under the pressure. He stopped attending the protests after visiting Minor. Still, they continued without him, thanks to the constant efforts of the Barakas and other activists.

It never occurred to Shawn or anyone else that they should have stayed out of civic affairs because they were drug dealers. They didn't think of themselves as only that. As far as they were concerned, they were businessmen and some of the only people with influence in their neighborhood. They thought they had a duty to be involved.

The Newark Police Department felt differently. Officers with the Fifth Precinct began a campaign of harassment against the Zoo Crew. They stopped and frisked members on the street and drove past Terrance's store a few times a day, just to let him know that he was being watched.

While everyone waited to see who'd blink first, Shawn was busy running his program, which had grown to include kids of all ages, boys and girls. That September, he had kids in three different age groups playing in the Below the Rim tournament, which lasted a whole week. To Shawn's delight, all three of his teams made it to the championship. His heart swelled with pride as people came up to him and congratulated him on the success of his program.

Shawn was lying in bed around 6 A.M. on the morning of the championship games when his phone rang. The speaker said, "It's Ras Baraka." Before Shawn could ask how he got his number, Baraka said the police were out rounding up other Zoo Crew members. Shawn didn't think to ask how he knew. He just took the call as a warning.

Shawn hung up and ran to his front door. There were two people meandering outside, waiting to be served. Shawn asked if they'd seen any police. One said she saw police raiding the store on Clinton Avenue. "They have on federal agent jackets," she added. Shawn felt sick to his stomach. He'd been in trouble before, but something in him said that this time was serious. He hadn't touched any drugs in months, but he had no idea how far back any investigation might have gone, what they might have on him.

Shawn got dressed and waited on his couch for the feds to come bursting through his door. The hours ticked by, but they never came. He left for the tournament eventually, feeling an uneasy relief. His worst fear was that the police might arrest him in the middle of coaching a game, but still, he couldn't let the kids down by not showing up. Shawn wasn't the praying type, but on the way to the game he found himself repeating the same promise to God: "They'll never get another chance. Unless I get a parking ticket. That's the only way."

Shawn coached that night like it was the last game he might ever see. The team returned his energy, playing their hearts out. All three teams won their championships and the police never showed up. It was a bittersweet day for the Zoo Crew.

36
—

CONSPIRACY
(1980–98)

MANY ARE ADAMANT THAT the crack epidemic was orchestrated by the U.S. government to disrupt communities of color, poor Black communities in particular. It's not a far-fetched theory, given this nation's penchant for terrorizing its Black citizens and the countless points at which the rising epidemic was noted by officials but ignored.

Crack's timing was also curious. It had mysterious origins and a convenient rise during a period when the government seemed desperate for an excuse to subdue urban America. The epidemic gave rise to tough-on-crime politics and politicians who refused time and time again to enact public-health solutions to a public-health crisis. Instead, they accelerated mass incarceration in the United States, creating what legal scholar Michelle Alexander describes in her book *The New Jim Crow* as "an enormous system of racial and social control." How could a phenomenon that accomplished so much well-timed, targeted destruction be an accident?

That's not to mention the laundry list of policies that produced the epidemic. Blacks and Latinos were economically isolated in ghettos. Compounding that vulnerability was a profound grief, the result of everything they lost in the sixties and seventies—assassinations of leaders, destruction of their communities from riots, a Civil Rights Movement that cost them so much but ultimately missed the mark of securing opportunity and freedom.

Add to that the U.S. government's unbelievably wrongheaded approach to eradicating drug use in America. Officials focused on marijuana and heroin as major threats to public health. Meanwhile, Americans were developing a taste for cocaine as the substance became cheaper and more widely available—coincidentally, due to the federal government's failure to effectively monitor the airways used by drug traffickers. Then, inexplicably, knowledge of the chemical process by which the alkaloid base could be "freed" from cocaine hydrochloride found its way to South Central Los Angeles, from which it spread to other urban centers around the country.

That's the story of the crack epidemic told through happenstance. Existing along the same timeline is evidence that government officials were well aware of the large quantities of cocaine coming into the United States. In fact, it appears that they facilitated it. Such a claim may seem wild on its face, but the evidence is hiding in plain sight—in news reports, government documents, and the firsthand accounts of individuals involved.

Ronald Reagan became president in 1981 and set out immediately to win the decades-long Cold War between the Soviet Union and the United States. Not only did Reagan seek an end to the Soviet Union, he wanted to wipe communism from the face of the earth. His plan wasn't to declare war on the communist nations of Europe, Asia, and the Americas but to destabilize them by providing overt and covert aid to anticommunist movements within their borders. The Reagan Doctrine, as it was called, meant actively interfering in the affairs of sovereign nations. It was imperialism through manipulation instead of conquest.

Nicaragua was central to these efforts. The United States had occupied the Central American country from 1912 to 1933. Following the occupation, Nicaragua oscillated between civil war and peace, marked by the installation of United States–backed dictators. This continued until 1979, when a socialist group known as the Sandinista National Liberation Front overthrew Anastasio Somoza Debayle, a dictator whose family had controlled the country with the support of the United States since 1936.

The rise of the Sandinistas would not be tolerated by Reagan and other cold warriors, who viewed it as a threat to global democracy and to U.S. economic interests in the region. After all, there were 168 U.S. businesses in Nicaragua before the Sandinistas came into power, including major corporations like IBM, Xerox, Citibank, Bank of America, Chevron, General Mills, Texaco, and Nabisco.

Upon assuming the presidency, Reagan halted economic aid to Nicaragua, citing the Sandinistas' support of a leftist uprising in El Salvador. Then, in November 1982, he signed the top-secret National Security Decision Directive 17. The document authorized $19 million for the CIA to recruit, train, and arm a five-hundred-man force of Nicaraguan rebels to conduct covert actions against the new Sandinista regime.

These Contras—Spanish for "against" and short for "counter-revolution"—were mostly ex-members of the Somoza-aligned Nicaraguan National Guard who'd retreated to nearby Honduras when the Sandinistas rose to power. With the support of the U.S. government, they initiated terror campaigns in Nicaragua, targeting civilians with kidnapping, torture, rape, and execution in an effort to put pressure on the Sandinistas.

The Reagan administration's proxy war in Nicaragua was unpopular from its inception. Upon learning of the CIA's activities, Representative Edward Boland of Massachusetts, chairman of the House Intelligence Committee, proposed legislation in December 1982 to prohibit the federal government from providing any military support "for the purpose of overthrowing the Government of Nicaragua." Reagan reluctantly signed the bill into law later that month but continued to advocate for assistance to the Contras.

His administration argued that no act of Congress could interfere with the president's powers as commander in chief of the armed forces. With that in mind, it set out to circumvent Congress by seeking secret aid for the Contras from private entities and foreign governments. Vice Admiral John M. Poindexter, who was the military assistant to the National Security Advisor under Reagan, and his deputy, Lieutenant Colonel Oliver "Ollie" North, were put in charge of the effort, which they called "the Enterprise."

With North as the point man, the administration solicited support from countries including Taiwan, South Korea, Israel, and Saudi Arabia. In fact, the administration was so adamant about supporting the Contras that it funneled funds to the fighters through a private, tax-exempt organization called the National Endowment for the Preservation of Liberty. The administration had even riskier schemes, however, and one became public in November 1986 when a Lebanese magazine revealed that a CIA-owned cargo plane carrying arms had been shot down over Nicaragua.

The sole survivor was a U.S. marine named Eugene Hasenfus, who started talking almost as soon as he was captured by the Sandinistas. Hasenfus admitted that he was part of a CIA mission to drop weapons to the Contras. He explained how he had been recruited by a friend in the CIA, that he had previously dropped supplies to CIA agents in Southeast Asia, and that two of the other men flying with him were Cuban American CIA agents and close associates of former CIA director George H. W. Bush, then vice president of the United States. Hasenfus would later recant his statements, but the connection to the U.S. government was confirmed when documents recovered from the downed plane, including a business card, were traced back to Ollie North's office.

The Iran-Contra Affair, as it was dubbed by the press, marked a low point for the Reagan administration. Officials were caught red-handed, and the details of the administration's criminal activity leaked out slowly through news reports, public statements, and congressional hearings. Indeed, the scandal was so major that it shifted attention away from Reagan's war on drugs at its height, months after the death of Len Bias and just one month after the passage of the 1986 Anti-Drug Abuse Act.

The two things, the Iran-Contra Affair and the war on drugs, seemed separate on their face, but buried in the stories of secret weapons shipments were whispers of Contra involvement in the trafficking of cocaine into the United States.

Connections were first made in December 1985, when the Associated Press published an investigation into cocaine trafficking by the Contras. Reporters Brian Barger and Robert Parry interviewed officials with the DEA, Customs, and the FBI, as well as Contra rebels and Americans who trained them. Based on those conversations, Barger and Parry detailed an operation wherein two CIA-linked Cuban Americans used armed Contras to guard airfields used by drug smugglers in northern Costa Rica.

At those airfields, cocaine was reportedly loaded onto planes to be later dropped near an "Atlantic coast port," where it was concealed on shrimp boats and ultimately unloaded in Miami. U.S. officials who monitored drug traffic from Colombia to the United States through Central America told the AP that they began receiving "reliable" reports of the operation as early as November 1984 after a Contra leader named Sebastian Gonzalez Mendiola was arrested and indicted in Costa Rica for drug trafficking.

Another Contra leader, unnamed in the AP's investigation, reportedly informed U.S. authorities that he had been approached by Colombian traffickers and offered $50,000 to guard a one-hundred-kilo cocaine shipment. In exchange for turning in the Colombian smugglers, he asked for $50,000 from the U.S. Embassy. When the request was rejected, he reportedly went forward with the smuggling arrangement and faced no consequences from U.S. authorities.

Months after the AP released its investigation, the *San Francisco Examiner* published another report on a Bay Area cocaine ring that used its sales to help finance the Contras. Based on information from federal court transcripts, government wiretap transcripts, and other documents, the article stated that Carlos Cabezas and Julio Zavala, both traffickers and Nicaraguan nationals, supplied the Contras with $500,000 before being busted in 1983. The aid was the proceeds of cocaine sales in the San Francisco Bay Area, Miami, and New Orleans.

"I was helping out with money and equipment, and sometimes I was helping out by making connections with people who had weapons," Zavala told the *Examiner*. The assistant U.S. attorney who prosecuted the case claimed there was no evidence that Cabezas and Zavala were doing anything other than "lining their own pockets," but sealed records uncovered by the *Examiner* revealed that the government returned $36,020 cash it had seized to Zavala after he presented letters from Contra leaders stating the money was for the "reinstatement of democracy in Nicaragua."

The following year, in April 1986, the AP published yet another report on Contras and cocaine. It revealed that the FBI had quietly launched an investigation into accounts of weapons shipments from the United States to Contra base camps in Central America, Contra involvement in drug smuggling, and a reported conspiracy to assassinate the U.S. Ambassador to Costa Rica. Several individuals interviewed by the AP confirmed the stories, sharing firsthand knowledge on the condition of anonymity.

Just one week later, the Reagan administration released a detailed response, the first of its kind, to allegations that its partners in Nicaragua were involved in smuggling cocaine into the United States. In a three-page report, the White House confirmed some instances where individual Contras acted as drug traffickers, but it downplayed the activity and shifted responsibility away from the Contras themselves to Congress, which withheld funding for the operation in Nicaragua.

"Drug traffickers were attempting to exploit the desperate conditions under which inadequately supplied resistance fighters were carrying on their battle in the field," the report read. "Individual members of the resistance, including those associated with the forces of [former Sandinista hero] Eden Pastora, may have engaged in such activity but it was, insofar as we can determine, without the authorization of resistance leaders."

The official explanation raised more questions than it answered. In search of the truth, Democratic senators John Kerry and Christopher Dodd called for the Senate Foreign Relations Committee to conduct hearings on the issue. The request led to the creation of the Kerry Committee and an investigation that would last three years.

The Kerry Committee report was finally released on April 13, 1989, and its findings were damning. According to the report, the committee found considerable evidence linking individual Contras to drug trafficking. Further, it found that in each case, "one or another agency of the U.S. government had information regarding the involvement either while it was occurring, or immediately thereafter."

Connections identified by the committee included direct involvement in trafficking by individual Contras; use of Contra supply networks by drug traffickers; assistance to the Contras from traffickers, including planes and pilots, cash, and weapons; and payments made by the U.S. State Department to four companies known by officials to be owned and operated by drug traffickers. These companies were paid a total of $806,401.20 to supply "humanitarian assistance" to the Contras. In each case, prior to the State Department entering contracts with the company, federal law-enforcement agencies received information that the individuals controlling them were involved in smuggling drugs into the United States.

Perhaps the closest the Kerry Committee got to proof of the federal government's intent to fund the Contras with drug money was a statement made by DEA officials before the House Judiciary Subcommittee on Crime in July 1988. According to those officials, Ollie North suggested to the DEA in June 1985 that $1.5 million in drug money acquired in a Medellín Cartel sting be given to the Contras. The suggestion was ultimately rejected by the DEA, but the fact that it was made, and by the Reagan administration's man in charge of "the Enterprise," illustrates an eagerness on the part of the administration to fund the Contras using the proceeds of drug trafficking.

The Kerry Committee report also detailed two years of stalling, obfuscation, and outright dishonesty on the part of federal authorities. "The failure of U.S. law enforcement and intelligence agencies to respond properly to allegations concerning criminal activity relating to the Contras was demonstrated by the handling of the Committee's own investigation by the Justice Department and the CIA," the report read.

One example came from a May 6, 1986, meeting between committee staff and representatives of the Justice Department, the FBI, the DEA, the CIA, and the State Department. In the days leading up to the meeting, spokesmen for the Justice Department made public statements that "The U.S. Attorney and the FBI have conducted an inquiry into all of the charges and none of them have any substance." But at the May 6 meeting, Justice Department officials privately contradicted those statements, even admitting to committee staffers that they were inaccurate.

Attempts to cover up the truth about the Contras became even more apparent on October 5, 1988, when the committee received sworn testimony from a Miami prosecutor who was handling a case involving the Contras and guns. In his statement, the prosecutor described a 1986 meeting between Justice Department officials where the topic of discussion was how to best "undermine" the Kerry investigation.

Major media outlets had, for years, disregarded accounts of Contra involvement in cocaine trafficking. They were, it seemed, unable to believe that the U.S. government would engage in illegal activity, even when the evidence was right before them. Reports from Nicaragua were accordingly ignored or downplayed as products of a conspiracy theory.

David Corn, then a Washington correspondent for *The Nation*, offered an example of mainstream media's dismissiveness from a November 1987 press conference related to the Iran-Contra hearings.

"In the midst of the questioning," Corn reflected in *The Nation*, "a journalist from an alternative weekly asked, 'Did the committees investigate the allegations of Contra drug dealing?' Before Arthur Liman, the chief counsel of the Senate Iran/Contra committee, could reply, a reporter from *The New York Times* loudly sneered, 'C'mon, ask a serious question.' And Liman, perhaps taking his cue from the *Times* reporter, moved on. I protested: Why not answer the question? But no other reporter joined in."

When the Kerry Committee report was finally released, it landed with a thud. *The New York Times* ran a short piece on page eight, the *Los Angeles Times* ran a 589-word story on page eleven, and *The Washington Post* ran a short article on page twenty that focused largely on alleged infighting within the committee. The report was all but ignored by the major news networks. For his trouble, John Kerry was characterized as a misguided crusader or, as *Newsweek* magazine called him, a "randy conspiracy buff."

It's worth noting that the period from 1985, when the AP first reported the Contra-cocaine connection, to 1989, when the Kerry Committee report was released, spanned some of the most treacherous years in the war on drugs. That period included two major anti-drug-and-crime bills, in 1986 and 1988. Indeed, at the very moment Ronald Reagan made his special address to warn the nation about crack, the Contras that his administration created were under investigation by the Kerry Committee. Moreover, as he signed legislation in 1986 and 1988 to increase penalties for American drug dealers and users, his administration was turning a blind eye to foreign actors bringing drugs into the country. Worse yet, the administration actively sought to fund its covert operations with the proceeds.

FOLLOWING THE UNDERWHELMING RECEPTION to the Kerry report, the story of the CIA's complicity in cocaine trafficking into the United States all but disappeared. It was resurrected in 1995 when "Freeway" Rick Ross was caught by federal agents with one hundred kilos of cocaine. His arrest and subsequent imprisonment led to a media firestorm that would once again shed light on the Contra-cocaine connection. But this time, a journalist named Gary Webb would draw a straight line from Reagan and the Contras to Ross and the crack cocaine epidemic.

In the years after Ross helped make freebase ubiquitous in Los Angeles, he grew to be a cocaine kingpin. It's estimated that he had thousands of employees across as many as forty-two cities and moved three tons of cocaine during his career. This reportedly earned him gross revenues of up to $900 million and profits of nearly $300 million. That all came crashing down in 1988 when a drug-sniffing dog found nine kilos of cocaine on a bus in Carlsbad, New Mexico. After the drugs were traced back to Ross, he and ten other individuals were indicted on drug-trafficking charges. Ross pleaded guilty and received a mandatory ten-year prison sentence, which he began serving in 1990.

Ross caught a break, however. Around the time that he was convicted, a federal investigation into the Los Angeles County Sheriff's Department was underway. Thirty-five deputy sheriffs and six others had been prosecuted on corruption charges ranging from beating suspects to planting evidence. Having worked with some of the department's crooked cops, Ross presented what he knew. In exchange for his testimony, his sentence was reduced from ten years to four.

Danilo Blandón, Ross's old friend and supplier, ran into his own trouble with the law just a few years after Ross had. He had been on the radar of local and federal authorities since the mid-eighties, but was finally indicted on federal drug-conspiracy charges in May 1992. Unlike Ross, who was initially sentenced to ten years, Blandón received just over four years behind bars. Then suddenly, after serving just two years in prison, he was released. By 1994, Blandón was a free man and once again involved in drug trafficking, or so it seemed.

Ross was also released from prison in 1994, and within a year the two men were back in contact. They first began discussing the possibility of rebuilding luxury cars in the United States and selling them in Nicaragua at a premium, but it didn't take long for their conversations to veer toward cocaine. Ross was strapped for cash and racking up debts, and he floated the idea of getting back in the game.

That opening was all Blandón needed. He soon began calling and paging Ross regularly to discuss the possibility of a drug deal. During one of their conversations, Ross happened to be with a friend named Leroy "Chico" Brown. A former dealer himself, Brown deciphered the substance of the conversation from Ross's side. Unlike Ross, he had the money for kilos and he wanted in. Brown convinced Ross that he could put up the $160,000 Blandón wanted as a down payment on one hundred kilos of cocaine. He promised to pay Ross a sizable commission for arranging the deal.

The deal took place on March 2, 1995, in the parking lot of a San Diego Denny's. A group including Ross, Brown, and Michael McLaurin, the man who first introduced Ross to cocaine, met with Blandón and another man, who Blandón identified as his supplier. After Brown handed a bag full of cash to the supplier, he was handed some car keys and directed by Blandón to the parking lot of the nearby Bonita Plaza Mall. There, he was told, the kilos of cocaine would be waiting in the back of a white Chevy Blazer.

Ross and company found the car and the cocaine inside. But just as they were about to leave the lot, DEA agents and local authorities swooped in to arrest them. Blandón, it turned out, had been working with federal authorities, and his supplier was actually an undercover DEA agent.

Ross and his friends were indicted in federal court on cocaine-conspiracy-and-distribution charges. He was found guilty of his third felony, and with that he was sentenced to life in prison without the possibility of parole. Blandón was paid $45,000 for his help in the sting.

Sometime later that year, Gary Webb, an investigative reporter for *The Mercury News,* a newspaper published in San Jose, California, received a tip about Danilo Blandón's ties to both the CIA and drug trafficking throughout California. The tip led Webb eventually to the Metropolitan Correctional Center, where Ross was being held. Through conversations with Ross, Webb learned the fine details of the empire he built off crack and how Blandón was there the whole way, supplying Ross with tons of cocaine. In the course of his reporting, Webb also learned the depth of Blandón's relationship to the Contras and the federal authorities.

Blandón fled with his family from Nicaragua to Los Angeles in 1979, the year of the Sandinistas' revolution. He began attending local Contra support meetings almost immediately, even founding a local chapter of the Nicaraguan Democratic Force. From there, Blandón met another Nicaraguan national named Norwin Meneses, who introduced him to cocaine trafficking for the Contra cause. Within a few years, he was the primary supplier for Ross's growing empire.

Federal authorities report becoming aware of Blandón's operation in 1986, when a confidential informant shared his name. The DEA opened a case targeting him, "his associates and source of supply." The Los Angeles County Sheriff's Department also opened an official investigation. Later that year, the department executed search warrants on properties associated with Blandón, but according to reports, the searches only turned up some records and a negligible quantity of drugs.

For the next five years, authorities including the L.A. Sheriff's Department, the FBI, and the DEA claimed that they collaborated on various investigations and task forces targeting Blandón. Still, none made an arrest. The closest he came to facing justice was in August 1991 when, during a random search of cars crossing the border to Mexico, U.S. Customs in San Diego found $117,040 in undeclared cash and money orders on Blandón and a companion. The two men were arrested, but charges against them were dropped after the Justice Department stepped in, purportedly so the agency could pursue a more complete case against Blandón.

Months later, officers with the Los Angeles Police Department arrested him once more in a sting that targeted a group of Colombian traffickers. Again, Blandón was in possession of a considerable amount of cash when authorities found him. And again, the charges were dropped.

Finally, on May 5, 1992, Blandón was indicted by a federal grand jury in San Diego on drug-conspiracy charges. He was arrested by DEA agents later that month and held without bail. He cooperated with the DEA within weeks and in turn was offered a plea deal that included a reduced sentence of just forty-eight months in prison and five years of probation. The following year, in September 1994, officials with the Department of Justice filed a motion asking the court to reduce Blandón's sentence even further. In a memo to a judge, a prosecutor wrote that Blandón had "almost unlimited potential to assist the United States" as a full-time, paid informant.

In the end, the court reduced Blandón's sentence to time served, and he was released from prison after serving just over two years behind bars. One month later, he received legal permanent-resident status from the Immigration and Naturalization Service and began his work as an informant for federal authorities. Within a year, Blandón would be on the phone with Ross, working to arrange the sting that would send Ross back to prison.

The Mercury News published Webb's reporting the week of August 18, 1996, in a three-part, twenty-thousand-word series titled "Dark Alliance." The series made several claims that culminated in an argument that a CIA-backed Blandón had supplied Ross with enough cocaine to kick off the crack epidemic. All of it was done, Webb claimed, to fund the Contras and covert operations in Nicaragua. Despite many of the revelations having already been exposed by the Kerry Committee, the "Dark Alliance" series set off a firestorm. It swept through Black talk-radio programs and attracted thousands of readers to *The Mercury News*'s website, making it one of the first viral news stories.

Black community leaders across the country demanded a response to the allegations from the federal government. Congresswoman Maxine Waters, whose district included South Central Los

Angeles, was especially vocal in her outrage and called for investigations by the CIA, the Justice Department, and the House Permanent Select Committee on Intelligence. By the end of September 1996, investigations by all three were underway. A fourth, by the L.A. Sheriff's Department, was announced soon after.

Federal law-enforcement officials were uncharacteristically quiet following the release of "Dark Alliance." The silence was filled, however, by the same media outlets that had largely ignored the Kerry Committee report just seven years earlier.

The Washington Post ran a lengthy front-page article on October 4, 1996, declaring in part that "available information does not support the conclusion that the CIA-backed Contras—or Nicaraguans in general—played a major role in the emergence of crack as a narcotic in widespread use across the United States." Alongside it, the *Post* published a companion piece on the Black community's susceptibility to conspiracy theories.

Weeks later, *The New York Times* published another long piece refuting the claims made in "Dark Alliance." The article concluded, as the *Post* had, that there was "scant proof to support the paper's contention that Nicaraguan rebel officials linked to the CIA played a central role in spreading crack through Los Angeles and other cities." As the *Post* had also done with its treatment of the series, the *Times* article closed with an examination of why Black Americans might be prone to believe such a story.

The most robust response to "Dark Alliance" came from the *Los Angeles Times*. The paper published "The Cocaine Trail," its own three-part series, from October 20 to 22, 1996. Leo Wolinsky, Metro editor for the *Times,* denied to a reporter for the *Columbia Journalism Review* that the series was meant to be a "knockdown of the *Mercury News* series," but its intentions were clear on the page. "The Cocaine Trail" painted a picture of crack's origins outside of Ross and Blandón. The piece argued that Blandón's contributions to the Contras were significantly less than the millions claimed in Webb's reporting. It was also fervent in its denials of CIA complicity.

Such an all-out offensive by the mainstream press is unusual. News outlets typically advance the work of others or allow bad reporting to wither on the vine. However, in the case of "Dark Alliance," *The New York Times,* the *Los Angeles Times,* and *The Washington Post* all saw fit to respond to Webb's story rather than suss out the truth themselves. Ultimately, the three papers committed more than thirty thousand words to refute "Dark Alliance."

To be sure, "Dark Alliance" was far from a perfect piece of journalism. In his eagerness to break the story of the CIA, the Contras, and crack, Webb overstated some key claims. It was not true, for example, that Blandón's drug ring "opened the first pipeline between Colombia's cocaine cartels and the black neighborhoods of Los Angeles." The piece also suggested in several passages that the CIA actively participated in Blandón's operation. As much as testimony points in that direction, Webb never presented a smoking gun.

What Webb could say with authority was exactly what the Kerry Committee had: that federal law-enforcement agencies, including the CIA, knew that Contra members were involved with the Colombian cartels and trafficking large shipments of cocaine to the United States. They also knew that a number of major U.S. drug rings controlled by Nicaraguan expats were helping to fund the Contras. Webb could have also said with authority that one of the Contra-cocaine connections known to the feds was Danilo Blandón, a trafficker who, it turned out, supplied Ricky Ross, the L.A. dealer who catalyzed the crack epidemic. Those were and are the facts.

National security expert Peter Kornbluh wrote about the collective editorial decision to "assault, rather than advance" "Dark Alliance" in an article for the *Columbia Journalism Review.* "Indeed, if the major media had devoted the same energy and ink to investigating the contra drug scandal in the 1980s as they did attacking *The Mercury News* in 1996, Gary Webb might never have had his scoop," Kornbluh concluded. "And having shown itself still unwilling to follow the leads and lay the story to rest, the press faces a challenge in the contra-cocaine matter not unlike the government's: restoring its credibility in the face of public distrust over its perceived role in the handling of these events."

Despite the many troubling facts exposed by "Dark Alliance," the media campaign against the story effectively ended Webb's career as a journalist. He resigned from *The Mercury News* in November 1997 and never again worked in a newsroom. In the years following, Webb worked as an investigator for the California State Legislature and published the occasional story as a freelancer. He was laid off from his job in 2004 and shortly after was found dead in his home with two gunshot wounds to the head. Coroners ruled Webb's death a suicide, to the continued disbelief of many.

Released July 23, 1998, the Justice Department investigation initiated by "Dark Alliance" found that "the allegations contained in the original *Mercury News* articles were exaggerations of the actual facts." The DOJ argued that Blandón was not a "significant" source of support for the Contras, and that his activities were not responsible for the rise of the crack epidemic. The report also concluded that previous government investigations into the Contras and cocaine trafficking suffered from a lack of coordination, "rather than anything as spectacular as a systematic effort by the CIA or any other intelligence agency to protect the drug trafficking activities of Contra supporters."

The CIA issued its own two-volume report on October 8, 1998. As the agency most closely tied to the Contras, investigators purportedly examined all information "relating to CIA knowledge of drug trafficking allegations in regard to any person directly or indirectly involved in Contra activities." The report also claimed that close attention had been paid to how the agency responded to reports of drug-trafficking activities associated with the Contras.

Still, the CIA claimed to find no evidence that "any past or present employee of CIA, or anyone acting on behalf of CIA, had any direct or indirect dealing" with any of the figures mentioned in "Dark Alliance," including Ross and Blandón. The report did admit, however, that there were instances where the CIA did not, "in an expeditious or consistent fashion, cut off relationships with individuals supporting the Contra program who were alleged to have engaged in drug-trafficking activity or take action to resolve the allegations." But to that it offered the curious caveat that, under an agreement in 1982 between Reagan attorney general William French Smith and the CIA, agents were not required to report allegations of drug trafficking involving nonemployees, defined as paid and nonpaid "assets."

The CIA's admissions were major. They implicated the U.S. government in cocaine trafficking during the eighties, and therefore in some of the devastation of the crack epidemic. There was some attention paid to the report, but overall, the revelations came and went.

With the Kerry Committee report, the lack of outrage was largely due to the media's ignoring the findings. With the "Dark Alliance," there was outrage, but it quickly dissipated as media outlets ripped the story apart, confusing readers about what was and wasn't factual in the process. The reports by the DOJ and the CIA faced neither response. They received fairly measured coverage by outlets including *The New York Times, The Washington Post,* and CNN. Still, the first-ever acknowledgment by federal law enforcement that it knowingly allowed drug trafficking into the United States while simultaneously waging a war on drugs was essentially met with a yawn.

Americans who might otherwise be interested were likely fatigued from more than twenty years of allegations and denials. The CIA, Contras, crack—it was all old news. Minds were already made up.

A smoking gun has yet to emerge proving a government conspiracy to poison communities of color using crack. But what the evidence supports is more insidious: the crack epidemic was the consequence of the anti-Blackness that permeated and continues to permeate every facet of American society and public policy. Reagan, the CIA, the cartels, and the Contras had no need to conspire, because the entire machinery of the United States was designed either to our detriment or with no regard for us at all. The crack epidemic was not the product of an anti-Black conspiracy but the product of an anti-Black system.

37

—

KURT

(1996-97)

KURT SCHMOKE WAS THRILLED to be Baltimore's mayor on the occasion of its bicentennial. He envisioned the milestone as another opportunity for rebirth. "It's going to be an international event," he told the *Sun*. "Baltimore's going to be the place to be in 1997."

The city was already turning a corner in one regard. Rates of crack use in Maryland began slowing around 1994, with researchers noting a decrease in cocaine-related admissions to both hospitals and treatment facilities. The decline of the crack epidemic in Baltimore was quiet, imperceptible to most, but by early 1996 it was beginning to manifest in less crime.

The *Sun* interviewed a number of police officials and residents about the drop. Many speculated that it was related to crack but ultimately attributed the decline in crime to a blizzard that disrupted open-air markets. "Obviously, the weather has had an impact on the level of violence that we normally deal with," Wendell M. France, commander of the homicide unit, told the *Sun*. "I think the mayor got the word out that people need to be patient. Everyone is taking the storm in stride."

Despite the promising numbers, crime remained a hot topic in Baltimore as local officials—folks who perceived Schmoke to be on his last lap as mayor—stoked concerns to raise their profiles. For example, in August 1996, Councilman Martin O'Malley led a delegation from City Hall to New York for a high-profile three-day visit to New York City Police Department headquarters.

O'Malley returned with an argument that New York was able to drive sharp reductions in crime over the years that Baltimore saw spikes because it embraced broken windows policing, the zero-tolerance model where even the most minor offenses—loitering, littering, open containers—were made priorities. "Clearly, what we are doing in Baltimore isn't working," O'Malley told reporters, despite evidence that crime in the city was also on the decline.

Schmoke's response was as pragmatic as always. He reminded O'Malley and others that zero-tolerance policing would require more police, and that it would clog the city's courts. He also noted there was little evidence that such a strategy had any effect on major crime.

Just as the fight over crime in Baltimore was getting underway, *The Mercury News* published "Dark Alliance," its three-part series detailing the connections among the CIA, a Bay Area drug ring, and the South Central Los Angeles dealer who helped introduce crack to cities around the country. The investigation caused shock waves in Baltimore's Black communities, and Schmoke was one of a few mayors who joined calls for a congressional probe into the matter.

"You know of the devastating impact that drugs have had on cities in the past two decades," Schmoke wrote in letters to presidents of the National Conference of Black Mayors, the United States Conference of Mayors, and the National League of Cities. "Many questions have been raised about our inability as a nation to control the flow of drugs into and throughout the country. Clearly, it is in our national interest to determine whether an agency of the United States government assisted, either directly or indirectly, the distribution of drugs in this country." Schmoke also sent letters calling for an investigation to

House Speaker Newt Gingrich, Senate Majority Leader Trent Lott, and members of the Maryland congressional delegation.

Crime in Baltimore continued to decline as the year unfolded. Statistics released at the end of 1996 by the Baltimore Police Department showed that it fell in most categories, but the city's homicide rate was a sticking point. That it lagged behind other measures spurred rumors that police leaders were cooking the books, reclassifying other crimes in their official reports to improve the city's stats—all except the one crime it's impossible to reclassify. The city, on the other hand, explained the rise in homicides as the result of deadlier handguns that made otherwise survivable shootings fatal.

The issue came to a head in the first week of January 1997, when a three-year-old boy named James Smith III was shot and killed in a West Baltimore barbershop, the random victim of an attack on another customer. "If we had embraced zero tolerance months ago, perhaps James Smith and many other murder victims of this city in the past few months might have been spared," council president Lawrence A. Bell told reporters at a press conference hours before the boy's funeral.

Schmoke defended his approach at a separate press conference. "The fact is the person who is alleged to have shot this boy was arrested by our city police and had been through the criminal justice system. So there's some sense that maybe we ignored this guy? No. Did the police release this guy? No. We put him in jail." Schmoke instead pointed the finger at the number of illegal weapons on the streets and pushed a gun buyback program run by the city. "We've got to figure out how we get to these young men to get the arms off the street and improve their sense of value, so they don't define their sense of manhood by carrying one of these weapons," he said.

Despite such high-profile incidents, crime continued to fall in Baltimore, with violent crime dropping 7.5 percent by July 1997 and property crime dropping 11.5 percent. Much to Schmoke's relief, homicides eventually dropped as well. One hundred and fifty-six slayings were recorded in the first half of 1997, compared to 168 the previous year. The trend would hold, and the city ended 1997 with 313 homicides, down from 333 in 1996.

Crime, violent crime in particular, had climbed steadily every year Schmoke had been mayor—it rose 40 percent between 1987 and 1995—but nearly every measure started to fall in 1996. Finally, Baltimore was catching up to other big cities, which had seen decreases in both crack use and crime as early as 1989. The reversal felt like a reward for Schmoke, who'd been steadfast for so long in his commitment not just to more policing but to smarter policing and investments in other city services.

ACT

VIII

–

RECOVERY

38

—

INTERVENTION

(1989-96)

THE CRACK EPIDEMIC DIDN'T end the way some expected. The drug warriors didn't gallop in on white horses and ride the bad guys out of town. Nor did federal law enforcement disrupt the flow of illegal substances into the United States, creating the long-promised drug-free America. What happened instead was more subtle: the drug trend ended as most trends do, because a new generation of young people simply refused to pick it up.

Rates of crack use in most cities hit their peak around 1989, plateaued, and started to decline soon after. Researchers are reluctant to declare an end to any epidemic. There are, for sure, individuals still using the substance in America today, but they're a small cohort of mostly veteran users, with fewer and fewer people opting for the drug each year.

"The crackheads, they're all 25 and up. They go walking around looking dirty and trifling, trying to sell $50 worth of food stamps for a real $20 bill. Kids aren't into that," one teenager told *The Washington Post* in a 1994 story about crack's end. "Gold is played out," she added as commentary on the drug dealer aesthetic.

Because their efforts were so public, many believe that drug warriors were responsible for the decline of crack and the violence that accompanied it. There is probably some truth to the idea that Nancy Reagan's anti-drug campaigns kept some young people off drugs. And maybe it is the case that casting a dragnet over poor communities of color prevented some young people from getting involved in the drug trade.

Other factors seem more salient in the decline of violent crime, including an improved economy. Poor economic conditions were, after all, responsible for the creation of highly competitive, often violent drug markets in urban America. And, in a way that Nancy Reagan never could, it appears the community and culture surrounding the most vulnerable young people demonstrated why they should just say no, rather than merely telling them.

According to a 2006 study published in *The Journal of Sociology and Social Welfare*, "Since the early 1990s, inner-city youths have been purposefully avoiding crack and heroin, having seen the devastation these drugs brought into the lives of older community members."

Research by the U.S. Department of Justice looking specifically at the epidemic in New York City backed that notion. "Ethnographic evidence suggests that the crack epidemic in New York City entered a decline around 1990 when youths began to disdain crack use," found one report by the agency. "They considered 'crackhead' a dirty word and even took to abusing crackheads. Such a change in attitude among youths heralded the beginning of the decline phase of the crack epidemic."

It's hard to overstate the significance of hip hop in this shift. The culture was blasted by the mainstream for its vulgarity, "gangsta rap" in particular. Just a cursory look at some of the most prominent popular albums and songs reveals, however, an anti-crack theme that emerged in the late eighties and continued on through the end of the epidemic in the mid-nineties.

New Jack City, Boyz n the Hood, and *Jungle Fever*, all released in 1991, depict the horrors of the crack epidemic. Written and directed by young Black filmmakers, these films were hip hop in style, tone, and subject matter. Barry Michael Cooper, the journalist behind *Spin* magazine's big crack feature in 1986, wrote *New Jack City*. The film depicted the rise and fall of a charismatic Harlem drug lord named Nino Brown. *Boyz n the Hood,* written and directed by John Singleton, took on the violence of the crack era. Spike Lee's *Jungle Fever* depicted the turmoil crack created within families. After these films, there followed a slew of others—*Juice* in 1992, *Menace II Society* in 1993, *Clockers* in 1995.

Just like the media messaging of the "just say no" era, these films all had anti-violence, anti-drug messages at their core. But what set them apart, in true hip hop fashion, was their commitment to centering the stories of those who'd been marginalized in the PSAs and made-for-TV movies of the eighties. As such, they became cult classics among young people of color and helped shape their perceptions of crack use and dealing.

Rap was also deeply engaged with the crack epidemic and the war on drugs. At the time, a common retort from rappers to criticism of their lyrics was that they were merely reflecting the reality of the streets. It was dismissed by some as an excuse, but when it comes to crack, they were telling the truth.

As crack use increased throughout the eighties, so did the release of rap songs warning users of its consequences. Kool Moe Dee released "Monster Crack" in 1986. Then in 1987, N.W.A. released "Dopeman," MC Shan dropped "Jane, Stop This Crazy Thing!" and Boogie Down Productions released "Say No Brother (Crack Attack Don't Do It)." The following year, Public Enemy released "Night of the Living Baseheads," N.W.A. dropped "Fuck tha Police," and Slick Rick released "Hey Young World."

There were other anti-crack hits: BDP's "Self Destruction," "Gimme No Crack" by Shinehead, "Just Say No" by Young MC, "Slow Down" by Brand Nubian, Notorious B.I.G.'s "Everyday Struggle." These songs did not glamorize drugs, as many rap critics claimed. On the contrary, they were practically uniform in their opposition. Moreover, they were hits played in heavy rotation by the young people who would ultimately put an end to the epidemic the songs reflected.

More than any other individual rapper, Dr. Dre deserves recognition for his role in helping turn the page on the crack epidemic. As a member of N.W.A. and producer for the group, he helped articulate the conditions of life in the ghetto on songs like "Dopeman," "Fuck tha Police," and "Gangsta Gangsta." Then in 1992, three years after leaving N.W.A., Dr. Dre dropped his magnum opus, *The Chronic.* The album is ranked by many, including *Vibe, Spin,* and *Rolling Stone,* as one of the greatest albums of all time. It also seems that during crack's decline, when a new generation was beginning its youthful experimentation, it presented an alternative to hard drugs.

On it, Dre perfected his "g-funk" sound, production marked by groovy basslines, layered synthesizers, funk and soul samples. The album contrasts those sounds of a bygone era with lyrics exploring the issues of the day. Songs like "The Day the Niggaz Took Over," "Lil' Ghetto Boy," and "A Nigga Witta Gun" are odes to street life during the crack era. More explicitly, Dre weaves documentary audio from the L.A. riots into intros and interludes throughout *The Chronic.*

On top of that, Dre layers on an homage to marijuana. "High Powered," "The $20 Sack Pyramid," "The Roach," "Let Me Ride," and other tracks from *The Chronic* exalt the benefits of smoking weed. In fact, the album's title is a slang term for high-grade marijuana, and the art for its cover references the packaging for Zig-Zag rolling papers.

Anti-rap crusaders like C. Delores Tucker decried *The Chronic*'s glamorization of marijuana. They speculated that the album would encourage young people to pick up the drug, and it appears they were right. According to the National Survey on Drug Use and Health, marijuana use among high school seniors had been on the decline since 1978, but it took off again in 1992, the year *The Chronic* dropped. The National Household Survey on Drug Abuse recorded a similar increase for individuals aged eighteen to twenty. Andrew Golub and Bruce D. Johnson, researchers with the Justice Department's National

Institute of Justice, dubbed this new cohort of young drug users the "blunts generation" and noted in a 2001 report that "the reemergence of interest in marijuana use was pioneered as part of the youthful, inner-city, predominantly black hip-hop movement."

Indeed, blunts were not mentioned at all in popular rap songs released before 1990, according to one analysis. But by the early nineties, 15 percent of rap songs mentioned blunts. Later in the decade, that figure nearly doubled to 29 percent.

"From a public policy perspective, a particularly important characteristic of the Blunts Generation is their disdain for hard drugs," observed Golub and Johnson. "Interestingly, this avoidance does not appear to be the result of shortages; indeed, the purity and availability of heroin and cocaine have reputedly increased during the 1990s, and the street price has declined. This avoidance may have been the result of increased law enforcement pressure and drug use prevention programs. On the other hand, many youths report that it was their direct personal observations of the ravages of crack smoking and heroin injection among their older siblings, parents, and members of the community that led them to avoid crack and heroin use."

Despite commonly held beliefs in Black complacency with drugs and crime, it's also clear that residents of the communities hardest hit by the crack epidemic played some part in its decline. In several cities, they formed neighborhood patrols and watch groups with the specific goal of driving out drug dealers and closing down crack houses, taking the dangerous work of securing their neighborhoods into their own hands. They also founded organizations, launching campaigns and initiatives to provide access to substance-abuse programs and job training, to beautify streets, build playgrounds, and mentor children.

People use the word "community" too loosely, especially when discussing marginalized Americans—Black Americans in particular. In the mouths of politicians and the like, "community" has become a border to draw around groups of folks who may or may not have anything in common. But real community, as honest and old as strangers huddled together in the bowels of ships, is what sustained

Black America through the trials and tribulations of the crack epidemic.

One study of the national decline of violence from the 1990s to the 2010s found that grassroots nonprofits focused on combating crime had a significant impact. Using data spanning 264 cities and more than twenty years, sociologist Patrick Sharkey and his team at New York University observed that for every one hundred thousand city residents, the addition of ten organizations led to a 9 percent reduction in the murder rate, a 6 percent reduction in the violent crime rate, and a 4 percent reduction in the property crime rate.

In a story that made national news, a local chapter of the Nation of Islam drove drug dealers out of the Mayfair section of Southeast D.C. Soon after building a mosque near the Mayfair Mansions and Paradise Manor projects in 1988, the Nation decided to take Mayfair on as a community development project. They held an anti-drug rally at Mayfair Mansions. Foot patrols soon followed. A command post was established in one Mayfair Mansions apartment and, armed with walkie-talkies and dressed in their signature suits and bow ties, Nation of Islam patrolmen confronted crack dealers and users in the neighborhood and pushed them out.

Residents of Fairlawn, another Southeast D.C. neighborhood, created the Fairlawn Coalition in 1989 with the sole mission of disrupting drug markets in the area. Led by a man named Eddie Johnson, a small group of neighbors patrolled Fairlawn, monitored suspicious traffic, and confronted drug dealers. In 1989 alone, the coalition's patrols led to nearly ninety arrests and the shutdown of a dozen crack houses.

That same year, a young activist named Mahdi Leroy J. Thorpe launched a sweeping anti-crack campaign in D.C.'s Shaw neighborhood, where he was a resident. Thorpe organized more than one hundred anti-drug rallies and coordinated raids of dozens of crack houses through his Red Hat Patrol.

There were other notable community groups in D.C.: the Marshall Heights Neighborhood Coalition, the Bloomingdale Civic Association, the Columbia Heights Neighborhood Coalition, the River Terrace Coalition, the Barney Circle Neighborhood Patrol, the Oakwood Coalition, the Parkview Coalition, the Randle-Highland Coalition, the Far Southwest Coalition, the Capitol Hill East Coalition, Washington View, and COPE.

Neighborhood patrols became so impactful in the district that the chief of police, Isaac Fulwood, Jr., praised them in a 1990 op-ed for *The Washington Post*. "We're beginning to see crime decrease in the areas in which these civic groups operate, and we believe the decrease can be attributed directly to the efforts of such organizations," wrote Fulwood. "By sending a message to the criminal element that illegal activity will not be tolerated, the dedicated citizens who are part of civic organizations have helped rid their neighborhoods of drug dealers."

Such stories exist in other neighborhoods around the country. In Philadelphia, for example, a man named Herman Wrice was pushed to action one day in 1988 when a star athlete from his Mantua neighborhood missed an important game because he was getting high. Concerned, Wrice went to the crack house where the young man was holed up, broke down the front door with a sledgehammer, and pulled him out. Wrice was so struck by what he saw in the crack house that he went on to found Mantua Against Drugs, a grassroots neighborhood watch organization that worked to identify drug dealers and run them out of Mantua.

MAD was composed of Mantua residents, and the group, in coordination with police, confronted street-level drug dealers and closed and demolished known crack houses. Doing so made Wrice and MAD unpopular among dealers. He faced death threats but never let intimidation deter him, going as far as to put up wanted posters featuring "the dealer of the week" around the neighborhood. His approach was revolutionary in its simplicity: stand up to them and they'll leave.

With the support of Wilson Goode, then mayor of Philadelphia, Wrice's methods were adopted by groups in other areas of the city.

Alliances formed between the neighborhood organizations, and before long there was a network of community watch groups working together with local police to push back against the tide of drug dealing and use. Of course, Wrice's "up with hope, down with dope" movement didn't save Philadelphia from being deeply impacted by the crack epidemic. Still, his methods kept Mantua and other neighborhoods from falling into utter disrepair during the late eighties and early nineties.

"The healthy forces in these devastated communities said they could take it no more, and mustered their collective strength to fight back," noted Jeremy Travis, former director of the National Institute of Justice, in a March 2, 1998, speech at the University of California, Los Angeles.

Even with all this activity, it seems most Americans failed to realize crack was on the decline because the epidemic left behind so much damage in its wake. Most obviously, the crack epidemic was a catalyst for mass incarceration in the United States. Federal anti-crack laws aside, fourteen states—Alabama, Arizona, California, Connecticut, Iowa, Maine, Maryland, Missouri, New Hampshire, North Dakota, Ohio, Oklahoma, South Carolina, and Virginia—rewrote their criminal codes to target crack. Most imposed harsher sentences for the substances than for powder cocaine. Others imposed mandatory minimum sentences. Iowa went so far as to adopt the federal government's one hundred to one (crack to powder cocaine) sentencing disparity.

More broadly, anti-crack fervor created a general tough-on-crime climate that led to more arrests, more convictions, and longer sentences. The result was a boom in the U.S. prison population. According to the Sentencing Project, there were 40,900 people incarcerated in 1980 for drug offenses. That number swelled to 489,000 by 2013. People of color absorbed much of the explosion in incarceration. In 1980, they comprised more than 40 percent of the state and federal prison population. By 2010, that number had grown to 68 percent—despite people of color accounting for just around 30 percent of the total U.S. population. What did the nation get for the widespread warehousing of citizens?

Many believe that the law enforcement response is what ended the violence that accompanied the crack era. New research suggests the availability of guns was a more salient variable. Economists Geoffrey Williams and W. Alan Bartley compiled handgun price and production data from the late eighties and early nineties from advertisements in *Gun Digest*. Comparing that data to crime rates revealed a "supply shock" of low-priced pistols, corresponding to higher levels of gun homicide among young Black men.

It turns out, just as crack was exploding, the federal government eased its oversight of the gun industry, and manufacturers kicked up production of cheap firearms, dubbed "Saturday night specials" by law enforcement due to the rate at which they showed up at weekend crime scenes. According to the analysis by Williams and Bartley, production of these guns peaked in 1993, the same year the murder rate peaked nationally. It was product-liability lawsuits, more funding for the Bureau of Alcohol, Tobacco, Firearms, and Explosives, and the Brady Bill that forced a decline in the production of cheap guns, and subsequently in the murder rate.

Beyond the quantifiable damage, the crack epidemic inflicted harms that cannot be measured—the attitudes, stereotypes, and preconceived notions that still linger in the hearts and minds of many Americans. The crack epidemic advanced in the American imagination the perception of Black people as sick and in need of a firm hand. This idea animated crime legislation to devastating effect, and it persists today in U.S. politics and domestic policy.

When the crack epidemic is mentioned now, it's usually as a punchline. Crack, crackheads, dope boys, and crack babies all get evoked to prove a point. Or they're referenced as fads of the late twentieth century—like *Dynasty*, shoulder pads, and acid-washed jeans.

There are, of course, other common uses of the crack epidemic.

Today's politicians brandish it like a shield, to both deflect and intimidate. In speeches, they invoke our national memory of the frightful period as an argument to maintain our criminal justice system. Or they use it as the Clintons did during Hillary's 2016 presidential campaign, to justify their role in a number of poor policy decisions related to Black life and death.

The ways we talk about the crack epidemic, or don't in some cases, reveal our deep misunderstanding of it. We don't discuss the crack epidemic properly because we barely understand what happened.

Media coverage was central to America's misunderstanding. In some ways, news stories about crack helped raise awareness about its dangers. However, a great deal of news coverage helped fan the flames of misinformation, panic, and hysteria surrounding the substance.

Perhaps some of the best research into the media's handling of the crack epidemic was conducted by Jimmie L. Reeves and Richard Campbell for their book *Cracked Coverage,* published in 1994. For the book, Reeves and Campbell studied some 270 network-news packages dealing with cocaine between 1981 and 1988 and, from that coverage, identified three phases of what they call the media's "cocaine narrative."

Phase one, the "trickle-down paradigm," lasted from about January 1981 to November 1985. It approached cocaine as a glamour drug that, through the rise of crack, threatened middle-class Americans. At this phase, the media emphasized the importance of public-health interventions. Between December 1985 and November 1986, coverage shifted to phase two, a "siege paradigm," which reframed the crack epidemic as a crisis originating in the "inner city." This phase of coverage racialized the substance and emphasized a law-enforcement response. Finally, after much criticism that the media was hyping the crack epidemic and engaging in harmful stereotyping, coverage shifted to a "post-crisis" phase, which returned to public-health solutions but maintained its focus on the inner city, continuing the racialization.

Television wasn't alone in its misrepresentation of the crack epidemic. According to researchers, early print coverage of the crack epidemic helped contribute to an outsized panic. A comprehensive examination of crack-related articles appearing in *The New York Times, Time,* and *Newsweek* from 1985 through 1995 found "an insidious bias in news coverage through its focus on the inner city, in spite of broader use of crack." The result of such coverage was a perception of the crack epidemic not as a drug trend like any other, but as a deadly plague associated with Black people that needed to be contained.

39
—
ELGIN
(1992-PRESENT)

SOME KIDS MIGHT HAVE plunged deeper into the street life after what Elgin went through. Instead, the events at home shook some sense into him. He wanted a way out of the nightmare and was surer than ever that a career selling drugs wasn't it. Once that sunk in, his thoughts turned to finishing school and getting a job and his own place, away from his dad.

Weeks after the incident with his clothes, something unexpected happened. Sixteen-year-old Elgin was hanging down the block with friends when he saw an unfamiliar car stop in front of his building. The driver, a white guy, dropped off a passenger, a Latino man, who hurried in. The man emerged a few minutes later and got back in the car. Elgin's friend Danny, who was also watching closely, turned to him and said, "Yo, that's the police. They're gonna raid your crib." Squad cars swarmed the block as if on cue.

Elgin stood still for the next few minutes, frozen, as police rushed into the building. He heard them bust down his apartment door. A lot of shouting followed, then the sound of three gunshots, and finally, quiet. It was unreal, Elgin thought as he looked up at the scene from the bottom of the hill. The pit bull the dealers got after the apartment was robbed had jumped out of a window and was balancing itself on the ledge.

Elgin and his friends went to the roof of a building across from his and watched as the police led everyone, including his father, out of the apartment and into police cars. He was devastated but also elated.

It was the beginning of a new life for Elgin. He continued to face challenges, especially in the days following the raid, but in the meantime he was finally free from his father's addiction and the chaos that accompanied it.

The next week was rough. He slept on the roofs of buildings in the neighborhood, in laundry rooms, and on friends' couches. All the while, word on the street was that the dealers from his apartment wanted Elgin dead. They'd decided that he was the one who put the police on to them, and in return they "put a number on his head." Elgin didn't know whether it was serious or guys just talking. Either way, he floated around Yonkers that week scared for his life and uncertain what to do next.

He was biding time at his friend Petey's house when Petey's mom, Linda, said to him, "Look, I know you ain't got nowhere to stay— I know you're out here. You can stay with us."

Elgin had been lying about his situation and telling people he'd found a place of his own. Embarrassed, he said, "I don't know what you talking about. I'm good."

But Linda wouldn't let it go. She said, "You can say whatever you want, but I know what's going on. If you want to come live with us, you can come live with us. I'm gonna leave it like that."

It was an unfamiliar situation, being offered help, and it made Elgin feel uneasy. Luckily, he had the good sense to accept it.

On television, kids like Elgin had their lives transformed when they moved in with new families. Petey's family—composed of him, his mom, his stepdad, and his sister—was far from perfect. They argued, struggled financially, and had other challenges, but there was always food in the refrigerator, and the house was clean. Moreover, they showed Elgin what it was like to have support. They worried about and cared for him.

At first, Elgin thought he might be able to hustle Linda and her husband, get as much as he could out of the situation and then move on. That was his mindset for probably the first six months. But little by little, he started to care about himself again, and the direction his life was going. He finally went back to school and even got a part-time job ringing up groceries at Finast Supermarket.

Things were looking up for Elgin. Still, he thought about his father more than he liked to admit. He worried about Stephen and how he was doing in jail. Elgin tried to see his dad once. He took a bus up to Westchester County Jail in Valhalla, New York, but was turned away because the only identification he had was a school ID. It felt to Elgin like a sign that he should just walk away from the situation—from his dad, the incorrigible addict—and never look back.

Over the eight months that Stephen was locked up, Elgin only heard from his father when Linda filed for custody of him. The process involved going to family court and asking a judge to sign off. Stephen put up a fight. He argued that he was clean and was the only person who could take care of his son. He went on at length about how much he loved Elgin and how different their life would be if he came home.

Thankfully, the judge saw through it and granted Linda full custody. Stephen was furious, with her and with Elgin. He went off on his son for turning his back on him. What his dad said got to Elgin a little, but he knew deep down that Stephen was still getting high, back in the streets and on his usual bullshit. He suspected his dad's reaction to losing custody had more to do with a decrease in his check from the state than any actual hard feelings.

Because he was so accustomed to life's many small catastrophes, Elgin managed not to panic when he learned in the summer of 1993 that his adopted family was moving to Puerto Rico. Linda was sick and wanted to go back home so she could get better, maybe for good.

She gave Elgin the option of going with them, but that seemed impossible to a seventeen-year-old whose entire world was New York. He decided to stay.

He was with them until their last day in Yonkers, fretting as they packed and the days wound down. His life before Linda's family had been one precarious situation after another. In a sense, uncertainty was the defining force in his life, and like the sun rising in the east, it had returned once again.

He said goodbye and scrambled to find a place to stay. He bounced between friends' apartments for a while before finally getting a room at Leake and Watts, the group home where he'd made friends a few years earlier. It was just another storm he'd have to weather, he told himself as he unpacked his things.

In the midst of it all, Elgin fell in love. He started off as friends with Artiesha, a girl he worked with at Finast. She was smart, he thought, and tough. Artiesha didn't take shit from anybody. She had no problem speaking up for herself and others, which Elgin liked. And the longer the two knew each other, the more he saw how sweet and supportive she could be underneath her tough-girl exterior.

Elgin asked his manager to put him on a register next to Artiesha's. Then he was all smiles and jokes. Like him, Artiesha came from a family in Yonkers that didn't have a lot. But unlike Elgin's, her family was big and together. She had both of her parents, an older brother, a younger brother and sister. She knew Elgin's situation at home, everything he'd been through with his dad—and never treated him differently because of it. As young people do, they bonded over their angst and dreamed together about how their lives would be when they "grew up."

Elgin's first big step toward security came one day while hanging out with Robert Scopino, a guy he'd known since he was five years old. Rob was an amateur boxer and knew some people outside of the neighborhood through boxing. He heard word of a busboy job at an Italian restaurant in Hartsdale, New York, a wealthier part of Westchester County. It was good money, Rob said, and all Elgin had to do was show up and he'd have the job. "Good money" was all that Elgin needed to hear. He took the bus to Hartsdale the next day.

He'd survived in some of the most dangerous neighborhoods in Yonkers but was never as nervous as he was when approaching the restaurant. It was like landing on another planet—pristine blocks, nice cars. He looked inside the large windows of the restaurant and what he saw only made him more nervous—a dining room full of white tablecloths, white napkins, and white people.

Elgin was white, but not the kind of white person who ate at restaurants full of white people. Would he be able to work there, he wondered, or would they figure him out as not one of them by something he said or did? He walked back to the bus stop and, for a moment, considered going back to the Bronx. But as he stood there waiting for the next bus, he thought about how embarrassed Rob would be that he never showed. He didn't want that, so Elgin rallied and returned to the restaurant.

He couldn't have predicted it, but the job would change his life. Elgin hit it off immediately with the family that owned the restaurant—an old Italian guy named Mitty and his daughter Tina. They liked Elgin, Mitty especially. The restaurateur had businesses all over. He saw Elgin had the same kind of hustle about him and took to mentoring him.

Elgin started making five hundred dollars a week, cash. He was good at the job—always on time, always quick clearing tables—so Mitty made him a food runner. Elgin excelled at that, too. He was just as fast, with the added skill of being able to handle customers when an order was wrong or if they needed something else from the kitchen. That led to a job as a waiter, where Elgin really shined. He was dealing with people more, which he liked, and he could rack up to eight hundred dollars a week in tips. The job was all hustle—personality, persuasion, getting people to splurge on just one more glass of wine or dessert. It wasn't too different from selling crack.

After a while, Elgin finally had enough money saved to move out of the shelter into his own place. He and Artiesha had been together for one year by then. He had come to trust her, but also to understand her better. Her relationships within her big family, all under one roof, were complicated. She shared with Elgin that she and her dad didn't exactly get along. He was in and out of the house, causing a great deal of emotional turbulence for Artiesha, her mother, and her siblings. Just like Elgin, Artiesha was ready to strike out on her own.

The two moved into a basement apartment in the Bronx in the winter of 1996. By 1999, they were expecting a baby. She gave birth to a baby girl they named Asia. Elgin worked even harder once Asia was born—in part because he wanted security for his new family but also because he loved making money. In a sense, he was addicted to the hustle. Work, more than anything, gave Elgin a sense of purpose. It also allowed him to live like he'd always wanted.

He and Artiesha soon moved out of their first apartment in the Bronx into a much larger place in Yonkers. They decked the new apartment out, and Elgin showered his daughter with everything he could think to buy. It gave him a real thrill to, on a whim, bring home new outfits for Asia or toys he thought she'd like. He also splurged on himself, buying three-hundred-dollar sweaters, five-hundred-dollar jeans, video games.

Elgin worked at the restaurant for nine years, being promoted eventually to head waiter, then manager. All the while, he got to know some of the regulars well. Most were upper-middle-class professionals who lived in Hartsdale and commuted to the city for work. They talked about their jobs, their businesses, and their investments. Conversations often turned to what Elgin wanted to do beyond working at the restaurant. It was not something he put a lot of thought into at first—he made eight hundred to a thousand dollars every week under the table—but the question started to nag him.

One day, a regular named Zach said, "Hey, I think you'd be good in the car business. Have you ever thought about it?" Zach worked at a dealership in New Jersey and offered to get Elgin an interview if he was interested. The thought of leaving what had become his career made Elgin nervous, but it also excited him. All his conversations with customers had opened up his imagination. When they talked about their jobs—these people he'd come to see as regularly as his friends from the block—Elgin imagined himself in their place on sales floors, on Wall Street, in corner offices.

He talked to Artiesha about leaving the restaurant, and she backed him without pause. She encouraged Elgin to go down to the dealership and interview, at least. "You can make a decision from there," she said.

It took a few months to work up the nerve to go, but when he finally did, Elgin had a great conversation with the general manager—a stern, older Irish guy named Jerry Cusick. Jerry offered him a job right there on the spot, which left Elgin with a choice to make. He could stay at the restaurant or he could take a leap of faith toward something more.

Despite his trepidations, he took the job at the dealership. Still, Elgin had a backup plan. He took a week-long vacation from the restaurant, telling his boss that he had to help a friend. The idea was to give the dealership a try, and if things didn't work out, he could easily go back.

Elgin got to the dealership just shy of 9:00 A.M., when the doors opened. He ambled around the floor while the rest of the staff sat in the office drinking coffee and eating breakfast. A customer strolled in around 9:15 A.M. He was a tall, heavyset Black man with a determined look in his eye. He was looking for a car for his mom, he said. Elgin started to look around nervously for someone to help the man, but when no one came to the floor, he just said, "Fuck it," and decided to walk him around himself.

He didn't know the inventory as well as the menu at the restaurant, but Elgin tried to sound confident as he read facts about each car off the sheets attached to their windows. That Elgin wasn't a slick-talking car salesman seemed to set the man at ease. By 9:35 A.M. or so, Elgin had his very first sale.

The sales that came after weren't nearly as easy, but that beginner's luck gave him the confidence he needed. Elgin had a commission check for about four thousand dollars by the end of his first week and he never went back to the restaurant.

Elgin came to love the car business, which he quickly learned wasn't too different from the drug trade. "Business is business," he'd tell himself. You had to stay ready, be able to read people and establish an instant rapport. Other parallels had to do with simple supply and demand—like how, if cars weren't moving, dealerships would slash prices or get creative with their marketing. It was the same thing dealers did when they changed their packaging to suggest they had a new product and came up with two-for-five deals.

Elgin's time on the block had also instilled in him a competitive spirit. He knew that he had to out-hustle his fellow salesmen—he had to get to work earlier, talk to more customers, and stay later to make more sales. It was high-pressure and competitive for sure, but it was like he was numb to some of the aspects of the job that scared others away. He had colleagues who stressed about meeting sales goals. Elgin took his sales goals seriously, but in one part of his mind, he always thought, "This isn't stress. A gun in your face is stressful. This is just something that we gotta figure out."

That mentality served him well. He was leading the dealership in sales in no time. From there, he received promotion after promotion and moved to bigger and better dealerships until he was sales director at an Audi dealership in Manhattan.

With a solid, legit career in place, Elgin became consumed with securing a home for his family. It was his next step toward a lifestyle that might make up for all he had suffered, the American dream. He was at work one day talking to Avery, a sales rep from Brooklyn who'd just moved about an hour outside the city to Orange County. Avery, who'd grown up like Elgin had, went on about how great Orange County was. The streets were clean and safe, he boasted. The houses were big, and the people looked happy.

Within a couple of days, Elgin and Artiesha were in Orange County looking at houses. They eventually found the perfect place. It was like something out of an ad for the suburbs—a two-thousand-square-foot, four-bedroom, two-and-a-half-bath, white, ranch-style house. It was in a cul-de-sac and sat on half an acre. There was even a finished basement.

After seeing the house and falling in love with it, Elgin promptly went to the bank and got a check for forty thousand dollars, the deposit. His stomach churned as he made it out, and every possible awful outcome swirled through his mind. What would happen if he lost his job, he wondered.

The good, in his imagination, outweighed the bad. He pictured Asia growing up in the house, having friends over and playing in the backyard. Elgin had never had that—a place in the world that he knew would still be his the next day, or two parents under one roof.

One week after buying the house, Elgin and Artiesha got married at City Hall. They'd been a couple for eleven years and it was a way to make things official, Elgin thought. There was no fanfare, no celebration or honeymoon. Indeed, in the years to come, the two celebrated not their wedding anniversary but, instead, the anniversary of the day they met.

Elgin tried to reconnect with his dad, even as life took him away from Yonkers. A part of him held out hope that they could find a way to be father and son again, or at least friends. Their meetings were awkward, like exes trying to rekindle a love lost. Stephen inevitably said something to hurt Elgin's feelings. He also seemed less sharp. The guy who'd been a genius, always a few steps ahead of everyone else, had trouble remembering simple things like phone numbers. His mind was deteriorating, Elgin thought, probably due to his decades of drug use.

He'd visit Stephen and be struck by the feeling that he needed to leave. He didn't feel any resentment toward him, any hate for all he'd been put through, but he'd sit talking with his dad and think, "I can't wait to get the fuck up out of here." He'd try to fight that feeling, but it was futile. Even if Stephen was clean, he was still the same person, and that person, sadly, wasn't someone Elgin wanted in his life.

The last time they were together was right after Elgin bought his first house. He shared the news with his dad, hoping to hear, "Good job, son. I'm proud of you." Instead, Stephen was skeptical. "Well, how much did it cost?" he asked. Elgin told his dad how much, and how much he'd put down, but Stephen was still suspicious. "Where'd you get that money from?" he asked. "Did one of your mother's sisters or your grandparents die and leave you the money? They had to leave you the money."

After all that he'd suffered and overcome because of his dad, that was a bridge too far. The awkwardness, the subtle slights, the lapses were all too much. Something inside Elgin snapped. He replied, "No, I bought it. I worked hard. I'm not like you. I work to get what I have." Elgin said goodbye to his dad after that and didn't look back.

TALK OF SUCCESS AND the American Dream rarely accounts for how focused dreamers must be to climb out of abject poverty to some degree of stability. You can't slow down, stop, or take detours. It's a never-ending grind to keep going, to create something from nothing and then maintain it. That plus the traumas sustained during the climb can produce an unhealthy desire for more—more money, more status, more things to confirm that you're safe.

No matter what he did or what he attained, Elgin felt like he needed something more. He loved his house, for example, but just three years after buying it, Elgin was ready to move on. "Home" started to feel less like a goal and more like an investment strategy as he became fixated on how the place where he lived should make him money. As with the rest of his life, "home" became a hustle.

He and Artiesha had been together for twenty-four years, fourteen of them married. They'd made a nice life together, but something had changed in him. He told himself that they'd come together at a point in their lives when they needed each other. They were bound together by their daughter. But as Asia grew up and needed less of their attention, all Elgin and Artiesha had to focus on was each other and themselves.

Elgin realized that his and Artiesha's decision to be together wasn't just about them being together. They became close because each needed a shoulder to lean on. They moved in together because each wanted out of the situation they were in. Then came Asia, and they decided to get married because it was the right thing to do. He wondered, Was that love? Was there more?

In the summer of 2017, Elgin met another woman via Instagram. They messaged each other here and there, with no intention of anything more. Then they crossed paths at a Puma store in the city. She was independent, pretty, and tough. Over the next four months, the two fell in love.

On New Year's Eve 2017, Elgin admitted to Artiesha that he was no longer happy. The two officially separated soon after, finalizing their divorce in late 2019. The result of the whole ordeal was a new life for Elgin, happier in some ways but also racked with guilt.

40

—

SHAWN
(1997-PRESENT)

SHAWN'S LIFE STARTED OVER on August 29, 1997. He was the same guy from Hayes Homes. He was still Zoo Crew. He still had to contend with the trials and triumphs that come with life in one of America's toughest cities. But now he was free from the narrow identity he'd worn for too long, that of a drug dealer.

He learned from news coverage that the feds had arrested twenty-one people as the result of an eighteen-month investigation into the Zoo Crew. They raided thirteen locations, seizing cash, weapons, and stockpiles of cocaine and heroin. They called the Zoo Crew a gang and "almost a drug supermarket operation." Shawn recognized only a handful of the people the police fingered as Zoo Crew. Among them were Abu, Lamar, Red, M.J., and Quan. Terrance, whom the feds called the "ringleader," was on the run.

Shawn's heart broke for his old friend. He was made out to be some scary underworld boss responsible for drowning Newark in drugs. Shawn couldn't help but see him as the kid who had shown him how to spin out on his Big Wheel. That kid didn't have any options besides hustling, Shawn thought, and he made the best of things. He even tried to bring his friends along.

Police finally caught up with Terrance in the Bronx five months after he went on the run. He was charged with conspiracy to distribute more than 150 kilograms of cocaine, a charge that carried ten years to life in prison.

Shawn dug deeper into coaching after the raid, in part because Bertina was expecting a baby. He kept the Zoo Crew Basketball Program going, and he also started a boys' summer high school league at the Hank Aaron Sports Complex on Springfield Avenue. Despite all that had happened, he named it the Zoo Crew Summer League. It was a controversial choice to say the least, and plenty of people said parents wouldn't let their kids play in a league named after drug dealers. It was a testament to what the Zoo Crew meant to people in Newark that the league flourished with that name.

As Shawn saw it, the kids in his program saved his life, and he would do whatever it took to save theirs. Inevitably, his commitment to the program created conflict with Bertina. She was pregnant and wanted a commitment herself from Shawn. He eventually came around, finally getting his own place and adjusting his schedule to spend more time with Bertina, but it was too late, and the two were broken up by September 1998, when their daughter, Jailen, was born.

Shawn came into his own over the next decade or so. He became a respected case manager at Essex County Mental Health. He also built the Zoo Crew Basketball Program into a force to be reckoned with. He expanded it to include kids from kindergarten to twelfth grade, he made it year-round, and his teams went on to win more than 125 championships.

Things truly came full circle in 2006, when Shawn became the boys' basketball coach at Central High School. Though it all happened within the confines of Newark, it was a long journey back.

41

—

KURT
(1998–PRESENT)

KURT SCHMOKE ANNOUNCED ON December 3, 1998, that he would not pursue reelection to a fourth term. It was a difficult decision but, after eleven years as mayor, he'd finally had enough of the job. He was out of ideas for treating the ills that plagued Baltimore. "My sense is it's time for change," he told reporters.

Over the years, Schmoke accomplished several feats. He demolished all four of Baltimore's high-rise projects and initiated redevelopment in neighborhoods such as Sandtown-Winchester and Pleasant View Gardens. He doubled the amount of money the city contributed to Baltimore City schools. It was controversial, but he also restructured the long-troubled school administration and wrestled away an additional $254 million in funding from the state.

Whereas neighboring cities such as Philadelphia and D.C. faced bankruptcy when the United States entered a recession in 1990, Schmoke kept Baltimore's budget balanced. He cut city bureaucracy in half by eliminating nearly 3,400 jobs—not with mass firings but through attrition. Schmoke also seized on the 1992 election of Bill

Clinton to bring much-needed federal funds to Baltimore, and he oversaw the erection of two new stadiums in the Inner Harbor.

"What I tried to do was keep the glittering things shining and address the rot under the glitter," Schmoke told *The Baltimore Sun* days after his announcement.

But despite all that he accomplished, Baltimore continued to operate as three distinct worlds: the Inner Harbor; the Suburbs, and the Underclass City. Much to Schmoke's disappointment, middle-class families continued to flee for the suburbs at a rate of one thousand per month, taking their tax dollars with them. And despite overall crime numbers having dropped in the city, Baltimore continued to produce more than three hundred homicides every year.

Schmoke's announcement was lamented in some circles. In an editorial for *The Baltimore Sun,* political analyst Juan Williams called Schmoke's legacy "a triumph over adversity." "Mr. Schmoke ran an honest government," noted Williams. "He tried new ideas. And he left the city better off than he found it when he was elected." Others, however, celebrated a changing of the guard. "Ain't soon enough," said Roberto Marsili, a Little Italy activist. "He's a charming guy, but he had unfulfilled promises and empty dreams."

A total of fifteen Democratic candidates entered the race to replace Schmoke. The front-runners were councilmen Carl Stokes and Lawrence Bell, both Black men, and Martin O'Malley, who was white. Bell and O'Malley rode Schmoke hard on the homicide rate in Baltimore, and both made promises of zero-tolerance policing the focus of their campaigns.

Truly, the 1999 mayoral contest called Schmoke's leadership into question as each candidate did their best to convince voters they had answers that apparently eluded Schmoke during his tenure. It's a testament to his work on drug policy, however, that drug treatment was an issue in the 1999 race, more than a decade after he proposed decriminalization to the United States Conference of Mayors.

All the leading candidates promised to implement treatment on demand. Both Bell and O'Malley insisted on tough-on-crime measures, but they also supported more funding for drug treatment and increasing the number of beds in residential programs.

"I have prosecuted drug addicts, and I've defended drug addicts, and I can say that government's response is woefully inadequate," O'Malley said at one point during the campaign. "I have represented a number of people who are addicted to drugs, and it took an arrest or maybe a subsequent arrest to coerce them to get help."

O'Malley went on to win the all-important Democratic primary with more than 50 percent of the vote as Stokes and Bell split much of Baltimore's Black vote. He then beat his Republican opponent, David Tufaro, by a margin of nearly nine to one. Despite their differences and O'Malley's loud opposition to his administration, Schmoke was magnanimous about it.

Schmoke did, however, in his first news conference following O'Malley's win, question how O'Malley might deliver on his promise of zero-tolerance policing, and on the implications of such a policy. "My concern would be a dramatic increase in cases of police abuse," Schmoke said.

Schmoke's concern would prove prescient nearly two decades later, after the death of a twenty-five-year-old Black man named Freddie Gray while in police custody led to a week of protest in Baltimore. The U.S. Justice Department launched an investigation into the Baltimore Police Department in the wake of the protests. Published in August 2016, the DOJ's report revealed a pattern and practice of abuse wherein officers routinely violated the constitutional rights of residents through unlawful stops and the use of excessive force.

Investigators found that misconduct rose alongside the zero-tolerance policies initiated under O'Malley. "The result was a massive increase in the quantity of arrests—but a corresponding decline in quality," the report noted. Officers interviewed by the DOJ said that even after O'Malley vacated City Hall after being elected governor of Maryland in 2007, BPD supervisors continued to push stops, searches, and arrests in certain areas.

The investigation found that of the approximately one hundred thousand arrestees that BPD processed through central booking in 2004, more than one in five were released without charge. Baltimore's Black residents were disproportionately the targets of this kind of policing. The report noted that of the more than three hundred thousand pedestrian stops made by officers between January 2010 and May 2015, roughly 44 percent were made in two small, predominantly Black districts that contain just 11 percent of the city's population.

The City of Baltimore would be forced into a consent decree with the federal government, an agreement that created a task force to monitor the BPD and mandated annual training on community policing, among other reforms.

Policing is but one area where time would prove Kurt Schmoke right. His early calls for a public-health response to drug addiction would only become more resonant as the panic over crack subsided and the public grew weary of the mass incarceration it fueled. Then, as an opioid crisis spread throughout the rest of the country, people looked again to Kurt Schmoke's time as mayor of Baltimore and the effectiveness of the needle-exchange program he championed, a program that stands as perhaps his most enduring achievement.

He practiced law at a private firm for a few years after leaving office. In 2003, Schmoke was appointed dean of the Howard University School of Law. Then, in 2014, the University of Baltimore announced that Schmoke would become its eighth president. The move brought him full circle to his 1987 campaign promise to improve education in the city, to make Baltimore "the city that reads."

He also appeared in two 2004 episodes of HBO's *The Wire,* a gritty series about life in Baltimore written by former *Sun* reporter David Simon. The episodes, entitled "Middle Ground" and "Mission Accomplished," featured Schmoke in a bit part. He portrayed a city health commissioner advising the fictional mayor after a rogue police major legalized drugs in a portion of the city.

When Schmoke became mayor of Baltimore more than three decades ago, many hoped his magic would rub off on the city. Indeed, Schmoke—who never lost anything—was expected to reverse white flight and deindustrialization, to reform a school system that had been failing for decades, to somehow stop the flow of drugs into the city—all while keeping taxes low.

He couldn't do those things, but what Schmoke did was still remarkable. He was a good steward of the city who, unable to transform it completely, did his best to guide it to sure footing through good governance. Schmoke's leadership wasn't the most thrilling, but his pragmatism and insistence on sound policy over politics probably saved Baltimore from a far worse fate.

42

—

LENNIE
(1990s–PRESENT)

SHE TRIED FOR AS LONG as she could to hide the fact that she was a prostitute. But it became harder to hide as she sank further into her addiction. Lennie did her best to keep herself up, to dress nicely and blend in, but crack took enough of a toll on her physically that it became impossible for her to work in Culver City without getting stopped by the police and questioned.

She started working where they weren't, closer to home, near Normandie and Western Avenues. She was selling her body for crack or just to eat, if she ate at all. She prided herself on never having a pimp, but crack became exactly that.

Lennie took some breaks, short periods where she'd put drugs on the back burner to handle some urgent business. At some point during her twenties, she tried getting clean and enrolling at West Los Angeles College, but she couldn't keep it up. She would have a drink, and that drink led to her smoking, and after smoking she felt like all her progress had been undone, so she just gave up.

She got a job at a call center during one promising period. She was selling home-improvement packages and was good at it. The boss told her so. She even managed to get her own apartment, a two-bedroom. Then Rudy, Lennie's oldest friend, was shot and killed. His murder threw her into an emotional tailspin that ended in relapse again.

There were also people from the neighborhood who remembered Lennie when she was a young girl just looking to make friends and hang out. Between them and the guys who knew Jay, she had a layer of protection from the random violence other women in her position faced.

Lennie was also a hustler and never lost her ability to negotiate and charm. Even on crack, she always had a place to live. She stayed at home for a while. When that was no longer possible, she hustled up materials from a construction site and convinced Uncle Archie to turn the screened-in back porch into a separate room. When she couldn't stay home any longer, she talked her way into apartments, where she'd stay as long as she could before getting evicted. Eventually, Lennie managed to get a voucher for the Section 8 program.

She was spared some of the trials other addicts faced but not all. One time, Lennie had agreed to go to a motel with a man. Everything was fine until she actually got in the room with him and two other men emerged from the bathroom. She knew that they would rape her, maybe kill her, but a calm came over her. She started thinking and talking fast. "Y'all's mamas would be so disappointed," she said. "Y'all are so cute. Why you gotta take pussy from a woman?" It was enough to put everyone at ease long enough for her to make a dash for the door and get away.

On another occasion, she was in a neighborhood where dealers were infamous for abusing addicts. She was trying to buy crack from a group of guys when she saw a woman she grew up with, obviously trying to get high, too. The woman started bargaining with the guys until they eventually said they'd give her a few rocks if she penetrated herself with an ear of corn. To Lennie's horror, the woman agreed. Having not debased her enough, the men asked if she'd have sex with a dog.

Lennie became so overcome with anger, she didn't care about getting high or what the men might do to her. She told the woman, "Get up," and dragged her out of there. Lennie again got away unscathed.

But she wasn't always so lucky. During her years in the streets, she crossed paths with people unlike any she'd met early on. She ran into rapists and sadists. She was threatened. She was beaten. She was stabbed, and even shot. She relied on her personality and her humor to get through it all, even the scariest situations.

It was two in the morning when Lennie jumped in the car with one trick. It was risky, she thought, but she'd taken many other risks by then and survived them. They were riding on their way to the man's place when he pulled a gun seemingly from nowhere. She barely had a chance to respond, because next the man was putting some kind of sheet over her head and yelling, "Get down, get down, get down." He'd blow her head off if she moved, he said.

Lennie's fear grew to terror when she realized that she was losing her sense of direction as the man drove in what felt like circles. It wasn't just a rape, she thought. The man then said, "I got a body in the back. You want to see it?" Lennie couldn't bring herself to answer at first, so he just kept repeating it. "I got a body in the back. I got a body in the back." Finally, she replied, "No, I don't want to see it."

The car eventually stopped. Lennie tried to stay calm, against every instinct she had, as the man got out of the car, opened her door, and guided her to a building. They went up some stairs, and then he finally pulled the hood off. Lennie opened her eyes and saw a normal bedroom, but right beside the door was a table covered with guns. Behind her, on the back of the door, was a meat hook. The man handcuffed Lennie and secured her wrists to the hook on the door.

Then it was like a switch had been flipped in him. The man went from calm and methodical to crazed and menacing. He started ranting about how Lennie was a demon, and how women like her shouldn't be on the streets. "You need help," he kept saying. All she could do was feel her way through it.

She didn't know what was going to happen next, but she just kept telling herself that all she had to do was get to a gun. If she could get to a gun, she thought, she could try to get him before he got her. He didn't go for a gun, though. Instead, he checked to make sure that her handcuffs were secure before stripping her and sodomizing her.

Lennie tried talking to him when it was over. She'd had enough close calls with men by then that she knew that she needed to get him to see her, Lennie, and not a "demon." She talked about how late it was, and how tired she was. Hanging there, she tried to crack jokes. Eventually, he let her down. She wanted to run, but something told her that wasn't a good idea. She still didn't know where she was, and he had so many guns.

After a while, the man said, "Put the hood back on," and he took her back out to the car. This was when Lennie became certain that she was going to be killed. Still, she stayed calm as he drove and drove and drove on, talking the whole while about the body in the back of his car.

Then something came over Lennie. Out of nowhere, she asked, "You got a cigarette?" He didn't respond, but she didn't let up. Every time he'd go on about the body, she'd say, "I need a cigarette." Eventually he got quiet, and that's when she said, "You're right. I shouldn't be out here. You are so right."

The next thing she knew, the car stopped, and he was uncovering her head. Lennie looked up and saw that he'd driven to a gas station. She held her breath as the man went into his pocket and pulled out money for her to buy a pack of cigarettes. He said he'd wait for her to give her a ride home, but Lennie went in and hid in an aisle until he was gone.

It was maybe the scariest thing that ever happened to her, in a life full of frightful events. The average person might have called the police to report the incident, but Lennie didn't. She couldn't. She was an addict and prostitute, after all, and she doubted that they'd care. So Lennie just thanked God for her life, went home, and tried to put the awfulness out of her mind.

Trauma and the endless pursuit of relief became the theme of

Lennie's life for the next two decades. Time flew by as she drifted through a series of lows and highs. It was a hard life, maybe the hardest any person could live, but it became normal to her after a while—mundane, even. She became a creature of the streets, and with every year that passed she drifted further away from the person she had been, from her family and the community that raised her.

Lennie's pipe was her only friend. She called it her baby. She fought with it, had sex with it, was arrested dozens of times with it. It was the center of her life.

So caught up, she could no longer hide that she was an addict. It didn't help to put on fresh clothes or fuss with her hair. People could tell no matter what she did. Some people were forthright about it, calling her names like "crackhead." However, most people showed it in little ways, like avoiding eye contact, putting physical distance between themselves and her. If they talked to her, their voices were both distant and cold.

It's one thing to be thought of as a bad person. It's another entirely to be thought of as so bad that you're no longer a person. Lennie felt like that's what was happening to her—she was so far outside of everything that she couldn't find a way back in. It hurt, but what hurt most was the impact it had on her son, Jamal.

He adored her when he was small. She spent as much time with him as her lifestyle allowed, and he lit up whenever she was in the room. That light seemed to dim as he got older.

Lennie didn't consider herself a good mother, but she loved her son. She never hit him, always tried to lift him up. "You can be anything you want in this world," she'd tell him. She hoped it was enough, but she knew it wasn't. Not enough to balance out the embarrassment and the hurt he likely felt. Over the years, Jamal just got angrier and angrier to the point that Lennie barely recognized him. It was devastating. Here he was, her only family in the world, and she'd made him into a stranger.

With nothing and no one else, Lennie eventually found herself homeless and strung out on L.A.'s infamous Skid Row. In 2006, Lennie was arrested once again for possession. She was facing five years in prison but, by the grace of God, was extended one last chance by the court. Prosecutors said that she could avoid the sentence if she got treatment for her addiction. Lennie saw the offer as a lifeline and eagerly accepted it.

MISS WOODLEY FINALLY GOT clean in 2006 after decades of using. She was homeless at the time and living on Skid Row. "I attribute that to God, my fear of prison, the twelve-step program of Narcotics Anonymous, and me making a decision not to use no more," she says.

"My son is the only reason I'm alive today," says Miss Woodley. "No matter what happened—the fights, the kidnapping, the rape, being shot at—I wouldn't let any of it keep me from getting home to my son."

Today, Miss Woodley is piecing her life back together. She found housing, then work. Then she went back to school and eventually received a degree in psychology from Los Angeles City College, where she continues to take classes. She also speaks all over Los Angeles at events focused on recovery and women's empowerment. Doing that work has forced her to sift through the past and make meaning of her years in the streets.

Sadly, many of her memories are incomplete or lost entirely in a haze of crack smoke. According to the National Institute on Drug Abuse, long-term cocaine use can lead to cognitive impairment, including memory loss. "My twenties and my thirties are completely gone," she says. "I can recall some stuff, but most of it—names, places, dates—it all kind of just runs together."

It is a gift and curse that she can't remember a great deal of the past. In many ways, having those memories locked somewhere inside her is what has allowed her to keep going. Otherwise, she might get caught in their undertow.

What she does remember, however, she embraces. "I have no regrets and no shame over any of the things that I've ever done or that were done to me in my life," she says. "You can never forget where you came from or the things that have shaped you. If you do, then how do you celebrate making it to the other side?"

In 2013, Miss Woodley signed up for AncestryDNA, a service that analyzes DNA samples from users to offer insights regarding health, ethnicity, and, as the name suggests, ancestry. It took five years, but in 2019, she was able to find her biological family using the service. A woman contacted her, suspecting from their results that she and Miss Woodley were related. Indeed, they were—first cousins on the woman's maternal side. From there, Miss Woodley found her biological mother.

She's also working on rebuilding her relationship with her son, Jamal. She was in and out of his life for so long, something that Miss Woodley knows had a negative impact. He got angry after a while. He started acting out and got in trouble with the law.

"You can't save nobody that don't want to be saved. It's like the devil couldn't get me, so he's going after mine," she says. Still, she does what she can to help, what she wishes others had done for her.

43

—

AFTER CRACK

THE CRACK EPIDEMIC HAS grown in legend since it tailed off in the mid-nineties, and the further away we get from its height, the more grotesque it has become in the American imagination. That's partly a product of memory itself, it seems, but also a consequence of which memories of the epidemic have been prioritized, and whose.

For more than three decades, we've listened to law-enforcement officials, politicians, and talking heads. Most of those people were never really touched by the epidemic, though, except perhaps for what they saw in the news or experienced in passing. For those people, the crack epidemic was and continues to be an idea that encapsulates everything bad about the eighties and nineties—the poverty, crime, gangs, violence, everything the ghetto represented in post–Civil Rights Movement America.

But for people who came face-to-face with the crack epidemic, it was as real as flesh and blood. Crack and its attendant misery permeated every aspect of our lives. For us, the crack epidemic was more than a collection of statistics used in an article or speech. It was a dominating force in our homes, families, and communities.

How we survived that with little to no assistance from the larger society is nothing short of amazing. Psychologists call it resilience: the mental process by which people accept loss, manage emotions, maintain confidence, and problem-solve in the face of adversity. Everyone has it, they say. Maybe so, but history has proven that nobody has it in abundance like Black Americans. We've proven resilient through centuries of challenge and change. The trick, it seems, is our very Blackness—not merely our color but something much deeper.

Resilience, psychologists say, is built on a foundation of caring and supportive relationships within and outside of families. "Relationships that create love and trust, provide role models and offer encouragement and reassurance help bolster a person's resilience," wrote Harvard psychiatrists J. Heidi Gralinski-Bakker and Stuart T. Hauser in their 2004 paper on resilience in vulnerable populations. If that's true, then it appears Black identity—a construct assigned to the darker peoples of the world for the purpose of discrimination—has become a shield, membership in a club that offers care and support through the toughest times.

And so it was that when the fires of the crack epidemic were finally extinguished, Black people emerged from the ashes together, having encountered untold defeats but still undefeated. That's the major takeaway of the crack epidemic: drugs like cocaine are addictive, mind-altering substances with the ability to shift cultures, generate fortunes, provoke hysteria, and disrupt communities. They are not, however, more powerful than the human spirit, hope, faith, second chances, the love and support of family, expressions of community care.

The process of recovery has been slow but steady. Much of the work has been invisible. Still, there are signs all around that Black America is healing itself from the inside out. High school graduation rates increased from a historic low of 87 percent in 1990 to 92 percent in 2017, according to the National Center for Education Statistics. Rates of Black teen pregnancy peaked in 1991 but have been falling ever since. Back then, for every 1,000 girls aged fifteen to nineteen,

118 had given birth. According to the most recent count by the Department of Health and Human Services, that number declined to 29 births for every 1,000 girls in 2016. Violent crime against and by Black people has also fallen sharply since it peaked in the nineties. There were, for example, 7,851 Black murder victims in 2017. Far too many, but that number is down considerably from its record high in 1991, when 10,660 Black men and women were killed.

In many ways, Black America is stronger post-crack than it was before. Millennials, individuals born between 1981 and 1996—the children of the crack epidemic—have surpassed previous generations in several respects. Since 1995, college enrollment for Black people aged eighteen to twenty-four has increased 9 percentage points. Black millennials are less likely than previous generations to do illegal drugs. The University of Michigan's government-funded "Monitoring the Future Survey" found, for example, that just around one percent of high school seniors had used cocaine in 1999, the year the oldest millennials became twelfth graders. That's compared to about three percent in 1989 and more than four percent a decade earlier.

Black millennials are also building new networks for and approaches to political and social activism. The clearest example of this is the Black Lives Matter movement, which sprang up following the shooting death of seventeen-year-old Trayvon Martin in 2012. While many of the groups within the movement target police violence against Black people primarily, Black Lives Matter more broadly was concerned with the conditions surrounding life for America's most vulnerable. To that end, the movement both attempted to carry out the unfinished work of the Civil Rights Movement and tackled head-on the indifference to Black suffering that facilitated the crack epidemic.

Years before Black millennials were organized around justice, they were organized around Barack Obama's campaign for the presidency. Just as the progressive movements of the sixties and the election of John F. Kennedy were expressions of the baby boomers' desire to correct the errors of previous generations, Obama's campaign marshaled the hopes of millennials—Black millennials especially. He rode the wave of our desire for a fairer system, one that acknowledged the plight of the most vulnerable instead of locking them up in droves.

Naturally, then, the Obama presidency ushered in a period of focus on racial justice. It also summoned levels of anti-Black racism unseen since the Reconstruction era. Those two currents came together to produce a moment in American history unlike any other: eight years during which race and justice were at the forefront of the national consciousness and the leader of the nation was a Black man.

Of Obama's reforms, *New Yorker* staff writer Jelani Cobb wrote, "The armchair forecast holds that the President's legacy will be anchored by his handling of two wars abroad. But history may have equal regard for the means by which he handles the one he inherited at home."

While many were disappointed in Obama's efforts to mitigate injustice in America, his administration did take significant steps to de-escalate the war on drugs. First, Obama signed the Fair Sentencing Act of 2010, a law that reduced the disparity between sentences for possession of crack and powder cocaine from a ratio of a hundred to one to eighteen to one. Next, in April 2014, the administration announced the Clemency Initiative, a program that encouraged federal prisoners to petition to have their sentences commuted or reduced by the president.

The initiative was controversial. It challenged decades of tough-on-crime politics and attitudes, but the administration followed through, and by the time he left office in 2016, Obama had commuted the sentences of 1,715 men and women, the majority of whom were nonviolent drug offenders.

Other moves by the Obama administration signaled a drawdown in the war on drugs. Under Obama, the Justice Department announced that the federal government would phase out its use of private prisons. Attorney General Eric Holder also encouraged Congress to overhaul federal drug-sentencing laws—and federal prosecutors to exercise more discretion in charging drug crimes, rather than always pursuing the toughest possible charges and sentences.

Just as important as its policy initiatives, however, was the Obama DOJ's public stance against the racism that animated crack-era politics and policy. "Though this nation has proudly thought of itself as an ethnic melting pot in things racial, we have always been, and we, I believe, continue to be, in too many ways, essentially a nation of cowards," said Holder during a February 2009 address to his staff. "Though race-related issues continue to occupy a significant portion of our political discussion, and though there remain many unresolved racial issues in this nation, we, average Americans, simply do not talk enough with each other about things racial."

In keeping with Holder's remarks, the Justice Department under Obama was aggressive in confronting racism in policing. Spurred by a string of high-profile police shootings and protests, it launched aggressive investigations in nearly two dozen cities, including Ferguson, Missouri; Cleveland; and Baltimore. Those investigations produced damning reports on racist patterns and practices in policing. Ultimately, Obama's Justice Department forced fourteen police departments into consent decrees, legal arrangements that forced them into reform and allowed for federal oversight.

Even as Obama's presidency approached its end, Black Lives Matter activists fought to keep reform on the national agenda by pressing the 2016 presidential candidates on justice issues. They applied pressure at campaign events, on social media, and in the press.

In July and August of 2015, activists interrupted campaign events to demand that Democratic candidate Bernie Sanders incorporate a racial-justice analysis into his critique of inequality in the United States. Others confronted candidate Hillary Clinton at a February 2016 fundraiser and demanded that she "apologize for mass incarceration" and answer for her use of the term "superpredator" to describe juvenile drug offenders in a 1996 speech. Months later, protesters showed up at a rally where Bill Clinton was speaking.

Much to the former president's chagrin, they interrupted his remarks with chants of "Black youth are not superpredators."

Hillary Clinton's eventual loss to Donald Trump threatened to halt efforts to reform the criminal legal system. Indeed, a major element of Trump's campaign to "make America great again" was an appeal for law and order right out of Richard Nixon's playbook. In speech after speech, he exaggerated the threat of drugs and crime in America and demonized Black Lives Matter protesters. Upon taking office, Trump began quickly reversing Obama-era reforms. His attorney general, Jeff Sessions, rescinded the Obama Justice Department's memos on private prisons and on charging and sentencing. And before resigning his post in November 2018, Sessions issued a memo limiting the Justice Department's use of consent decrees.

Despite those setbacks, there's still broad consensus that America's system of mass incarceration is immoral and unsustainable. Most Americans also recognize that the war on drugs has been a waste of taxpayer dollars and other resources. According to a 2018 Rasmussen poll, a whopping 75 percent of Americans said they didn't believe the government was winning it. The same share of Americans said the criminal justice system needs "significant" reform. In fact, the movement created by Black Lives Matter activists was so resonant that even the Trump administration was obliged to support some justice reforms.

In June 2018, Trump commuted the sentence of Alice Marie Johnson, a woman serving life in prison for conspiracy to possess cocaine, attempted possession of cocaine, and money laundering. Then in December 2018, he signed the bipartisan First Step Act into law. One of the legislation's major provisions made the Fair Sentencing Act retroactive, opening a path for nearly 2,600 federal inmates to have their sentences reduced. It also eased mandatory minimum sentences under federal law, including lowering the infamous "three strikes" penalty from life in prison to twenty-five years. The First Step Act also authorized increased funding for vocational and rehabilitative programs within prisons—$50 million per year through 2023.

Trump's motives for supporting reform were questionable. Nevertheless, the very existence of a First Step Act, passed overwhelmingly by the U.S. Senate and signed into law by a Republican president, signals that maybe America is ready to end its decades-long war on drugs, crime, and urban America.

We know that drug epidemics come and go. Like the flu or the common cold, they infect the body politic when our systems are compromised. We are presented with options when these epidemics occur. We can shore up the weakened systems that allowed the epidemic to take hold. We can rally around vulnerable communities, providing them with resources and support to survive. Or we can turn our backs on those suffering. Worse yet, we can attack them as though they are affliction itself instead of the afflicted.

There is no guarantee that future generations will not repeat the mistakes of the crack epidemic. Young people tend to experiment with drugs, after all, and there always seems to be a new substance around the corner, or an old one made cheaper and more accessible. Still, no drug trend should devastate a people the way crack did Black America.

I'VE BEEN ALL OVER the country and have interviewed hundreds of people whose lives were touched by crack, but never have I met a "crackhead." I met people—dealers who thought they'd have just one hit, party girls who stayed at the party a little too long, men and women who simply started experimenting with drugs in the wrong decade. Their stories were buried by that word.

I think often of my old neighbor Michelle From Down the Street and wonder what became of her. I like to imagine that she left the neighborhood for treatment—that she got clean and moved into a big house with her daughter, who can't remember a time when they weren't attached at the hip.

Years of covering the criminal legal system tell me that outcome is unlikely, though. It's more probable that she was criminalized for her addiction and gobbled up by the system. If Michelle is alive today and clean, she probably lives with the residue of the epidemic—a criminal record, chronic illness, trauma, guilt, and shame.

For her sake and those of so many others, it's past time that we reconcile the crack epidemic with the rest of Black history and identity. We must take its measure, make meaning of it, and incorporate that meaning into the greater story of who we are.

It's time we begin the difficult work of excavating the real stories of the individuals, families, and communities who were swept up in the crack epidemic. A part of that work is putting ideas like "crackhead," "crack baby," and "superpredator" to rest.

They were always constructs, after all, distortions of flesh-and-blood people. It wasn't those people—our people, us—who should have been the objects of our fears but the forces that created them.

I got to the end of my reporting on the crack epidemic in 2018 after spending nearly a year on the road. I settled in Atlanta and began the hard work of writing this book. It was tough from the very start. Indeed, I'd tried to write what I was learning as I learned it but couldn't. For the first time in my entire career as a journalist, I had writer's block. It was like an out-of-body experience, sitting down at my keyboard and freezing at the sight of the blank page. And there was no getting by it, no nifty techniques to summon the words to describe everything I'd experienced.

Before long, I'd break out in hives when I thought about writing (hives, another first). Next came the nightmares that made me awaken violently in the middle of the night and left me gasping for air. I'd dealt with anxiety and panic attacks before as an undergrad and again in grad school, but those episodes didn't hold a candle to the experiences I had attempting to put the crack epidemic into words. At times, it felt like the story wanted to kill me.

As I struggled through each chapter, each moment in the lives of Kurt, Elgin, Lennie, and Shawn, the story fought back. Throughout the writing process, I had brain fog, insomnia, stomach pains, heart palpitations. On more than one occasion I visited the ER, certain that

I was dying. Doctors and nurses would check my vitals; all normal. Then they'd ask me if I had any major stressors or if I'd experienced any recent trauma.

One of the valleys of the experience came in 2020, at the height of the COVID-19 pandemic and after a summer of protest. On a break from book writing, I attempted to report on something else, a local topic that would provide an outlet for my creative energies and ground me firmly in the present.

The nearest story to me was that of Atlanta's "water boys": groups of young men who peddle bottles of water at a dollar a pop, all over the city and my downtown neighborhood. Water boys are a part of the landscape in Atlanta. Like hydrangeas, lavender, and other perennials, they appear as the days get longer and temperatures rise. Their curbside operations are usually a welcome sight in a city known for its heat. That summer changed that, however, as a climate of fear and desperation threatened to weed out the water boys and maybe do worse.

A handful of violent incidents that summer were responsible for the shift. First, a fourteen-year-old boy threatened a man with a handgun after he refused to buy water. The very next day saw a similar incident with another boy. Then later, an altercation between water boys ended with eighteen-year-old Jalanni Pless shot and killed by another teen.

Atlanta mayor Keisha Lance Bottoms announced soon after an initiative to curb unpermitted water sales, and ultimately the water boys. "We appreciate the entrepreneurial spirit of youth who are selling water to motorists," said Mayor Bottoms. "But we have seen an increase in unsafe and violent activity in some locations and cannot allow it to continue."

Tensions mounted, and I was once again transported back in time as city officials debated whether to arrest the boys or put them in jobs programs, or maybe even issue citations to their parents. I couldn't help but worry about what was around the corner in a moment when Black death and suffering were more visible than ever, when calls to end police brutality still went unanswered, when nearly twenty-nine thousand Black Americans were dead from COVID and almost one-third of Black Americans knew someone who'd died from the illness, when mass evictions were threatening to further destabilize Black communities, when architects and advocates of mass incarceration had been elected president of the United States, when the response to Black boys hustling on corners (water this time) was still the police.

All it would take was the right substance—novel, cheap, and abundant—for us to be right back where we were a few decades ago, I thought. I hoped for everyone's sake that it didn't come along.

I'm ashamed to say how long it took me to put two and two together. Truly, for most of that very trying time, I attributed the way my body was reacting to either "book jitters" or a medical mystery that would require the world's finest internists to solve. But little by little, I came to accept that what was happening was something theorists had proposed: the trauma of the crack epidemic—that which I'd experienced firsthand growing up, and that which I had absorbed talking to Kurt, Elgin, Lennie, and Shawn—was wreaking havoc in my body and creating classic symptoms of post-traumatic stress disorder.

I would like to say that the symptoms went away with the revelation, but they didn't. They persisted even after I cranked out a 110,000-word manuscript. They were compounded as I looked around and saw glimmers of the past.

I saw the way hope succumbed to fear and how fear fueled a violent backlash, how the backlash created trauma and trauma laid the groundwork for a substance that promised escape. I was triggered when Donald Trump promised "law and order," as Richard Nixon had; triggered as COVID devastated communities of color, as HIV/AIDS had; triggered seeing police beat Black protestors in the street, as they had in the sixties and seventies.

It took months of counseling, prayer, yoga, medication, and reflection for me to come to grips with the fact that my grief over what had already happened and my apprehension about what was to come were collapsing time—the past, the present, and the future—into a whole mess of hurt.

When Crack Was King is, hopefully, a narrative intervention that will help heal the hurt. The book is my earnest effort to make history out of memories. Not an attempt to discredit or exclude dissonant notes, but to synthesize them into a harmonious whole. I hope *When Crack Was King* has done that for the people who spent hours piecing their life stories together with me. And I hope that their stories, together, will produce something that helps us all make sense of both the crack era and where we are today.

The crack epidemic is over. We should celebrate that, and the fact that Black America survived it and the war on drugs that followed. People of good conscience should also hold to account the individuals and entities that helped spread the epidemic, and those that organized a draconian response merely for political gain. Then and only then can we begin the work of healing and repair—reversing unjust laws, challenging the myths of the era, treating PTSD in survivors.

If we fail to do this, to reckon with this history, we are doomed to repeat it.

—

ACKNOWLEDGMENTS

I reserve the greatest measure of gratitude for Lennie Woodley, Elgin Swift, Kurt Schmoke, Shawn McCray, and the many other sources who entrusted me with their memories. They believed in me despite the inherent difficulty of telling a story such as this. Thank you for seeing me and allowing me to see you. It is my deepest hope that this book honors your lives and does your remarkable stories justice.

When Crack Was King is the culmination of five years of research, conversations, and writing. I was supported along the way—carried at times, really—by my extraordinary editor, Nicole Counts. Thank you, Nicole, for your patience and understanding, for being a sister, and for always reminding me to get out of my head and back into my body.

My gratitude also to the team at One World and Penguin Random House: Chris Jackson, Victory Matsui, Oma Beharry, Greg Mollica, Carla Bruce-Eddings, Avideh Bashirrad, Cecilia Flores, Angela Orlando, Greg Kubie, Andrea Pura, and Tiffani Ren. I cannot thank you enough for your editorial help and ongoing support in getting this work to readers. A special acknowledgment to Matthew Martin, Evan

Camfield, and Howard Cohn for polishing the manuscript into a real book that is inarguably better because of their contributions.

When Crack Was King began in earnest with a prompt from Rich Benjamin, the genius writer and then–director of fellows at Demos. He encouraged me, in 2014, to write out five big goals on a sheet of paper before beginning my fellowship. One of those goals was to write a book proposal. That prompt became a proposal, which ultimately became this book. Thank you, Rich, for teaching me to take time to dream.

I would not be the writer and thinker I am without the guidance of David Wall Rice and the Identity, Art & Democracy Lab. Dr. Rice, your scholarship within identity psychology is the foundation of my own writing on race. Your use of language and commitment to *us* is a constant source of inspiration. Thank you for lifting me up while also holding me accountable.

My steadfast, honest, and true appreciation to the Morehouse College community, especially Ron Thomas, Jann Adams, Duane Jackson, Bryant T. Marks, Sr., Sinead Younge, Asha Ivey, Tina R. Chang, Jeanine D. White, and Cynthia Hewitt, for ensuring that I had an understanding of journalism and social science that accounted for people who look and live like me.

I would be remiss not to acknowledge the other educators who invested their time and care into me. Thank you, Amara Eddings, Michael Owens, Stan Embry, and all of the Mamas and Babas at the Columbus Africentric School. Thank you for grounding me at an age when so many young people drift. Thank you also to Giuseppina DiRosario, Eric East, Marvin Beculhimer, and the faculty at Fort Hayes Metropolitan Education Center.

A career in journalism is impossible without a community of people who value your voice, who will read your work and extend opportunities to you. I've had more of those helping hands than I deserve, including Joy-Ann Reid, David A. Wilson, Miles Marshall Lewis, Gordon Hurd, Jason Parham, Chris Gayomali, Rachel Dry, Kierna Mayo, and Jamil Smith. Special thanks to Kristina Moore, Rebecca Nagel, and the team at the Wylie Agency. And a big thanks to Reeves Wiedeman for introducing us.

I have also benefited enormously from conversations, critiques, and kind words from colleagues, including Alexis Garrett Stodghill, Aaron Ross Coleman, J Wortham, Kimberly Drew, Fatimah Asghar, Safia Elhillo, Jay Ellis, Sara David, Reniqua Allen-Lamphere, Vann Newkirk, Robin Walker, Crystal Hayes, and Taylor Eldridge.

Farnoosh Torabi, Danyel Smith, Heather McGhee, and Liz Flowers have given me invaluable mentorship throughout my career. You all have also led by example. I am so grateful to you each for checking in on me, putting in good words, putting me onto game. I will continue to pay it forward wherever I can.

Because *When Crack Was King* links together so much existing knowledge and understanding, I am indebted to entire bodies of scholarship and to those who have contributed to the archives I sought to advance. I am grateful for the work of so many journalists, historians, sociologists, psychologists, and artists.

This book might also not exist without the work of Isabel Wilkerson, Khalil Gibran Muhammad, Ta-Nehisi Coates, Nikole Hannah-Jones, James Forman, Jr., Ibram X. Kendi, Bryan Stevenson, Roland G. Fryer, Jr., Carl Hart, Johann Hari, Carol Anderson, Michael Javen Fortner, Brenda Wall, bell hooks, Keith L. Alexander, Michelle Alexander, Barry Michael Cooper, Andrew Golub, Bruce D. Johnson, Michael Itzkoff, Toni Morrison, Colson Whitehead, Mat Johnson, Philip Roth, Spike Lee, John Singleton, Albert and Allen Hughes, Mario Van Peebles, Maxine Waters, John Kerry, Cornel West, Derrick Bell, William Julius Wilson, Gary Webb, Jay Z, the Notorious B.I.G., Tupac Shakur, Dr. Dre, Kendrick Lamar, and W.E.B. Du Bois. Thank you all for your contributions and examples.

A very special thanks to Adam Culbreath, Christina Voight, and the Open Society Foundations Soros Justice Fellowships, Joan Berry, and Stanford's McCoy Family Center for Ethics in Society Manuscript Workshop. *When Crack Was King* is a better book because of your generous support.

I'm eternally grateful to my ever-loving community. They believed in me and in this project perhaps more than anyone else. Their words of encouragement and loving presence kept me going when the work got hard. I am better for loving them and being loved by them.

Thank you, ancestors: Grandma, Aunt Do, Uncle Walter, Aunt Brenda, Aunt Kathy, Tony, Gaylon, Baby Dexter, and Ben E. Boots. I have felt you each lifting me up and working on my behalf. Thank you to my dear friends: Travers Johnson, Morris Borenstein, Christina Coleman Mullen, Alexandros Orphanides, Gerren Keith Gaynor, Trevor Burton, Zak Cheney-Rice, Josie Duffy Rice, Rosa Duffy, Christian Nwachukwu, Jr., Saada Ahmed, and Samuel Alicea.

I am blessed to have more loving aunts, uncles, cousins, nieces, and nephews than I can name here. I love you all beyond measure. More love to my brilliant dad and to dear Mimi for giving me my missing pieces and so much more. Thank you, Janice Wiggins and Rita Hamilton, my godsent godmothers. Thank you, Kacie, Cory, Gabby, Cole, and Bella. Thank you, Brittany, for being my first friend and always having my back.

I know for certain that this book would not exist without the love and help of Antonio M. Johnson, the best person I know. I am renewed every day by your love, brought closer to God and myself. Thank you for always being there for me, for traveling with me while I researched this book, and for listening to me read every word aloud as I was writing and rewriting it. Thank you, Tone, for loving the rough drafts of me and my work.

Thank you to my amazing mother, who loved me to life. Thank you, Mommy, for your unconditional love and unwavering support. Thank you for always listening and for always encouraging me. Long before this book was a thought, you demonstrated for me how to speak from my heart, how to lead with love and fight like hell when I must. I owe you everything.

Last but not least, all credit is due to the Most High from whom all truth and love flow. Only the mistakes have been mine.

—

BIBLIOGRAPHY

Abusaid, Shaddi. "After Latest Shooting, Atlanta Police Consider Citing Parents of 'Water Boys.'" *Atlanta Journal-Constitution,* May 7, 2021. ajc.com/news/atlanta-teen-shot-during-fight-over-bottled-water-sales/ZEDV54C57NBMHGE46P5EC43TFU/.

———. "Atlanta Police, City Officials Cracking Down on Roadside Water Sales." *Atlanta Journal-Constitution,* July 25, 2020. ajc.com/news/atlanta-police-city-officials-cracking-down-on-roadside-water-sales/54FSZVBRYZGVNIUYER5W3LGDEY/.

Agnew, Spiro T. "Opening Statement." Speech, Baltimore, Md., April 11, 1968.

Aiken, Jonathan. "C.I.A. Admits It Overlooked Contras' Links to Drugs." CNN, November 3, 1998. cnn.com/US/9811/03/cia.drugs/.

Alexander, Keith L. "Decades After Three People Were Killed in a D.C. Park, Their Families Learn It Was Over $20 Worth of Cocaine." *Washington Post,* February 16, 2018. washingtonpost.com/local/public-safety/decades-after-three-people-were-killed-in-a

-dc-park-their-families-learn-it-was-over-20-worth-of-cocaine/2018/
02/16/0ce7e516-125a-11e8-9570-29c9830535e5_story.html.

Alexander, Michelle. "The Nation: The New Jim Crow." NPR, March
15, 2010. npr.org/templates/story/story.php?storyId=124687663.

———. *The New Jim Crow: Mass Incarceration in the Age of Colorblind-
ness.* New York: The New Press, 2012.

Allen, Jonathan. "Bill Clinton Defends Wife's 'Super Predator' Comment to Protesters." Reuters, April 7, 2016. reuters.com/article/
us-usa-election-billclinton-idUSKCN0X42NS.

American Addiction Centers. "Drug and Alcohol Abuse Across Generations." August 2, 2022. drugabuse.com/featured/drug-and
-alcohol-abuse-across-generations/.

American Psychological Association. "Resilience." apa.org/topics/
resilience.

AP News. "Report: Cocaine Ring Finances Contras." March 16, 1986.
apnews.com/article/e91b543900c3e8736ea34a290dc87010.

———. "US Concedes Contras Linked to Drugs, But Denies Leadership Involved." April 17, 1986. apnews.com/article/bb7394e75625
a363b8c0bf9b0d6cf969.

Apperson, Jay. "'Drug Court' Offers Treatment and Job Advice, Not
Jail." *Baltimore Sun,* March 30, 1994. baltimoresun.com/news/
bs-xpm-1994-03-30-1994089005-story.html.

Apple, R. W., Jr. "Washington's Suburbs Offer Tsongas a Chance to
Win Again." *New York Times,* February 27, 1992. nytimes.com/
1992/02/27/us/1992-campaign-maryland-washington-s-suburbs
-offer-tsongas-chance-win-again.html.

Applebome, Peter. "Death Penalty; Arkansas Execution Raises Questions on Governor's Politics." *New York Times,* January 25, 1992.

nytimes.com/1992/01/25/us/1992-campaign-death-penalty
-arkansas-execution-raises-questions-governor-s.html.

Associated Press. "Baltimore Mayor Supports Legalization of Illicit
Drugs." *New York Times,* September 30, 1988. nytimes.com/1988/
09/30/us/baltimore-mayor-supports-legalization-of-illicit-drugs
.html.

———. "Bias Report Disputed." *New York Times,* September 14, 1986.
nytimes.com/1986/09/14/sports/bias-report-disputed.html.

———. "Evidence Indicates Bias Had Smoked Pure Form of Drug."
Los Angeles Times, July 10, 1986. latimes.com/archives/la-xpm
-1986-07-10-sp-22181-story.html.

———. "Study Ties Cocaine Use to Theft." *New York Times,* September 20, 1983. nytimes.com/1983/09/20/science/study-ties
-cocaine-use-to-theft.html.

———. "Youth Is Arrested for Selling Crack That Bush Displayed."
New York Times, September 27, 1989. nytimes.com/1989/09/27/
us/youth-is-arrested-for-selling-crack-that-bush-displayed.html.

Baldwin, Lewis V. "Malcolm X and Martin Luther King, Jr.: What
They Thought About Each Other." *Islamic Studies* 25, no. 4 (Winter 1986): 395–416. jstor.org/stable/20839793.

Balko, Radley. *Rise of the Warrior Cop: The Militarization of America's
Police Forces.* New York: PublicAffairs, 2013.

Baltimore Sun. "Mayor Has Had Enough After 11 Years in Office City
Hall: Schmoke's Decision Not to Seek Reelection Should Trigger
Intense Debate on Baltimore's Future." December 4, 1998.
baltimoresun.com/news/bs-xpm-1998-12-04-1998338128-story.html.

———. "Spotlight on Schmoke and Mikulski." July 17, 1992.
baltimoresun.com/news/bs-xpm-1992-07-17-1992199036-story.html.

Banisky, Sandy. "Baltimore May Rewrite Anti-Drug Policy Focus on Arresting Traffickers, Treating Addicts, Panel Says." *Baltimore Sun,* September 9, 1993. baltimoresun.com/news/bs-xpm-1993-09-09 -1993252005-story.html.

———. "Drug Problems as Health Issue: Schmoke Task Force Shows Way." *Baltimore Sun,* September 12, 1993. baltimoresun.com/news/ bs-xpm-1993-09-12-1993255195-story.html.

Barger, Brian. "FBI Reportedly Probes Contras on Drugs, Guns." *AP News,* April 10, 1986. apnews.com/article/4c28d082f93d4d08d4fc 2b41a968a1f4.

Bartley, William Alan, and Geoffrey Fain Williams. "The Role of Gun Supply in 1980s and 1990s Urban Violence." June 27, 2015. dx.doi .org/10.2139/ssrn.2623253.

Baum, Dan. "Legalize It All." *Harper's Magazine,* April 2016. harpers .org/archive/2016/04/legalize-it-all/.

Bennett, David A. "Rescue Schools, Turn a Profit." *New York Times,* June 11, 1992. nytimes.com/1992/06/11/opinion/rescue-schools -turn-a-profit.html.

Berke, Richard L. "Bennett Asks Tougher Drug Fight, Declaring Crack 'Biggest Problem.'" *New York Times,* August 1, 1989. nytimes .com/1989/08/01/us/bennett-asks-tougher-drug-fight-declaring -crack-biggest-problem.html.

———. "For Baltimore Mayor, A Shaky Incumbency." *New York Times,* September 7, 1995. nytimes.com/1995/09/07/us/for-baltimore -mayor-a-shaky-incumbency.html.

Berman, Emily. "D.C. Residents Caught Amid Crack's Bloody Turf Wars." WAMU, January 30, 2014. wamu.org/story/DC-Residents -Caught-Amid-Cracks-Turf-Wars/.

Black Enterprise. "Black Bourgeoisie Revisited: Two Views." December 1978. books.google.com/books?id=dA4VzDQqOcsC&printsec

=frontcover&dq=black+middle+class&hl=en&sa=X&ved=0ah
UKEwi1q-Kc7OrdAhVdHzQIHZezAVsQ6AEITTAJ#v=onepage
&q=black%20middle%20class&f=false.

Blakeslee, Sandra. "Crack's Toll Among Babies: A Joyless View, Even
of Toys." *New York Times,* September 17, 1989. nytimes.com/1989/
09/17/us/crack-s-toll-among-babies-a-joyless-view-even-of-toys
.html?pagewanted=all.

Boo, Katherine. "Crack's Crash." *Washington Post,* August 26, 1994.
washingtonpost.com/archive/politics/1994/08/26/cracks-crash/
6f376d48-387f-4273-adbf-33f4388faf50/.

Boyd, Gerald M. "Reagan Signs Anti-Drug Measure; Hopes for 'Drug-
Free Generation.'" *New York Times,* October 28, 1986. nytimes
.com/1986/10/28/us/reagan-signs-anti-drug-measure-hopes-for
-drug-free-generation.html.

Bradner, Eric, "Bill Clinton Spars with Black Lives Matter Protesters."
CNN, April 8, 2016. cnn.com/2016/04/07/politics/bill-clinton
-black-lives-matter-protesters/.

Brinkley, Joel. "Anti-Drug Law: Words, Deeds, Political Expediency."
New York Times, October 27, 1986. nytimes.com/1986/10/27/us/
anti-drug-law-words-deeds-political-expediency.html.

Broder, David S. "Clinton's Gamble with Jesse Jackson." *Washington
Post,* June 17, 1992. washingtonpost.com/archive/opinions/1992/
06/17/clintons-gamble-with-jesse-jackson/42afc01e-4199-4d0c-b4d9
-41d53961a429/.

Brown, DeNeen L. "Residents Have Drug Sellers on the Run." *Washington Post,* June 4, 1989. washingtonpost.com/archive/local/
1989/06/04/residents-have-drug-sellers-on-the-run/19954794
-5dcd-4276-9a10-033821213ca9/.

Bush, George H. W. "National Drug Control Strategy 1." Speech,
Washington, D.C., September 5, 1989.

Butterfield, Fox. "Drop in Homicide Rate Linked to Crack's Decline." *New York Times,* October 27, 1997. nytimes.com/1997/10/27/us/drop-in-homicide-rate-linked-to-crack-s-decline.html.

Cannon, Carl M. "Clinton Gives Cities Hope, Schmoke Says That Zeal Spurred His Decision to Stay." *Baltimore Sun,* October 1, 1993. baltimoresun.com/news/bs-xpm-1993-10-01-1993274048-story.html.

Carmichael, Stokely. "Black Power." Speech, Mississippi, June 6, 1966.

Carson, E. Ann. "National Prisoner Statistics (NPS) Program." Bureau of Justice Statistics. bjs.ojp.gov/data-collection/national-prisoner-statistics-nps-program.

Carstairs, Catherine. "'The Most Dangerous Drug': Images of African-Americans and Cocaine Use in the Progressive Era." *Left History* 7, no. 1 (2000): 46–61. doi.org/10.25071/1913-9632.5410.

Carter, Daryl A. *Brother Bill: President Clinton and the Politics of Race and Class.* Fayetteville: University of Arkansas Press, 2016.

Cassie, Ron. "Back to the Future." *Baltimore Magazine,* April 2018. baltimoremagazine.com/section/health/thirty-years-ago-kurt-schmoke-openly-advocating-for-decriminalization-of-marijuana/.

Castañeda, Rubén. *S Street Rising: Crack, Murder, and Redemption in D.C.* New York: Bloomsbury, 2014.

CBS News. "MLK: A Riot Is the Language of the Unheard." August 25, 2013. cbsnews.com/news/mlk-a-riot-is-the-language-of-the-unheard/.

Celis, William. "Private Group Hired to Run 9 Public Schools in Baltimore." *New York Times,* June 11, 1992. nytimes.com/1992/06/11/us/private-group-hired-to-run-9-public-schools-in-baltimore.html.

Chasnoff, Ira J., William J. Burns, Sidney H. Schnoll, and Kayreen A. Burns. "Cocaine Use in Pregnancy." *New England Journal of Medi-*

cine 313, no. 11 (September 1985): 666–669. nejm.org/doi/full/ 10.1056/NEJM198509123131105.

Children's Hospital of Philadelphia. "Poverty More Damaging Than Gestational Drug Exposure." October 21, 2013. chop.edu/news/ poverty-more-damaging-gestational-drug-exposure.

Childress, Sarah. "Michelle Alexander: 'A System of Racial and Social Control.'" *Frontline,* April 29, 2014. pbs.org/wgbh/frontline/ article/michelle-alexander-a-system-of-racial-and-social-control/.

City of Atlanta, Georgia. "Atlanta Mayor Keisha Lance Bottoms Announces Initiatives to Further Curb Unpermitted Water Sales." July 25, 2020. atlantaga.gov/Home/Components/News/News/ 13418/672?backlist=%2F.

Clines, Francis X. "A Divisive Mayoral Race in Baltimore." *New York Times,* August 8, 1999. nytimes.com/1999/08/08/us/a-divisive -mayoral-race-in-baltimore.html.

Clinton, William J. "Remarks on Signing the Violent Crime Control and Law Enforcement Act of 1994." September 13, 1994. govinfo .gov/content/pkg/PPP-1994-book2/pdf/PPP-1994-book2-doc -pg1539.pdf.

Clymer, Adam. "Crime Bill Approved, 61–38, But Senate Is Going Home Without Acting on Health." *New York Times,* August 26, 1994. nytimes.com/1994/08/26/us/decision-senate-overview -crime-bill-approved-61-38-but-senate-going-home-without.html.

Cobb, Jelani. "A Drawdown in the War on Drugs." *New Yorker,* August 29, 2016. newyorker.com/magazine/2016/08/29/a -drawdown-in-the-war-on-drugs.

Cobbs, Chris. "Widespread Cocaine Use by Players Alarms NBA." *Washington Post,* August 20, 1980. washingtonpost.com/archive/ sports/1980/08/20/widespread-cocaine-use-by-players-alarms-nba/ 0eb819b3-bd92-412a-b14c-baed1a9e7c68/?utm_term=.8730dd0ca91e.

Cockburn, Alexander, and Jeffrey St. Clair. *Whiteout: The CIA, Drugs, and the Press.* London: Verso Books, 1999.

Columbia University Press. "An Interview with Marianne Hirsch." cup .columbia.edu/author-interviews/hirsch-generation-postmemory.

Cooke, Janet. "Jimmy's World." *Washington Post,* September 28, 1980. washingtonpost.com/archive/politics/1980/09/28/jimmys-world/ 605f237a-7330-4a69-8433.

Cooper, Edith Fairman. *The Emergence of Crack Cocaine Abuse.* Hauppauge, N.Y.: Nova Publishers, 2002.

Cooper, Kenneth J. "House Approves $28 Billion Crime Bill." *Washington Post,* April 22, 1994. washingtonpost.com/archive/politics/ 1994/04/22/house-approves-28-billion-crime-bill/8d0f4935-0740 -4413-8ef8.

———. "House Passes $30 Billion Crime Bill, 235 to 195." *Washington Post,* August 22, 1994. washingtonpost.com/archive/politics/1994/ 08/22/house-passes-30-billion-crime-bill-235-to-195/c1780662-ae99 -42b3-a698-21b270d46a52/.

Corn, David. "How I Got That Story." *The Nation,* April 6, 2015. thenation.com/article/archive/how-i-got-story/.

Council of Economic Advisors. "15 Economic Facts About Millennials." October 2014. obamawhitehouse.archives.gov/sites/default/ files/docs/millennials_report.pdf.

COVID Tracking Project. "COVID-19 Is Affecting Black, Indigenous, Latinx, and Other People of Color the Most." March 7, 2021. covidtracking.com/race.

CQ Almanac. "Bush Signs Stripped-Down Crime Bill." 1990, 46th ed., 486–99. Washington, D.C.: Congressional Quarterly, 1991. library .cqpress.com/cqalmanac/cqal90-1113148.

————. "Lawmakers Enact $30.2 Billion Anti-Crime Bill." 1994, 50th ed., 273–87. Washington, D.C.: Congressional Quarterly, 1995. library.cqpress.com/cqalmanac/cqal94-1103448.

Daemmrich, JoAnna. "Schmoke Sworn in for 3rd Term as Mayor: He Calls for All Citizens to Work Together for City." *Baltimore Sun,* December 8, 1995. baltimoresun.com/news/bs-xpm-1995-12-08 -1995342025-story.html.

Daley, Steve. "CBS Gets Libel Jitters." *Chicago Tribune,* September 30, 1986. chicagotribune.com/news/ct-xpm-1986-09-30-8603130156 -story.html.

Denton, Herbert H. "Janet's Race." *Washington Post,* April 26, 1981. washingtonpost.com/archive/opinions/1981/04/26/janets-race/ 9628c9e6-8c2d-45be-9b99-bcfdaa9f9ce5/.

Desert Sun. "Black Panther Greatest Threat to U.S. Security." July 16, 1969. cdnc.ucr.edu/?a=d&d=DS19690716.2.89&e=-------en--20 --1--txt-txIN--------1.

Devroy, Ann, and Kenneth J. Cooper. "$30 Billion Voted to Combat Crime." *Washington Post,* July 29, 1994. washingtonpost.com/ archive/politics/1994/07/29/30-billion-voted-to-combat-crime/ 6301936d-3e07-4237-b0d7-2ca7ae834978/.

Diamond, Jeremy, and Kaitlan Collins. "Trump Commutes Sentence of Alice Marie Johnson." CNN, June 6, 2018. cnn.com/2018/06/06/ politics/alice-marie-johnson-commuted-sentence/index.html.

Dimock, Michael. "Defining Generations: Where Millennials End and Generation Z Begins." Pew Research Center, January 17, 2019. pewresearch.org/fact-tank/2019/01/17/where-millennials-end -and-generation-z-begins/.

Dowd, Maureen. "White House Set Up Drug Buy in the Park for Bush TV Speech." *New York Times,* September 23, 1989. nytimes

.com/1989/09/23/us/white-house-set-up-drug-buy-in-the-park-for
-bush-tv-speech.html.

Drum, Kevin. "Lead: America's Real Criminal Element." *Mother Jones,*
January/February 2013. motherjones.com/environment/2016/02/
lead-exposure-gasoline-crime-increase-children-health/.

Duke, Lynne. "Black Leaders Press Action on Crime, Youth." *Washington Post,* January 9, 1994. washingtonpost.com/archive/politics/
1994/01/09/black-leaders-press-action-on-crime-youth/95ab7fdf
-85ae-42d5-895d-02dc6872311d/.

———. "For Pregnant Addict, Crack Comes First." *Washington Post,*
December 18, 1989. washingtonpost.com/archive/politics/1989/
12/18/for-pregnant-addict-crack-comes-first/1058f8f5-d7a8-43e3
-bbc0-273df79cc09d/.

Dunlap, Eloise, Andrew Golub, and Bruce D. Johnson. "The Severely-
Distressed African American Family in the Crack Era: Empowerment is not Enough." *Journal of Sociology and Social Welfare 33,*
no. 1 (February 2006): 115–39. ncbi.nlm.nih.gov/pmc/articles/
PMC2565489/.

Ebony. "The Black Middle Class Defined." August 1973. books.google
.com/books?id=YKXsm19fBpkC&lpg=PA30&pg=PA30.

———. "The Muslims to the Rescue." August 1989. books.google
.com/books?id=xswDAAAAMBAJ&pg=PA136.

Eizenstat, Stu. "Memorandum: Policy Review on Youth Employment." April 11, 1979. jimmycarterlibrary.gov/digital_library/sso/
148878/113/SSO_148878_113_08.pdf.

Englund, Will. "The Superintendent, the Schools and the Bureau-
crats." *Baltimore Sun,* December 13, 1990. baltimoresun.com/news/
bs-xpm-1990-12-23-1990357022-story.html.

Frazier, E. Franklin. *Black Bourgeoisie.* New York: Free Press, 1997.

Frece, John W. "Schaefer Reluctantly OKs Needle Exchange." *Baltimore Sun*, May 2, 1994. baltimoresun.com/news/bs-xpm-1994-05 -03-1994123057-story.html.

Freud, Sigmund. "Über Coca." 1884.

Fryer, Roland G., Jr., Paul S. Heaton, Steven D. Levitt, and Kevin M. Murphy. "Measuring Crack Cocaine and Its Impact." *Economic Inquiry* 51, no. 3 (July 2013): 1651–81. scholar.harvard.edu/fryer/ publications/measuring-crack-cocaine-and-its-impact.

Fuerbringer, Jonathan. "Making the Punishment Fit the House's Politics." *New York Times*, September 14, 1986. nytimes.com/1986/ 09/14/weekinreview/making-the-punishment-fit-the-house-s -politics.html.

Fulwood, Isaac. "As a Community, We Can Lick Crime." *Washington Post*, May 13, 1990. washingtonpost.com/archive/opinions/1990/ 05/13/as-a-community-we-can-lick-crime/615f406f-4e18-4fa2-99b5 -66e5b6ed6dc2/.

Gately, Gary. "City's Bicentennial Logo Is Unveiled: Mayor Says Baltimore Will Be Renowned as 'The Place to Be in 1997.'" *Baltimore Sun*, June 15, 1996. baltimoresun.com/news/bs-xpm-1996-06-15 -1996167004-story.html.

Genius. "Grandmaster Melle Mel—White Lines (Don't Do It) Lyrics." genius.com/Grandmaster-melle-mel-white-lines-dont-do-it -lyrics.

———. "Ice Cube—A Bird in the Hand Lyrics." genius.com/Ice -cube-a-bird-in-the-hand-lyrics.

———. "Nas—Life's a Bitch Lyrics." genius.com/Nas-lifes-a-bitch -lyrics.

———. "The Notorious B.I.G.—Everyday Struggle Lyrics." genius .com/The-notorious-big-everyday-struggle-lyrics.

———. "Tupac—Keep Ya Head Up Lyrics." genius.com/2pac-keep
-ya-head-up-lyrics.

George, Justin. "What's Really in the First Step Act?" The Marshall
Project, November 16, 2018. themarshallproject.org/2018/11/16/
what-s-really-in-the-first-step-act.

Golden, Tim. "Though Evidence Is Thin, Tale of C.I.A. and Drugs
Has a Life of Its Own." *New York Times*, October 21, 1996. nytimes
.com/1996/10/21/us/though-evidence-is-thin-tale-of-cia-and-drugs
-has-a-life-of-its-own.html.

Goldstein, Amy, and Emily Guskin. "Almost One-Third of Black Americans Know Someone Who Died of Covid-19, Survey Shows." *Washington Post*, June 26, 2020. washingtonpost.com/health/almost
-one-third-of-black-americans-know-someone-who-died-of-covid
-19-survey-shows/2020/06/25/3ec1d4b2-b563-11ea-aca5-ebb63d
27e1ff_story.html.

Golub, Andrew Lang, and Bruce D. Johnson. "Crack's Decline: Some
Surprises Across U.S. Cities." *National Institute of Justice Research in
Brief* (July 1997). ojp.gov/pdffiles/165707.pdf.

———. "The Rise of Marijuana as the Drug of Choice Among Youthful Adult Arrestees." *National Institute of Justice Research in Brief*
(June 2001). ojp.gov/pdffiles1/nij/187490.pdf.

Gottlieb, Adam. *The Pleasures of Cocaine.* Berkeley: Ronin Publishing,
1978.

Gov Track. "H.R. 3355 (103rd): Violent Crime Control and Law Enforcement Act of 1994." govtrack.us/congress/votes/103-1994/
h416.

Green, Bill. "The Players: It Wasn't a Game." *Washington Post*, April 19,
1981. washingtonpost.com/archive/politics/1981/04/19/the
-players-it-wasnt-a-game/545f7157-5228-47b6-8959-fcfcfa8f08eb/.

Greenhouse, Steven. "The Economy; Despite Recession's End, Bush May Face Unusually Harsh Public Judgment." *New York Times,* May 11, 1992. nytimes.com/1992/05/11/us/1992-campaign-economy-despite-recession-s-end-bush-may-face-unusually-harsh.html.

Gross, Jane. "A New, Purified Form of Cocaine Causes Alarm as Abuse Increases." *New York Times,* November 29, 1985. nytimes.com/1985/11/29/nyregion/a-new-purified-form-of-cocaine-causes-alarm-as-abuse-increases.html.

Guerino, Paul, Paige M. Harrison, and William J. Sabol. "Prisoners in 2010." *Bureau of Justice Statistics* (December 2011). bjs.ojp.gov/content/pub/pdf/p10.pdf.

Haldeman, H. R. *The Haldeman Diaries: Inside the Nixon White House.* New York: G. P. Putnam's Sons, 1994.

Hari, Johann. *Chasing the Scream: The First and Last Days of the War on Drugs.* New York: Bloomsbury, 2015.

Harriston, Keith. "Warning Preceded Execution-style Slaying in NE." *Washington Post,* April 25, 1991. washingtonpost.com/archive/local/1991/04/25/warning-preceded-execution-style-slaying-in-ne/e5219fed-5fd3-4e86-a855-eed1f52d894a/.

Hart, Carl. *High Price: A Neuroscientist's Journey of Self-Discovery That Challenges Everything You Know About Drugs and Society.* New York: Harper Perennial, 2014.

Hartman, D. M., and A. Golub. "The Social Construction of the Crack Epidemic in the Print Media." *Journal of Psychoactive Drugs* 31, no. 4 (October–December 1999): 423–33. pubmed.ncbi.nlm.nih.gov/10681109/.

Hawthorne, Nathaniel. *The Scarlet Letter.* New York: Signet Classics, 1988.

Henig, Jeffrey R., and Wilbur C. Rich. *Mayors in the Middle: Politics, Race, and Mayoral Control of Urban Schools.* Princeton, N.J.: Princeton University Press, 2020.

Herbers, John. "Changes in Society Holding Black Youth in Jobless Web." *New York Times,* March 11, 1979. nytimes.com/1979/03/11/archives/changes-in-society-holding-black-youth-in-jobless-web-young-blacks.html.

Herd, Denise, "Changes in Drug Use Prevalence in Rap Music Songs, 1979–1997." *Addiction Research and Theory* 16, no. 2 (2008): 167–80. doi.org/10.1080/16066350801993987.

Hermann, Peter. "Violent Crime Drops in City's Snow Week but Drug Dealers Continue to Operate in Many Sections." *Baltimore Sun,* January 13, 1996. baltimoresun.com/news/bs-xpm-1996-01-13-1996013069-story.html.

Hermann, Peter, and Keith L. Alexander. "Police Arrest Two Suspects in 25-Year-Old Triple Slaying in Northeast." *Washington Post,* February 17, 2016. washingtonpost.com/local/public-safety/police-arrest-two-suspects-in-25-year-old-triple-murder-in-northeast/2016/02/17/44dabfc8-d591-11e5-b195-2e29a4e13425_story.html.

Himmelman, Jeff. *Yours in Truth: A Personal Portrait of Ben Bradlee.* New York: Random House, 2017.

Hirsch, Arthur. "In Schmoke's World, It's Slow and Steady, Never Mind the Dramatics: Mayor Serene." *Baltimore Sun,* August 31, 1995. baltimoresun.com/news/bs-xpm-1995-08-31-1995243136-story.html.

Holmes, Steven A. "Blacks Relent on Crime Bill, but Not Without Bitterness." *New York Times,* August 18, 1994. nytimes.com/1994/08/18/us/blacks-relent-on-crime-bill-but-not-without-bitterness.html.

Hoover, J. Edgar. "The FBI Sets Goals for COINTELPRO." *SHEC: Resources for Teachers,* March 4, 1968. shec.ashp.cuny.edu/items/show/814.

Hopkins, Ellen. "Childhood's End: What Life Is Like for Crack Babies." *Rolling Stone,* October 18, 1990. rollingstone.com/culture/culture-news/childhoods-end-what-life-is-like-for-crack-babies-188557/.

Hornick, Ed. "Holder 'Nation of Cowards' Remarks Blasted, Praised." CNN, February 19, 2009. cnn.com/2009/POLITICS/02/19/holder.folo/.

Hosler, Karen. "Black Caucus Yields on Crime Bill." *Baltimore Sun,* August 18, 1994. baltimoresun.com/news/bs-xpm-1994-08-18-1994230118-story.html.

Ifill, Gwen. "Debate; Economy, and Brown, Are Focus of a Democratic Round Table." *New York Times,* March 6, 1992. nytimes.com/1992/03/06/us/the-1992-campaign-debate-economy-and-brown-are-focus-of-a-democratic-round-table.html.

———. "The Democrats; Clinton, in Houston Speech, Assails Bush on Crime Issue." *New York Times,* July 24, 1992. nytimes.com/1992/07/24/us/1992-campaign-democrats-clinton-houston-speech-assails-bush-crime-issue.html.

Isikoff, Michael. "Bennett Seeks Wider State Penalties for Drug Crimes." *Washington Post,* July 20, 1989. washingtonpost.com/archive/politics/1989/07/20/bennett-seeks-wider-state-penalties-for-drug-crimes/2e9a631f-9a45-4849-bb86-4decf57481a3/.

———. "Drug Buy Set Up for Bush Speech." *Washington Post,* September 22, 1989. washingtonpost.com/wp-srv/local/longterm/tours/scandal/bushdrug.htm.

Jacobsen, Sally. "U.S. Firms Hang on in Nicaragua." *Washington Post,* October 11, 1987. washingtonpost.com/archive/business/1987/

10/11/us-firms-hang-on-in-nicaragua/ed803579-45c6-4d95-8113
-fcadd01a3948/.

Jaffe, Harry S., and Tom Sherwood. *Dream City: Race, Power, and the Decline of Washington, D.C.* New York: Simon & Schuster, 1994.

Johnston, David. "Bush to Seek Death Penalty for Drug Chiefs." *New York Times,* October 15, 1989. nytimes.com/1989/10/15/us/bush -to-seek-death-penalty-for-drug-chiefs.html.

Jouzaitis, Carol. "Ex-N.Y. Police Boss Nominated for Drug Czar." *Chicago Tribune,* April 29, 1993. chicagotribune.com/news/ct-xpm -1993-04-29-9304300013-story.html.

Karch, Steven B. *A Brief History of Cocaine.* 2nd ed. London: Routledge, 2005.

Katz, Jesse. "Tracking the Genesis of the Crack Trade." *Los Angeles Times,* October 20, 1996. latimes.com/archives/la-xpm-1996-10 -20-mn-59169-story.html.

Kelling, George L., and James Q. Wilson. "Broken Windows." *The Atlantic,* March 1982. theatlantic.com/magazine/archive/1982/03/ broken-windows/304465/.

Kennedy, John F. "Civil Rights Announcement." Speech, Washington, D.C., June 11, 1963.

Kennedy, Robert F. "Statement on Assassination of Martin Luther King, Jr." Speech, Indianapolis, Indiana, April 4, 1968. jfklibrary.org/ learn/about-jfk/the-kennedy-family/robert-f-kennedy/robert-f -kennedy-speeches/statement-on-assassination-of-martin-luther -king-jr-indianapolis-indiana-april-4-1968.

Kerr, Peter. "Anatomy of the Drug Issue: How, After Years, It Erupted." *New York Times,* November 17, 1986. nytimes.com/1986/11/17/ us/anatomy-of-the-drug-issue-how-after-years-it-erupted.html.

———. "The Unspeakable Is Debated: Should Drugs Be Legalized?" *New York Times,* May 15, 1988. nytimes.com/1988/05/15/us/the -unspeakable-is-debated-should-drugs-be-legalized.html.

———. "U.S. Drug 'Crusade' Is Seen as Undermining Itself." *New York Times,* October 26, 1987. nytimes.com/1987/10/26/us/us -drug-crusade-is-seen-as-undermining-itself.html.

Kifner, John. "F.B.I. Sought Doom of Panther Party." *New York Times,* May 9, 1976. nytimes.com/1976/05/09/archives/fbi-sought-doom -of-panther-party-senate-study-says-plot-led-to.html.

Kihss, Peter. " 'Benign Neglect' on Race Is Proposed by Moynihan." *New York Times,* March 1, 1970. nytimes.com/1970/03/01/archives/ benign-neglect-on-race-is-proposed-by-moynihan-moynihan-urges .html.

King, Martin Luther, Jr. "I Have a Dream." Speech, Washington, D.C., August 28, 1963.

King, Wayne. "Heavy Use of Cocaine is Linked to Surge in Deaths and Illnesses." *New York Times,* June 26, 1981. nytimes.com/1981/ 06/26/us/heavy-use-of-cocaine-is-linked-to-surge-in-deaths-and -illnesses.html.

Kohn, Howard. "Cowboy in the Capital: Drug Czar Bill Bennett." *Rolling Stone,* November 2, 1989. rollingstone.com/politics/ politics-news/cowboy-in-the-capital-drug-czar-bill-bennett-45472/.

Kornbluh, Peter. "Crack, the Contras, and the C.I.A.: The Storm Over 'Dark Alliance.'" *Columbia Journalism Review,* January/February 1997. nsarchive2.gwu.edu/NSAEBB/NSAEBB2/storm.htm.

Krauthammer, Charles. "Children of Cocaine." *Pittsburgh Post-Gazette,* August 2, 1989. news.google.com/newspapers?nid=1129&dat =19890802&id=zrFRAAAAIBAJ&sjid=W24DAAAAIBAJ&pg =6587,202482&hl=en.

Kurtz, Howard. "Janet Cooke's Untold Story." *Washington Post,* May 9, 1996. washingtonpost.com/archive/lifestyle/1996/05/09/janet -cookes-untold-story/23151d68-3abd-449a-a053-d72793939d85/.

Labaton, Stephen. "Surgeon General Suggests Study of Legalizing Drugs." *New York Times,* December 8, 1993. nytimes.com/1993/12/ 08/us/surgeon-general-suggests-study-of-legalizing-drugs.html.

Lacayo, Richard. "Do The Unborn Have Rights?" *Time,* November 8, 1990. content.time.com/time/subscriber/article/0,33009,971585,00 .html.

Langone, John. "Crack Comes to the Nursery." *Time,* September 19, 1988. content.time.com/time/subscriber/article/0,33009,968449 ,00.html.

Levy, Peter B. *The Great Uprising: Race Riots in Urban America During the 1960s.* 1st ed. Cambridge University Press, 2018.

Lewis, Neil A. "Quitting, Bennett Blames Others for Work Undone." *New York Times,* November 9, 1990. nytimes.com/1990/11/09/us/ quitting-bennett-blames-others-for-work-undone.html.

Lind, Dara. "Black Lives Matter vs. Bernie Sanders, Explained." *Vox,* August 11, 2015. vox.com/2015/8/11/9127653/bernie-sanders -black-lives-matter.

Lindsey, Robert. "Pervasive Use of Cocaine Is Reported in Hollywood." *New York Times,* October 31, 1982. nytimes.com/1982/ 10/31/us/pervasive-use-of-cocaine-is-reported-in-hollywood .html.

Litsky, Frank. "Player Tells of Wide Drug Use in N.F.L." *New York Times,* June 10, 1982. nytimes.com/1982/06/10/sports/player-tells -of-wide-drug-use-in-nfl.html.

LoLordo, Ann. "Baltimore Homicides for 1991 Reach 304, 1 Under '90 Record: Shooting of Woman Marks First of '92." *Baltimore*

Sun, January 2, 1992. baltimoresun.com/news/bs-xpm-1992-01
-02-1992002004-story.html.

Lopez, German. "The First Step Act, Explained." *Vox,* February 5,
2019. vox.com/future-perfect/2018/12/18/18140973/state-of-the
-union-trump-first-step-act-criminal-justice-reform.

Los Angeles Times. "Bush Balks at Criticism of D.C. Mayor." April 11,
1989. latimes.com/archives/la-xpm-1989-04-11-mn-1907-story.html.

Los Angeles Times Graphics Staff. "L.A. Riots by the Numbers." *Los
Angeles Times,* April 26, 2017. latimes.com/local/1992riots/la-me
-riots-25-years-20170420-htmlstory.html.

Malleck, Daniel. *Drugs, Alcohol and Addiction in the Long Nineteenth
Century: Volume II.* 1st ed. London: Routledge, 2020.

Mansnerus, Laura, and Katherine Roberts. "Drug Poll Raises Questions for TV." *New York Times,* September 7, 1986. nytimes.com/
1986/09/07/weekinreview/ideas-trends-drug-poll-raises-questions
-for-tv.html.

Maraniss, David A. "Post Reporter's Pulitzer Prize Is Withdrawn."
Washington Post, April 16, 1981. washingtonpost.com/archive/1981/
04/16/post-reporters-pulitzer-prize-is-withdrawn/9cf4b4dc-c9a9
-438d-8fa1-c2e1cf53fcf9/.

Marsh, Robert. *Agnew: The Unexamined Man: A Political Profile.* Lan-
ham, Md.: M. Evans, 1971.

Massing, Michael. "D.C.'s War on Drugs, Why Bennett Is Losing."
New York Times, September 23, 1990. nytimes.com/1990/09/23/
magazine/dc-s-war-on-drugs-why-bennett-is-losing.html.

———. "The War on Cocaine." *New York Review of Books,* December 22, 1988. nybooks.com/articles/1988/12/22/the-war-on
-cocaine/.

Matthews, Robert Guy. "Zero Tolerance on Baltimore Crime Pushed:
Some on City Council Favor New York Policy; Mayor, Frazier

Don't." *Baltimore Sun,* August 23, 1996. baltimoresun.com/news/
bs-xpm-1996-08-23-1996236059-story.html.

McFadden & Whitehead. "Ain't No Stopping Us Now." Lyrics.com
.lyrics.com/lyric/14055076/Ain%27t+No+Stopping+Us+Now.

Memoryretro. "Bill Clinton's Sister Souljah Moment—JUNE 13,
1992." YouTube. April 9, 2016. Video, 2:32. youtube.com/watch?v
=xtSifopiL1g&ab_channel=Memoryretro.

Miller, Bill. "Jailed Killer's New Weapon Is a Pen, Prosecutors Say."
Washington Post, October 23, 1996. washingtonpost.com/archive/
local/1996/10/23/jailed-killers-new-weapon-is-a-pen-prosecutors
-say/3f9263b0-7835-4508-8d1d-510e5260940a/.

Miller, George. Interview. *NBC News,* October 25, 1988.

Miller, Marjorie. "Hasenfus Says CIA Supervised Flights: 2 Salvador-
Based Agents Named by Captive American." *Los Angeles Times,*
October 10, 1986. latimes.com/archives/la-xpm-1986-10-10-mn
-5178-story.html.

Milloy, Courtland. "A Time Bomb in Cocaine Babies." *Washington
Post,* September 17, 1989. washingtonpost.com/archive/local/
1989/09/17/a-time-bomb-in-cocaine-babies/634afdf8-3c4c-499c
-9fc8-8a1dbe4058cf/.

Movieclips. "Jungle Fever (9/10) Movie CLIP—Gator's Last Dance
(1991) HD." YouTube. June 1, 2011. Movie scene, 3:26. youtube
.com/watch?v=Bu2PFyl689w&ab_channel=Movieclips.

Murakawa, Naomi. *The First Civil Right: How Liberals Built Prison
America.* Oxford: Oxford University Press, 2014.

Murrell, Peggy J. *Wall Street Journal,* September 11, 1969.

National Center for Education Statistics. "Educational Attainment."
nces.ed.gov/fastfacts/display.asp?id=27.

Navasky, Victor S. "The Torch Is Passed." *New York Times,* June 2, 1968. nytimes.com/1996/04/14/magazine/race-and-rights-june-2-1968-the-torch-is-passed.html.

New York Times. "The Atlanta Riots." September 25, 1906. nytimes.com/1906/09/25/archives/the-atlanta-riots.html.

———. "Coast Police Chief Accused of Racism." May 13, 1982. nytimes.com/1982/05/13/us/coast-police-chief-accused-of-racism.html.

———. "Cocaine Risk Seen in Pregnancy." September 12, 1985. nytimes.com/1985/09/12/us/cocaine-risk-seen-in-pregnancy.html.

———. "Crack's Smallest, Costliest Victims." August 7, 1989. nytimes.com/1989/08/07/opinion/crack-s-smallest-costliest-victims.html.

———. "Excerpts from a Speech on Halting Drug Abuse." September 15, 1986. nytimes.com/1986/09/15/us/excerpts-from-speech-on-halting-drug-abuse.html.

———. "Limited Success Seen in War Against Drugs." December 9, 1987. nytimes.com/1987/12/09/us/limited-success-seen-in-war-against-drugs.html.

———. "Malcom X." February 22, 1965. nytimes.com/1965/02/22/archives/malcolm-x.html.

———. "The Cost of Not Preventing Crack Babies." October 10, 1991. nytimes.com/1991/10/10/opinion/the-cost-of-not-preventing-crack-babies.html.

———. "Transcript of President Bush's Address on the State of the Union." January 29, 1992. nytimes.com/1992/01/29/us/state-union-transcript-president-bush-s-address-state-union.html.

———. "Transcript of Reagan's State of the Union Message to Nation." January 26, 1988. nytimes.com/1988/01/26/us/transcript-of-reagan-s-state-of-the-union-message-to-nation.html.

New York Times Editorial Board. "Slandering the Unborn." *New York Times*, December 28, 2018. nytimes.com/interactive/2018/12/28/opinion/crack-babies-racism.html.

Newsweek. "Like Dom Perignon and Caviar." May 30, 1977.

Newton, Jim. "DARE Marks a Decade of Growth and Controversy: Youth: Despite Critics, Anti-Drug Program Expands Nationally, but Some See Declining Support in LAPD." *Los Angeles Times*, September 9, 1993. latimes.com/archives/la-xpm-1993-09-09-mn-33226-story.html.

Nixon, Richard. "Address Accepting the Presidential Nomination." Speech, Miami Beach, Fla., August 8, 1968.

———. "Special Message to the Congress on Drug Abuse Prevention and Control." Speech, June 17, 1971. presidency.ucsb.edu/documents/special-message-the-congress-drug-abuse-prevention-and-control.

———. "State of the Union Message to the Congress on Law Enforcement and Drug Abuse Prevention." Speech, March 14, 1973. presidency.ucsb.edu/documents/state-the-union-message-the-congress-law-enforcement-and-drug-abuse-prevention.

———. "Statement on Establishing the Office for Drug Abuse Law Enforcement." Speech, January 28, 1972. presidency.ucsb.edu/documents/statement-establishing-the-office-for-drug-abuse-law-enforcement.

Noah, Timothy. "It's Not Easy Being Mayor." *Washington Post*, May 27, 1990. washingtonpost.com/archive/lifestyle/magazine/1990/05/27/its-not-easy-being-mayor/226f2529-097d-44c3-b56c-3383f9ba4ddb/.

Norman-Eady, Sandra. "State Cocaine Sentencing Policies." *Connecticut General Assembly*, October 3, 2003. cga.ct.gov/2003/olrdata/jud/rpt/2003-R-0700.htm.

O'Connor, Julie. "Former Drug Dealer Makes Community Basketball League a 'Safe Zone' for City's Youth." *NJ.com,* August 16, 2009. nj.com/news/2009/08/from_newark_street_gang_to_sum.html.

O'Toole, Thomas. "Heroin, Cocaine Overdoses Rise Young Americans Cut Use of Marijuana." *Washington Post,* February 4, 1983. washingtonpost.com/archive/politics/1983/02/04/heroin -cocaine-overdoses-rise-young-americans-cut-use-of-marijuana/ 17092b9e-6e8c-4f2e-8310-41fe01eb5e48/?utm_term=.6af562d84b91.

Ockerman, Emma. "The Eviction Crisis Is Already Here and It's Crushing Black Moms." *Vice,* July 24, 2020. vice.com/en/article/ 7kpega/the-eviction-crisis-is-already-here-and-its-crushing-black -moms.

Office of Population Affairs. "Adolescent Health." opa.hhs.gov/ adolescent-health?adolescent-development/reproductive-health -and-teen-pregnancy/teen-pregnancy-and-childbearing/trends/ index.html.

Office of the Historian. "Central America, 1981–1993." *Milestones.* history.state.gov/milestones/1981-1988/central-america.

Okie, Susan. "Crack Babies: The Epidemic That Wasn't." *New York Times,* January 26, 2009. nytimes.com/2009/01/27/health/27coca.html.

Parry, Robert, and Brian Barger. "Nicaraguan Rebels Operating in Northern Costa Rica . . ." *AP News,* December 20, 1985. apnews .com/article/c69eaf370de9884f907a39efd90337d3.

Penn, Ivan. "Schmoke Asks O'Malley to Detail How He Would Implement Zero-Tolerance Policing; Mayor Fears Policy Would Increase Police Brutality." *Baltimore Sun,* September 17, 1999. baltimoresun.com/news/bs-xpm-1999-09-17-9909170185-story .html.

People Staff. "Richard Pryor's Tragic Accident Spotlights a Dangerous Drug Craze: Freebasing." *People,* June 30, 1980. people.com/

archive/richard-pryors-tragic-accident-spotlights-a-dangerous
-drug-craze-freebasing-vol-13-no-26/.

Perlstein, Rick. "Exclusive: Lee Atwater's Infamous 1981 Interview on the Southern Strategy." *The Nation,* November 13, 2012. thenation .com/article/archive/exclusive-lee-atwaters-infamous-1981 -interview-southern-strategy/.

Perot, Marin. "Chris Rock Dope Fiend." YouTube. June 15, 2010. Movie scene, 0:21. youtube.com/watch?v=UE2tPyGJStQ&ab _channel=MarinPerot.

Perry, Charles. "Freebase: A Treacherous Obsession." *Rolling Stone,* May 1, 1980. rollingstone.com/culture/culture-news/freebase-a -treacherous-obsession-73987/.

Petersen, Robert C. *Cocaine, 1977.* 13th ed. U.S. Government Printing Office, 1977.

Pinchevsky, Tal. "A Drug Kingpin and His Racket: The Untold Story of Freeway Rick Ross." *Vice,* May 11, 2015. vice.com/en/article/ jpz79y/a-drug-kingpin-and-his-racket-the-untold-story-of-freeway -rick-ross.

Pincus, Walter. "C.I.A. Ignored Tips Alleging Contra Drug Links, Report Says." *Washington Post,* November 3, 1998. washingtonpost .com/archive/politics/1998/11/03/cia-ignored-tips-alleging -contra-drug-links-report-says/d7ade266-803e-4987-9d01 -ce7d98d9ea13/.

Pogatchnik, Shawn. "Death Penalty Bills Target Drug Traffickers, Terrorists." *Los Angeles Times,* March 15, 1990. latimes.com/archives/ la-xpm-1990-03-15-mn-290-story.html.

Public Opinion Strategies. "Memorandum Re: National Poll Results." January 25, 2018. politico.com/f/?id=00000161-2ccc-da2c-a963 -efff82be0001.

Ramsey, Donovan X. "A Triple Murder, a Broken Family, and the Long Tail of the Crack Era." *Vice,* August 29, 2016. vice.com/en/article/7bmx3e/triple-murder-washington-dc-crack-era-curtis-pixley-langdon-park.

Rangel, Charles B. "Legalize Drugs? Not on Your Life." *New York Times,* May 17, 1988. nytimes.com/1988/05/17/opinion/legalize-drugs-not-on-your-life.html.

Rasmussen Reports. "Voters Have Little Faith in War on Drugs." January 10, 2018. rasmussenreports.com/public_content/politics/general_politics/january_2018/voters_have_little_faith_in_war_on_drugs.

Reagan Library. "Address to the Nation on Drug Abuse Campaign, September 14, 1986." YouTube. Address, 19:50. youtube.com/watch?v=pwpciZ7R8UU&ab_channel=ReaganLibrary.

Reagan, Ronald. Executive Order 12368: Drug Abuse Policy Functions. June 24, 1982. archives.gov/federal-register/codification/executive-order/12368.html.

———. "The President's News Conference." Speech, Washington, D.C., March 6, 1981. presidency.ucsb.edu/documents/the-presidents-news-conference-995.

———. "Remarks on Signing Executive Order 12368, Concerning Federal Drug Abuse Policy Functions." *Public Papers of the Presidents of the United States: Ronald Reagan, 1982.* June 24, 1982.

Reed, Todd. "Crack Baby Myth Goes Up in Smoke." Al Jazeera America, March 10, 2015.

Reed, Todd, and Sarah Hoye. "Former Crack Baby: 'It's Another Stigma, Another Box to Put Me In'." Al Jazeera America, March 10, 2015. america.aljazeera.com/watch/shows/america-tonight/articles/2015/3/10/crack-baby-myth.html.

Reeves, Jimmie L., and Richard Campbell. *Cracked Coverage: Television News, the Anti-Cocaine Crusade, and the Reagan Legacy.* Durham, N.C.: Duke University Press, 1994.

Reinarman, Craig, and Harry G. Levine. "The Crack Attack: Politics and Media in the Crack Scare." In *Crack in America: Demon Drugs and Social Justice* (Berkeley: University of California Press, 1997): 18–51. us.corwin.com/sites/default/files/upm-binaries/4006 _Newman_Reader___Chp_3_The_Crack_Attack_Final_Pdf.pdf.

Risen, James. "C.I.A. Says It Used Nicaraguan Rebels Accused of Drug Tie." *New York Times,* July 17, 1998. nytimes.com/1998/07/17/world/cia-says-it-used-nicaraguan-rebels-accused-of-drug-tie .html.

Robison, Jennifer. "Decades of Drug Use: The '80s and '90s." Gallup, July 9, 2002. news.gallup.com/poll/6352/decades-drug-use-80s -90s.aspx.

Ronald Reagan Presidential Foundation and Institute. "Nancy Reagan: Her Causes." reaganfoundation.org/ronald-reagan/nancy -reagan/her-causes/.

Rosenthal, Andrew. "Taking Message on Road, Bush Pushes Crime Bill." *New York Times,* January 24, 1990. nytimes.com/1990/01/24/us/taking-message-on-road-bush-pushes-crime-bill.html.

Rule, Sheila. "Racial Issues; Rapper, Chided by Clinton, Calls Him a Hypocrite." *New York Times,* June 17, 1992. nytimes.com/1992/06/17/us/the-1992-campaign-racial-issues-rapper-chided-by -clinton-calls-him-a-hypocrite.html.

Sager, Mike. "Say Hello to Rick Ross." *Esquire,* September 25, 2013. esquire.com/news-politics/a25818/rick-ross-drug-dealer -interview-1013/.

Scott, Eugene. "Black Lives Matter Protesters Confront Clinton at a Fundraiser." CNN, February 25, 2016. cnn.com/2016/02/25/politics/hillary-clinton-black-lives-matter-whichhillary/index.html.

Seelye, Katharine Q. "Accord Reached on Sweeping Bill to Battle Crime." *New York Times,* July 29, 1994. nytimes.com/1994/07/29/us/accord-reached-on-sweeping-bill-to-battle-crime.html.

———. "Crime Bill Fails on a House Vote, Stunning Clinton." *New York Times,* August 12, 1994. nytimes.com/1994/08/12/us/crime-bill-fails-on-a-house-vote-stunning-clinton.html.

———. "House Approves Crime Bill After Days of Bargaining, Giving Victory to Clinton." *New York Times,* August 22, 1994. nytimes.com/1994/08/22/us/crime-bill-overview-house-approves-crime-bill-after-days-bargaining-giving.html.

Select Committee on Narcotics Abuse and Control. "Drug Paraphernalia." November 1, 1979. babel.hathitrust.org/cgi/pt?id=purl.32754078079153.

Sentencing Project. "Trends in U.S. Corrections." May 2021. sentencingproject.org/app/uploads/2022/08/Trends-in-US-Corrections.pdf.

Shakur, Tupac. "Changes." Genius. genius.com/2pac-changes-lyrics.

Sharkey, Patrick, Gerard Torrats-Espinosa, and Delaram Takyar. "Community and the Crime Decline: The Causal Effect of Local Nonprofits on Violent Crime." *American Sociological Review* 82, no. 6 (2017): 1214–1240. doi.org/10.1177/0003122417736289.

Sheffy, Gillian. "Non-State United States Support for the Contras During the Reagan Era." Honors Thesis, Bucknell University, 2013. digitalcommons.bucknell.edu/honors_theses/145.

Shenon, Philip. "Bush Officials Say War on Drugs in the Nation's Capital Is a Failure." *New York Times,* April 5, 1990. nytimes.com/1990/04/05/us/bush-officials-say-war-on-drugs-in-the-nation-s-capital-is-a-failure.html.

———. "Nominee for 'Drug Czar' Has Tough-Talking Past." *New York Times,* January 13, 1989. nytimes.com/1989/01/13/us/nominee-for-drug-czar-has-tough-talking-past.html.

Shields, Gerard. "Candidates Plot Strategy for Drug Battle; Several Mayoral Hopefuls Support 'Treatment on Demand.' But How Would the City Pay for the Proposal?" *Baltimore Sun,* August 15, 1999. baltimoresun.com/news/bs-xpm-1999-08-15-9908211594 -story.html.

———. "Schmoke Leaving Mixed Legacy; Mayor Said He Tried to 'Address the Rot Under the Glitter.'" *Baltimore Sun,* December 5, 1999. baltimoresun.com/news/bs-xpm-1999-12-05-9912050068 -story.html.

Sides, Josh. *L.A. City Limits: African American Los Angeles from the Great Depression to the Present.* 1st ed. Berkeley: University of California Press, 2006.

Siegel, Eric. "Schmoke Joins Call for Probe of CIA-Drug Charges." *Baltimore Sun,* September 19, 1996. baltimoresun.com/news/ bs-xpm-1996-09-19-1996263036-story.html.

Simon, Roger. "A Few Debate Factoids to Reinvigorate Your Day." *Baltimore Sun,* October 18, 1992. baltimoresun.com/news/bs -xpm-1992-10-18-1992292009-story.html.

———. "Schmoke Says Legalization of Drugs Is Now Inevitable." *Baltimore Sun,* February 11, 1994. baltimoresun.com/news/bs -xpm-1994-02-11-1994042050-story.html.

Smart, Charlie. "Obama Granted Clemency Unlike Any Other President in History." *FiveThirtyEight,* January 19, 2017. fivethirtyeight .com/features/obama-granted-clemency-unlike-any-other -president-in-history/.

Smith, Benjamin T. "New Documents Reveal the Bloody Origins of America's Long War on Drugs." *Time,* August 24, 2021. time.com/ 6090016/us-war-on-drugs-origins/.

Smith, Sally Bedell. "Mrs. Reagan Takes Her Anti-Drug Campaign to Television." *New York Times,* October 11, 1983. nytimes.com/1983/

10/11/us/mrs-reagan-takes-her-anti-drug-campaign-to-television
.html.

South Florida Sun-Sentinel. "Bennett Faces an Uphill Battle as America's New Anti-Drug Czar." January 22, 1989. sun-sentinel.com/news/fl-xpm-1989-01-22-8901040730-story.html.

Spencer, Jim. "The Drug Warrior: My Job Is to Free America of Addiction." *Chicago Tribune,* October 26, 1986. chicagotribune.com/news/ct-xpm-1986-10-26-8603200589-story.html.

Spillane, Joseph F. *Cocaine: From Medical Marvel to Modern Menace in the United States, 1884–1920.* Baltimore: Johns Hopkins University Press, 2002.

St. Louis Post-Dispatch. "Disaster in Making: Crack Babies Start to Grow Up." September 18, 1990.

State of California Department of Industrial Relations. "Negroes and Mexican Americans in South and East Los Angeles." Report, 1965. files.eric.ed.gov/fulltext/ED022589.pdf.

Stevens, William K. "Muslims Keep Lid on Drugs in Capital." *New York Times,* September 26, 1988. nytimes.com/1988/09/26/us/muslims-keep-lid-on-drugs-in-capital.html.

Stone, Andrea. "Drug Epidemic's Tiny Victims: Crack Babies Born to Life of Suffering." *USA Today,* June 8, 1989.

Stone, Andrew. "Crack, a Tiffany Drug at Woolworth Prices: SPIN's 1986 Feature." *SPIN,* February 1986. spin.com/2015/08/crack-a-tiffany-drug-at-woolworth-prices-spins-1986-feature/.

Sullivan, Ronald. "N.F.L. Says Players' Cocaine Use Could Threaten Integrity of Game." *New York Times,* June 27, 1982. nytimes.com/1982/06/27/sports/nfl-says-players-cocaine-use-could-threaten-integrity-of-game.html.

Suro, Roberto, and Walter Pincus. "The CIA and Crack: Evidence Is Lacking of Alleged Plot." *Washington Post,* October 4, 1996. washingtonpost.com/archive/politics/1996/10/04/the-cia-and -crack-evidence-is-lacking-of-alleged-plot/5b026731-c5de-4234 -b3bd-9e0fd2e21225/.

Teixeira, Ruy, and Alan Abramowitz. "The Decline of the White Working Class and the Rise of a Mass Upper Middle Class." In *The Future of Red, Blue and Purple America* (April 2008). The Brookings Institution. brookings.edu/wp-content/uploads/2016/06/04 _demographics_teixeira.pdf.

Thomas, Pierre. "Elders Drug Comments Repudiated." *Washington Post,* December 8, 1993. washingtonpost.com/archive/politics/ 1993/12/08/elders-drug-comments-repudiated/460bf2f9-3e82 -49f6-82e2-310721011fa6/.

Thomas-Lester, Avis. "An Agony of Uncertainty." *Washington Post,* April 23, 1998. washingtonpost.com/archive/local/1998/04/23/ an-agony-of-uncertainty/ab0ae3fd-3982-4ec6-893b-ddae2ba628f7/ ?tid=a_inl.

Thompson, Hunter S. *Fear and Loathing in Las Vegas.* 2nd ed. New York: Vintage Books, 1998.

Time. "Dukakis' Deadly Response." 1988. Video, 0:40. content.time .com/time/specials/packages/article/0,28804,1844704_1844706 _1844712,00.html.

———. "Middle-Class Blacks: Making It in America." June 17, 1974. content.time.com/time/covers/0,16641,19740617,00.html.

Toufexis, Anastasia. "Crack Kids: Innocent Victims." *Time,* May 13, 1991. content.time.com/time/subscriber/article/0,33009,972924, 00.html.

Travis, Jeremy. "Declining Crime and Our National Research Agenda: A New Yorker's View." Speech, New York, March 9, 1998. nij.ojp

.gov/speech/declining-crime-and-our-national-research-agenda
-new-yorkers-view.

Twain, Mark. *The Adventures of Huckleberry Finn.* London: William
Collins, 2010.

Uniform Crime Reports. "2017 Crime in the United States: Expanded
Homicide Data Table 1." ucr.fbi.gov/crime-in-the-u.s/2017/
crime-in-the-u.s.-2017/tables/expanded-homicide-data-table-1.xls.

U.S. Congress. *District of Columbia Appropriations for 1969.* U.S. Government Printing Office, 1968.

———. *Legalization of Illicit Drugs: Hearing Before the Select Committee
on Narcotics Abuse and Control, House of Representatives, One Hun-
dredth Congress.* U.S. Government Printing Office, 1989.

———. "S.756—First Step Act of 2018." congress.gov/bill/115th
-congress/senate-bill/756/text.

U.S. Department of Justice. "Chapter II: Oscar Danilo Blandon." oig
.justice.gov/sites/default/files/archive/special/9712/ch02p1.htm.

———. "The C.I.A.–Contra–Crack Cocaine Controversy: A Review
of the Justice Department's Investigations and Prosecutions." December 1997. oig.justice.gov/sites/default/files/archive/special/
9712/index.htm.

———. "The Cocaine Threat to the United States." March 1995. ojp
.gov/pdffiles1/Digitization/154678NCJRS.pdf.

———. "Crime Control: Federal Initiatives." *Congressional Quarterly,*
1993. ojp.gov/pdffiles1/Digitization/148292NCJRS.pdf.

———. "Crime in the United States 1991." August 30, 1992. ojp.gov/
pdffiles1/Digitization/138839NCJRS.pdf.

———. "Department Policy on Charging Mandatory Minimum Sentences and Recidivist Enhancements in Certain Drug Cases."

August 12, 2013. big.assets.huffingtonpost.com/HolderMandatory MinimumsMemo.pdf.

———. "The Fair Sentencing Act of 2010." August 5, 2010. justice .gov/sites/default/files/oip/legacy/2014/07/23/fair-sentencing -act-memo.pdf.

———. "Historical Statistics on Prisoners in State and Federal Institutions, Yearend 1925–86." May 1988. bjs.ojp.gov/content/pub/pdf/ hspsfiy25-86.pdf.

———. "K. Allegation That Blandon Received Special Treatment in the 1992 San Diego Prosecution of Him." oig.justice.gov/sites/ default/files/archive/special/9712/ch02p6.htm.

———. "National Advisory Commission on Civil Disorders." Report, 1967. ojp.gov/ncjrs/virtual-library/abstracts/national-advisory -commission-civil-disorders-report.

———. "Phasing Out Our Use of Private Prisons." August 18, 2016. justice.gov/archives/opa/blog/phasing-out-our-use-private-prisons.

———. "Prisoners in 1987." April 1988. bjs.ojp.gov/content/pub/ pdf/p87.pdf.

———. "Race of Prisoners Admitted to State and Federal Institutions, 1926–86." April 1991. bjs.ojp.gov/content/pub/pdf/rpasfi2686.pdf.

———. "Review of the Department's Clemency Initiative." August 2018. oig.justice.gov/reports/2018/e1804.pdf.

———. "Timeline of Significant Events Related to Danilo Blandon." oig.justice.gov/sites/default/files/archive/special/9712/appe.htm.

———. "Tracking the Crack Epidemic in New York City Using Data from the Drug Use Forecasting Program." November 16, 1994. ojp.gov/pdffiles1/Digitization/151225NCJRS.pdf.

U.S. Senate. *Drugs, Law Enforcement and Foreign Policy: Report by the Committee on Foreign Relations, U.S. Senate.* Diane Publishing, 2004.

Valentine, Paul W. "Baltimore Killings Break '72 Record." *Washington Post,* December 30, 1992. washingtonpost.com/archive/politics/1992/12/30/baltimore-killings-break-72-record/3adc525c-9a52-4043-a225-0b76d857ba60/.

Washington Post. "It's Crack/Cocaine Awareness Month—Retroactively." November 18, 1986. washingtonpost.com/archive/politics/1986/11/18/its-crackcocaine-awareness-month-retroactively/d6bd0ab6-862a-4803-85df-eea23c36c648/.

Washington Post Editorial Board. "The End of the 'Jimmy' Story." *Washington Post,* April 16, 1981. washingtonpost.com/archive/politics/1981/04/16/the-end-of-the-jimmy-story/bbb40958-98ca-4b49-9da6-bcff88ede045/.

———. "New Schoolmasters in Baltimore." June 13, 1992. washingtonpost.com/archive/opinions/1992/06/13/new-schoolmasters-in-baltimore/1e0d2554-5c1b-40cf-9d9c-e1e9d1fb6669/.

Weinreb, Michael. "The Day Innocence Died." ESPN, June 1986. espn.com/espn/eticket/story?page=bias.

Wheeler, Linda. "Anti-Drug Crusade Intensifies in Shaw." *Washington Post,* June 3, 1989. washingtonpost.com/archive/local/1989/06/03/anti-drug-crusade-intensifies-in-shaw/56d387e4-d774-4b22-9350-c1d02d443854/.

Whitehead, Colson. *Sag Harbor.* New York: Doubleday, 2009.

White House. "National Drug Control Strategy." September 15, 1989. ojp.gov/pdffiles1/ondcp/119466.pdf.

———. "National Security Decision Directive on Cuba and Central America." January 4, 1982. irp.fas.org/offdocs/nsdd/nsdd-17.pdf.

Wikipedia. "1968 Democratic National Convention." en.wikipedia .org/wiki/1968_Democratic_National_Convention.

———. "Prenatal Cocaine Exposure." en.wikipedia.org/wiki/Prenatal _cocaine_exposure.

Wilkinson, Francis. "Benign Neglect." *New York Times,* June 11, 2008. archive.nytimes.com/campaignstops.blogs.nytimes.com/2008/ 06/11/benign-neglect/.

Will, George F. "Peanut's Prison Tale." *Washington Post,* January 30, 1994. washingtonpost.com/archive/opinions/1994/01/30/peanuts -prison-tale/db84cbdb-6a47-40fa-8c9d-8c0d3e52b415/.

Williams, Edward Huntington. "Negro Cocaine 'Fiends' Are New Southern Menace: Murder and Insanity Increasing Among Lower-Class Blacks." *New York Times,* February 8, 1914.

Williams, Juan. "Schmoke Legacy Is Triumph Over Adversity." *Baltimore Sun,* December 15, 1999. baltimoresun.com/news/bs-xpm -1999-12-15-9912160362-story.html.

Winerip, Michael. "Revisiting the 'Crack Babies' Epidemic That Was Not." *New York Times,* May 20, 2013. nytimes.com/2013/05/20/ booming/revisiting-the-crack-babies-epidemic-that-was-not.html? _r=0//.

Woody, Christopher. "Here's What's Driven Changes in Cocaine Prices on US Streets Since the 1980s." *Business Insider,* October 26, 2016. businessinsider.com/us-cocaine-prices-change-2016-10.

Wright, Hamilton. "Report on the International Opium Commission and on the Opium Problem as Seen Within the United States and Its Possessions." *Opium Problem: Message From the President of the United States* (February 1910).

Wright, Richard. *The Outsider.* New York: Harper Perennial, 2009.

Zorzi, William F., Jr. "Baltimore School Deal Tough Sell for Schmoke: Mayor Encounters Opposition at Home and in Annapolis." *Baltimore Sun,* February 24, 1997. baltimoresun.com/news/bs-xpm-1997-02-24-1997055002-story.html.

INDEX

ABOUT THE AUTHOR

DONOVAN X. RAMSEY is a journalist, author, and voice on issues of race, politics, and patterns of power in America. His reporting has appeared in *The New York Times, The Atlantic, GQ, Gawker, BuzzFeed, Vice,* and *Ebony,* among other outlets. He has been a staff reporter at the *Los Angeles Times, NewsOne,* and *theGrio.* He worked as an editor at The Marshall Project and *Complex.* Ramsey holds a master's degree from the Columbia University Graduate School of Journalism and a bachelor's degree in psychology from Morehouse College.

To inquire about booking Donovan X. Ramsey for a speaking engagement, please contact the Penguin Random House Speakers Bureau at speakers@penguinrandomhouse.com.

donovanxramsey.com
Twitter: @donovanxramsey
Instagram: @donovanxramsey
@whencrackwasking
@blackmagcovers

—

ABOUT THE TYPE

This book was set in Dante, a typeface designed by Giovanni Mardersteig (1892–1977). Conceived as a private type for the Officina Bodoni in Verona, Italy, Dante was originally cut only for hand composition by Charles Malin, the famous Parisian punch cutter, between 1946 and 1952. Its first use was in an edition of Boccaccio's *Trattatello in laude di Dante* that appeared in 1954. The Monotype Corporation's version of Dante followed in 1957. Though modeled on the Aldine type used for Pietro Cardinal Bembo's treatise *De Aetna* in 1495, Dante is a thoroughly modern interpretation of that venerable face.